LITERATURE'S REFUGE

translation/TRANSNATION

SERIES EDITOR **EMILY APTER**

A list of titles in the series appears at the back of the book.

Literature's Refuge

REWRITING THE MEDITERRANEAN
BORDERSCAPE

WILLIAM STROEBEL

PRINCETON UNIVERSITY PRESS
PRINCETON & OXFORD

Copyright © 2025 by Princeton University Press

Princeton University Press is committed to the protection of copyright and the intellectual property our authors entrust to us. Copyright promotes the progress and integrity of knowledge created by humans. Thank you for supporting free speech and the global exchange of ideas by purchasing an authorized edition of this book. If you wish to reproduce or distribute any part of it in any form, please obtain permission.

Requests for permission to reproduce material from this work should be sent to permissions@press.princeton.edu

Published by Princeton University Press
41 William Street, Princeton, New Jersey 08540
99 Banbury Road, Oxford OX2 6JX

press.princeton.edu

All Rights Reserved

Library of Congress Cataloging-in-Publication Data

Names: Stroebel, William, 1982- author.
Title: Literature's refuge : rewriting the Mediterranean borderscape / William Stroebel.
Description: Princeton : Princeton University Press, 2025. | Series: Translation/transnation | Includes bibliographical references and index.
Identifiers: LCCN 2024021516 (print) | LCCN 2024021517 (ebook) | ISBN 9780691266053 (paperback) | ISBN 9780691266046 (hardback) | ISBN 9780691266091 (ebook)
Subjects: LCSH: Greco-Turkish War, 1921–1922—Literature and the war. | Greek literature, Modern—20th century—History and criticism. | Turkish literature—20th century—History and criticism. | Population transfers in literature. | BISAC: LITERARY CRITICISM / Comparative Literature | SOCIAL SCIENCE / Refugees | LCGFT: Literary criticism.
Classification: LCC PA5230.G74 S77 2025 (print) | LCC PA5230.G74 (ebook) | DDC 889.09/3589495072—dc23/eng/20240928
LC record available at https://lccn.loc.gov/2024021516
LC ebook record available at https://lccn.loc.gov/2024021517

British Library Cataloging-in-Publication Data is available

Jacket credits (*top to bottom*): a private codex from the family library of Joanna Sitterlet; Bayerische Staatsbibliothek, Cod. Graec. 593; Princeton Firestone Library, Special Collections, Q-001243; Mehmet Yashin, *Sınırdışı Saatler*; the Stratis Doukas collection of the Modern Greek Literature Archive, Department of Modern Greek and Comparative Studies, Aristotle University of Thessaloniki; first edition of Halide Edib's *Ateşten Gömlek*, held in the University of Toronto Libraries; Princeton Firestone Library, Special Collections, Q-001243; a private codex from the family library of Kurtuluş Öztürk; a private codex from the family library of Giorgos Kallinikidis; the Stratis Doukas collection of the Modern Greek Literature Archive, Department of Modern Greek and Comparative Studies, Aristotle University of Thessaloniki. Stitched together across languages and alphabets, we might translate all these scraps as a pastiche poem of sorts:

> *God made the moon and the sun and set them in the sky,*
> *a work well known, at least,*
> *but the weather here, it rains, rains, and rains,*
> *and the streets are so quiet, and on everyone's face, turned inward to the depths—*
> *oh for the love of the Lord who created us, don't cast me off in this foreign place.*
> *I was looking for a way to go when the door opened again*
> *and the people coming here, they weren't enemies: they were us.*
> *You saved the nightingale, Şani, when it was in its throes,*
> *[you] won [it] with POEMS that most consider shameful,*
> *but I hold you as a father in my heart.*

This book has been composed in Arno

10 9 8 7 6 5 4 3 2 1

For Giota,

θαύμα, θαυματουργό, και πιο δύσκολα απ' όλα σύντροφο

Μ' αεροπλάνα και βαπόρια
και με τους φίλους τους παλιούς
τριγυρνάμε στα σκοτάδια
κι όμως εσύ δε μας ακούς

δε μας ακούς που τραγουδάμε
με φωνές ηλεκτρικές
μες στις υπόγειες στοές
ώσπου οι τροχιές μας συναντάνε
τις βασικές σου τις αρχές.

By plane and by ship
with our old friends near us
we wander in the shadows
but you don't hear us

you don't hear the songs we perform
with electric voices
in the underground stoas—
not till our lines of flight conform
to the norms you've set before us.

—from "zeibekiko," a
refugee ballad performed
by dionysis savvopoulos
and sotiria belou (1972)

CONTENTS

Acknowledgments xi

Preface xv

Note on Transliteration and Translation xxi

Introduction   1

Chapter one, in which Şānī and his readers save the nightingale   35

Chapter two, in which Cavafy is scattered and gathered up
    and scattered again   68

Chapter three, in which witnesses to war tell their truths   116

Chapter four, in which displaced books make a place   163

Chapter five, in which the script is rewritten   196

Afterword   239

Notes 245

Bibliography 267

Index 287

ACKNOWLEDGMENTS

THIS BOOK was researched and written during a fifteen-year trek through the highways and byways of Greek- and Turkish-language literature. I could never have done it alone. Look closely and you'll see the footprints of that journey stretching out beyond this book: They are scattered across various classrooms, faculty and staff offices, state archives, special collections, and community libraries; they wend their way between Michigan, Turkey, Princeton, Greece, and again Michigan; and if their trail has led at last to the pages of a book, it's thanks only to the helping hands and warm support of dozens of people with whom I sojourned along the way and whom I thank here.

It's customary in such acknowledgments to save our closest for last, but I want to foreground from the start my partner, Giota Tachtara. Her emotional and intellectual support and her labor have made this book possible. Truth be told, *Literature's Refuge* has been a hard slog, and as a working parent I will say the quiet part out loud: years of economic precarity before the tenure track, followed by years of COVID disruptions to public schooling, caregiving, and emotional well-being, have weighed heavily not just on this book but on my immediate family. Without Giota, this book would not have made it to your hands.

Among my colleagues, I single out first my mentors: Vassilis Lambropoulos and Artemis Leontis, whose unflagging support shaped the early stages of my doctoral studies even as they continue to offer their wisdom today. Karen Emmerich has provided an early model for the kind of intellectual work I want to put out into the world. Yopie Prins as both a department chair and a senior colleague has enthusiastically championed my project from the first. Brent Hayes Edwards, Karen Emmerich, and Pam Ballinger generously guided my manuscript through its workshop phase. Emily Apter, Anne Savarese, and James Collier believed in this book before it was a book and safely steered it from peer review to production. Sara Lerner and Karen Verde deftly pushed my book through production phase, Felix Summ designed the cover, and

Derek Gottlieb drew up the index, and I am grateful to them all. I likewise want to thank Susan Clark, Steve Stillman, and all the others at Princeton University Press whom I did not meet, as well as the anonymous readers and the editorial board for their helpful feedback.

Hadji Bakara, Catherine Brown, Aaron Coleman, Aileen Das, Nicoletta Demetriou, Kristin Dickinson, Christi Merrill, Taymaz Pour Mohammad, Renée Ragin Randall, Niloofar Sarlati, and Antoine Traisnel have offered me their time and guidance as both readers and friends. More generally, to my colleagues in the Comparative Literature Department, the Classical Studies Department, and the Modern Greek Program at University of Michigan, I am grateful for the intellectual ether and day-to-day back and forth that keeps me going. Among current and recent graduate students, CC Barick, Ali Bolcakan, Samet Budak, Georgios Douliakas, Amanda Kubic, Graham Liddell, Jaideep Pandey, Aliosha Pittaka Bielenberg, and Berkay Uluç have helped me open new windows through their conversations. When I myself was a graduate student, crucial to my early research and writing were Tatjana Aleksić, Harry Kashdan, Jeff Knight, Kader Konuk, Erol Köroğlu, Tina Lupton, and Karla Mallette, some of whom still offer me insight today. I owe a big thank you to Gottfried Hagen and Evangelia Balta, who helped me immensely in my early days of Ottoman and Karamanli Turkish, respectively, and continue to support me today, as well as to Evyn Kropf and Pablo Alvarez for their codicological wisdom. Kathryn Babayan, Cameron Cross, Michael Pifer, Adi Saleem, Ron Suny, and Ryan Szpiech have been fruitful interlocutors from across campus. The broader institutional support I've received here has likewise been crucial in pushing me across the finish line: a fellowship from the Institute for Humanities, under Peggy McCracken, allowed me two semesters to guide my book to contract, while the rock-solid backing of my chairs and the LSA College during a wave of acute physical and mental health crises within my family have allowed me the headspace to be both a scholar and a parent. For this, I am deeply grateful to Celia Schultz and Chris Hill, as well as the LSA College. To the staff of my departments: Jeff Craft, Stephanie Hart, Judy Gray, Michelle Biggs, Julie Burnett, Katie Colman, Tarah Hearns, Sarah Kandell, Elaine Medrow, and Zach Quint. Only God knows the tally of my debt to you all collectively.

During my time at Princeton, the Seeger Center for Hellenic Studies offered me a crucial refuge to pivot away from the dissertation through a postdoctoral fellowship, followed by a lecture position. Dimitris Gondicas showed an abiding trust in my early book project and in me. Paul Babinski, Sandra

Bermann, Emmanuel Bourbouhakis, Richard Calis, Kristina Gedgaudaitė, Tony Grafton, Molly Greene, Soo-Young Kim, AnneMarie Luijendijk, Georgios Markou, Alexander Nehamas, Argyro Nicolaou, Dan-el Padilla Peralta, Katerina Stergiopoulou, Berke Torunoğlu, and Christos Tsakas brightened my years at Princeton with a delightful constellation of ideas and conversations. Beyond Princeton, Yorgos Dedes, Johanna Hanink, and Veli Yashin generously read through portions of chapters and my ideas. I am grateful as well for the invitations to give lectures and workshops of my book at the Hellenic Studies Program at Yale University, the Modern Greek Seminar at Columbia University, the Program in Translation and Intercultural Communication at Princeton University, Brian Catlos and Sharon Kinoshita's itinerant Mediterranean Seminar, the Cavafy Summer School at the Onassis Foundation, and the Greek Studies Now Network in Oxford and Amsterdam, spearheaded by Maria Boletsi and Dimitris Papanikolaou.

In addition to the Institute for Humanities Fellowship mentioned above, earlier financial support during my PhD research from the Mellon Foundation and the Social Science Research Council made possible a year of research in Turkey; a Princeton Firestone Library Grant deepened my research on Cavafy; a scholarship from the Rare Book School in Virginia gave me critical training in analytical bibliography; a number of fellowships from across the University of Michigan funded summer research trips overseas. During my time on site, I accrued many debts to the staff at the National Library of Greece, the Library of Parliament of Greece, the Centre for Asia Minor Studies, the Modern Greek Studies Archive at Aristotelian University in Thessaloniki, the Ottoman and Turkish Periodical archive at Atatürk Library in Istanbul, the Rare Books Division at Boğaziçi University Library, the National Library of Turkey in Ankara, and the Bavarian State Library in Munich. Alongside these institutions, I'm equally grateful to the individuals who have opened their libraries up to me, particularly Giorgos Kallinikidis, Joanna Sitterlet, and the congregation of Saint Nicholas Orthodox Church of Ann Arbor.

Small slivers of chapters two, three, and four have appeared, respectively, in "Some Assembly Required," *Book History* vol. 21 (2018), 278–316; "Distancing Disaster," *Journal of Modern Greek Studies* vol. 32, no. 2 (2014), 253–285; and "Longhand Lines of Flight," *PMLA* vol. 136, no. 2 (March 2021), 190–212. I reprint small portions of this material here by permission of Johns Hopkins University Press and Cambridge University Press. I am grateful to the anonymous readers and editorial staff of these journals, including Sara Pastel and Joe Wallace, whom I was unable to thank publicly for their care and oversight of my article at the *PMLA*. I am also grateful to Jeff Knight and the *MLQ* editorial team for their understanding in 2021, when I reached the difficult decision to withdraw a submission after peer review; I thank the anonymous readers for their time and thoughts.

Finally, let me turn my gaze back closer to home. I'm grateful to my father and mother for their help through the lean years of grad-school parenting (and afterward), and to my second family in Greece, including my brother-in-law Thanos Tachtaras, who always puts a smile on his nephews' faces. I'm grateful as well to my labor union, I.W.W. Ypsilanti. And on every page of this book hide the fingerprints of Orpheus and Leandros, two children whose creativity and warmth and startlingly complex lives have rewritten my own life from scratch and will only write more as we grow older. But I'm most grateful—and here I've gone and smuggled her into the ending as well—to Giota, for helping day after day to cultivate that creativity and warmth, sometimes in the most difficult of circumstances. I dedicate this book to her.

PREFACE

THIS IS A GUIDEBOOK of sorts. It will walk you through a mostly uncharted geography of refugee and diasporic literature between Europe and the Middle East, pushed off the grid a century ago as modernity took shape. Modernity has of course taken many shapes across the globe, but along the rim of the Eastern Mediterranean, from Southeastern Europe down through the Levant, it was marked by massive projects of human displacement, ethnic cleansing, and genocide. *Literature's Refuge* will focus in particular on the Greek- and Turkish-speaking borderlands of this geography, where some of the core mechanisms of modern border logic were tried and tested in the early twentieth century. During the collapse of the Ottoman Empire, the institutions of the nation-state radically reshaped the region through a series of population movements and border-making, one of the most violent of which was the Greco-Turkish Population Exchange of 1923, which uprooted almost two million people and aimed at ethno-religious and racial homogenization: displaceable peoples were bandied about and traded like hundreds of thousands of cattle, Christians prodded this way out of Turkey and Muslims that way out of Greece. The Exchange carved up the edges of Europe and West Asia between two faiths; between two languages and alphabets; between two continents and indeed two "civilizations." But it did not stop there; more broadly, it bequeathed to global geopolitics a working template for the solution of so-called minority problems and continues to haunt many human geographies today.

These border upheavals have been chronicled several times over by historians, a number of whose works I can commend to my readers, such as Bruce Clark's *Twice a Stranger*, Onur Yıldırım's *Diplomacy and Displacement*, or Dimitris Kamouzis's *Greeks in Turkey*. This book, however, plies its trade not in histories but in stories. It is a work of comparative literature, in other words, not historiography. The difference is important, and the stories in these pages deserve a broad audience, because they open windows onto alternative cultural imaginaries that can help rewrite not only the literary history of the region but the larger civilizational logic of modern borders writ large. A precious small number of comparative literary studies have blazed a trail toward the Exchange and its aftermath,[1] but these concern themselves with mainstream national literatures on both "sides" of the conflict, a choice that tends to repeat rather than replace the border logic of the Exchange. *Literature's Refuge* aims at something different: to recover the stories and storytellers hiding in the chinks and crannies of the border itself. In some cases, this means digging down beneath the surface of canonical works—for example, the popular fiction that I treat in chapter three—in order to recover the messy plurality of human geographies, languages, texts, and contexts that were once intertwined within these stories, before the latter were canonized and standardized. Other works of literature that I detail in this book are mostly or entirely unknown: fugitive stories hidden away in unpublished manuscript codices, such as Greek-language Islamic poetry in the Arabic alphabet (written by Greek-speaking Muslims from Greece) or Turkish-language novels in the Greek alphabet (written by Turkish-speaking Orthodox Christians from Turkey). These literary traditions, which tied their languages to the alphabet of their community's holy scriptures, introduced unwelcome if not embarrassing complications to national and civilizational narratives of belonging. Unsurprisingly, therefore, they were uprooted not only from the physical geographies that they called home but from literary histories on both sides of the civilizational border. Decimated, disoriented, and displaced, these poems and narratives have nonetheless miraculously survived a century or more in manuscript formats and bits of print, passed from hand to hand in refugee communities or held in limbo in special collections half a world away from the lands where they belonged. They are what Heghnar Zeitlian Watenpaugh calls "survivor objects."[2] What kind of literary refuge have they forged since their displacement? What refuge can I offer them in this book?

That brings me to the book's title. Given the fact that neither Greece nor Turkey showed much institutional interest in preserving many of the texts and scraps of text that I trace out here, the "refuge" in my title cannot and should not be understood as formalized asylum; this refuge is constituted not by state bureaucracies but by a series of community-based or ad hoc relationships of care, centered on stories and texts. Weaving these textual networks together and placing them in dialogue with one another, *Literature's Refuge* builds a larger regional border refuge based on principles of horizontal solidarity—not unlike the solidarity movement in Greece today, as documented for example by Katerina Rozakou and Zareena Grewal.[3] It is in these horizontal relationships of care that I invest the energies of my book, not in any given state or its structures of protection—and this includes the Ottoman state as well, as will become clear already in the first chapter. My book harbors no nostalgia for the Ottoman imperial past or for the present-day Neo-Ottomanism of the Turkish Republic, whose aims are geopolitical expansion and the imposition of state interests in the region. The refuge of this book seeks its legitimacy in neither Greek nor Turkish nor Ottoman nor Neo-Ottoman state institutions but in the fugitives of those institutions, whose words and worlds I place side by side from one chapter to the next.[4]

In an earlier draft of this book, I had considered the title "Undocumented Literatures of the East-West Borderscape," but I foreclosed this possibility for two reasons: first, I do not wish to appropriate the experiences of contemporary undocumented people, with whom this book certainly shares affinities but is not directly concerned.[5] Second, I do not want to front this book with a negatively charged title. True, some of the stories featured herein (and many of the people who have handled them and kept them alive) were indeed denied access to philological documentation in Greece and Turkey, documentation such as printed editions, editorial prefaces, academic articles, or monographs that survey or study a given literary tradition and thus create broader interest and publishing opportunities for it. These kinds of print documentation, which traditionally depended on decisions made by professors, chairs, or researchers of this or that national literature, had the potential to lift an otherwise philologically undocumented story out of material precarity into some degree of sustainability, whereas the absence of such documentation over the course of the twentieth century ensured ongoing institutional neglect and the real possibility of physical annihilation from the historical record.[6] I do not shy away from pointing out these conditions of institutional precarity in the pages that follow—particularly in my introduction—yet rather than highlight them in my title, I want instead to signal the core concern of my work: elevating and elaborating the literary survivors themselves.

I see my task here as one primarily of curation and assemblage: to give a print platform to these refugee and diasporic narratives and to articulate them together in a shared space. To make place for the displaced, in other words. But I do so not by expanding national literary histories to make room for these texts; rather, I remap the literary geography from the ground up, placing known works of literature (e.g., Cavafy's poetry) and unknown works of literature (e.g., Şānī's poetry) alongside one another on equal footing. I want to shape this refuge not on the terms set by institutional philology but on the decentered, reader-centric protocols of many of the texts that I foreground. That means not only rearranging the furniture of this or that literary canon but, crucially, opening up the canon and indeed the academy to the active input of my own readers, who, as I discuss in the introduction that follows, will hopefully include a modest but diverse swath of reading publics beyond the academy as well. The book itself is just one step in a larger public invitation to engage in the work of recovery and curation, which I plan to continue on site in Greece, Turkey, and the United States in the form of workshops, open-access translations, and interconfessional dialogues.

This kind of work inevitably highlights my outsider status, as someone who identifies as neither Greek nor Turkish and has lived in both Greece and Turkey with the relatively privileged status of a documented alien and visa-holder. Still, my pathway to this book has been a long haul in its own way. It has benefited not only from training in standard Greek and Turkish but, after this, from an insistent exploration of less-traveled roads within those languages, breaking past the national guardrails and veering off into nonstandard dialects, unconventional alphabets, and unexpected media and formats that, for readers of twentieth- or twenty-first-century literature, might at first appear illegible mismatches—or they simply don't appear at all.

The novelist China Miéville has a word for this: *unseeing*.[7] Many contemporary readers have indeed been trained to "unsee" parts of the literary world around us, which we sequester into invisibility. But if you "breach"— that is to say, if you stop unseeing and train your eyes on these fugitive worlds within your world—"you can't come back from that . . . you'll never unsee again."[8] You'll find Islam at home in unexpected corners of Greek literature; you'll find Greek Orthodoxy not only in the earliest novels of the Turkish language but in the darkest years of Kemalist homogenization nearly a century later; you'll see worlds and worlds of rich literary traditions interlocked like the warp and woof of a tapestry. But to truly understand them on their own terms, we need to learn their languages and scripts, their media and formats.

This program of graduate training is a key pathway forward for literary studies today. It is no longer good enough to critique the status quo; we ought to set ourselves the demanding task of recovering and elevating literary systems that have survived the status quo, often along its borderlands.[9] Thankfully, there are many more scholars—and many of them more skilled than I— pushing this kind of research agenda. My own agenda has been beset by occasional dead ends and frustrations, and even among the works that have made it into this book, certain turns of phrase or patches of text continue at times to puzzle me. I hope that my humble sense of discovery helps keep the following chapters fresh and exciting (and open to the additions or corrections of my readers). Yet I also want to emphasize the real work that I have put into refining and polishing these literary excursions, which I have done with an aim to honor the texts and scraps of text themselves *as literature*. In the rare instances when they were not ignored wholesale by institutional philologists, the refugee traditions that I examine in several of the chapters here were taken up only to be downgraded into subliterary genres—folklore, oral history, etc.—and dismantled for parts in the footnotes of national historiography. Their works were deemed "derivative," their storytellers were dismissed as "illiterate," their prosody was denigrated as "displeasing to the ears," and their language was called a "pollution." I have taken great pains therefore to do justice to these literatures not only with my analyses but with my translations as well. I want to render these stories as vibrant and colorful works of literature worthy of a place in the belletristic traditions of the region, and I want to invite my nonspecialist readers into those traditions. I can think of no better way to honor the displaced literatures of my study than by winning them a place among the broad readerships that they deserve.

NOTE ON TRANSLITERATION AND TRANSLATION

THIS BOOK charts out a fraught geography of wayward words and alphabets: Greek in the Greek script, Greek in the Arabic script, Turkish in the Arabic script, Turkish in the Greek script, Greek and Turkish in the Latin script, even a patch of Greek in the Hebrew script. How to navigate such a landscape in English? My priority is to keep things simple and hospitable for all interested readers, yet I also strive, as best I can, for the precision demanded by specialists and indeed deserved by the literature itself. This is why original languages and oftentimes original scripts are presented alongside my English translations in a place of parity on the page, rather than shunted into the endnotes at the back of the book. When transcription is preferred, I generally follow the transliteration systems of the *International Journal of Middle East Studies* and the *Journal of Modern Greek Studies* for the Ottoman and Greek alphabets, respectively (though I apply a lighter touch to my transcriptions of Halide Edib's Ottoman Turkish in chapter 3). Some proper names have been altered to match common English spellings or the preferred usage of the persons themselves, such as Singopoulos for Σεγκόπουλος.

But what about place names? How to name a city with multiple toponyms, each of which bears a political charge in the aftermath of ethnic cleansing and deportation? Two such cities appear in this book—the one variously known as Selanik, Salonico, Solun, or Thessaloniki and the other as Smyrna or İzmir. Let me take the latter first, which is a port city on the coast of West Asia: called "İzmir" by Turkish speakers, the city was known to its large Greek-speaking population as Smyrni (conventionally Smyrna in English). Greeks were ethnically cleansed from the city in the autumn of 1922, whereafter it gained a Turkish supermajority almost overnight. Thessaloniki, on the other hand, as it is known today, is a major port city in northern Greece. During the later Ottoman period, Greeks were a small minority in the city, which was known to its large Sephardic Jewish population as Salonico and Selanik to its Ottoman

Turkish population (conventionally Salonica in English). The city was annexed by the Greek state in 1912 and the city's Muslims were deported in 1924, while the Jewish population was decimated by the Holocaust twenty years later. I try to navigate the political difficulty of ethnically cleansed toponyms by actually marking it—*naming* it, if you will—such that one will read here of "Smyrna" before 1923 and "Izmir" thereafter, or similarly of "Salonica" before 1923 and "Thessaloniki" thereafter.

LITERATURE'S REFUGE

Introduction

THE GRECO-TURKISH War of 1919 to 1922 was a watershed moment in the twentieth century. Not only did it draw the final curtain on the First World War; it simultaneously redrew the human geography between Europe and the Middle East. The conflict, which was marked by atrocities on both sides, reached its bloody conclusion in September 1922 with the victory of Turkish nationalists and the irregular flight of Greek occupation forces from Anatolia. Yet Greek soldiers weren't the only ones fleeing. Swept up in the chaos, nearly a million Ottoman Greek civilians abandoned their ancestral homes in Turkey and sought refuge across the sea in Greece. Over the long winter months that followed, while these refugees bundled up as best they could in makeshift tents and rags, Greek and Turkish diplomats and representatives of the Great Powers and the League of Nations were working feverishly to answer this one question: what to make of so much human misery?[1]

What these diplomats eventually made was the Population Exchange of 1923. It entailed the wholesale uprooting of all remaining Greek Orthodox Christians from Anatolia (several hundred thousand had stayed on in their homes even after the conclusion of the war and the flight of the first million refugees) and their forced deportation to Greece, which in turn uprooted nearly all of its Muslims (some four hundred thousand) and deported them to Turkey. To resolve the refugee crisis, it seemed, more refugees would have to be created. The Exchange was an unparalleled act of mutual state-sponsored ethnic cleansing, and it was legitimized by a Nobel Peace Laureate: Fridtjof Nansen.[2] In his capacity as the League of Nations High Commissioner for Refugees, Nansen acknowledged the "very considerable hardships, perhaps very considerable impoverishment" that this solution would necessarily impose upon the now displaceable peoples of Turkey and Greece, but he nonetheless endorsed it. As he declared during the negotiations, "I know that the

Governments of the Great Powers are in favor of this proposal because they believe that to unmix the populations of the Near East will tend to secure [its] true pacification."[3] In the eyes of Nansen and his peers, this massive, ethnic "unmixing" of the so-called Near East was not simply the price of peace but the means of imposing it.

Paradoxically, however, the unmixing in fact hinged on a massive remixing of peoples. The Greek Orthodox Christians of Ottoman Anatolia displayed a startling cultural and linguistic diversity that found little ground for expression in the Greek state, which was at pains to homogenize its population. Several Greek dialects from Turkey bore witness to rich and heavy contact with Turkish and/or Levantine cultures, while hundreds of thousands of Greek Orthodox Christians from the interior in fact spoke Turkish as their only tongue, writing it in the Greek alphabet of their gospels. The Population Exchange tore all these groups from their regional cultures and languages and shunted them into Greece, where they were often ostracized as "Turkish spawn." Many of the Muslims of Greece, meanwhile, found it difficult to integrate into Turkey for similar reasons, due to cultural or linguistic difference (not a few Muslims spoke Greek) that they often had to suppress amidst the cultural reforms of the Kemalist state, which also aimed at national homogenization at all costs.[4] Refugees on both sides of the Aegean had been unmixed from their homes, cultures, and languages only to be violently remixed into what others had decided was their true home. This is what it meant to "pacify" the Middle East. The global foundations of modern humanitarianism were being set in the shifting sands of ethnic cleansing.[5]

Let me pause for a moment over that last term. Race and ethnicity were in fact key vectors of the Exchange and the international standards that it set. While the final official agreement defined the displaceables by their religion, a careful reading of the notes, memoranda, and initial reports before the convention—where off-hand and unguarded turns of phrase reveal the ideological assumptions and aims of the participants—suggest that religion was actually a proxy for race.[6] As Kristina Gedgaudaitė and I have argued elsewhere, the imbrication of race and religion in the negotiations betrayed a larger state project to mark not just the refugees but "the entire civic body of each country in blood-based terms of racialized homogeneity."[7] It took many more years of state policy to realize this vision of racialized majoritarianism in Turkey and Greece, yet it was at the Treaty of Lausanne that such a vision was first enshrined and diplomatically normalized. Indeed, Aslı Iğsız has argued that the Greco-Turkish Population Exchange was a definitive moment in the

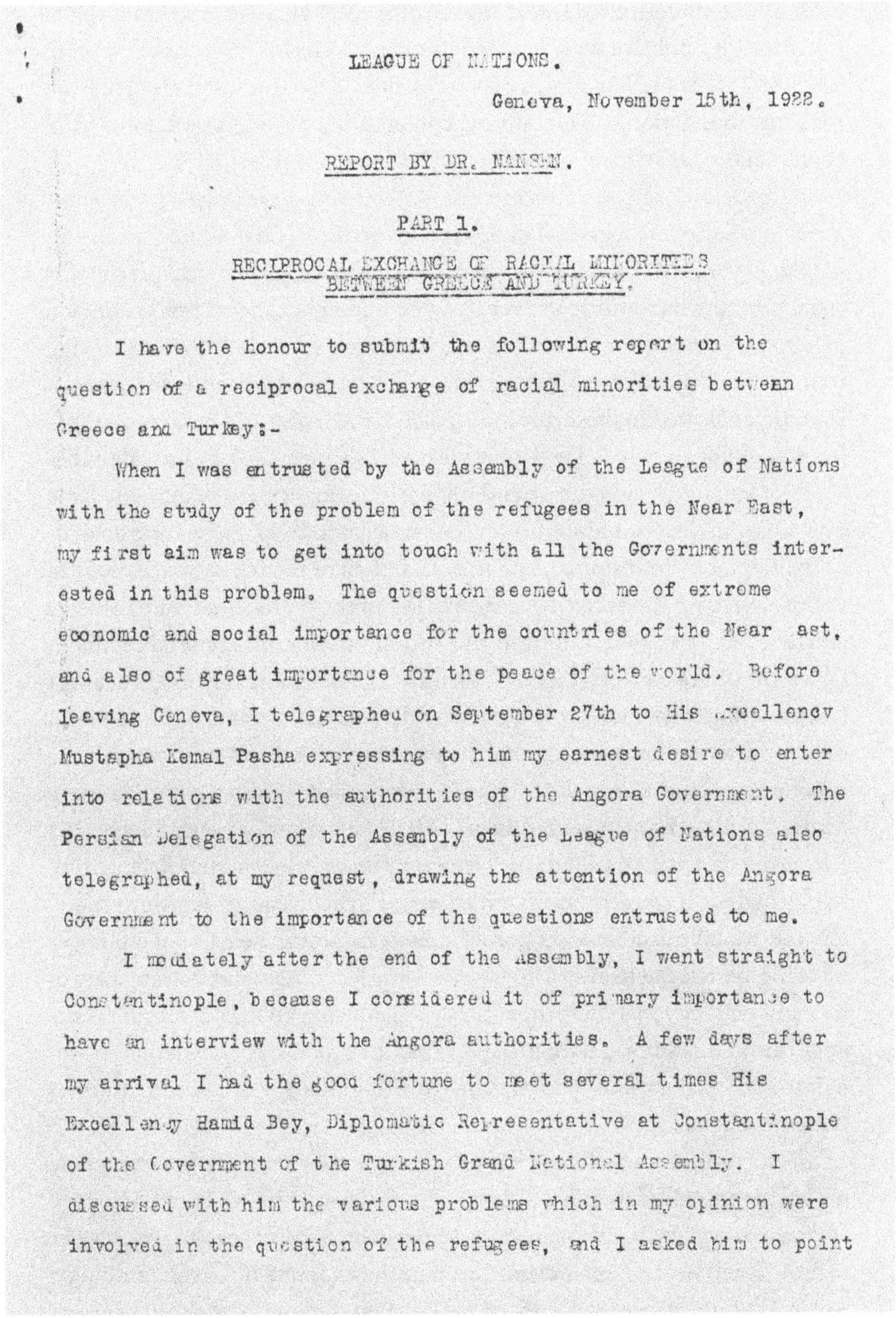

LEAGUE OF NATIONS.

Geneva, November 15th, 1922.

REPORT BY DR. NANSEN.

PART 1.

RECIPROCAL EXCHANGE OF RACIAL MINORITIES
BETWEEN GREECE AND TURKEY.

I have the honour to submit the following report on the question of a reciprocal exchange of racial minorities between Greece and Turkey:-

When I was entrusted by the Assembly of the League of Nations with the study of the problem of the refugees in the Near East, my first aim was to get into touch with all the Governments interested in this problem. The question seemed to me of extreme economic and social importance for the countries of the Near East, and also of great importance for the peace of the world. Before leaving Geneva, I telegraphed on September 27th to His Excellency Mustapha Kemal Pasha expressing to him my earnest desire to enter into relations with the authorities of the Angora Government. The Persian Delegation of the Assembly of the League of Nations also telegraphed, at my request, drawing the attention of the Angora Government to the importance of the questions entrusted to me.

Immediately after the end of the Assembly, I went straight to Constantinople, because I considered it of primary importance to have an interview with the Angora authorities. A few days after my arrival I had the good fortune to meet several times His Excellency Hamid Bey, Diplomatic Representative at Constantinople of the Government of the Turkish Grand National Assembly. I discussed with him the various problems which in my opinion were involved in the question of the refugees, and I asked him to point

FIGURE 1. An early draft report of the "Reciprocal Exchange of Racial Minorities" by Fridtjof Nansen. Copyright held by United Nations Archives at Geneva. Folder R1761/48/24318.

birth of the modern border regime, infusing the border with a thinly veiled eugenicist biopolitics that, as she demonstrates in her book *Humanism in Ruins*, took root and blossomed over the course of the twentieth century. Even today, its foundational logic informs contemporary borders and population control across the region, from Israel-Palestine to Cyprus.[8]

In short, the Exchange set a precedent. Yet it also drew on past precedents, some of which were legal and diplomatic in nature—what we might call *procedural precedents*[9]—while other, more fundamental ideological precedents came from the humanistic sciences—what we might call *first principles*: who belonged where, where belonged to whom, and what were the identifying features of a collective people and their collectivity? Among the branches of learning dedicated to these questions, one of the oldest and most central pillars was philology, which I will examine here. I define philology broadly as the study of languages, literatures, and textual transmission, an admittedly large domain whose edges and subfields are somewhat fuzzy (ranging from analytical bibliography to historical linguistics), but all of them in essence concern themselves with the recovery and curation of the stories that humans have conveyed across space and time and the languages and material media in which they have conveyed them.[10] Defined as such, philology might seem at first an unlikely tool for parsing out populations, but it came to be used not only for drawing lines of filiation between texts or tongues but, through the movements of those texts and tongues, for drawing lines of categorical division across racialized human geographies.[11] In the interstices between Europe and Western Asia, where the linguistic geography was so unyieldingly diverse, philology had been an early and essential player in articulating questions of belonging, mobility, and assimilation. Philology in fact can help us put our finger on some central questions of the modern border: Where did the language of race and ethnicity that these diplomats were drawing upon come from? What linguistic and cultural paradigms informed their vision of population movements and borders, and what was the role of philology in the formation of these paradigms?

The focus here on philology has to a certain extent been predetermined by my training as a literary scholar, but I nonetheless insist that the philological endeavor has played a crucial role in the larger ideation of the modern border regime. I will bear out this claim through the example of Greek philology, which I choose rather than Turkish philology not because the latter is in any way innocent of similar border violence—it is not[12]—but rather because Greek as a concept lies at the historical core of philology and informs not only the regional border politics of the Aegean but the larger ideological machinery of Europe and the West writ large. I will have occasion to revisit Turkish literary history at several critical points in the following chapters, but my focus here is on Modern Greek philology, which was established in the shadow of European classical philology and found its voice in an often tense and asymmetrical dialogue with the latter.[13] Greek had always lain near the heart of European philology, yet with the material and institutional expansion of the discipline over the course of the nineteenth century, the study of Greek and the construction of a Greek-language corpus gained immense institutional capital and extended its methodological and intellectual hegemony over ever greater swaths of world literature and indeed of the world itself.[14] There was thus much at stake in demarcating who could lay a claim to the Hellenic and who could not.[15] Determined to validate and protect its share in Hellenism's cultural and institutional capital, Modern Greek philology made large strides over the course of the nineteenth century and broke ground toward the philological border regime that I am tracing out here.

In the decades leading up to the Population Exchange, the terms of the debate had already been rehearsed through an explicit philological border regime of mixing and unmixing. As Greek intellectuals attempted to trace a throughline from antiquity to the present, they found it impossible to ignore the many mass movements of peoples and texts over the lands they claimed for their own. The border regime that they eventually developed to manage these population movements and textual traditions was subtler than a simple apartheid wall (although several forms and degrees of exclusion were applied); equally important were the internal mechanisms of assimilation, value extraction and partial omission, which thrust peoples and texts into several gray zones of semi-inclusion and -exclusion, semi-mobility and -immobility. Drawing from the field of border studies, we might call these mechanisms (and the peoples and texts moving through them and against them) a *borderscape*, which is to say a dynamic clockwork of funnels and filters and contested mobilities across an entire geography.[16]

Within this philological borderscape, which continued and expanded in the years and decades after the Exchange, certain diasporic textual bodies like the poems of C. P. Cavafy in Egypt could be absorbed and admitted into national Greek literature and mainstream media, but only after being subjected to significant reformatting and reframing. Other stories and storytellers, like the Turkish-language ballads of one or two refugee poets, found a partial foothold in minor regional press shops but were actively excluded from mainstream publishing, literary anthologies, libraries, textbooks and, of course, from classrooms. Even less lucky were others, like the poetry of Greek-language Islam, which was almost entirely banished from the annals of literary history and left to cross the borders of world literature in manuscript formats that until today remain largely undocumented by national philology. At the same time, a given manuscript or oral performance by refugees was occasionally transcribed, reworked and rewritten by mainstream Greek authors, who supplied their own versions to a national publishing apparatus that in turn supplied them to foreign-language publishers, where we can now read, for example, *A Prisoner of War's Story* or *Farewell Anatolia*, whose title pages attribute the works to single, recognizably Greek authors (Stratis Doukas and Dido Sotiriou, respectively). Teasing the category of "literature" out from within these and similar contexts, I would thus define it as a modern philological invention, at the core of which lie mechanisms of partial inclusion, exclusion, extraction, and the production of institutional value. At the borderscape between Europe and the Middle East, philologists, critics, and publishers *made* literature by picking apart, pruning, and separating out a complex geography of texts and their human handlers (such as writers, oral storytellers, copyists, scholiasts, readers, binders, translators, etc.). Some of these pieces were reconstituted and printed as canonical works and authors, while others have wound up pushed into supplementary footnotes, appendices, archival ephemera, or singular manuscripts of various shapes and sizes in special collections or the ad hoc libraries of third- or fourth-generation refugee communities.

Literature's Refuge spans this entire literary spectrum. Breaking known and unknown literature down into its constituent parts, I ascribe literary value to each and every one of those parts (some of which have traditionally been denied literariness). Taken together, the chapters of this book raise important methodological questions for the larger discipline of literary studies. Over the past twenty years, the idea of "world literature" has come to frame many of the poems, novels, and stories that academics study and compare across national borders, yet not all texts can claim citizenship to the world as we have made it; not all texts bear the proper documentation to move freely through the checkpoints of modern philology,[17] which ultimately forces certain border crossings underground. In short, the border logic initiated by the Population Exchange didn't just displace peoples from their place in the world; it has also displaced many of their stories from a place in world literature.

This book aims to open up a space to foreground and honor the border crossings of such stories and, in doing so, to reconsider and revise the larger philological borderscape through which texts pass. As Kader Konuk has done in a different context, I work hard to recover the "multiple attachments" that often extend across exile, forced displacement, and partition.[18] To trace out these attachments is not simply to insert new textual objects into the existing economies of exchange that structure transnational publishing and circulation networks; it is to set our sights on alternative networks altogether and, by sifting through their material records, to seek more democratic protocols of textual transmission and exchange. These protocols draw their strength not from some core assimilatory power of institutional Hellenism or Turkishness but rather—and this is crucial—from a decentralized federation of languages and texts that identify in some way with localized Greek Orthodox or Islamic cultures, or those that do not identify but have coexisted alongside these cultures and claim a place in the cultural tapestry. This is a book of humble means— using for the most part what we might call the manuscript and ephemeral detritus of national philology—but its goal is lofty: to provide an alternative cartography of the eastern Mediterranean borderscape, which is a small but constitutive mechanism of the larger global border system that regulates our world today. Who belongs where, and who gets to decide? *Literature's Refuge* attempts over the following five chapters to articulate some preliminary answers to those questions in the discipline of literature. Before that, however, I must sketch out in greater detail the philological border regime as it exists today and the methods and first principles that have helped shape it.

No Greece Left in Greece

To whom does the legacy of Greece and Greek belong? Already in the fifteenth century, European philologists had begun to question whether contemporary speakers of Greek could lay claim to their own tongue. Writing of his experiences in the final years of the Byzantine Empire, where he had traveled to learn Greek, Francesco Filelfo warned against

> linguam vulgarem [. . .], quae et plebeia erat et depravata atque corrupta ob peregrinorum mercatorumque multitudinem qui quottidie [sic] Constantinopolin confluebant in urbemque recepti incolae Graecisque admixti locutionem optimam infuscarunt inquinaruntque. Nam viri aulici veterem sermonis dignitatem atque elegantiam retinebant, in primisque ipsae

nobiles mulieres, quibus cum nullum esset omnino cum viris peregrinis commercium, merus ille ac purus priscorum Graecorum sermo servabatur intactus.[19]

the vulgar [Greek] language of the plebs, perverted and corrupted by the multitude of migrants and merchants who flowed into Constantinople every day. Welcomed as residents in the city, these travelers mixed in with the Greeks and tainted and defiled the Greeks' most beautiful manner of speech. For the ancient dignity and elegance of speaking was retained only by members of the court—first and foremost, by the noblewomen, who had no commerce whatsoever with foreign men and thus kept the uncontaminated and pure language of the ancient Greeks intact.*

Filelfo argued here that the Greek spoken in the capital had been tainted and defiled—or, if we translate the verb *inquinare* more literally, the language had been "shat into" by (and mixed up with the feces of) the migrant multitudes. The fatal mistake had been to "welcome" these migrants as "residents." The ancient dignity of the language, according to Filelfo, had thus been perverted and corrupted by the unchecked "flow" of non-Greeks into the city, and it was only by walling itself off from this mass of human migration that a small cadre of Greek nobility (particularly women) had been able to preserve the Greek tongue from contamination. Linguistic integrity depended on a class-based border regime against the unregulated flow of human bodies in and out of the city. Europeans looking to learn Greek, he warned, would thus do well to similarly wall themselves off from the language of the masses and seek out tutors among the nobles.

In later centuries, after the collapse of the Byzantine Empire, many European philologists held increasingly deep suspicions of their Greek contemporaries, whose language they viewed as irreparably corrupted by a long series of population movements.[20] Daniel Heinsius, one of the most renowned scholars at Leiden University in the seventeenth century, penned a witty epigram in ancient Greek bemoaning,

Οὐκ ἔτι δὴ μένεν Ἑλλὰς ἐν Ἑλλάδι· τίς κε πίθοιτο;
Ἑλλαδικῇ γλώσσῃ μίγνυτο Βαρβαρική.

---

*Throughout this book, translations are my own unless otherwise noted. Block quotations, like the one above, will provide both the English and non-English text, while shorter quotations will shift the non-English text to footnotes.

Φωναὶ δ᾽ ἀλλήλῃσι πάλαι μίγεν· οὐδ᾽ ἴα γῆρυς
Ὀψιγόνοισιν ἔην τοῖς ποτὲ γενομένοις.[21]

No Greece left in Greece now—who'd believe it?
Into Greece's tongue was mixed the barbaric;
all voices long since mixed together and not a single voice
remained to those lately born too late.

The verbs of mixture (μίγνυμι) immediately catch one's eye, continuing the same conceit of Filelfo, yet one finds a subtler and more devastating innovation in Heinsius's verses: the confusion of land and language. You will note that in my translation of the second line of the excerpt I write not "the Greek tongue" but rather "Greece's tongue"; Heinsius geographically marked the language as *Helladic* (rather than *Hellenic*), an adjective that means "of the Greek lands." If there is no Greek tongue—or at least nothing that European scholars acknowledged as a Greek tongue—left in Greece, then surely there is no Greece left there either, Heinsius quips. Not only does he dispossess Greeks of their speech and language, he simultaneously dispossesses them of their land. Born too late into a language and a soil no longer their own, these linguistic outcasts belong nowhere but to the roving masses of barbarians.

The prolific philologist Claude Saumaise happily piled on a few decades later, opining offhandedly in his *De Hellenistica Commentarius* that "today, vulgar Greek has in all its aspects been disfigured into such barbarity that it is hardly recognizable."* Ironically, Heinsius and Saumaise were in a bitter feud over the status of Koine Greek in the septuagint and the New Testament (this was the actual topic of the latter's *Commentarius*), yet the barbarity of modern Greek remained a point of common agreement between the two. Over the longue durée of ensuing decades and centuries, many Western intellectuals consolidated such remarks into a philological trope that could be picked up and widely repeated with or without citation.[22] At the turn of the next century, for example, Johann Michael Lange endorsed the idea that "by now the Greek tongue has totally spiraled into barbarity" since it had "admitted innumerable barbarian voices: those of Arabs, Hungarians, Spaniards, Gauls, Italians, and other peoples. Therefore the Greeks of today must learn the Greek tongue just as we do: from tutors and from the books of the

---

* "Hodie vulgaris Graeca ex omni parte ita barbarie deformata est, ut vix agnoscatur" (Saumaise, *De Hellenistica*, 32).

ancients."* Through the successive migrations of non-Greeks, the argument went, Greeks had corrupted their own language to such a degree that they were in fact on equal (if not worse) footing with the West. Perhaps, it was implied, it was time for Greeks to study under European tutelage if they were to understand themselves.

Up to the cusp of the nineteenth century, these kinds of philological attacks on contemporary speakers of Greek were often driven by the theological schism of Eastern Orthodoxy and Western Christianity. The central crux of the debate lay in the textual authority of the New Testament and whether Greek Orthodox Christians could even understand it. Nonetheless, the repeated metaphors of contamination, corruption, miscegenation, and purity had primed the soil for the racialist discourses that were to blossom soon enough. In 1830, just as the modern Greek state was in its final birth throes, a Bavarian historian named Jakob Fallmerayer published his *Geschichte der Halbinsel Morea während des Mittelalters* (*History of the Morean Peninsula in the Middle Ages*), which argued that successive waves of Slavic immigration into Byzantine lands in late antiquity had effectively wiped out the "race of the Hellenes." As a result, "Not the slightest drop of undiluted Hellenic blood flows in the veins of the Christian population of present-day Greece."[23] Modern Greeks, he implied, were not only culturally illegitimate heirs to the title, they were *racially* illegitimate too. While Fallmerayer remains a minor figure in the history of German thought, it is difficult to overstate his colossal impact in Modern Greece, where he continues to this day to haunt and shape the national culture.[24] Admittedly, his thesis may have harbored a broader geopolitical aim beyond Greece—namely, to bolster the Ottoman state against Russian expansion[25]—but his only lasting effects were limited to Greece, where the Greek intelligentsia of subsequent generations (who by no means remained passive observers, as I will discuss in the next section) responded with a reactive cultural agenda of their own, in which questions of racial belonging were to be answered definitively through language and literature.

Importantly, Fallmerayer helped to frame this agenda at least partially by partaking in discourses of scientific racism and colonialism, best seen in a

---

*"Nostra hac aetate, Graeca lingua plane in barbariem prolapsa est [...]. Innumeras admisit voces barbaras, Arabicas, Hungaricas, Hispanicas, Gallicas, Italicas, aliarumque gentium. Ideo hodie [ ] Graecam linguam Graeci illi, non minus ac nos, a praeceptoribus et e libris veterum debent addiscere" (Lange, *Differentia Linguae*, 5). Lange is quoting an unnamed source here that I have been unable to determine.

lecture he delivered in 1835 (i.e., five years after the publication of his initial thesis) to the Bavarian Academy of Sciences:

> The Greek nation, which from the Trojan war until the sixth century after Christ lived in the Peloponnese and the mainland to the north, no longer exists today. Due to unfortunate circumstances of every kind, the Greek nation perished, or it melted into totally insignificant dregs and was so intermixed with foreigners that the initial character of the Greeks was snuffed out completely [...]. This doctrine, which was initially just an historical experiment, enters henceforth into the ranks of undebatable historical truths. It has become a fact that no one can deny save by self-delusion. This is not a political matter, it is of a purely scientific nature and is intended only for those who are seriously interested in the proper knowledge of the past and present. [...] It is a matter of mental exercise in the European fashion. Such exercises that only a European can bring to fruition [...] have sharpened the acuity of the mind of those who live in this region of the world [i.e., Europe] and have led them to such discoveries in the fields of nature, art, and science, that with their wise institutions and their skillful use of physical force have gained dominance over the entire human race.[26]

Fallmerayer buttressed his argument within a vocabulary of phylogenetic miscegenation and decline (though his evidence as such was not genetic but philological[27]), which was just starting to solidify into pseudoscientific discourse. Concepts of "racial families" and the presumed hierarchies that obtained among them had been circulating since at least the eighteenth century, in the taxonomies of Linnaeus and the offhand pronouncements of a Hume or a Kant,[28] yet they gained a concerted institutional force in the nineteenth century. Channeling this force into a linguistic analysis, Fallmerayer harnessed it to present his thesis as scientific fact and to foreclose debate. In the final sentence of the excerpt above, however, his rhetorical excess spills even further outward into the geopolitical manifestations of that racial discourse: empire and colonization, which Fallmerayer explicitly links to European knowledge production.

In the following paragraph, Fallmerayer turns this colonial lens back to modern Greece, but under a different light than that with which he had made his initial argument in 1830. In the intervening five years, the newly established state of Greece had become a "Kingdom," and a young Bavarian prince, Otto Friedrich Ludwig, had been imposed upon the people of Greece as their king. This new status quo led to an important twist in Fallmerayer's thesis:

Otto I was chosen by providence to deliver the benefices of this European superiority of intellect to the new, savage and unschooled, but energetic race of Greeks, who have taken the place of the ancient, physically and morally atrophied children of Deucalion. Like a second Kekrops, Otto came from a foreign land to Athens in order to meld together, with new legislation, the scattered and internally disparate races [living in Greece] and to seal all their minds with the common form of a new Hellenic intellect, bestowed by Europe: the rule of law and respect for the king.[29]

The peoples living in Greece are marked here as primitive and ignorant, racially bastardized and dissimilar from one another—spilled across the lands of Greece through successive migrations. To rehabilitate these peoples, Fallmerayer calls on Otto to impose the civilizing mission of European law and acculturation, just like other populations in the colonies of Europe. Despite being stigmatized as illegitimate heirs to the Hellenic past, the peoples of Greece are nonetheless invited to participate in Hellenism if only they apprentice themselves to the true heirs of that tradition: the Europeans.[30] Fallmerayer extended to the people of modern Greece a kind of provisional invitation to Greekness, but only to the degree that they colonized their minds and bodies under the tutelage of Europe.

To be sure, Fallmerayer's attacks represent but one extreme of a larger and varied discourse, and there were many Europeans who expressed support for both modern Greeks and their independence. Nonetheless, these philhellenes tended to conform to and hence confirm the same paradigm as that of Fallmerayer, since they usually justified their support only by resort to classical Greece and its supposed Western European legacy.[31] Rather than denigrating modern Greeks as barbarized, most philhellenes simply sifted through the supposed barbarism of the East to salvage the broken "ruins" of the West's ancient past that they wanted to see there, in the "living museums" of the modern Greeks.[32] Even more complicated manifestations of philhellenism, such as those of revolutionary Italian circles or of feminist empowerment, often fell into similar antiquarian tropes.[33] Much of philhellenism, in other words, staked its defense of Greece on the same terms as anti-hellenism, playing by the same rules for the same prize: a classical culture "uncontaminated by foreign elements."[34] Situated within this system of thought, which legitimized a perceived pure Greek core in fifth-century Athens and devalued any cultural manifestations of Greekness to the degree that they diverged from the core, the twin faces of anti-hellenism and philhellenism had a profound and lasting effect on the trajectories that modern Greek historiography and philology followed.[35]

Hellenism at the Crossroads

Over the nineteenth century, self-identifying Greek intellectuals defended their language and history as legitimately Hellenic on many of the same basic terms set by European Hellenism. Most famously (and as a direct response to Fallmerayer) the Greek historiographer Konstantinos Paparrigopoulos wrote the five-volume Ἱστορία τοῦ Ἑλληνικοῦ Ἔθνους (*History of the Hellenic Nation*, 1860–1874), which rehabilitated Byzantine history and offered it as the crucial missing link between ancient and modern Greece. The "Helleno-Christian" culture of Byzantium was institutionalized as a kind of narrative bridge—one that, through the stories they told about themselves, modern Greeks could traverse in reverse and lay claim to the ancient past lying on the other side.[36] There was, however, an important point of difference with European Hellenic studies of that period, which often seemed so obsessed with a static image of the fifth-century BCE: Paparrigopoulos, to the contrary, readily admitted that his model of continuity was founded on change and adaptation. Hellenism's three-thousand-year adventure, he argued, was one not of stasis but of movement, which he categorized across four periods: Hellenic antiquity; Hellenistic late antiquity; Byzantine Hellenism; and contemporary Hellenism. Hellenism had survived in a single continuous lineage from antiquity to today not in spite of but because of its dynamism. Interestingly, however, Paparrigopoulos injected into this dynamism the same precise terms as Fallmerayer: colonial conquest and domination. Just as the Greek culture of fifth-century Athens seemed ready to collapse into extinction, Paparrigopoulos wrote,

> Αἴφνης ἀναφαίνεται περιβαλλόμενος τὴν μοναρχικὴν πορφύραν καὶ ἐπιχειρῶν δι' αὐτῆς τὴν εἰς μέγα μέρος τῆς Ἀσίας καὶ τῆς Ἀφρικῆς διάχυσιν τῶν ἀπείρων διανοητικῶν, τεχνικῶν, πολιτικῶν θησαυρῶν ὅσους παρήγαγε καὶ ἐτελείωσε καὶ ἐσώρευσεν ἐν τῇ μικρᾷ ταύτῃ γωνίᾳ τῆς γῆς κατὰ τὴν πρώτην τῆς ἱστορίας αὐτοῦ περίοδον. Τὴν δ' ἀρετὴν ταύτην τῆς ἀναμορφώσεως μετέδωκεν ὁ πρῶτος Ἑλληνισμός, διὰ τοῦ δευτέρου, καὶ εἰς τὸν τρίτον, διὰ δὲ τοῦ τρίτου καὶ εἰς τὸν καθ' ἡμᾶς Ἑλληνισμόν.[37]

suddenly it reappeared invested in the royal gowns [of Alexander the Great] and, by means of its royal scepter, it poured out its infinite intellectual, technical, and political treasures upon a large swath of Asia and Africa— treasures that it had produced, perfected, and amassed in that small corner of earth during its first period of life. This virtue of reconfiguration was passed from the first Hellenism to the second, and from the second to the third, and from the third on to our own Hellenism.

In Paparrigopoulos's narrative, which mirrored in striking ways the encomiastic narratives that European scholars were crafting about their own empires, Hellenism survived through territorial and linguistic conquest, expanding and assimilating foreign lands and foreign tongues to itself, and through that assimilation, reformulating itself in turn.

And this survival strategy did not end with Alexander's ancient conquests. Even in the Byzantine period, where the dominant narrative at this point was Greek decline amidst the population movements of so-called barbarians, Paparrigopoulos simply shifted the terms of the debate. While admitting to "miscegenation" (ἐπιμιξία), he chose to focus not on race or blood but on language and culture: "Fallmerayer had made the claim, with every assurance, that the Greek language had been wiped out from Greece [. . .]. We do not deny that Slavic blood was mixed up into the Greek blood in the Greek heartlands, but in the end it was Hellenism that overpowered Slavism," which essentially meant that "the Slavic tongue was wiped out and the Greek tongue dominated absolutely."* Amidst the population movements of the Middle Ages, Paparrigopoulos used the tools of philology to argue that Byzantium had preserved its Hellenism through linguistic and cultural domination. In this way, Paparrigopoulos bequeathed at least one core element to subsequent modern Greek narratives about Greekness: the rhetoric of miscegenation was not to be rejected but accepted and at times even celebrated—but only up to a certain point. So long as this border crossing could be managed, so long as the dominant assimilatory power belonged to Hellenism, such mixing was allowed a place in the pages of Greek historiography. If, on the contrary, any

---

* "Ὁ δὲ Φαλλμεράυερ εἶχε προβῆ μέχρι τῆς βεβαιώσεως ὅτι ἡ ἑλληνικὴ γλῶσσα ὅλως ἐξωστρακίσθη ἐκ Πελοποννήσου καὶ ἐκ τῆς Στερεᾶς [. . .]. Δὲν ἀρνούμεθα ὅτι αἷμα σλαυικὸν ἀνεμίχθη μετὰ τοῦ ἑλληνικοῦ αἵματος καὶ εἰς αὐτὰς τὰς νοτιωτάτας ἑλληνικὰς χώρας. Ἐπὶ τέλους ὅμως ὁ ἑλληνισμὸς κατίσχυσε τοῦ σλαυισμοῦ [. . .] ἐξηλείφθη ἡ σλαυϊκὴ γλῶσσα, ἐπεκράτησε δὲ αὐτῆς ἀπολύτως ἡ ἑλληνική" (Paparrigopoulos vol. 3, 391; 382).

so-called miscegenation threatened the core elements of Greek continuity, the offending parties would have to be displaced from Greek memory, their heritage dispossessed or detained in the footnotes and appendices. For it was only in this way that Paparrigopoulos could claim that "the Greek nation did not cease to exist over the whole course of three whole thousand years [...] always speaking this same language, and bearing this same sentiment, spirit, and name."* Ultimately, continuity depended on a kind of cultural demographic numbers game, one that was played out in the realm of mass migrations.

How did Paparrigopoulos's model translate into literary history, though? The dynamic of miscegenation and assimilation presented some initial difficulties here, because the object of study was no longer populations but individual authors and intellectuals, in whose person migration and "mixing" often equated to crossing religious borders or even to religious conversion.[38] Konstantinos Sathas was the first to make sense of the literary terrain with his *Νεοελληνικὴ Φιλολογία* (*Modern Greek Philology*, 1868), which was essentially a massive biographical index of authors and their bibliographies.[39] As one would expect, Sathas viewed Greek literature primarily through the twin prisms of language and religion, yet he also allowed for exceptions and differentiated degrees of "Greekness," as seen for example in his entry on Leo Allatios, a Greek convert to Catholicism who spent a good part of his career railing against the supposed heresies of the Greek Orthodox faith. Despite his anti-Orthodox writings, Allatios finds a welcoming and sympathetic host in Sathas's *Modern Greek Philology*, which praises the former's gift for locution and poetry and makes excuses for his anti-Greek polemics: "By necessity he became a strident critic of Orthodox Christianity, but not a supercilious reviler of the faith, like other renegades [*drapetidai*]."† Sathas expels most Greek converts to Catholicism from the Greek tradition, lumping them under the category of *drapetidai*—a derogatory term used by the Orthodox Church to mark converts literally as "fugitives" from Orthodoxy—but he opens the canon to those few whom he sees as deserving of attention, such as Allatios, and excuses their attacks on Greek orthodoxy as a matter of necessity. It was

---

*"Ἡ Ἑλληνικὴ ἐθνότης δὲν ἔπαυσεν ὑπάρχουσα ἐπὶ τρισχίλια ὅλα ἔτη, [...] ἀείποτε δὲ τὴν αὐτὴν λαλοῦσα γλῶσσαν, καὶ τὸ αὐτὸ ἔχουσα αἴσθημα, πνεῦμα, ὄνομα" (Paparrigopoulos, vol. 1, 877).

†"Ἠγέρθη καὶ οὗτος ἐξ ἀνάγκης δριμὺς τῆς ὀρθοδοξίας ἐπικριτής, οὐχὶ ὅμως καὶ ὑπερφίαλος ὑβριστής, ὡς ἄλλοι δραπετίδαι" (Sathas, *Νεοελληνικὴ Φιλολογία*, 270).

his way of managing cultural contact and border crossing without sacrificing the Hellenic core.

Since Sathas was willing to make exceptions for certain Greek-speaking Catholics in Europe, one might ask: did he extend the same courtesy to Greek-speaking Muslims of the Ottoman Empire? This is a critical question, and one that brings us to the heart of the Hellenic border regime. For, while early philologists and historiographers like Sathas and Paparrigopoulos were often willing to search out hybrid forms of Hellenism in the borderlands of Catholic and Slavic Europe, Ottoman Islam constituted the ultimate limit case. As I will discuss in chapter one, Greek-language Islam did in fact exist within the Ottoman Empire and developed its own literary traditions, which productively drew both from Greek Orthodox prosody and from Turkish, Arabic, and Persian Islamic genres and narratives. For the most part, this Greek-language literature was written not in the Greek alphabet but in the modified Arabic script of Ottoman Islam.

To my knowledge, throughout his career Sathas only recorded one Greek-language poem by a Muslim, the *Alipashiad*, an epic ballad sung by Haxhi Shehreti at the court of Ali Pasha in the early nineteenth century.[40] But even as he published an excerpt of the poem Sathas reviled it as "barbarous" and "illiterate" and went out of his way to displace it from the Greek canon. Sathas treated it not as a work of literature but as an historical curiosity from which he could strip-mine any data of interest to national Greek historiography. This assessment was later taken up and repeated by Vasilis Pyrsinellas, who, as far as I know, was the only scholar in Greece to survey Arabic-script Greek literature. Yet rather than extolling his object of study, Pyrsinellas deemed Greek-language Islam aesthetically insignificant: "Regarding the poetic value of these works, there is nothing to speak of. The presence of Turkish and Arabic words, which were a source of intellectual flair for the Turks [i.e., Greek-speaking Muslims], creates for us ['Greeks'] a series of ugly and displeasing phonetic impressions without anything poetic to add to the prosaic nature of the Greek verses."* He concluded by admitting that the only value of this literature is of a purely historiographic or ethnographic nature, thus solidifying the trope begun by Sathas.

---

* "'Όσον ἀφορᾶ δὲ περὶ τῆς ποιητικῆς ἀξίας τῶν ἐν λόγῳ ἔργων, οὐδεὶς λόγος δύναται νὰ γίνῃ. Ἡ παρουσία τῶν τουρκοαραβικῶν λέξεων, ἡ ὁποία ἦτο διὰ τοὺς Τούρκους πηγὴ πνευματικῆς ἐξάρσεως, εἶναι δι' ἡμᾶς αἰτία δυσαρέστων μόνον ἠχητικῶν ἐντυπώσεων χωρὶς οὐδὲν ποιητικὸν νὰ προσθέτῃ εἰς τὴν πεζότητα τῶν ὑπολοίπων στίχων" (Pyrsinellas, "Ὁμολογίες," 164).

What was the reasoning behind this systematic circumscription of Ottoman Islam? Sathas hints at an answer in his *Τουρκοκρατουμένη Ἑλλάς* (*Greece during Turkish Rule*, 1869), where he opines that after Greek Byzantium had been hit by the so-called Asiatic deluge (ἀσιανὸς χείμαρρος) of Ottoman Islam, Hellenism "rose up into the mountains, where it set up camp during those long and stormy years. It bore itself bravely under oppression, and while it sometimes met victory and sometimes met defeat it always preserved itself pure and untouched, just like the pure and untouched mountains that had rescued it."* The key concept here is "pure and untouched" (literally: "virgin"), which applies both to the physical mountains of Greece and to the faithful Greeks atop them. Climbing up into the hills and engaging in guerrilla warfare for centuries, these Greeks kept themselves high above the supposedly murky and impure waters of the Asian deluge that had come flooding into erstwhile Greek territories below. In the decades leading up to the Population Exchange, this is how Greek philology seems to have narrated Ottoman cultural contact. Philologists defended Hellenism's pedigree by categorically displacing Islam beyond the bounds of literary or aesthetic value. It was allowed a place on the page only inasmuch as it provided raw facts to the historiographic archive of the nation. As Konstantinos Tsitselikis pointedly remarks, Muslims were denied the possibility of integration into the Greek narrative; the best that they could hope for was "invisibility."[41] According to this paradigm, any Greeks who converted to Islam (or, more generally, any Muslims who spoke Greek) necessarily forfeited their claim to a place in the Greek canon.

Half a century later, most Muslims necessarily forfeited their claim to a physical place in Greece as well, when they were deported to Turkey as part of the Population Exchange.[42] And of the Greek Orthodox Christian refugees who came to take their place, at least a couple hundred thousand did not in fact speak Greek; they spoke Turkish, writing it in the Greek alphabet of their bible. As I will discuss in chapter four, these refugees, known as Karamanli Christians, were likewise dispossessed of their place in the Hellenic canon, for despite their Greek alphabet and the shared Greek Orthodox cultural reservoir from which they drew, in the eyes of Greek nationalists their language was contaminated and unfit for direct integration. In both these and other cases,

---

*"Ὁ Ἑλληνισμὸς ἀμέσως ἀνακύψας καὶ ἐπὶ τῶν ὀρέων κατασκηνώσας κατὰ τὸν μέγαν ἐκεῖνον καὶ πολυχρόνιον κλύδωνα, ἠνδροῦτο διωκόμενος, καὶ ἐναλλὰξ νικῶν καὶ νικώμενος παρθένος διετηρήθη, ὡς οἱ διασώσαντες αὐτὸν παρθενικοὶ βράχοι" (Sathas, *Τουρκοκρατουμένη*, α΄).

like those of Armenian refugees in Greece, the stories and the status of such communities were discounted and ignored. Their uprootings remain always "minor losses" within the larger narratives of national loss, internally displaced within them.[43]

In the years following the Exchange, the literature of both Turkish-speaking Greek Orthodox Christians and Greek-speaking Muslims was stripped for parts and relegated to the footnotes of Greek literary history.[44] Other minorities who remained in Greece, such as the Turkish- and Slavic-speaking Muslims of Western Thrace, the Cham Albanians of Epirus, and the Slavic-speaking Orthodox Christians of Macedonia, were likewise denied entry into literary histories and sometimes targeted for outright linguistic suppression at the hands of the state. The absence of these voices was papered over by a louder, more systematic nationalist philology. In 1926, just a year after the first phase of the Population Exchange had been completed, the Academy of Athens was founded and charged with salvaging and studying the "national heritage." In 1929, Nikolaos Tomadakis submitted the first doctoral dissertation in Modern Greek philology to the University of Athens; his topic was the editions and manuscripts of Dionysios Solomos, author of what had become Greece's national anthem. In 1931, the Academy announced its plans to publish the *Greek Library* series, devoted to Ancient Greek titles in modern translation. By 1936, the figurehead of a new generation of philologists, Ioannis Sykoutris (whom we will meet again in chapter two), was arguing for the need to apprentice Greek philology explicitly to Western European knowledge production—as a defense, in part, against so-called Eastern despotism.[45] These and other philological pronouncements, initiatives, and organizations further cemented the implicit categorical limits on what kind of Greek literature was institutionally visible.

In the years following the Population Exchange, as the Greek state struggled to integrate and assimilate nearly one and a half a million refugees from Turkey, to many intellectuals it seemed as though the only appropriate response to the crisis was national revival. Greek-language Islamic poetry or Turkish-language Greek Orthodox refugee ballads were perhaps the farthest thing from the minds of most in Athens. But the problem was deeper than the discipline's ignorance of such textual traditions at a given historical moment or a given political crisis; there was a structural problem embedded in the discipline's basic definitions and first principles. The major histories of Modern Greek Literature written in the following decades—for example, those of K. Th. Dimaras (1949) and Linos Politis (1978)—subtly but categorically delimit Hellenism in ethno-linguistic if not racial terms and document its border crossing only in the West.[46]

Nonetheless, one important new trope to emerge in Greek philology after the Exchange was the idea of Greek literature as a "crossroads between East and West." How, one might ask, could Greek literature function as a crossroads between East and West when so-called Eastern traditions like Greek-language Islam and Karamanli Turkish had been denied entry? What kind of a crossroads was Greek literature when the philological gatekeepers had, more generally, foreclosed Ottoman Islam as a possible contact point? Yet it was precisely *because* such literary cultures had been dispossessed and immobilized, I believe, that Greek philology was able now to safely use them as props to playact its crossroads metaphor, embracing it as a core component of the Hellenic tradition. Islam and Islamicate literary traditions were not deported wholesale from Greek philology, in other words; they were stripped of their specific value and generalized as the "East" of Greece's crossroads. Instructive here is Dimaras, whose Ἱστορία τῆς Νεοελληνικῆς Λογοτεχνίας (*History of Modern Greek Literature*) was and remains formative. He writes, "Greece's geographic position gives it an additional importance. It is located between two major civilizational masses that stand ever apart from one another [...]. East and West meet atop Greek lands, which thus become a crossroads where two fundamental forms of civilization constantly clash."* Anticipating Samuel Huntington's notion of civilizational clash, Dimaras paints a picture of two opposing worlds destined to stand in unceasing conflict. Between them lies Greece, which is traversed by each of the two. It is important to note that such a language robs Greece of any political agency and likewise excuses it of any political responsibility for its own role in such clashes or the forced migrations that they spark. Be that as it may, even amidst the geopolitical tensions and violence of such a geography, Dimaras seizes on the cultural advantages that it lends to Hellenism, which, since it is a crossroads, has thus been trained to "exercise its assimilatory power" ("νὰ ἀσκήσει τὴν ἀφομοιωτικὴ του δύναμη") over the foreigners who travel across its lands. Recycling a key trope from Paparrigopoulos, Dimaras latches on to "assimilatory power" as the essential tool for his literary history, because it is only after he has assimilated

---

* "Ἔρχεται νὰ δώσει μιὰ πρόσθετη βαρύτητα ἡ γεωγραφικὴ θέση τῆς Ἑλλάδας. Βρίσκεται ἀνάμεσα σὲ δύο μεγάλους πολιτιστικοὺς ὄγκους, ποὺ ξεχωρίζουν πάντα [...]. Ἡ Ἀνατολὴ καὶ ἡ Δύση σμίγουν ἐπάνω στὰ ἑλληνικὰ ἐδάφη, ποὺ γίνονται ἔτσι ἕνα σταυροδρόμι ὅπου ἀδιάκοπα συγκρούονται δύο πρωταρχικὲς μορφὲς πολιτισμοῦ" (Dimaras, Ἱστορία, 5).

and thereby disarmed them that Dimaras can go on to celebrate the foreign elements that give Hellenism its dynamism: "Hellenic civilization, then, expresses itself within a ceaseless renewal sparked by its contacts with foreign cultures."*

To better encapsulate this idea, Dimaras later coins one of the key conceptual metaphors for Hellenic culture, one that epitomizes the intellectual project of Greek philologists since the 1860s: "I might even speak of a kind of border-guard logic to our literature."† Given its importance, I should unpack the word "border-guard" in my translation here, which stands in for the Greek concept of *akritai*: i.e., Byzantine border guards along the Eastern frontier. These guards were essentially irregular military units of the Byzantine Empire whose task it was to police the empire's outermost lands neighboring the Muslim states to the east. These border guards' participation in the frequent wars between Byzantium and its opponents led to a series of folk songs and epic poems in Demotic Greek—most famously, the *Epic of Digenis Akritas*. The name *Digenis* means "born to two [peoples]" and belongs to a mythical border guard whose father was a Muslim and his mother an Orthodox Christian. The former converted to Orthodoxy before their child was born, thus ensuring that the boy would be fully raised within Greek Orthodoxy, albeit at its outermost territorial limits. Growing up in this borderland, Digenis goes on to offer his service to the Byzantines and, roaming the limits of Hellenism, he protects its territorial integrity by means of his own cultural hybridity. His person thus symbolizes the exact assimilatory miscegenation that Greek philology had been at such pains to manage and control from the start. In naming Greek literature a "border guard" literature, Dimaras thus completes the circle begun by Paparrigopoulos.

Yet the *Akritai* poems are only one example that Dimaras lists for his notion of a "border guard" literature. This poem cycle reached its apex in the late Byzantine and early Ottoman periods and thenceforth fell into general obscurity until the late nineteenth century.[47] What other, more recent examples of frontier literature does Dimaras list? In fact, all the remaining examples are situated not in the East but in the West, among Italianate influences: the Cretan Renaissance of the sixteenth and seventeenth centuries, which was under

---

* "Ὁ ἑλληνικὸς πολιτισμός, λοιπόν, ἐκφράζεται μέσα στὴν ἀδιάκοπη ἀνανέωση τὴν ὁποία προκαλοῦν οἱ ἐπαφὲς μὲ τοὺς ξένους πολιτισμούς" (Dimaras, Ἱστορία, 5).

† "Θὰ μιλοῦσα ἐδῶ γιὰ ἕναν ἀκριτικὸ χαρακτῆρα τῆς λογοτεχνίας μας" (Dimaras, Ἱστορία, 6).

Venetian rule and thus blended Greek and Italian; or the nineteenth-century poetic output of the Ionian islands, likewise under Venetian rule for centuries. That such spaces constitute all of Dimaras's other literary frontiers is no coincidence. Contact with the East is all well and good when situated in the nearly mythical world of the *akritai*, who were active during the apex of Byzantine power a millennium ago, yet one would be hard pressed to find Dimaras recording more recent literary contact, exchange, or hybridity among Greek and Turkish, Arabic, or Islam in later centuries.[48] Such forms of contact continued to exist, as I demonstrate in this book, but they had been (and remain today) informalized and pushed to the margins of literary histories like those of Dimaras, where they can be alluded to vaguely and capitalized on as needed for the construction of "crossroads" or "gateways."

Reassembling the Hellenic Borderscape

Broadly understood, such is the institutional Hellenism that has been handed down to us today. Western discourses of purity and miscegenation, which from the fifteenth through the nineteenth centuries obsessively focused on the population movements of peoples across the Hellenic world, were internalized and slowly reformulated by Greek philologists in the nineteenth and twentieth centuries. Rather than accept the dominant Western parameters of debate wholesale, they gradually pruned away some concepts and re-articulated others, slowly developing what we can now recognize as core elements of the modern border regime. Under the care of successive scholars from Paparrigopoulos to Sathas to Dimaras, institutional Hellenism no longer denied population movements or "mixing"; it channeled them, micromanaged them, assimilated what it could, and displaced into gray zones what it could not. In this way, philologists pioneered a method of "extraction and displacement."[49] Foreign elements deemed of value were incorporated into the Hellenic project while the foreign cultures from which that value had been extracted were often diverted or displaced.

Seen through the prism of this intellectual history, Greece becomes not a solid rampart of "Fortress Europe" but a borderscape—which, again, denotes a network of semi-inclusions and -exclusions that permeates the whole of a given geography. This is not to underplay the role of hard borders along the edges of Greece; rather, it is to see how those borders redound inward as well. As Mezzadra and Neilson have argued in their book *Border as Method*, the modern border regime may indeed draw hard lines in the sand, but behind these lines it simultaneously filters and funnels people across a series of internal borders through a process of "differential inclusion."[50] In other words, even after they had crossed the hard and fast geopolitical borders of the Eastern Mediterranean, the refugee and diasporic stories that you will read in this book remained entangled in an internal borderscape that sometimes displaced them out of print, at other times detained them at the edges of print in footnotes and appendices, or, on occasion, reformatted and reappropriated pieces of them into mainstream commercial print. In each case, institutional philology was extracting value of one kind or another from these texts. And while the concept of "value extraction" should remind us of the larger economic stakes of the modern border, where precaritized labor draws down wages in the wider economy,[51] the differential inclusion on which it depends is not only of an economic nature but linguistic and cultural as well. Such interlocking forms of differential inclusion structure many of the modern world's borderscapes, as seen in the situation of migrant workers and refugees in Greece today,[52] yet early traces of this system were already emerging in the Population Exchange of 1923, where the economic predation and exploitation that awaited many of the "exchanged" peoples in their host countries was often justified by their linguistic and cultural differences[53]—differences that had largely been systematized and institutionalized by philology.

How might we reform such a philological system? It goes without saying, of course, that I am not the first to ask this kind of question. Over the past forty years, a growing number of literary scholars have aimed trenchant critiques at the internal mechanisms of institutional Hellenism, placing a spotlight on the Global North's intellectual and material colonization of modern Greece while also documenting Greek participation in that colonial model.[54] My book draws on the discoveries and connections charted out by this work, even as I move in a slightly different direction from much of it. For, although I share the desire to decolonize the Hellenic, I will do so not primarily through a critique of its core institutions (many incisive critiques already exist) but by tracing out lesser-known and complementary voices hiding within those institutions: texts and fragments of texts that have for a century or more been quietly held in limbo inside the internal borders or just outside the external borders of institutional Hellenism. Konstantina Zanou has written that there is "an entire universe of the 'in-between'" that has gone missing from our historical memory and will remain institutionally invisible "if we stick to conventional national and state divisions of historical writing."[55] And while she focuses on the nineteenth century, as empire just began to give way to nation-state, it is my contention that this "universe of the in-between" remains legible into the twentieth and even twenty-first century, if we only commit the time and patience to apprentice ourselves to its media formats, scripts, and tongues. But I also do not want to reify these voices and texts as inherently "in-between"; I trace them back to the foundational and more recognizable forms of Hellenism and thus open spaces for dialogue between them. In other words, I build bridges between the margin and the mainstream and in doing so attempt to re-envision both as lateral coordinates in a shared topography. In this endeavor, I draw inspiration from recent scholars working in other disciplines or periods, such as Konstantina Zanou, Heath Cabot, Katerina Rozakou, and Michael Pifer, among others, whose ethos of care and curation I hope to bring to the refugee and diasporic literatures featured here.

This does not mean that I will abandon criticism, which has already played an important role in this introduction and will maintain a persistent albeit smaller footprint in each of the following chapters.[56] It does mean, however, that even in moments of structural critique I take care to use a diplomatic language that respects and approximates the divergent and disparate experiences of my potential readerships.[57] Because ultimately I aim to gain the broadest possible audience for this literary refuge. My book provides new voices, models and tools to a range of readers in the academy, but I also want to extend the conversation further to readers in and of the borderscape that I study, at the edges of Southeastern Europe, West Asia, and North Africa.[58] This is a complex and heterogenous set of audiences, some of whom may indeed have grown disenchanted or dissatisfied with the stories that national philology has told them; others of whom were never represented by such stories in the first place; but also a great many others who remain deeply invested in those stories and identify with them. I want to speak to and assemble as many of these audiences as I can within a shared narrative.

Such a narrative remains available to us today through looseleaf papers, bits of ephemeral print, chapbooks, second-hand testimonies, reader marginalia scrawled onto flyleaves, entire manuscript codices written out and bound together by hand and passed from hand to hand among refugee communities, other manuscript codices redirected into the state libraries of Europe, or even printed books that one can purchase in a bookstore in Athens or in Istanbul, if one knows how to read between their lines. Taking up each of these in turn, I attempt to document philology's undocumented. Crucially, I elevate these texts and their handlers not simply for the sake of diversity—a gesture that, if left to itself, would ultimately amount to a kind of empty tokenism—but also to learn from them more participatory forms of textual transmission, migration, and exchange. This is an essential claim of my book and bears emphasis: stripped of philological power, several of the texts and stories that I examine survived not despite but thanks to the decentralized and lateral networks of their handlers. There are of course tensions in these networks, and greater or lesser degrees of power asymmetries may be hiding just beyond my field of vision. Nonetheless, I maintain that literary studies, whose textual conscience has been forged in the smithy of a strictly top-down philology, has much to gain from dialogue with the case studies in this book. This is particularly true at a moment when, spurred on by the call for a public humanities, a growing number of scholars attempt to open our universities to the publics and the undercommons that lie beyond their facilities.

There are of course limits to what this book can accomplish. Much of the material damage is irreversible and it would be irresponsible to pretend that my work here offers any tactile reparations or an actionable political agenda (even as I feel both to be urgent needs). Many of the communities documented in the following chapters have been uprooted and decimated by the Exchange and the modern border regime that it helped create, and *Literature's Refuge* can neither undo that violence nor restore lost homelands, just as it cannot undo the ongoing legal grey zones, hotspot buffer zones, and systematic labor exploitation that continue to define the borderscape today. Such is the project not of a book but of on-the-ground organizing and broad coalition-building. Despite its limits, however, what this book *can* offer is a paradigm shift in the ideological mechanisms of the borderscape and, at its most ambitious scale, a blueprint for rebuilding those mechanisms. No longer bound to a system of linguistic and cultural extraction and displacement, the new borderscape that this book envisions would instead decentralize philological control and put it at the service of those on whose backs it has been built. As I wrote earlier in this introduction, the stories of such a borderscape might best be gathered under a kind of loose federation: Greek- or Turkish-language texts, non-Greek or non-Turkish language texts adjacent in some way to Greek or Turkish or Orthodox or Islamic culture, and other textual traditions that do not identify with Greek or Turkish but claim a place in the cultural tapestry. My logic is thus not merely comparative per se but what Lital Levy, in a different context, calls "integrative."[59]

To be sure, my study cannot hope to integrate all the threads of this tapestry, but it does take up a number of key strands, ranging from Epirus in the north to Egypt in the south, from Greek-language Islam in the west to Turkish-language Greek Orthodoxy in the east. The journey that this book makes across that itinerary marks a small but necessary step in a larger collective project of the humanistic sciences today: rethinking the border regime not only of Greece but of the Global North *in toto*, whose institutions have for too long monopolized and weaponized the Hellenic.

A Road Map

Despite the word "global" in the previous sentence, this is not a book about world literature. When occasion demands I follow the texts of my study to far-flung corners of the globe, but for the most part I remain grounded in the borderscape of the Eastern Mediterranean, which straddles Europe and the Middle East. Nevertheless, the slow and regionally bounded mobility of my book, which reflects similar patterns of mobility among most of the refugee and diasporic actors whose stories I tell, may perhaps be able to speak productively to world literature in one small respect. But first let me clarify the terminology here: what do we mean when we say *world literature*? On its face, it gestures toward transnational networks of literary texts, translated and transited across borders and offering readers a window into the larger world around them.[60] For more than a decade, much literary scholarship written in English has been wrestling with a decidedly Western constellation of the term, namely Anglophone publishing conglomerates and Euro-American academic disciplinary formations—both of which have been critiqued for their practices of knowledge extraction, homogenization, and appropriation.[61] Change is in the air, though. Building on but also pushing beyond these critiques, important and exciting work is now expanding our understanding of world literature in new directions, focusing on global South-to-South translation networks or explicitly communist or maoist publishing ventures in the soviet or Bandung sphere.[62] These recent research agendas are reshaping the geographies of intellectual history and breathing new life into the category of world literature.

To my mind, however, at least one problem remains unresolved: the many bibliographic gaps torn open by forced displacement. What place in world literature can the displaced hope to claim? And let me be specific by what I mean with the category of "displacement": I gesture here neither to this or that author exiled from their homeland,[63] nor even to the wholesale displacement of peripheral national literatures from large-scale transnational publishing[64]— instead, I mean those displaced from the very categories of authorship and national literature in the first place. This might correspond, on the one hand, to entire textual traditions such as Greek-language Islam or Turkish-language Greek Orthodoxy, uprooted from national literature, from modern authorship, and from the institutional visibility that both of them secure. But on the other hand, it also corresponds to canonical texts such as the poetry of C. P. Cavafy or popular fiction from the Greco-Turkish war, which have been fully integrated into the canon. Scratch the surface of these texts and here too you find a wealth of human voices, media constellations, texts, paratexts, and contexts that were once bound up in these literary works and their authors, only to be sloughed off by philology as it curated and nationalized them. Because ultimately, the canonical text is also a site of displacement, a residue of all that has been shorn or torn from the authorized story.

Of course, it should go without saying that the problem here is not the author-writer as an individual agent, who is in any case a relatively insignificant force in the alignment of global intellectual property regimes.[65] Looking to postcolonial authorship, for example, Sarah Brouillette and Caroline Davis have carefully demonstrated that if authorial brands sometimes function as important linchpins in global literature, the writers themselves often have less power than the material and legal infrastructure amassed around them.[66] The problem thus is clearly one of institutional infrastructures, access to which overdetermines how a text will move (or not move) across geographies of transnational publishing. I look for alternative visions of textual mobility by narrowing my focus to what I call "textual handlers" operating along the outermost edges of this infrastructure: writers, editors, printers, binders, readers, copyists, oral storytellers, translators, and others—most often refugees or diasporic peoples. Some of these textual handlers have been entirely displaced and forgotten, such as the writer, copyists, and readers of the Islamic codex discussed in chapter one, while others have seen their labor and their value extracted and reinvested into national authorship, such as the refugee narrator Nikolas Kazakoglou treated in chapter three. By tracing out these and other creative patchworks hiding beneath the surface of authorship, the following chapters attempt to gaze beyond the proprietary claims (that are made on stories, on texts, on knowledge) in national and transnational publishing and offer some sketches of alternative models.[67]

These alternative models bring with them alternative mobilities. As I intimated at the start of this section, texts that have already been displaced from national philology and national publishing networks tend to navigate a slower, less formalized circuit of mobility, spread across community libraries, coffeehouses, village squares, family archives, private collections, and the rare book holdings of a state library here or there—usually *there*, in foreign states. And this last point is worth unpacking a little further: despite their provisional and precarious infrastructure, the refugee and diasporic textual networks that my book examines are often international in scale and geographically extensive in their own right, each node hundreds or sometimes even thousands of miles from the other or from the point of origin of the texts with whose care they have been charged. Constitutionally different from large publishing conglomerates, this displaced geography has nonetheless silently helped to shape the contours of many transnational publishing networks—precisely through its silence. Because if Greek and Turkish literary history can teach us anything in this book, it is that the national literatures upon which transnational publishing has traditionally relied for most of its acquisitions sometimes place themselves on a map only by displacing their "others." And this displacement is both epistemological and physical in nature, for when texts are *philologically* displaced, they are simultaneously rendered *geographically* displaceable, along with the communities that produced them.[68]

How to build back a place for such displaceables? How to chart out their passage across the Mediterranean borderscape? Questions of method are particularly important here. In the chapters that follow, my main recourse will be to the history of the book, which studies literature as physical objects that are made and circulated from hand to hand. The book historian's toolbox includes (but is not limited to) textual criticism, analytical bibliography, codicology, and network analysis. Some of these terms might benefit from a brief explanation: textual criticism is the comparison and close analysis of the multiple manuscripts and/or print editions that comprise the material traces of a given literary work's production and transmission over time (think of the *Iliad*, which is commonly understood as a single work but exists in multiple versions in ancient papyri fragments from Egypt, in medieval manuscript codices from Constantinople, in early Renaissance printed editions from Venice, in scholarly editions over the past hundred years, in translations based on one or several of the former, etc.). Analytical bibliography and codicology, on the other hand, are the analysis and documentation of a specific textual object within that transmission chain (think of a single manuscript witness of the *Iliad*) and the stories hidden within its material components, such as paper sources, ink, binding, scribal and/or reader marginalia, colophons, etc. Together, textual criticism and bibliography allow us both to follow textual transmission networks over time and space and to pause and zero in on particular socio-material nodes within a given network. Using these various scales of analysis, the history of the book can accommodate everything from a single textual object's history to the national or transnational book networks within which it is assembled, transmitted, copied, consumed, reproduced, and recycled. Under a different name, book history might justly be described as a kind of philology in its own right. The two share many of the same methods, and this overlap is no coincidence. My book in fact seeks explicitly to take up some of the tools of traditional philology and to use them to elevate the border crossings traditionally driven underground by that same philology. I take to heart Aamir Mufti's assertion that elaborating new uses for these older philological tools stands as one of the most critical tasks of literary studies today.[69]

If traditional philology has used its tools to construct authors, authorized texts, and canons, I use those tools instead to reverse engineer the process. I take a given work and disassemble it like the engine of a car, piece by piece, spreading it out across a flat surface as a mechanic does upon a workbench. Having done so, I set about examining the inner logic and interconnections of the work's constituent parts, using multiple scales as noted above, both within a single text and across the larger infrastructure supporting its reproduction and transmission.[70] Careful attention to these components and the relationships between them makes clear that literature often moves in explicitly nonlinear ways back and forth across multiple media (manuscript to print, print to manuscript, composite codices, oral to manuscript to oral to print, print to oral, etc.); across multiple bindings (unbound newspapers and broadsheets, commercial case bindings, through-the-fold stitching, saddle stitching or even single cotter pins); across multiple editions (first edition, revised edition, critical edition, expanded edition); across multiple alphabets and languages (Greek-script Greek, Arabic-script Greek, Arabic-script Turkish, Latin-script Turkish, Greek-script Turkish); and most importantly, from one textual handler to the next, each of whom might variously read the work, mark it up, take it apart, reassemble it, remediate it, or indeed multimediate it.

Without this kind of reverse engineering, most of the stories that I want to tell are difficult to recover, cordoned off and silenced behind the standardized books of modern commercial publishing, which project an aura of fixity, finality, and singularity. This aura is powerful, but it is of course a fiction. Print brought many changes to human communication, but it by no means brought standardization.[71] True, the late nineteenth century did see a growing consensus that stable, standard texts could and did exist, driven by faith in new print technologies, philological institutions, and international law. To take just this last domain as an example, by the turn of the twentieth century a web of international copyright agreements (both bilateral treaties and larger conventions such as Berne) seemed to foreclose most legal forms of unlicensed translation and reprint across many national borders.[72] Nonetheless, it's worth noting that such agreements failed to achieve global dominance for much of the century (in Turkey, for example, unlicensed translation and adaptation of foreign works remained legally protected until 1952). More importantly, while unlicensed copying is certainly a significant factor in the destabilization of texts, I don't want to reduce the question of textual fluidity and variation to so-called piracy. All textual reproduction is inherently social in nature and hence it is open to the transformative agencies of many. Whether we are speaking of copying, compiling, rebinding, revising, reinscribing, editing or otherwise, all textual objects—even printed books in bookstores—remain indices not of stability and fixity but of a messy pluriform network. My book locates literature at this latter level, collapsing formats, media, and actors into one another, spreading them out across a flat plane to reveal less linear, more multidirectional movements and mobilities between textual handlers.

I follow these mobilities on two scales: textual and geographic. The easiest and perhaps most helpful way to join the two is to follow the movement of texts through space, which B. Venkat Mani has usefully termed "bibliomigrancy."[73] This kind of textual mobility is important for me, but by itself it would have a hard time accounting for some of the more informal ways that literature is moved not just across geographies but between pages and media formats as well. To make this kind of mobility more visible, I would add a second scale of bibliomigrancy, one that Mani himself hints at: "Biblio may be opened up to acknowledge all kinds of books: written and oral, printed and handwritten, bound and unbound, stationary and portable."[74] Such categories are not stable; they can be made and unmade, assembled, disassembled, and reassembled into one another. I can take a printed book and undo its binding, interpolate my own manuscript writing between the pages, and rebind them all together; I can take another book and read it aloud while my friend copies it down; I can take yet a third book and jot a poem onto its flyleaf. The migration of literature, as these examples demonstrate, simultaneously occurs across both geographic and bibliographic borderscapes. In fact, the two scales of migration might sometimes be mutually implicated in one another almost like a mathematical fractal—from the largest geographic units of analysis down to the smallest typographic marks upon a page. Indeed, *Literature's Refuge* argues that one can quite literally read the transformations of the larger region on the pages of the literary texts as they are reproduced, transmitted, and transformed

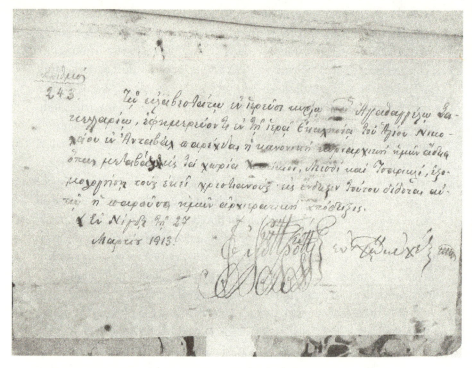

FIGURE 2. Pastedown binding of *Το βιβλίον Ψυχωφελέστατον*. Courtesy of Giorgos Kallinikidis.

over time. Examples big and small abound in the chapters that follow, but to make my meaning clear here I offer a simple case in point, as seen in figure 2.

What you see here is a pastedown—i.e., a piece of paper that has been integrated into the binding of a book, joining the leaves of the text to the boards of its binding. The book belongs to Agathangelos, a Turkish-speaking Greek Orthodox refugee poet whom I detail in the fourth chapter. Look closer, though, and you will see that this pastedown is living a double life, recycled from an earlier context. In his native Cappadocia (in what is today central Turkey), Agathangelos had served not only as a poet but as a priest. In 1913, he was granted permission by the Orthodox Church to perform his priestly duties beyond his home village of Andaval in the surrounding parishes of Hasaköy (Χασάκιοϊ), Misti (Μισθί), and Çarıklı (Τσαρικλί) as well. This official permission, written out and signed in an ornate calligraphic font by the bishop of Niğde, was an important document for Agathangelos's livelihood and status, yet it was drained of all meaning by the Exchange a decade later. The bishop's seat in Niğde was annulled, the villages that his office had overseen were ethnically cleansed of their inhabitants, and over time the entire region's history was buried under new Turkish toponyms. Uprooted from this geography (which was itself changing), Agathangelos nonetheless retained the document that preserved a piece of it and bound it into a book that he was reconstructing by hand, now half a world away in exile. As this example demonstrates in brief and broad brushstrokes, by tracing out the material migrations within and across texts, the following chapters simultaneously trace out the shifting geopolitical borderscape of the larger region embedded within them.

Chapter one begins in Ioannina, the major metropole of what is today northwestern Greece. My goal here is to pluralize the Greek tradition from within Greece itself, mapping out some important contours of one understudied site in Greece's literary landscape: Greek-language Islam. I focus on an early example of this small and scattered corpus, the *Tuḥfe-i Şānī be Zebān-ı Yūnānī* (*The Gift of Şānī in the Greek Tongue*), a seventeenth-century religious work of rhyming Greek couplets written in the Arabic script of Ottoman Islam. I draw on David Damrosch's notion of "scriptworld"—i.e., a self-contained multilingual literary system joined under the umbrella of a single alphabet— and set out for the borders of such a world. Where does one scriptworld end, where does the other begin? What literary contact points might we chart out between scriptworlds? Şānī explicitly defends his Greek and argues forcefully for Greek's place in Islam's ecumenical vision. Taking Şānī's words to heart, I expand not only the Greek-language canon but the role of local readerships in shaping that canon. For this latter goal, the provenance and date of the surviving codex are critical; recovering what I can of the work's transmission history, I speculate on its importance for the larger community of Greek-language Muslims in north-western Greece, although its current location—in a German state library far removed from Ioannina—is indicative of the fate of Greek-language Islam, uprooted and devastated by the Exchange.

Chapter two charts out the opposite phenomenon: not the displacement of an indigenous Greek literature from Greece's borderscape but rather the assimilation of a diasporic Greek literature into it—but only on the terms set by Hellenic philology. Using the poetry of C. P. Cavafy, I trace the processes of philological consolidation that gradually reshaped Hellenic literature throughout the first half of the twentieth century. I begin by examining the scattered, polymorphous Greek publishing world during Cavafy's lifetime, with its multiple centers in Alexandria, Athens, and Istanbul, and how this world was, over the course of fifty years, slowly and painfully consolidated on the two scales discussed in the previous paragraphs: geopolitically, as Greek diasporas were destroyed and reconsolidated within the Greek state; and textually, as Cavafy's own fluid and polymorphous texts were supposedly consolidated by the philologist George Savidis. My goal here is twofold: first, to situate Cavafy's fluid poetic practices within the analogous fluidity of the larger Mediterranean ambit beyond the Helladic state in the early twentieth century; and second, to document some of the more destructive border-guarding practices of traditional Helladic philology that developed in the decades following the Population Exchange and the collapse of most major Greek diasporas in the Eastern Mediterranean.

Chapter three turns its attention more insistently to the Population Exchange itself. I focus here on testimonial fiction from the war, a genre that since its initial circulation has enjoyed a significant status among Greek and Turkish readerships and both national literary canons. Literary historians in both countries have spoken of these "eye-witness" testimonials as if they offered readers direct historical access. They are, as one early critic remarked, "a valuable document for the world to learn what happened there in the East [...]. The truth emerges from facts, not from rhetorical flairs."* I revisit this assessment by comparing the complicated textual history of two key testimonials—Stratis Doukas's *A Captive's Story* (*Η ιστορία ενός αιχμαλώτου*) and Halide Edib's *Shirt of Flame* (*Ateşten Gömlek*). Examining successive editions and their emendations, this chapter will pause over the multiple hands through which they have passed—witnesses, interviewers, writers, editors, translators, and transcribers—and their role in shaping and reshaping the narratives therein. Particularly important for my analysis here is the role of Nikolas Kazakoglou, the refugee survivor whom Doukas interviewed for the basis of his published testimonial. Through careful analysis of the textual fragments that survive from Kazakoglou and a comparison with Doukas's revisions and later publications, this chapter aims to further pluralize authorship and hence the textual handlers who can lay a claim to textual authority within the canon.

Kazakoglou's language straddled both Greek and Turkish, yet his story found legitimate commercial expression only in the standard Greek of Doukas. Was this the common fate of all refugees who could not (or would not) tell their stories in the national vernacular? My fourth chapter seeks out other possibilities, foregrounding the handmade and handwritten codices of a

---

*"Είνε καὶ ἕνα πολύτιμο ντοκουμέντο γιὰ τοὺς λαοὺς γιὰ ὅ,τι ἔγινε ἐκεῖ στὴν Ἀνατολή [...]. Ἡ ἀλήθεια βγαίνει ἀπὸ τὰ πράγματα καὶ ὄχι ἀπὸ ρητορισμούς." Rodas, "Book review."

Turkish-speaking refugee poet from central Turkey: Agathangelos. As noted earlier, his was a Turkish used by a sizeable group of Greek-Orthodox Christians from the interior of Anatolia, written in the Greek script of their bible and popularly known today as Karamanli Turkish. Karamanli print networks of the nineteenth century were robust, producing newsprint, educational materials, and fiction for Anatolia's hundreds of thousands of Turcophone Greek Christians. With the mass deportations of the Exchange, however, their print apparatus vanished almost overnight. In Greece, they were discriminated against and soon excluded from Helladic publishing networks, but their literature continued and survived beneath the radar of commercial publishing, in short-lived newspapers, small chapbooks, and, as chapter four documents, in manuscript and composite codices. The patchwork books written, translated, adapted, bound, and rebound by Agathangelos bypassed national print networks and their authorial regimes—not through recourse to the global market but, crucially, by means of the displaced readerships who kept these works alive even after Agathangelos himself had long since died.

The fifth and final chapter of this book traces out the twenty-first-century survival of such textual pluralisms. I focus here on Mehmet Yashin's *Sınırdışı Saatler—Σηνηρδησι Σαατλερ* (The Deported Hours), which, despite being written in Turkish and distributed by a major Istanbul publisher, places large portions of its text in the Greek script. This alphabetic multiformity was supposedly decimated by modernity, yet rather than telling that story (which has already been told well by scholars like Nergis Ertürk), I want to trace the transformative revival of these mixed scriptworlds even in the present. The protagonist of Yashin's novel is a fictional Karamanli refugee; resurrected and tossed headlong into twenty-first-century Turkey, he searches frantically for the writer who brought him back to life, a Cypriot named "Mehmet Yashin." To find his author, the protagonist passes through Hell (Istanbul's underground prisons), Purgatory (Northern Cyprus), and Heaven (a multinational publishing house with a branch in Southern Cyprus), yet in each realm he fails to find what he's looking for: his own language, demoted now to a dead dialect. The author "Mehmet Yashin," in the meantime, is also searching for something: a manuscript *Book of Hours*, first assembled in sixteenth-century Cyprus, which houses his own threatened Cypriot dialect. Indeed, Yashin turns out to be not an author per se but a reader, spurred to rewrite this *Book of Hours*, which has passed from generation to generation of Cypriots and with each new handler accumulated new sections and new scripts: Ottoman Turkish, Greek-script Turkish, Greek-script Greek, and Latin. Functioning as a book-within-the-book, the codex and its several hands constitute the true textual homeland of Yashin and his Karamanli double, blurring the institutional partitions between authors and their others and, in doing so, forging unauthorized pathways between geographies, languages, scripts, and confessional communities.

Such are the stories that I tell in this book. A century or more of philologists, historiographers, and diplomats have done much to untell them, dispossessing and displacing them across two racialized religions and indeed two civilizations. The damage has been immense. The border lines that European, Greek, and Turkish intellectuals threw down upon their pages gave rise, like ripples in the water, to a thousand more lines of refugee caravans, crisscrossing one another from Crete, from Thessaly, from Epirus, from Macedonia, from Thrace, from Ionia, from the Black Sea, from Cappadocia, from Cyprus and elsewhere, torn from their homes and their homelands and "unmixed" into new lands. But even here the border regime was not yet done with them; extracting value from their cultures, stories, languages, and scripts, the nation-state assimilated and authorized certain aspects of its refugees, emigres, and migrants even as it circumscribed other bits and pieces of them into gray zones, purgatories, partial inclusions and exclusions that continue to this day.

From this status quo, *Literature's Refuge* pries open a place for literature's displaced: those who against all odds transited their words and worlds across the Mediterranean borderscape, beneath the radar of national and world literature. From chapter to chapter, I follow the pathways of survival that many of them forged between Europe and the Middle East, through years of deportations, repatriations, expropriations, assimilations, or delegitimization and isolation, in Greek, in Turkish, in manuscript or print, across the margins of pages or on unbound scraps of paper. In following them thus, my aim is more than just to string together a series of vignettes or insert a new cast of characters into the existing literary landscape; I want to *change* that landscape, to re-envision it from the bottom up. Of course, what follows are only a few initial threads in a much larger tapestry, one whose restoration and elaboration will require many hands and many capacities beyond my own. My hope is that others will continue where I leave off and bring us, one page at a time, to a new vision of the borderscapes that rack our world today.

Chapter one, in which Şānī and his readers save the nightingale

WHAT IS GREEK literature and to whom does it belong?

This chapter explores that question through a sustained engagement with the *Tuḥfe-i Şānī be zebān-ı yūnānī* (*The Gift of Şānī in the Greek Tongue*[1]), a seventeenth-century poetic guide to the tenets of Islam. Written by and for Greek-speaking Muslims along the western edge of the Ottoman Empire, the *Tuḥfe* is indeed in the Greek tongue as its title promises but uses the Perso-Arabic alphabet of Ottoman Islam—a modified Arabic script that I will henceforth call the "Ottoman" alphabet. Şānī's Greek boasts a witty, versatile, and at times beautiful prosody that reflects a studied familiarity with traditional Greek versification, yet the work has been ignored wholesale by Greek philology, unpublished and unexamined until now. Thus is the shared fate of nearly all Greek-language Islamic poetry.[2] For as I argued in the introduction, the sad but unsurprising truth is that during the nineteenth and twentieth centuries Greek philologists assembled and secured Hellenism's patrimony only after they had picked apart and neutralized any textual traditions (foremost among them, Islam) that introduced unwelcome complications to their narrative of Greek continuity. Today, disciplinary perspectives on Islam have changed, but our knowledge of Greek literature is still largely bounded by this early exclusionary narrative. What kind of a philological reorientation might expand our horizons? How might literary scholars not only welcome back those Greek voices orphaned by the institutionalization of the Greek canon but, on a more fundamental level, reconfigure the deeper disciplinary protocols that orphaned them in the first place?

There is a certain urgency to these questions. In the public imagination today the Greek tradition reproduces many implicit or explicit exclusionary

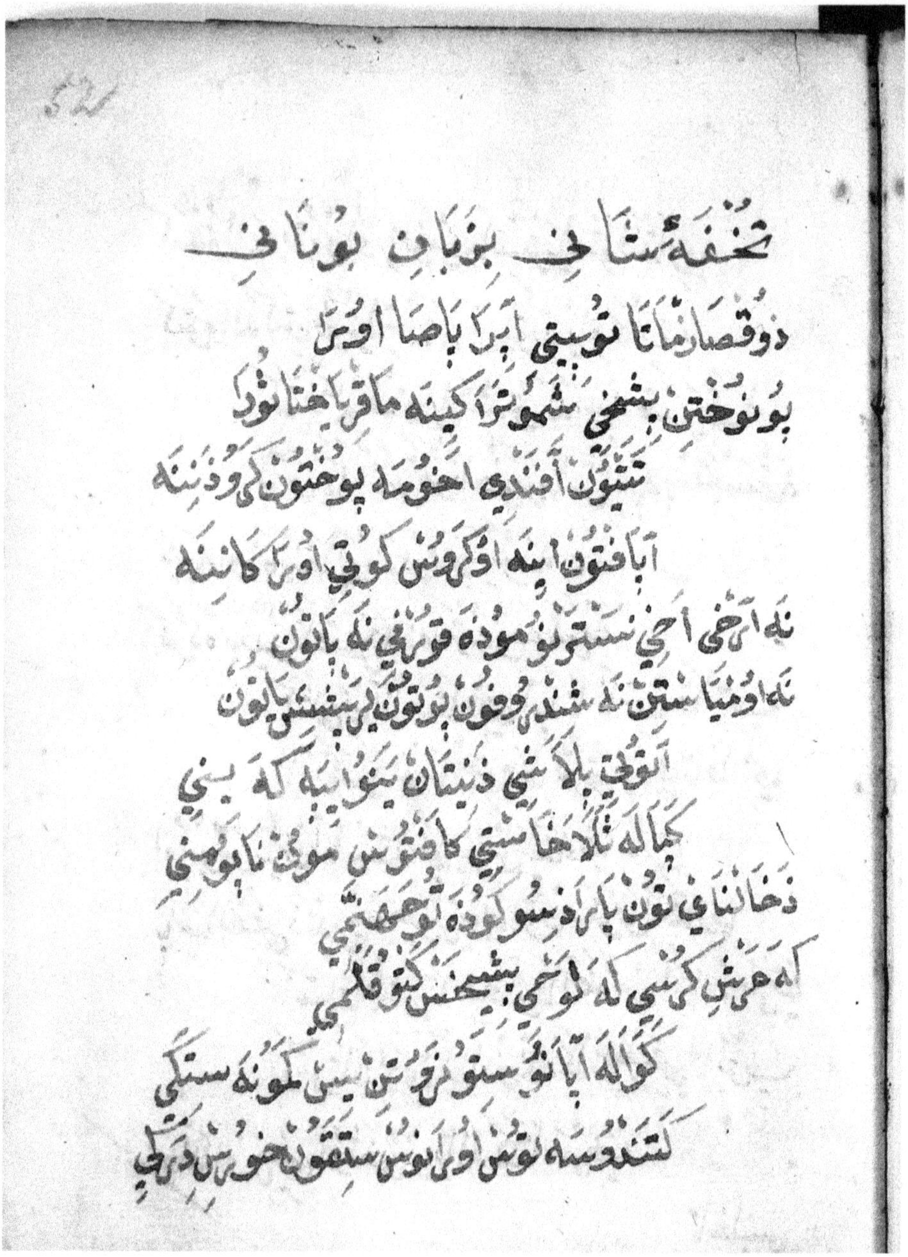

تُحْفَهْ مْنَافِ بُرْبَانْ يُونَانِ

ذُوقْصَانْ مَانَا قُوسِيجِي أَبْرَا بَاصَا اوِيرَا
بُو يُوخْتِنْ بِشْمِجِي نِشْمُو تْرَا كِنْدَ مَاقْ بَاخْتَا نُوذَا
سْنْيُونْ أَفْنْدِي احْوُومَه بُوخْتُون كِي وَذَنَّه
آبَافْتُون إنْدَ اوْكَمُسْ كُوتِي اوِرَا كَانِنْه
نَه اَخِي اَخِي نِسْتُرُنُو مُودَه قُورِنِي نَه بَانُون
نَه اُومْيَاسْتِنْ نَه شْنْدْ وَقُوفْ بُوتُون يِنْشِكِي بَانُون
اَنْوفْتِي بِلَاسِي ذْنِتَانْ يِنْوَابْيَه كَه بِنِي
كِمَالَه تِلَاخَاسْنِجِي كَأَنْتُوسْنِي مُوذَه نَابُومِنِي
ذَخَانَانَا غِي نُون بَارَه اذْسُوكُودَه اوْجَهَنْجِي
كَه هَرْمِشْ كَمْسِي كَه لُوجِي بِشِيخْنِي كُوفْلَمْ
كُولَه آبَانُو سْتُو نَرْعَ سْتَنْ يِسِي لْكُونَه سْتْكِي
لَنْدُوسِسَه تُوسْنِي اوِرْ اوْنِسْ سْتُقُون خُورِنْ دَرْجِي

FIGURE 3. The opening passage of the titular volume of the *Tuhfe*. Bayerische Staatsbibliothek, Cod. graec. 593, folio 52a.

paradigms, which in turn inform a range of problematic policies and ideologies. Think for example of the proliferation of Spartan helmets, *meandroi* insignia, and *Molon Labe* flags and face masks among the far right in both Greece and the United States. Greek fascists, whose flash raids on immigrants in Athens and elsewhere have resulted in at least nine hundred beatings and knifings—six hundred of which targeted Pakistanis—drew their inspiration from the ancient Spartan *Krypteia*, an organization of Spartan elite who assigned themselves the task of terrorizing their own underclass.[3] It was in this spirit for example that Shahzad Luqman was stabbed in the heart and left to die in the streets of Athens in 2013. Such far-right deployments of Greek symbols and Greek words would be unsettling even as standalone anomalies, but they are especially troubling precisely because they are not anomalies; they draw their strength from the institutional lineage discussed above and are evidence that some core components of this ideological machinery remain functional today, subtly shaping what is (and is not) Greek and who can lay a claim to it.

Şānī's *Tuhfe* can help both to push back against this system and to offer something new in its place: a decentralized federation of Greece's literary traditions. It does so not just by virtue of its Islamic identity but also through an explicit politicization of language and textual authority. At multiple points throughout the *Tuhfe*, Şānī foregrounds and defends his own Greek-language project, arguing for the textual autonomy of his local Greek-speaking Muslim audience, which was under pressure to assimilate to the linguistic norms of the capital. This spirit of autonomy pervades the codex at nearly every level, from its content to its form to its script.

That last word may lead some of my readers to think of David Damrosch's "Scriptworlds." A scriptworld, in Damrosch's view, arises when a particular alphabet—take, for example, the Latin alphabet—bridges a set of distinct languages, joining them within a cohesive and exclusive cultural system. Scriptworlds has sustained an ongoing and productive discussion across area studies, particularly in a 2016 special issue of the *Journal of World Literature* devoted to the concept.[4] Yet, as Etienne Charrière has recently argued, the concept may be less attuned to the special dynamics of the Ottoman context, which was marked not so much by a centralizing scribal culture but a decentralized pluralism based on the holy scriptures of a given confessional community: Turkish in Ottoman script, Turkish in Armenian script, Turkish in Greek script, Greek in Ottoman script, Greek in Hebrew script, Greek in the Greek script, Greek in the Latin script, to name the most common scripts for but two of the empire's several major languages. Charrière calls this pluralism a "complex traffic in script," which at times produced a sense of acute misalignment and at other times afforded a generative dialogue between scriptworlds and their cultural productions.[5] On a global scale, a language may have a significantly harder time crossing several alphabets than an alphabet several languages, yet careful examination of the former instance, when and where it does occur, is critical to uncovering literary genealogies and relations that have long lay hidden from—or been marginalized by—the discipline of literary studies. In this spirit, then, I situate Ṣānī's *Tuhfe* not within a particular scriptworld per se but rather in what Damrosch calls the "porous" interstices between them,[6] for the poem is equally at home in its traditional Greek prosody and its intertextual dialogue with the Turkish and Arabic corpus of Ottoman Islam. This inbetweenness is important, because scriptworld border regimes are often tied up in larger political border regimes that for too long have warped philology's view of cultural contact and exchange.

Nowhere is this more clear than in the philological and political border regimes of modern Greece and Turkey, whose current status quo was solidified with the Population Exchange. It was here that the textual archives of Greek-language Islam, which were primarily in manuscript formats (since they had failed to attract the attention of Greek philologists and publishers), were lost or scattered along with the local communities that had cared for them.[7] Ottoman-script Greek became a refugee literature. Not simply a literature *of* refugees: the literary corpus itself was made into a refugee, its legacy sustained only by piecemeal textual survivors hiding away in private collections or chance archives and libraries in Turkey, Germany, or elsewhere. To this day, Greek philology has yet to come to terms with either the surviving fragments of this Greek-language literature or the professional principles that have categorically precluded Islam from the start.

How to open up the borders of such scriptworlds? The answer to that question depends in part on how one answers the more fundamental question of authority: By what authority are literature's borders demarcated and maintained, and by what mechanisms are texts integrated or not? Who gets to place their hands on the levers of these mechanisms? In a modern book, one might look for example to the copyright page, which not only announces legal ownership and copying permissions but often catalogues the work's genre and its subject headings and library call numbers (e.g., the LCSH, the LCC, or the DDC[8]) and hence its categories of belonging. Beyond this page extends a network of institutions and conventions—many of them located in or alongside the university—that subtly encourage and discourage specific uses and relationships for a given book:

for example, the syllabi that scholars draw up, the classes they teach, and the research they publish. While they have used different tools and methods over the centuries, these kinds of institutions and norms have long shaped books and our interactions with them—and Şānī's poem is no exception. In this chapter, then, I am interested in how specific textual communities (and textual authorities) read (or did not read) Şānī's Greek, how they embraced (or censured) it, and how they copied it and recirculated it (or ignored it). To wit, I am interested in broader questions of the philological conventions and procedures that govern communities of readers and writers. Ultimately, in reading Şānī's *Tuḥfe* back into the scriptworlds that have displaced it, my broader aim is twofold: first, to question received notions of which texts can be authorized as Greek; and second, to reexamine the philological protocols of authorization itself, sketching out a more collective paradigm of textual authority, negotiated by the community of a text's own writers, readers, and recyclers.

Şānī's Gift in the Greek Tongue

The *Tuḥfe-i Şānī be zebān-ı yūnānī* was composed in the 1660s and is among the earliest examples of Ottoman-script Greek. Today, you'll find it as Cod. graec. 593 in the Greek Manuscript collection of the Bayerische Staatsbibliothek, where, due to its Ottoman alphabet, the original cataloguer identified the work as a Turkish manuscript (see figure 4). The library lacks an acquisitions record so I cannot determine with certainty when or how the codex reached Bavaria.[9] What I know about the work's author Şānī (whose nom de plume means *glorious*) is likewise limited to what biographic details I have drawn from the codex itself: that he was a scholar and jurist from Ioannina, in what is today North-Western Greece.[10] The city of Ioannina, which has functioned as a major regional metropole throughout its history, surrendered peacefully to the Ottomans in 1430. Along with the peaceful transfer of power, city representatives negotiated favorable privileges and protections for the Greek Orthodox majority, yet many of these were lost two centuries later after a chaotic and destructive peasant revolt led by the cleric Dionysios of Larissa in 1611. After this, Ottoman authorities forced the Christian community to live beyond the walls of the inner citadel. The loss of such privileges likely contributed to an increase in conversions to Islam and bolstered what had been a tiny minority beforehand. By the time Şānī was writing in the latter half of the century, the city seemed to have regained its equilibrium and both Christian and Muslim communities were on friendly terms.[11]

FIGURE 4. The first leaf of the *Tuḥfe* in its current binding. Bayerische Staatsbibliothek, Cod. graec. 593.

As was true of many of the towns and cities of Epirus and Thessaly to the East, and Crete in the south, the first and often only tongue of Ioannina's local Muslims was Greek. I should point out that the term "Greek," as it applied to people, was an entirely religious category at the time (i.e., Greek Orthodox Christian, or *Rūm / Romios*) and hence these Muslims would not have identified as such. This creates an even more complex question of identification today, as the terms *Greek* and *Turk* have now expanded into the legal category of citizenship—even as they maintain in popular understanding the exclusionary biases of ethnicity. In this chapter, then, I want to avoid calling these Muslims "Greek," yet they certainly spoke the language and hence partook in its cultural reservoir. This is corroborated by Evliya Çelebi, whose famous *Seyāhatnāme* (*Book of Travels*) is roughly contemporary with Şānī and the *Tuhfe*. During his visit to Ioannina, Evliya Çelebi described the predominance of Greek in the city, adding that literacy was not uncommon among the broader populace. When people speak, he writes, "their language is charming and eloquent, but they speak something close to the Greek dialect. They know an elegant and artful form of Greek and read and write it too, because Ioannina is the most select city of the Rumeli province."*

From within this "select" milieu, a few gifted intellectuals moved on to illustrious careers in the imperial capital, integrating themselves into Istanbul's scholarly culture and leaving behind a significant body of Arabic- or Turkish-language literature.[12] But the majority of the city's population stayed local—and they stayed primarily (and often exclusively) Greek-speaking. Indeed, according to Avram Galanti, who was writing in the 1920s, Ioannina's Muslims remained Greek-speakers up to the twentieth century. Even in the final years of Ottoman rule (Ioannina was annexed by Greece in 1913, less than a decade before the Population Exchange), Muslims appearing in court needed a translator, since most knew only Greek and the magistrates appointed and sent from Istanbul knew only Turkish.[13] In the same passage Galanti further informs us that Istanbul's Director of Education, who was from Ioannina, learned Turkish as a foreign language and that his mother still wrote to him in Ottoman-script Greek—but with *munfaṣıl* (separated) letters and *ḥarakāt* diacritics, e.g., سَ فِ لُ تَ مَ تْ یَ سُ, (se fi lo ta ma t ya su / σε φιλώ τα μάτια σου; *I kiss your eyes*). This woman later confirmed to Galanti that the city's Muslims still composed Greek-language poetry in the Ottoman alphabet.

---

* "Söze gelseler bedī'u'l-beyān ve faṣīḥü'l-lisāndırlar ammā lisānları Urūm lehçesine meyyāl kelimāt ederler. Ve faṣīḥ ü belīğ Rūmca bilüp okuyup yaz[a]rlar, zīrā Rūmeli vilāyetinin güzīde yeridir" (*Seyāhatname*, vol. 8, 291).

Unable to understand either the Arabic verses of their prayers or the Turkish glosses that translated them, these Greek-speaking Muslims had a pressing need to access the tenets of their faith. Writing in the middle of the seventeenth century, just as the city's Muslim community was growing, Ṣānī noted this issue and devised a solution. He wrote,[14]

پُو تُو غْرَاپْسِه رُومَيِقَا پَانْدَخُو ذَنْتُو ولَاوِي
پَذِي يِنَقَا تَاغِرقَاي كَنوُمُو ثَلِي لَاوِي
تِذوُ بِنَكَسْ پُويْتَا توُرِكِقَا قَانْ ذَقْسَرُونْ
پِو لَسْ تُو صَلَوَاتِتوُسْ ذَقْسَرُونْ نَا تُو فَروُنْ

f. 157b, line 10

f. 157b, line 10
    pu to ġrapsa romeyika pandaḫu ðento volevi
    peði yineka ta ġrikay kenomo theli lavi
    tiðo yinekes pu'peta turkika ḳan ðe ḳserun
    pu les to ṣalavātitus ðe ḳserun na to ferun

f. 157b, line 10
    Whatever's abstruse, I wrote it out in Greek;
    now women and children can hear and learn our creed.
    Because women here know not even Turkish,
    let alone the *salawat*[15]—their mouths can't word it.

Ṣānī's aim in other words was to use Demotic Greek as a tool for empowering the Muslims of his community—particularly women and children (although as I will show later with other passages, men were in need of the same tools). Of course Ṣānī was not working in a vacuum; he was drawing on and adapting directly from a larger textual tradition in Ottoman Islam known as ʿIlm-i ḥāl, or Islamic catechism. The basic function of this genre was to convey the principles of the faith to a mass, nonspecialized and non-Arabophone audience, and several popular exemplars existed in Turkish.[16] Nonetheless, the social conditions and motivations of the Turkish-language genre were significantly different from those of Greek-speaking Ioannina, where a smaller, more localized community had its own needs and demands that directly shape the text. While there is no shortage of dogmatic pronouncements in Ṣānī's writing, at several key passages he evinces a genuine interest in providing interpretive tools (rather than merely talking down to) the undereducated Greek-speaking Muslims in his city. Ṣānī's work, in other words, aspired to place his audience in the hermeneutic driver's seat.

He did so through two volumes (bound together in the codex from which I am working), which adapted established Sunni teachings into rhymed Greek couplets of fifteen syllables. This verse form was by far the most popular in

Demotic Greek, known commonly as *politikos stichos,* and while the basic rhyme structure (rhyming couplets) mirrors the popular Islamic form of the *masnavi,* the fifteen-syllable meter pulls the poem distinctly closer to Greek-language traditions. There is only one significant difference: while demotic Greek poetry had reserved this verse form for secular themes and genres, Şānī redirects it toward religion. The first volume translates and explicates the five pillars of the faith, although it is unfortunately missing several of its initial pages, whose fate is unknown (see figure 4). Missing entirely is the first pillar of the faith: the *shahada* or profession of faith. The manuscript begins with a passage on ablution before prayer, followed by a series of subtopics on prayer, which takes up the lion's share of the volume (ff. 1–40). The remaining pillars of the faith follow in quick succession, capped with a conclusion. The second volume expands into broader philosophical and practical issues, ranging from the creation of the world to a survey of sins and life after death.[17]

In both volumes, Şānī demonstrates a proficiency in the canonical body of Ottoman Islamic law (*fiqh*), with citations that range from Abu al-Layth al-Samarqandi (10th c. CE) to al-Marghinani (12th c. CE), from Devletoğlu Yusuf (15th c. CE) to Ibrāhīm al-Ḥalabī (16th c. CE), but such citations never over-burden the poem and are always integrated into an animated and approachable Greek. There are indeed many passages that reveal Şānī's true gift for Greek prosody, such as his magnificent description of the creation of the world, with which he begins the second tome:

f. 52a
ذُوْقْصَارْمَاتَا تُوْبِيتِى آپْرَا يَاصَا اوْرَا
پُونُوخْتِنْ پِشِخِى شَمُوتَرَا كِينَه مَاقْرِيَا خْتَا ثُورَا
تَتِيُونْ آفَنْدِى اَخوْمَه پُوخْتُونْ گَرُو ذَنِنَه
آپَافْتُونْ اِينَه او گَرُوسْ كُوْتِى اوْرَا گَانِنَه

line 5
نَه آرْخِى اَخِى نَسْتَرْنُو مؤوْذَه قُورْفِى نَه يَاتُونْ
نَه اوْمْيَاسْتِنْ نَه شِنْدِرُوفُونْ پُو تُونْ بِرَپْشِسْ يَاتُونْ
اَتوْتِى پِلَاشِى ذَنِيتَانْ يَنُو اِپِه كَه بِنِى
كَپَالَه ثَلَا خَاسْتِى كَآفْتُوسْ مُونْ نَاپومِنِى
ذَخَالْنَاىْ تُونْ پَارَاذِسُو كُوذَه تُو جَهَنَّمِى

line 10
كَه عَرْش كُرْسِى كَه لَوْحِى پِشِخَسْ كَتُو قَلَمِى
كَوَالَه آپَانُو سِتُو نَرُو تِنْ پِس كَموْنَه سِتَكِى
كَتَنْدُوسَه تُوسْ اوْرَانُوسْ سِتَقُونْ خُورِسْ دِرَكِى

f. 52b
كَسْتُولِسَه تُوسْ اوْرَانُوسْ مَاسِتَرْيَا مَتُو فَنْقَارِى
كَتُوَالَه كَتِنْ فُوتْيَا تِسْ مَرَاسْ پُونْ يَادِگَارِى
كَفْرِفْتِكَه خْتِنْ پِلَاشْتِنُو كَه اِپِه قِسَرِتَمَه

44 CHAPTER 1

پوُسْ اِیمَة اَنَاسْ موُنَاخوُسْ مَاسْ اِیپِة پِسْتَپْسْتَمَه
كِیپِة اوُدَهْ یَنِقًا كوُذَهْ پوُتَهْ یَنِیوُمَه   line 5
كوُذَهْ یَنِیوُ نَا قْسَرَتَهْ نَهْ تْرُغوُ [18] نَهْ كِموُمَه
كَثَلِی تِنْ آنَاسْتَاشِی أَپَاتَا نَا تِن قَامِی
تَا وَانْگَلاَ توُمَارْتِروُنْ توُتوُ بَذِی تَاذَامِی
اوُپِیوُسْ یَاتِن آنَاسْتَاشِی پوسْ یَنَّهْ ثِیَامَازِي
پَاصَانِقْشِی ذَنْدروُنْ خوُرْتِیوُنْ توُنْ سِتوُلُو نَا كِتَازِي   line 10
كَاسْكِتَاقْشِی تَاشِغْنوُفَا آنَموُسْ اوُنْدَا سَرْنِي
پوُسْ تَانَالأَيْ كَخَانوُنْدَه كَانَالِپْشِی تَا یَرْنِي
كَانْدَا اوُرِیشِی اوُتَغوُسْ پَاله كَمَتَا سَرْنِي
تَاغْلِیسْ كَانَاسْتَه نوُنْدَه سِتوُنْ طِپوُ توُسْ تَا فَرْنِي   f. 53a

f. 52a   ðoksazmata tu piti apira paşa ora
pu'n'oḫ'tin[19] pşiḫi şamutra k'ine makriya 'ḫ ta thora
tetyon afendi eḫume pu'ḫton kero ðen'ine
ap'afton ine o keros k'o,ti ora k'anine
line 5   ne arḫi eḫi nesterno m'uðe korfi ne paton
ne omyastin ne şindrofon pu ton yirepşis ya ton
etut' i plaşi ðenitan yenu ipe k' eyini
kepale 'thele ḫasti k'aftos mon' n'apomini
ðeḫalnay ni ton paraðiso k'uðe to cehennemi[20]
line 10   ke 'arş kürsī ke levḫ-i pşiḫes keto kalemi[21]
k'evale apano sto nero tin yis kemone steki
ketendose tus uranus stekun horis direki
f. 52b   ke stolise tus uranus m' asterya meto fenkari
ke tuvale ke ti fotya tis meras pu'n' yādigāri[22]
kekriftike oḫtin plaşitu ke ipe kserteme
pos ime enas monaḫos mas ipe pistepsteme
line 5   k'ipe uðe yenika k'uðe pote yeniume
k'uðe yenyo na kserete ne [ ]troğo ne kimume
ketheli tin anastaşi epeta na tin kami
ta vangelya tomartirun tuto peði t' aðami
opyos ya tin anastaşi pos yenete thiyamazi
line 10   paş' anikşi ðendron ḫortion ton stolo na kitazi
k'askitakşi ta şiğnufa anemos ond'da serni
pos t'analey keḫanonde k'analipşi ta perni
k'anda orişi o Theġos pale kemeta serni
f. 53a   ta ġlepis k'anastenonde ston topo tus ta ferni

f. 52a	Endless praises give Him each hour you're alive,
	whom you see with your soul but is far from your eyes.
	Such a Lord we have that he does not come from Time;
	no matter the hour, Time comes from our Lord Divine,
line 5	who has nor beginning nor end, nor bottom nor top,
	nor commensurate nor companion to be sought.
	This world was not; "*Become*" He said and it became.
	And still all this will be lost and He'll remain
	together with both Paradise and Jehennem,[23]
line 10	the exalted 'Arsh, the tablet of souls and the pen.
	And atop the water He placed the solid earth
	and stretched sky above, which stands without pillars.
f. 52b	And He adorned the sky with stars, with the moon's rays,
	and as a keepsake He gave flame to the day,
	and He hid from his creation and said "*Know me*
	and believe in me, know that I am one and only.
line 5	*Neither was I begotten nor did I beget,*
	just as never do I eat nor do I rest."
	And He will hereafter bring the resurrection,
	as God's good news has testified, o child of Adam.
	Whoever wonders what the resurrection brings,
line 10	just watch the fleet of leaves and grass rise each spring,
	and look too at the clouds when the wind drags them,
	how it dissolves them and the Ascension takes them,
	and when God wills it once more and draws them in,
f. 53a	you see He's resurrected them in their place again.

This passage offers a beautiful window into Ṣānī's prosody.[24] While occasional lines of the Greek meter run one syllable under or over the required fifteen, Ṣānī is generally quite dexterous in observing even the finer rules of the *politikos* verse form, the most important being the subdivision of each line into two smaller units: one eight-syllable and one seven-syllable syntactical cluster, separated in the middle by a caesura—i.e., a brief pause in sense or the introduction of a new clause. Most lines of the codex deploy this regularized form of 8[/]7, where the division in the line is introduced by a natural breath in the syntax or a conjunction or subordinate clause. Oral recitation of the lines reveals other rich ornaments, such as unexpected rhymes across languages (e.g., rhyming the Greek *fengari* of f. 52b line 1 with the Persian *yadigâri* of the next line); alliteration (e.g., f. 52a line 1, with its quick succession of "p" sounds); asyndeton and anaphora (e.g., f. 52b line 1, where "με" /"with" is repeated twice without an intervening conjunction); as well as polysyndeton, both in isolated lines (e.g., f. 52a line 10) and across the broader passage, as it stacks "and" atop "and" atop "and" in an increasingly breathless list of the miracles of creation. To lend both immediacy and grandeur to these miracles, Şānī also makes use of natural sublime imagery, from sea to sky to firmament above. On the other hand, he is also capable of drawing the reader down to the minute scale of grass and leaves in his extended simile of the resurrection.

Beyond its prosody, this passage is also brimming with intertextual allusions to both Islamic and (albeit more subtly) Orthodox Christian concepts and reveals the rich cultural milieu in which Greek-speaking Muslims were operating. Already in the second line Şānī's description of God seems to be translating and synthesizing key passages from the Quran[25] and the hadith[26] traditions, by which God is understood to be invisible to the eye but visible to the soul. More explicit is the description of creation: "Become, he said, and it became" (Γένου είπε κ' εγίνη, f. 52a l. 7), which is a Greek calque of the key Quranic term *kun fayakun* (كن فيكون, "Be and it is"), alluding to God's easy will to creation and voiced at multiple points throughout the Quran. Similarly, Şānī's description of the creation of the sky (f. 52a, l. 12) finds a direct parallel in the language of the Quran,[27] while the allegory of clouds for the resurrection, which comes at the end of the passage, likewise gestures toward a Quranic parallel but with a slight modification in Şānī's Greek, for while the Quran envisions clouds as the agents of resurrection, bringing new life to the flora and fauna with their rain,[28] Şānī figures them as objects of God's resurrection.

More important than such passing imagery is the first and most fundamental pillar of the faith: the Tawhid, or the indivisible oneness of God, reworded in the extended excerpt above into Modern Greek. To understand how and where the Tawhid is woven into the text, let me first provide its Quranic counterpart from the 112th surah: "(1) Say: He is God, the one and only; (2) God, the Eternal, Absolute; (3) He begetteth not, nor is He begotten; (4) And there is none Like unto Him."[29] The fourth and final verse of the surah is carried up toward the beginning of Şānī's poem, in line 6 of folio 52a, while the first and third verses are joined together and deferred to the following page (folio 52b, lines 4 through 6[30]), which is now rendered as a direct quotation of God's speech—in Demotic Greek.

This last point holds important implications for the language politics surrounding Şānī's book, but it is also important to note that alongside the Greek one finds some explicit Arabic words for other religious concepts, such as those in lines 9 and 10 of fol. 52a: Hell (*cehennem / jahannam*), the Throne of God (*al-'Arsh*) or God's Tablet (*Lawh*). Such translanguaging is to be expected, particularly for religious terms,[31] but even so, Arabic does not monopolize the conceptual vocabulary of Islamic piety. Other concepts, like "God," are almost invariably voiced in Greek (*Theos* rather than *Allah*), while some terms yoke Greek and Arabic side by side, like "Tablet of Souls" (*levh-i pṣyhes*), where "tablet" is Arabic and "souls" is Greek (ψυχές).[32] Such combinations may jar modern readers, but for Şānī and his audience the intermingling of Arabic and Greek (as well as Persianate and Turkish syntax within the Greek syntax[33]) were the everyday linguistic *realia* of their lived experience, and Şānī combines them to good effect.

Hiding within the Islamic religious vocabulary, one also finds certain key conceptual terms drawn from Orthodox Christianity—not translated but transposed into the Islamic context. The most striking example here can be seen in what I've translated as "God's good news" (f. 52b, line 8). In fact, what Şānī actually writes is *ta evangelia*, or "Good tidings," which is one and the same with the Christian gospels. To be sure, Şānī likely means not the Christian gospels in isolation but the sum of God's revelation—i.e., the Torah, Gospels, and Quran. Even so, its presence here is an indication that Şānī and his readers were conversant with both Islamic and Greek Orthodox traditions. And it is not an isolated instance. In the first moments of the poem (lines 3 and 4), Şānī also writes of God's exteriority from time, and in doing so he uses the philosophically and theologically loaded Greek term *kairos*. This concept was already fully developed in Platonic and Aristotelian thought, meaning the decisive or critical moment of intervention, but in early Christianity *kairos* came to mean God's appointed time. Islam quickly developed its own philosophy of time in dialogue with the Aristotelian and Neoplatonic traditions,[34] yet to reimpose that Islamic tradition back into the Greek language, as Şānī does here, unavoidably places it in close proximity to the word's hefty Orthodox Christian index of meaning. Denoting God's eschatological time, Orthodox Christian *kairos* seems aptly contrasted in Şānī's poem to the linear chain of "hours" (*ores*) marking human time. Şānī draws several other concepts from Orthodox Christianity as well, such as "ascension" (*analepsis*), which is one and the same with the Greek term for the assumption of Christ.

48 CHAPTER 1

Given Şānī's insistence on using Greek and his borrowings from Orthodox terminology, what kind of pushback was he expecting from the Turcophone elite of the centralized Ottoman state? I'll let Şānī answer in his own words:

ف. 49a   تُو تَارِيخ تُو كِتَاپيُو پُويِنكِه نِشَانِي

line 6   خِيلِيُوسْ اَوْذُومِنْدَا اَفْتَا اِيتَانْ كَه رَمَضَانِي

پُو تُوقْرِنَا رُومِيقَا تُوْيِيي 35 اُوتي تُوُولَاوِي 36

اَسْرُوتِشِي عَالمِدَسْ اُوْپُو نَا قَاتَالَاوِي

نَايْذِي پُو تِنْ عَرَابِكِي مُونْ سِتِنْ تمِي خُورِيزُونْ

line 10   تِسْ غِلُوسَسْ پُوخُونْ اِيَاتْرُوْبْ قَاتُوسْ ثَلُونْ پِرِيزُونْ

مُونْ مِيرُوتِشِي اَكِينُوسْ پُوذَنَنَه قِسَرْتَاذَسْ

پُوتُو فَاكُولِي سِترُونْكِلُو ذِيَاوَازُونْ صَا خُوجَاذَسْ

مِتُوسْ اَرْثِي بَارَاقْسَنُو اوخِتِنْ آذُوكْشَا تُوسْ

ف. 49b   كِمِي تُويِيُونْ مُونْ تِيُوتَاسْ تِيَارُونْ تَا مْيَالَاتُوسْ

اِينْ كِيُولِي پُونْ فِرُونِمي آيَافْتُوسْ نَا سُو فَرُو

يَافْتُو پُو ذَنْ تُو قْسَرِي مُونْ تُو لَيْ پُو ذَنْتُو قْسَرُو

اَكِنِي پُو تُو غْرُونِصَانْ اوخْتُو سْترَاوُ تُو اِيشُو

line 5   شِنْبَاثْيُو پِرْنُو آفْتُونُونْ مَا تُونْ ثَعُو پَرِيشُو

تُو ثْلِمَا مُو اَكِنُونْ تُونْ لُوغُو لَنْ نَا قْسَرُو

قِسَرُونْ ذَنِقْسَرُونْ مُونْ تُوسْ قُوسْ تُو لَنْ اُوتِي تُو قْسَرُو

اَفْتِنته مُؤنِه مَكِنُوسْ تُوسْقُوزْمِقُوسْ دَمَني

اُوپُو تُو لَنْ اِغْلُوصَا مَاسْ مُونْ تُوركِقَا نَا قْرَنِي

line 10   آنْ لَنْ وَانْكَلُو سِتِلْثكه سَتُوتِنْ كَتِنْ تمُومَه

ذَنْ اِرِثَه سَتُوتِنْ آذَرْفِه پُويِنه 37 پُونَا تُويِذُومَه

آنِنه پُونَا تمِيثِي اِغْلُوصَا خْتُو وَانْكَلُو

اِغْلُوصَا اِيرُومَيكِي ذَنَخِي آنَايلُو

ف. 50a   آنِيُونْ تِي اُوخِي تُوركِقَا قْرَنِي اُو وَاشِلَازْمَاسْ

كَتُّومَه آقْلُوثْرْمَا تِخَنِي تِسْ تُورْكَازْمَاسْ

آنِنه يَا تَا قْلُوثْرْمَا عَارِ ابِقَا تِخَنِي

تِتَا قْرِنِه اُوْپِرُوفِتِسْمَاسْ پْلُولُوغُوسْ ذَسَونِي

line 5   ثَامَازْمَا مَغَا تَا خْرِتْيَا تَا تمْيَا تَا كِتَاپْيَا

ذَنه مَارْتِرِيسَانْ نَايِيُونْ قَالِي اِغْلُوصَا قَاپْيَا

اِيقُوزْمِكِي پُو تُوغَالَانْ اَتُوتُو بِذعَاتِي

اُوپُو ذَنِقْسَرُونْ نَاندُوسْ پِي تثَالَايْيِي رَكعَاتِي

f. 49a   to tarihi tu kitapyu puyin[e] ke nişāni
line 6   ḫilyus evðominda efta itan ke ramazāni
         pu to 'krina romeyḳa [t]o ipi oti to volevi

SAVE THE NIGHTINGALE 49

           asrotişi ʿalimiðes[38] opu na ḳatalavi
           nayði pu tin ʿarabiki mon stin timi ḫorizun
line 10   tis ġloses puḫun iyathrobi ḳathos thelun yirizun
           mon mirotişi ekinus pu ðen[i]ne ḳsertaðes
           pu to fakuli strongilo ðiyavazun ṣa ḫocaðes
           mitus erthi paraḳseno oḫtin aðoḳşa[39] tus
f. 49b   kemi tuypun mon tipotas tiparun ta myala tus
           in' kepoli pu'n' fronimi ap'aftus na su fero
           p'afto pu ðen to ḳseri mon' tu leyi pu ðento ḳsero
           ekini pu to ġronisan[40] oḫ'to stravo to işo
line 5   şinbathyo perno aftonon ma ton Theġo perişo
           to thelima mu ekinon ton logo len na ḳsero
           ḳserun ðenḳserun mon tus kus to len oti to ḳsero
           aftine mone mekinus tusḳozmikus ðemeni
           opu to len iġloşa mas mon turkiḳa na ḳreni
line 10   an len vangelyo stilthike setutin kaytin timume
           ðen irthe setutin aðerfe puiyne pu na toyðume
           anine pu na timithi iġloşa ḫto vangelyo
           iġloşa iromeyki ðeneḫi anayelyo
f. 50a   an pun ti oḫi turkiḳa kreni o vaşilyaz mas
           kethelume aḳluthizma tiḫeni tis turkyaz mas
           anine ya t'aḳluthizma ʿarabika tiḫeni
           titaḳrine o profitismas polevloġos ðe se vani
line 5   thamazma meġa ta ḫartya ta timya ta kitapya
           ðen emartirisan naypun ḳali iġloşa ḳapya
           iḳozmiki tovġalan etuto bīd ʿāti[41]
           opu ðenḳserun nandus pi titheleypi rek ʿāti[42]

f. 49a   To seal my poem let me get the date tacked on,
line 6   one thousand seventy-seven,[43] during Ramadan.
           I judged it fitting to write in the Greek tongue;
           go ask scholars to examine what I've done.
           Arabic's place, you'll see, is solely honorific;
line 10   the languages we have are those we stick with.
           But just make sure that you consult wise peers,
           not those hacks who simply add a smart veneer
           by reading with a magnifying glass. I fear
           that if you pose them a question that's obscure

f. 49b   they'll blather themselves into a furor.
         True, I could mention many reasoned scholars too,
         who admit when they lack answers to an issue.
         They can tell right from wrong. From these, by God,
line 5   I beg a thousand pardons. No, I mean those slobs
         who, regardless of their knowledge on a matter,
         always have at hand opinionated answers.
         They're allied with those secular authorities
         who say Turkish is the only tongue we can speak.
line 10 They tell us, "*God's word was sent in Turkish and we respect it.*"
         No it wasn't, friends! Where's that text? Let me inspect it.
         If we're to honor tongues in which God's word was sent,
         Then the Greek tongue is nothing to scoff at, my friends.
f. 50a   And then they'll say, "*But Turkish is our king's tongue
         and we want worship to conform with Turkdom.*"
         With that logic, though, we should follow Arabic,
         because our blessed Prophet spoke to us with it.
line 5   But wonder great! The sacred books and holy tracts
         never said this or that tongue was good or bad;
         secular authorities made this heterodoxy after the fact,
         they who couldn't explain the meanings of rak'at![44]

As before, there is a lot of rich material here, but I will focus on the most important strands. In the first section, as Şānī prepares to seal his work, he pauses for an intriguing invitation: he challenges any Islamic scholar to scrutinize his decision to write in Greek. So long as that scholar is honest and qualified, Şānī maintains, they will sanction his decision. The problem lies in the many scholars who are neither honest nor qualified and whose sophistries will find a way to discredit Greek. While Şānī does not name any of his opponents, we should note that he was writing during a period of general upheaval in Ottoman religious life, due largely to the agitation of a group of fundamentalist revivalists known as the Kadızadelis (named after the initial leader of the movement, Kadızade Mehmed).[45] This movement, whose prime period of activity was from 1630 to 1660, attacked what it viewed as decadent and dangerous religious and cultural "innovations" that were supposedly leading the faithful astray. Turkish-language catechisms often reflected and embodied this fundamentalist drive to police religious boundaries. Occasionally, they even singled out the Ottoman Empire's western territories—of which Ioannina constituted an important metropole—as particularly "heretical" and called upon centralized authorities to watch these suspect populations more vigilantly.[46] While it remains unclear to me to what degree Kadızadeli fundamentalists were specifically attacking Şānī and his fellow Greek-speaking Muslims in Ioannina, the doctrinal tensions and generally heightened atmosphere that they created had no doubt reached the city.

According to Şānī's text, however, religious jurists are not the only ones engaging in such unwanted policing. They are allied with secular authorities, whose stance appears even more pointedly hostile to Şānī's project. His use of the word "secular" indicates that he is pushing back against some part of the Ottoman state apparatus—most likely the administrators in Istanbul or their appointed representatives in Ioannina. After the Greek peasant revolt in 1611 CE, which was violently suppressed by the Ottoman state, there may have been lingering suspicion against the region's Greek cultural dominance. It might have been the case then that certain secular authorities sent from Istanbul wished to separate Greek-speaking Muslims from their language in order to fully assimilate them. Yet even if such an explicit program of assimilation was absent, one can find historical precedents for a more general tension between the Turkish-speaking ruling elite, imported to the provinces from Istanbul (for what was often a brief term of service), and the local lower-order jurists and scholars who more often represented the interests of the indigenous population.[47] Language barriers were not an inconsequential factor in these tensions.

Whatever the specific historical details may have been, Şānī's codex depicts the ultimate aim of his adversaries in stark terms: to eradicate the Greek language from Islamic piety. The two main lines of attack as Şānī depicts them are as follows: first, that Greek-speaking Muslims must abandon Greek for Turkish because the latter is the language of God's revelation. Şānī's response to this is swift: there are no Turkish scriptures; that language has come late to the table; Greek conversely *is* one of the languages of God's revelation in the Abrahamic tradition.[48] The second line of attack leans more on the secular power of the state: the idea that the Ottoman Sultan speaks Turkish and hence so should his subjects when performing ritual prayer. Here again Şānī deflects the argument by pointing out that when Muslims are capable of switching languages during prayer, the only true choice is the Arabic of the Prophet.

Şānī's ultimate aim is not to reverse the hierarchy of tongues in favor of Greek but to level that hierarchy altogether. Yes, he praises Greek as one of the languages of the Abrahamic scriptures (while Turkish is not), but he raises the specter of such an argument simply to turn the religiously based attacks of linguistic chauvinists on their heads. *No matter how you turn it*, he seems to say ironically to his antagonists, *you're playing at a losing game here*. Ultimately, as Şānī makes clear in the generous passage that closes the excerpt above (fol. 50a, lines 5–8), God's word never deigned to categorize particular languages as good or bad; this was a latter-day heterodoxy invented by secular authorities and their hacks. In contrast to them, Şānī embraces Islam's universalism and in doing so defends Greek not as a better or worse language but as an integral part of his religion's ecumenical vision:

غِرَافِي مَصَا سِتُونْ عِمَادِي مُوتِغْلُوصَا ثَلِيشِي   f. 50a
تُونْ ثُوْ كُوتِيُورِسَه اُوْ ثُوسْ لَي آسْمَارْتِرِيشِي   f. 50b
صُو لَي تُوْ اِيمَانِتُوْ مُوتِي غِلُوصَا ثَلِيشِي
مُوپْيَا غِلُوصَا تُوْ نُومُوْ تُوْ تُوْ قُوزْمُوْ نَا مِلِيشِي
تُوِيذَا كَمَسْتُوْ مُلْتَقَه پُوْ لَي ذَنْ تُوْ خْرِيزِي
مُوپْيَا غِلُوصَا تُوْ نُومُوْ تُوْ تُوْ قُوزْمُوْ نَا مِلِيشِي   line 5
أَغُوْ أَتُوْتُونْ تُونْ دَعْوَا سِتُونْ أَخُوْ سِتُونْ تُخْفَمُوْ
أَكِينُوْ اُوپُوْ ذِيَالِصَا كَه اِيذَسْتُوْ آذَرِفَه مُوْ

f. 50a   ġrafi mesa ston 'Imādī[49] m'o,ti ġloṣa thelişi
f. 50b   ton Tho k'o,ti orise o Thos, leyi, as martirişi
        su leyi to imanitu m'o,ti ġloṣa thelişi
        m'opya ġloṣa tonomo tu tu ḳozmu na milişi
        toyiða ke mesto Mülteḳa pu lei den tu ḫrizi
line 5   m'opiya ġloṣa tonomotu tu ḳozmu na milişi
        eġo etuton ton da 'vā[50] s'ton eḫo ston tuḥfemu
        ekino opu ðiyalişa ke iðes to aðerfemu

f. 50a   Ebussuud writes about this language business:
f. 50b   To God and God's commands let each bear witness
        and tell their faith in whatever tongue they choose.
        Speak God's laws to people with the tongue you use.
        I read it also in the Multaqā al–Abhur:
line 5   you don't need [Arabic]. Use the tongue that's yours.
        My *Tuhfe* argues this until the bitter end,
        that's the analysis you saw here, my friend.

The references here to Ebussuud Efendi and the *Multaqa al-Abhur* are important and I will unpack them in due course, but first I need to lay out the larger stakes at play in this passage. By "bearing witness" and "telling the faith," Şānī likely means not only public confession of the faith and catechismal teaching but also the performance of daily ritual prayer.[51] In essence he seems to be arguing that in the mosque it was acceptable for his Greek-speaking coreligionists to pray in their native (and for most of them, their only) tongue.

Such a claim is by no means uncontroversial in Islam. Most legal schools of Sunni Islam do not recognize translated ritual prayer as such, even while translation in non-ritual contexts is of course widespread across all forms of Islam, from interlinear Qurans to exegeses (*tafsirs*). Latching onto the former prohibition against ritual translation and ignoring the multiform uses of translation elsewhere, many popular understandings of Islam and indeed even some influential scholarship have until recently promoted the idea that Islam prohibits all Quranic translation in all contexts. The prominent orientalist Bernard Lewis wrote, for example, that "the text is divine, inimitable, uncreated and eternal, and to translate it would be an act of presumption and impiety."[52] Thankfully, more recent scholars such as Travis Zadeh and Bret Wilson have been pushing back against this monolithic and inaccurate view to paint a finer-grained picture of multiple practices and positions vis-à-vis Quranic translation in several Islamic cultures. Most investigations of translation in Islam pivot on the Hanafi legal school, because Hanafi jurisprudence was the most liberal legal tradition on the issue of translation. Conveniently for Şānī, it was this legal school that had also been adopted by the Ottoman court as the empire's official form of Islam.

Abu Hanifa, from whose name the Hanafi school is derived, was particularly clear in his support of translated prayer. When asked whether Muslims could pray in translation—even if they had a command of Arabic—Abu Hanifa reportedly answered that yes, even in such a case their ritual prayer is valid. It was only later that his disciples Abu Yusuf and Muhammad al-Shaybani, who took a slightly more conservative view on the issue, declared that one could only resort to translated prayer if one lacked command of Arabic.[53] It was this qualified position that was repeated and elaborated by Şānī's source material in the passage above: Ebussuud Efendi, the celebrated sixteenth-century Shaykh al-Islam of the Ottoman Empire, and the *Multaqa al-Abhur*. Written by the jurist Ibrahim al-Halabi in the sixteenth century, the *Multaqa* in particular became a touchstone for Ottoman Islamic law, and its position on translation was clear: "If [the person praying] . . . is incapable of reading Arabic, then it is valid for her/him to recite not in Arabic but in Persian . . . Like Persian, this is true for other languages as well during the Profession of Faith."[54]

54 CHAPTER 1

The fact that the *Multaqa* upheld Hanafi opinion on this point offered a crucial shield for Şānī. Translating Islamic piety into Greek on the edge of the empire, his work gives multiple indications that he and his fellow Greek-speaking Muslims had been experiencing linguistic discrimination by Turkish-speaking, Arabic-reading jurists and scholars. Look for example to this passage later in the codex:

f. 161b
line 7

تُومُورِيسَه كَه اَيْپَسَه تُو مُحَمَّدْ پِروُفِتِي
نَا قْرَاقْشِي قُوزْمُونْ كَه فِيلَسْ سِتُونُومُو كَسِتِين بِسْتِي
ذَنِيپَه غِلوُصَا توُسْ قَاكِي يَسْتوُسْ نَا تِنْ آفِسوُنْ
موُنْ اِيپَه بِسْتِتوُسْ قَاكِي يَسْتوُسْ نَا سَقْلوُثِسوُنْ

line 10

ذَنْ اِيپَه پوُ ذَنْ اَقْلُوثَايْ تِغْلوُصَا سوُخِي پَاثِي
موُنْ اِيپَه پوُ ذَنْ اَقْلوُثَايْ تِنْ بِسْتِتوُ اَخَاثِي[55]
اَمَا ذَنْتُويْپَه اُو ثَغوُسْ كَموُذَه بَيْغَمْبَرِسْ
اِغْلوُسَسْ اوُلَسْ موُنْ مِيَانَه اكِنِي نَا تِنْ قْرَنِيسْ

f. 162a

مَتِيموُروُنْ[56] پَارَ اوُلِي نَايْپوُمَه اوُخْتِنْ بِسْتِي
اوُپوُ قْرِينَه روُمَيِقَا اَپَسَه كَقْرَ هَمِسْتِي
تِسْ غِلوُسَسْ اوُلَسْ اُو ثَغوُسْ تِسْ اَذوُسَه تِقْتَمَه
مَاقَرِي نَا يَنوُمَاسْتَانْ سِتَارَابِقَا مِسْ لَمَه

line 5

مَغْلوُصَا پوُ يَنِثِقَامَانْ قْرَنوُمَه موُلوُغوُمَه
مَتوُ كَفَالِي پوُخوُمَه مَتَافتوُ پْروُشْكِنوُمَه

f. 161b tom'orise ke epepse to Mohammed profiti
line 7 na ḳraḳşi ḳozmon ke filés sto nomo kestin bisti
ðenipe ġloṣa tus ḳaki pestus na tin afisun
mon ipe bistitus ḳaki pestus na s'aḳluthisun
line 10 ðen ipe pu ðen aḳluthay tiġloṣa su'ḥi pathi
mon ipe pu ðen aḳluthay tin bistitu eḥa[th]i
ama ðentoyipe o Theġos m'uðe peyġamberis
iġloses oles mon' mya'ne ekini na tin ḳrenis
f. 162a ma[s] timo[r]un para oli naypume oḫtin bisti
opu 'ḳrine romeyiḳa epese keḳremisti
tis ġloses oles o Theġos tis eðose tifteme
maḳari na yenomastan st'arabiḳa mis leme
line 5 meġloṣa pu yenithiḳamen ḳrenume moloġume
meto kefali pu'ḫume metafto proşkinume

f. 161b God revealed his book and sent Muhammad
line 7 to call all peoples to his faith as Prophet.

He didn't say, "*Tell them their language is taboo!*"
He just said, "*Their faith's wrong, tell them to follow you!*"
line 10   He didn't say, "*Who follows not your tongue will suffer!*"
He just said who follows not his faith is lost forever.
If neither God nor the prophet said differently,
all tongues are but one, so speak it freely.

f. 162a   But they punish us, even though we all confess the faith.
"*Whoso speaks Greek has forfeited his soul!*" they say.⁵⁷
God gave all tongues, though, we've nothing to atone for.
If only we spoke Arabic at birth—but we don't, for
line 5   we speak and pray with the tongue we're born with,
with the head our shoulders are adorned with.

Şānī cuts through the debates on language and returns us to the roots of Islam, the true engine driving the Quran and its revelation to the Prophet Muhammad. God's commands concerned not linguistic heresy but the pillars of good faith. It was a decisively universal message, directed at the whole world over—think, for example, of Quran 21:107 or 38:87—and to anchor that universalism in a particular tongue (i.e., Arabic) necessarily created a deep and abiding tension, one that lies at the heart of all debates around translation in Islam. Şānī however dispels this tension by positing a divine umbrella language of which all human tongues are so many regionally and culturally localized manifestations. In an ideal world, he argues, we would all speak Arabic, but such is the world as God has made it and we each view creation through the lens of our own, equally valid tongue. The only problem was that some tongues were being invalidated, as the final lines of the excerpt insinuate. The criticism in this particular instance focuses on the use of Greek in ritual prayer, but as other passages have made clear, Greek was also stigmatized more generally as an inappropriate tongue that should be abandoned for Turkish.

Ironically, Turkish-language authors in earlier centuries had also made use of the same Hanafi position toward the same ends: to promote their own vernacular translations from Arabic into Turkish. One such early author was Devletoğlu Yusuf, whose Turkish translation of Hanafi law was an early milestone in Turkish vernacularism. Although Devletoğlu Yusuf was active two centuries before Şānī, the two projects share several common aims: to adapt Arabic-language tenets into the language of their regional coreligionists, and to do so in rhymed couplets. Devletoğlu Yusuf in fact makes a brief cameo in the *Tuhfe* of Şānī, when the latter quotes the former's defense of Turkish as evidence that one can and should do the same with Greek. Şānī writes:

قُوسَه كَقَاپْيَا بِيتْيَا ذوْ پوْيْيَه مُلاَ يوُسُفِسْ   f. 162b

سِتوُ مَنْظُومْ فِقْهِ توُرْكِي يَا نَا مِتوُ پِسَفْتِشِسْ   line 3

بَيْتْ تُرْكِي

تُركْچَه دِرْ دَرْسِي مُدَرِسْلَرْ اَخِي   هَمْ مُحَدِّثْلَرْ مُفَسِّرلَرْ دَخِي   line 5

بوُ حَنِيفَه كِيم اوُلْدُرْ⁵⁸ صَاحِبِ اوُصُلْ   مَعْنِدِرْ قُرْاَنْ بِرْ قَوْلْ اوُلْ

پَارْسِجَه قُرْاَنْ جَائِزْ كُوْردِي بَسْ   كِيْم نَمَازْدَه اوُقُسوُنْ قِلْسِنْ هَوَسْ

اَيْلَه اوُلْسَه هَرْ نَه دِلْجَه اوُلْسَه كَرْ   لَفْظْلَرْ آلَتْ مَعْنِي اوُلْدِرْ مُعْتَبَرْ

f. 162b   ḳuse keḳapya beytya ðo pu ipe Molla Yūsufis
line 3   sto Manẓūmi Fıḳıh⁵⁹ tūrkī ya na mito pseftişis
         beyt turkī
line 5   türkçedir dersi müderrisler aḫi [/] hem muḥaddisler müfessirler daḫi
         bu Ḥanīfe k[im] oldur sāhib-i usul [/] ma'nidir Ḳur'ān bir ḳavl ol
         parsice Ḳur'ān cā'iz gördi bes [/] kim namāzda oḳusun ḳılsın heves
         öyle olsa her ne dilce olsa ger [/] lafzlar ālet, ma'nī oldur mu'teber

f. 162 b   Listen to some of Molla Yusuf's verses,
line 3   and, so that you'll believe me, in his own Turkish:
         Turkish Verses
line 5   At madrasa the teachers' lessons are in Turkish;
         as with scholiasts and exegetes of hadith verses.
         Abu Hanifa was a master analyst. He averred
         the Qur'an's essence is its meanings, not its words.
         He viewed the Qur'an in Farsi as legitimate,
         so long as whoso reads it makes their prayers passionate.
         And so no matter the tongue you're speaking,
         words are a tool; what matters is the meaning.

Devletoğlu Yusuf begins by pointing out that much of the religious education and research within formal Ottoman settings is already taking place in Turkish, not Arabic. He then justifies this status quo by tying it to the authority of Abu Hanifa himself. Abu Hanifa, Devletoğlu wrote, had implicitly located the divine essence of the Quran not in its language but in the underlying meaning. The Arabic prosody thus became a well-wrought but non-essential vehicle. Make no mistake, this was a highly controversial claim. The majority of Islamic jurists agree that to translate the Quran is to compromise its holy essence, which is part and parcel of the Arabic text's inimitable prosody.[60] Abu Hanifa's position as represented by Devletoğlu Yusuf thus stands in the minority. But within Ottoman Islam it held major sway and had offered a conceptual spark to Turkish vernacularization two centuries earlier. It was this same spark—along with its Turkish-language text—that Şānī was now taking and ingeniously using on behalf of Greek. In other words, he was turning some of the foundations of Turkish vernacularism against the very Turkish authorities who, more than two centuries later, he understood to be censuring Greek vernacularism.

Despite their shared reliance on Hanafi law, Devletoğlu's Turkish vernacular project and Şānī's Greek vernacular project have one important difference in their goals. While the Greek-speaking Şānī had at best a tense relationship to the secular authorities of the imperial capital, Devletoğlu was *allied* with these authorities. Early Hanafi law had located legal power in the autonomy of jurists and conceded little ground to secular authorities, but with the rise of the Ottoman Empire more and more scholars, shaped by a centralized curriculum and appointment system, anchored their vision in the authority of the Sultan. Nonetheless, as Guy Burak has argued, the farther away you marched from Istanbul the more resistance you could find from the margins.[61] Just compare these two passages, the first from Şānī and the second from Devletoğlu:

> [Secular authorities say] *"But Turkish is our king's tongue
> and we want worship to conform with Turkdom."*
> [...]
> But wonder great! The sacred books and holy tracts
> never said this or that tongue was good or bad;
> secular authorities made this heterodoxy after the fact,
> they who couldn't explain the meanings of rak'at!   (Şānī f. 50a)

And here is Devletoğlu:

> For in this world order is
> caused by the Lord of all creatures.
> From among his servants God chooses one sultan
> to rule over all people by edict.
> He is God's deputy among the faithful;
> as such, they accept his authority.[62]

Şānī's passage, as I have already discussed, pushes back against the Turkish of the Ottoman court and its authorities. In Şānī one finds a "Turkish king" whose representatives stand at fairly explicit odds with God's mission. Devletoğlu Yusuf however writes in clear praise of both the Sultan and his authority, which are neatly packed into a hierarchical taxonomy of the universe that descends from God to the Sultan and thence to his subjects beneath him.⁶³ The one vernacular project, in other words, is easily aligned with the imperial vision of centralized authority; the other betrays certain irreconcilable differences with centralization. Why? Periodization might help in part explain this difference, since the Ottoman state was still expanding in the fifteenth century, but the different cultural geographies seem to me even more important.

One possible factor lies in the ideological charge of Greek, which was sometimes identified as a "Christian" language. For this we can look to a late eighteenth-century Greek-Turkish dictionary written by the Greek-speaking Cretan Muslim Nūrī. In his introduction, Nūrī takes a defensive stance and concedes (to his Turkish-speaking Muslim readers from the mainland) that Greek is a "crude" (*pek kaba*) tongue, a tongue that belongs, moreover, to the infidel (*kâfir*), and it is therefore "shameful" (*ayıbdır*) for Muslims to adopt it—or, more literally, to "imitate" (*taklīd*) it, a verb that presumes Greek to be intrinsically alien to Muslims.⁶⁴ While Nūrī eventually reverses this position and celebrates the virtues of Greek, it is clear from such apologetic language that Greek-speaking Muslims could sometimes be made (by the imperial Turcophone core) to feel shame for their native tongue, due to its close proximity to Christianity. These particular language politics may perhaps shed some light on the motivations behind Şānī's stated resistance to centralized authority.

To my mind, however, an even more important factor lies in the specific audiences of the two works. While Devletoğlu Yusuf had dedicated his work to the Sultan with an eye toward a court appointment, Şānī was addressing his fellow Greek-speaking Muslims in Ioannina. In the codex Şānī betrays no pretensions to state power. In fact he makes explicit references to wresting power from Turkish-speaking scholars and investing it directly into the hands of his local audience. He writes,

آفْتِي پوُ قُرَنوُنْ توُرْكِكًا خِرِيا اِينْ پوُنْ خَامَنِي   f. 159a
حَاشَا اَفْتِي قَاقوُ توُرْكِي قِرِينَانْ كِتَابِي   line 5
اِيذَانْ پوُلِي ذَنْ اَغْرِيقوُنْ مَعْلوُسَاسِبْروُ عَرَبِي
كِيَانْدَخوُنْ اوُخْتوُنْ نَعوُ پوُرْمِنِيْسَانْ ثَوَابِي
مَعْلوُصَا يَاغْرِيقوُنْ پوُلِي اَكِينوُ توُ كِتَابِي
كَانِنْ سَكِينوُ توُ توُرْكِي كَعْرَافِي يَا توُ نوُموُ

SAVE THE NIGHTINGALE 59

اَكِينُوسْ اوْپُو تُو پْسَفْتَايْ بِسْتِتُو اَخِي فُووُو   line 10
اوْتِي كَافْتِي تُوْ عَرَبِي كِتَازُونْ كَاپَهْ پَرْنُونْ
تِتْلُونْ تِنَا تُوسْ ذَحْتِي كَتُورْكِكَّا تُو قْرَنُونْ
يَا نَا غْرِيكَايْ اَقْسَرِيغُوسْ تِنْ بِسْتِي اَنَانْكَازِي
وَارْيَانَه تُوْتُورْكِي اَفْتُونُو اوُرْمِكَّا ذَنْ اَذْرَازِي   f. 159b
نَا قْرِنِيسْ اَنُوْ تُورْكِكَّا اوُپُو نَا مِنْ تَا قْسَرِي
مُوسْتَكِي كَسَتِيرَايْ ذَنَحِي خَبَرِي

f. 159a afti pu krenun turkika hriya[65] in' pu'n' ḥameni
line 5   ḥāṣā[66] afti kako türkī krinan kitābi
         iðan poli ðen aġrikun meġlosa asbro 'arabī
         k'apandeḥun oḥton Theġo p'orminepsan ṣevābi
         meġlosa p'aġrikun poli ekino to kitābi
         k'anin' sakino to türkī keġrafi ya to nomo
line 10 ekinos opu to pseftay bistitu eḥi fovo
         oti k'afti to 'arabī kitazun k'apepernun
         tithelun tina tus ðeḥti keturkika tu krenun
         ya na ġrikay akseriġos tin bisti anankazi
f. 159b varya'ne to türkī aftunu ormiña ðen aðrazi
         na krinis eno türkika opu na min ta kseri
         mo[n'] steki kesetiray ðeneḥi ḥaberi

f. 159a Scholars who speak vulgar Turkish are lost souls.
line 5   God forbid they read a faulty book in Turkish:
         seeing that most here don't know Arabic, they wish
         to earn reward from God for their so-called piety
         with a book whose language people know more readily.
         If these scholars explain God's law based on bad Turkish texts,
line 10 [the Greek speaker] fears for his faith when he objects,
         thinking they know Arabic and can scold him into silence.
         They want only [the Greek speaker's] dumb compliance,
         and so they use Turkish when they speak to him,
         and he's forced to listen to the faith in ignorance.
f. 159b Turkish is a burden for him, he just can't grasp it.
         If you start speaking Turkish when you explain the faith,
         he'll stare back at you with a blank and clueless face.

According to Şānī, some Turcophone religious scholars were explicating scripture and the tenets of Islam based on Turkish texts to which local

Greek-speaking Muslims had limited linguistic access. Taking advantage of this power imbalance, such Turkish-speaking scholars were speaking down to Greek-speaking Muslims when they dared question or push back against the former's interpretations. It was for these Greek-speaking Muslims that Şānī was writing, to give them the tools to defend themselves against the tyranny of and dependence on Turkish-language scholars. If Şānī himself had any kind of patron or dependence, it was not upon the Ottoman court but the local readers and listeners for whom he was writing. Because ultimately the survival of his text depended on them. In the final lines of the codex he writes,

f. 166a
نَاخِي اَغْكَا اوْپِوْ توُيْذِي اوُمُوْرْفَا نَا تِرِيشِي
مِپِي تِنْ قُوپُوسْ پْسَفْتِقُوسْ 67 اِپنهَ كَتوُ قْلوُجِشِي
اَكِپِنوُنْ توُنْ پَرِيقَالوُ اوْپِوْ توُ بَيَنْدِشِي
كَنَا توُغْرَايْشِي آپاَ تَا قَرْذِيَا توُ نَا ثْلِيشِي
line 10

f. 166a na'ḫi eġña opu toyði omorfa na tirişi
mipi tin ḳopos pseftikos ine keto ḳlocişi
ekinon ton pariḳalo opu tobeyendişi
line 10 kena toġrapsi ape t[in] ḳarðia tu na thelişi

f. 166a May my readers have a care to preserve
the things that they find beautiful in my oeuvre.
Don't let them say *"what faithless drudgery!"*
and kick it in the garbage heap.
I pray that anyone who takes joy in my art
line 10 will wish to write it from the bottom of their heart.

Admittedly such gestures are not uncommon in manuscript culture, yet for a geographically marginal text in a linguistically minor language with no pretensions to state patronage, its call to readers must be understood not only as a formulaic trope but also as an acknowledgment of real readerly power. Whether Şānī's text survived depended not on the largess of a courtly patron or that patron's scriptorium (*kitaphane*) but on local readers, whose hands kept this work alive—both by copying it out and by preserving those copies against all odds of fire, water, moisture, parasites, and degradation. Their task was also necessarily social, since to copy an Ottoman-script manuscript one also had to have another person read it aloud, as was characteristic of Islamic book cultures. Transmission by dictation was common in mosques and madrassas, where a work was recited aloud while student-copyists took down the recitation in rough form. The scale of textual reproduction must have been smaller for Ottoman-script Greek, but the dictation took on added value since the alphabet was (at this early stage at least) a novel and demanding form for the language. Errors were apparently more common, as Şānī explicitly notes:

اوْتِنَه غِلوُصَا يوُنَانِي كَسَارِ ابِي تُوْ غُرَامَا   f. 166a

خُورِسْ اوُسْتوُنْ نَا ذِيْاوَاسْتِي أَخِي قوُپيوُنْ تُوْ ثِيَامَا   f. 166b

[...]

نَا تَا كِتَاقْشِي او قْسَرِتِسْ پوُسْتُوْ مِيلَازوُنْ   line 6

تِپوُ تُوْ غْرَافوُنْ شِكَازوُمَه تَا حَرْفِيَا تُوْ تَالَازوُنْ

تِتوُتوُنَه روُمَيِقَا كَخِي مَغَالوُنْ قوْپوُ

تِتوُسْتوُنِي تُوْ حَرْفِتوُ نَالَاقْسوُنْ ورِسْقوُنْ توُپوُ

f. 166a   oti'ne ġloṣa yūnānī ke's'arābī toġrama
f. 166b   horis [tonus][68] na ðiyavasti eḫi ḳopon to theyama
[...]
line 6   nata kitaḳşi o ḳsertis posto milazun
          tipu to ġrafun şkiâzome ta harfiya tu t'alazun
          tituto'ne romeyiḳa ke'ḫi meġalon ḳopo
          tituston[us] tu ḥarf[y]u nalaḳsun vriskun topo[69]

f. 166a   The tongue is Greek and the letter Arabic;
f. 166b   without diacritics, your eyes get tired quick.
[...]
line 6   Let someone in the know check how it's read aloud:
          in copying, I fear, letters will get changed around.
          See, this is Greek and it's a big headache
          since in lettering there's wide room for mistakes.

Ottoman-script Greek is no walk in the park, Şānī tells us. The multilayered system of diacritic markings, from the *i'jām* baseline of the consonants to the *ḥarakāt* symbols of vowelization, present ample opportunities for omission, misplacement, and misreading. For this reason, he calls out directly for collaboration and cross-checking among his readers, stressing the momentous task they've been assigned. And given this critical importance, I want to introduce you to the copyist of this surviving witness—the reader to whom, in a very real sense, I owe my chapter. He identifies himself as Hasan Bey Osman Zade in the colophon of the first tome and in fact includes a short Greek-language poem of his own in the final page of the codex (f. 167b), where he presents himself on more intimate terms as *Hasanis*. The poem offers a parting valediction to both the book and its readers and deserves a place in this book as well:

كِرْيَمُو أَفْخَارِسْتِسَه تُو شَانِي تِنْ پِشِخُولاً
مَتوْرَ رَحْمَتِسُوكِرْيَه كَمَتِيسْ خَارَسُولاً
اوْتِي پَاشْكِسَه كَقَامَهَ پوْسُوْنْ قُپوْ
يَا نا دْقْشِي تِسْتِرَاتَا سوْ كْپِروْفِتِيوْسُو ذِرومُو
كِرْيَه كَتوْنْ قَاقُونْ كَتوْنْ عَاصِي حَسَنْ
كِرْيَه پَارْتَامَانَاتِسُو آپَافْتوْنْ مَه اِسْلَامِي
كِرْيَه مَاتِنْ [اَخَارِپِسوُ] پوْخِسْ تُوْ مُحَمَّدِي صلى الله عليه وسلم
كِرْيَه سِتِسْتِرَاتَا آفْتوُنُو سِقوْتُوْ تُوْنْ حَسَنْ
اوْپِيوُسْ نَا ذِيَاوَاشِي رَحْمَتِي تُوْ حَسَنْ
كِرْيَمُوذوْسْتوْاَكِينوُ لَيْموُشِنِي مَغَالِي
اوْپوْ ذِيَاوَاشِي فَاتِحهَ آپَانوْ سْتوُنْ حَسَنْ
كِرْيَمُوْ سَه پَارَاقَلُو سِتِنْ بِيصَا مِتوْ وَانِسْ
تَا قرِيمَاتَا توْ پوْلاَ نَه كِرْيَمُو خَارِي قَانِسْ

kirye mu efḫaristise tu Şānī tin pṣiḫula
meto raḥmetisu kirye kemetis ḫares s'ola
oti paṣkise keḳame poson ḳopo
yana ðikṣi tistrata su keprofityu su ðromo
kirye keton ḳaḳon keton âṣî Ḥasani
kirye par t'amanatisu apafton me islāmi
kirye metin eḫarisu puḫis to Mohammedi ṣallâllahu 'aleyhi ve sellem
kirye stistrata aftunu siḳoto ton Ḥasani
opyos na ðiyavaṣi raḥmeti tu Ḥasani
kiriye ðostu ekinu leymoṣini meġali
opu ðiyavaṣi fātiha apano ston Ḥasani
kirye se paraḳalo stin biṣa minto vanis
taḳrimata tu pola 'ne kirye ḫari ḳanis

My Lord show favor on Şānī's dear soul,
with your mercy, o Lord, and your graces all,
for he labored and toiled and never stopped but
showed us your path and the way of your prophet.
And Lord, as for lowly Hasanis: however great his sins,
receive with his *islam* this book that you entrusted him.
Lord, by the blessing you have in Muhammad (*sallallahu alayhi wa salaam*),

Lord, on your prophet's path lift up Hasanis,
and whoever prays for Hasanis's *rahmet*,
Lord, grant them even greater *eleemosyne* yet.
Whoever will recite *fātihas* upon Hasanis's soul,
Lord, I beg you spare them from eternal flames,
their sins are great, Lord, but greater is your grace.

This poem follows a fairly standard formula, delivering a brief eulogy for the author, a prayer for the copyist, and a blessing for any future readers who might perform a *fātiha*—i.e., a ritual recitation of the first chapter of the Quran—for the latter's soul. Behind the formulaic structure of these verses, however, I see at least a couple points worthy of remark. First, the subtle play of language, which I've tried to signal in my English translation, weaves the Greek in and out of Arabic, with a pun on the core meaning of *islam* (i.e., submission) and a twinning back and forth between *rahmet* and *eleemosyne*, which mean "mercy" in Arabo-Turkish and Greek respectively. Beyond this, there is not much in Hasanis's modest prosody to bedazzle the reader's imagination, but that is not his aim. For within the humble intimacy of this poem lies the promise of a truly awesome undertaking: an intergenerational transmission network that joins Şānī to Hasanis and thence to us, the readers of their textual project today, which binds us up within it and makes it ours as well.[70]

The power of this transmission network is borne out by the date and place of the manuscript's production, which Hasanis provides in the colophons of the second and first volumes respectively. The date he gives his work is 1786 CE—i.e., a hundred and twenty years after Şānī. And the place of its production is recorded as the "district of Fener," likely the city of Fanari in Thessaly, a day's journey south of Trikala. Look on any map and you will see that the distance between Şānī's Ioannina and Hasanis's Fanari is substantial, but just as important, the two cities are also divided by the greater part of the dense and rugged Pindus Mountains.

The journeys—both geographic and temporal—that Şānī's words made in order to reach Hasanis warrant some final remarks here. First, the work must have been copied by multiple hands in multiple nodes along a larger network.[71] This in turn suggests that however localized Şānī's message and intent may have been, the work struck a chord with a wider audience of Greek-speaking Muslims across central Greece. Why? Certainly much of the enduring value that such communities placed in Şānī's poem derived from its practical utility: the careful explication of their faith in Greek. In providing this explication it also accomplished something bigger, though: it granted Greek a place at the table of Islam. Such a place was by no means a given, as I have tried to show from Şānī's spirited defense of the language in the face of Ottoman Islamic higher learning, whose centralized institutions and norms did not always hold Greek in high esteem. While the *Tuhfe* likely never even reached the echo chamber of Ottoman-Turkish higher learning, its local audience lay elsewhere, closer to home, and this audience seems to have found significant value in the work.

Şānī foresees this lasting value of his work in the closing couplet of the first tome. Just before the colophon, he ends with a clever and suggestive couplet (fol. 50b, lines 8–9), which has likewise inspired the title to this chapter:

بِوُتَّه تُو اَصوُسَسْ شَانِي تَايْذوُنِي اوُنْداَ سْقوُزِي
ثَارُو تُوتَسْ اِيتَانْ كَقَدِرْ كَمَرَا تُو نَوْروُزِي

pote to esoses Şānī t'aydoni onda skuzi
tharo totes itan keḲadir kemera tu Nevruzi

Şānī, you saved the nightingale when it was in its throes,
it must have been both Qadr Night and the day of the Nevruz.

The meanings of this couplet are dense but can be coaxed out through careful analysis. The nightingale is a common trope in Persian and Ottoman poetry. In most instances the bird is paired with a rose, to which it calls out in sweet and plaintive song and laments their separation. The symbolism of this image had its beginnings in love poetry, in which the nightingale was a figure for the disconsolate lover and the rose his beloved, but with the rise of Sufi poetry this symbolism attained a second, higher level in which the rose came to represent God's perfection and the nightingale the human soul seeking it out. The Greek couplet activates this second level, where the nightingale stands in for the souls of Greek-speaking Muslims, who were crying out in pain for the absence not so much of their God but of the Greek-language tools to reach him.

The second line's "Qadr Night," traditionally commemorated during the last ten evenings of Ramadan, is the night when God revealed the Quran to the Prophet. It is considered a particularly holy and blessed moment when Islam was first made known to the faithful. In the couplet, however, the Night of Qadr is juxtaposed to the Nevruz, or the Persian New Year—a combination that may at first seem perplexing. The Nevruz was a public holiday in the Ottoman Empire, celebrating the coming of spring, the blossoming of trees, and the creation of Adam from mud. It was the celebration of new life. To understand its place here, we must recall that Şānī had dated his work to 1667 CE during the season of Ramadan. It just so happened that in 1667, Ramadan (and hence Qadr Night) coincided with the Nevruz. Noting this coincidence, the couplet above thus seizes the symbolic value of the two festivals' convergence and likens the *Tuhfe* to both a moment of revelation (Qadr Night) and a joyous rebirth (Nevruz), when the reeling Greek-speaking Muslim community was brought back to life by Şānī's teachings.

And if the poem still held that potential over a hundred years later as Hasanis copied it out on the far side of the Pindus Mountains, it was thanks not only to Şānī but to the readers who continued to read and reproduce his work along the margins of the empire. Şānī authored the initial text; it was his audience who *authorized* it again and again in the decades that followed.

Şānī's Gift to Readers Today

Şānī's *Tuhfe* may have saved the nightingale of Greek-language Islam for a time, but the combined ideological and institutional forces of Greek and Turkish nationalisms ultimately drove that bird to flight in the first decades of the twentieth century. While Greek nationalism had been philologically excluding Greek-language Islam since the nineteenth century, only with the Population Exchange of 1923 did this cultural partition reach its devastating geopolitical conclusion, when all of Greece's Greek-speaking Muslims were dumped like so much human trash into Turkey—where Turkish nationalism received them with equal suspicion and hostility.[72] Today, a hundred years later, I believe the time has come to welcome indigenous Islam back to the pages of Greek philology and the Greek tradition.

The *Tuhfe* can offer us a helpful model toward that end. Sifting through the scripts and traditions of Greek prosody and Ottoman Islam, Şānī and his readers sorted out the felicities and infelicities of both and took what they needed from each. This kind of free-ranging across domains is rich with potential, particularly when it serves to decentralize systems that have grown rigid through the centralization of authority.[73] Reassembling the scripts and protocols from the borders of literary systems can help, even in small ways, to decalcify texts, providing opportunities for each textual handler (like Şānī, as he sifted through his Arabic and Turkish sources and his Greek-language prosody; or like Hasanis, as he listened to a recitation of Şānī's text and copied it down anew) to reassess, renegotiate, and ultimately reassemble the texts that they've been given by both local and translocal networks of transmission.

Working slowly and assiduously along the borderscape of Greek literature and Ottoman Islam, Şānī and his subsequent handlers charted out their own space within a more open-ended literary landscape.

To be sure, this landscape has always been subject to historical erasure, or what we might more aptly call "circumscription." From the indifference or contempt of centralized Ottoman Sunni scholarship to the institutionalized hostility of foundational national philologies in the region, literatures like those of Greek-language Islam were systematically circumscribed and categorically neutralized. To the few national philologists who deigned to consider Greek-language Islam, it mattered little what the Greek-speaking Muslims themselves thought of their own texts. Only the philologists could decide the place of those texts—a place far away from literature proper, internally displaced within historical appendices and ethnographic sidenotes. And as I wrote at the start of this chapter, many of the humanistic sciences are today more mindful of such biases, yet the understanding that readers bring to the Greek tradition still abuts the internal limits set by the borderscape of early institutional philology.

How to break down these boundaries? How to reformulate the canon not as a core national or Western legacy but as its own ecosystem of Greek-language, Greek-adjacent, and outright non-Greek traditions, such as texts of Turkish-language and Albanian-language Islam produced in what is today Greece? If Şānī's *Tuhfe* has any answers to contribute to these questions, I feel that they come not only from Şānī himself but also from the community of readers, listeners, and copyists whom his text sustained and who in turn sustained it. For them, it was not merely a question of piecing together Arabic- and Turkish-language juridical texts and Greek-language prosody; more fundamentally, it was a question of claiming and reclaiming for themselves the texts, teachings, rhythms, and rhymes that they told and retold to one another, in dialogue with several literatures and philologies but beholden to the higher authority of none. Seen from this perspective, to truly rethink Greece's cultural borderscape will require offering a place at the philological table not only to orphaned texts like those of Greek-language Islam but to the communities who have produced, reproduced, and cared for them. The Greek canon cannot be opened up to a wider range of authors if it is not first opened up to a wider range of authorizers.

What does this mean in practice today? Whether or not such literatures are still actively being produced—this is a question whose answer we will only begin to explore in the final sections of this book—even as family or community archives they have a critical role to play in the twenty-first century. At its most ambitious scale, Şānī's vision might translate today into a sustained public outreach toward the descendants of Greek-speaking Muslims torn from their homes a hundred years ago. Working with community leaders and local associations in Turkey, an initiative of this kind might aim toward the creation of a community-driven and collectively owned digital library. These texts and their online infrastructure might in turn help facilitate larger dialogues between Greece's majority Christian population and its past and present Muslims, including the tens of thousands of new Muslim immigrants in Greece today whose children you might find on a given national holiday marching alongside their classmates in the streets of Athens—sometimes at no small risk to their safety.[74] At their most fundamental level, such dialogues necessarily lead to some difficult questions about the Greek tradition and the Greek canon. What does it mean to speak Greek or to write oneself into its tradition, and who gets to authorize that decision? Deftly crossing back and forth between the borderscapes of scriptworlds to tell and retell their stories, Şānī and his textual community can help us begin to answer these questions, if we but listen.

Chapter two, in which Cavafy is scattered and gathered up and scattered again

I WONDER what Constantine Cavafy would have made of Şānī's Greek. Where would the former have situated the latter in the human geographies that his poetry explored? And what of Cavafy himself? Where should we situate him geographically? Today, Cavafy is perhaps one of the few Greek-language poets who can claim some enduring global visibility, as refracted for example through world literature anthologies like those of Norton or Longman. Over the past century, Cavafy's poetic corpus has slowly but methodically multiplied across a dizzying number of translations and languages, inspiring even more readings and essays in a series of interlocking academic fields: modern Greek literature, European modernism, queer theory, translation studies, classical reception, and postcolonial studies, to name but the most prominent. By 2013, the 150th anniversary of the poet's birth, Cavafy was seemingly everywhere, circulating through the most unexpected of media.[1] In Athens, you could find his words on the side of any number of public buses or share a train with stanzas of his poems, laminated on the backs of seats and walls. Beyond Athens, Cavafy found new life in Istanbul, in Cairo, and in New York,[2] through forms as divergent as editorials (written by, among others, Orhan Pamuk), choreographic poems (such as Dimitris Papaioannou's *K.K.*), and musical compositions too numerous to cite here. Ten years later, in 2023, the Onassis Foundation expanded the celebrations further afield with its week-long "Archive of Desire," drawing in artists as diverse as Nick Cave, Robin Coste Lewis, Vijay Iyer, Julianne Moore, Nadah El Shazly, and Rufus Wainwright. Across a network of installations, musical adaptations, and visual art, Cavafy appears to have exploded onto the world scene.

Crucially, this explosive multiplicity does not so much revolutionize Cavafy's original poetic project as reiterate and augment it: adaptability and fluidity were constitutive elements of the poems when Cavafy himself was drafting and circulating them in the earliest decades of the twentieth century. Most notably, he repeatedly rejected the possibility of publishing a commercial edition of his poems, choosing instead to stitch, glue, and pin together shifting sets of "collections." During the last couple decades of his life, he circulated hundreds of copies of a dozen different, handmade books that he assembled himself and mailed off to far-flung readers across the Mediterranean and beyond. His fellow Alexandrian I. A. Saregiannis vividly sets the scene: "Cavafy's book-bindery—let's call it that—was in his house. It was a naked room [...] with assorted stacks of his poems [...]. He'd go in and out of his office and erase and write again the variation that he now preferred. [...] I never imagined that it would be such a huge process to [...] send his *Poems*. But which *Poems*?"* Utilizing multiple bindings, experimenting with alternative orderings of the poems, making manuscript inscriptions atop or alongside the printed words on the page (over and over again for each copy), and shifting through multiple imprints and emendations within each collection, Cavafy's books were difficult to pin down—not unlike the diasporic and queer Hellenisms that he explored within them.

But those books and their Hellenisms did not emerge from a vacuum. More important than Cavafy's books themselves—in the present chapter, at least—are the larger social and material networks of transnational Greek-language print within (or against) which his poems took shape, crisscrossing the Mediterranean. Some nodes of these print networks, like those in Alexandria, were deeply diasporic and peripheral to the Greek nation while also closer to imperial and postcolonial debates that we can now recognize as core concerns of Modernism. Other nodes to the contrary were bound up in the Helladic nation, either at its core in Athens or along its own periphery, in places like Thessaly

---

*"Τὸ βιβλιοδετεῖο, ἂς τὸ ποῦμε ἔτσι, τοῦ Καβάφη βρισκόταν στὸ σπίτι του. Ἦταν ἕνα δωμάτιο γυμνό [...] γεμάτο μὲ [...] διάφορες στίβες τὰ ποιήματά του [...]. [Π]ήγαινε καὶ ξαναπήγαινε κάθε φορὰ στὸ γραφεῖο του κι' ἔσβηνε κ' ἔγραφε τὴν παραλλαγὴ ποὺ τώρα προτιμοῦσε [...]. Δὲ φανταζόμουν ποτέ, πὼς ἦταν τόσο μεγάλη διαδικασία τὸ νὰ σταλ[οῦν] [...] τὰ 'Ποιήματά' του. Ποιά ὅμως Ποιήματα;" (Saregiannis, *Σχόλια στον Καβάφη*, 33–34).

or Macedonia. Each of them made particular claims to the Hellenic legacy that were staked on local and regional differences and affinities. Operating within these networks, Cavafy's shifting publication strategies necessarily activated the Mediterranean's shifting registers of Greekness.

Setting Cavafy's poems against this larger backdrop allows us to articulate a series of important questions: Beyond the walls of Cavafy's own "book bindery," in what ways might the broader world of Greek-language print have influenced or encouraged Cavafy's fluid poetics and publishing strategies? Second, in the years and decades following Cavafy's death, how did subsequent attempts at a complete edition narrate and justify themselves to later readerships? And, finally, what can such narrations tell us about the shifting human geography of the Eastern Mediterranean?

There were admittedly vast distances and weak media infrastructures between some of these geographies, particularly during Cavafy's lifetime. Rather than try to mitigate or explain away those distances and weaknesses, my aim here is to embrace them. True, the field of modernist studies has long centered on the *close* friendships and *strong* social ties between writers, but Paul Saint-Amour's notion of "weak theory" points us to (among other things) a more recent turn toward *weak* social ties, such as one-off or passing exchanges of writers, editors, publishers, and readers who will never meet in person.[3] These weak connections do not just expand the geographic interplay of modernisms; they also have the potential to reshape larger meta-narratives—none more important for me here than those of Hellenism and Greek modernity. What might happen, in other words, if we read Cavafy not only through his circle of friends and contacts but also through more distant voices of readers and editors at several ports of call along the Eastern Mediterranean? What new light might such a method shed on the stakes of Greekness and alterity at the borderscape between West and East?

After the creation of the Greek state in 1830, it was soon clear that this tiny kingdom, which hugged the peninsulas of Attica and the Peloponnese in mainland Greece, remained dwarfed by the larger Greek networks that continued to thrive beyond its borders. Large populations of Greek Orthodox Christians and/or Greek speakers were scattered across the Eastern Mediterranean, running from the Balkans deep into Anatolia, and thence down the Levant to Egypt. Over the next century, in an attempt to bring these vast Hellenic diasporas of the Eastern Mediterranean under its territorial, administrative, and ideological control, the Greek state embarked upon an irredentist project of territorial expansion. Known in Greek as the *Grand Idea* (*Μεγάλη Ιδέα*), this policy was ostensibly promulgated in the name of "unredeemed Greeks" (*ο αλύτρωτος ελληνισμός*) within Ottoman territories. Yet the relation of these *Hellenic* communities to the *Helladic* state was not always clear. Despite the admiration that many of them expressed for Greece, diasporic Greeks were nonetheless something more than just Greek citizens—and usually not citizens at all. Until the middle of the twentieth century, the diasporas that were writing their words on the margins of the Greek world had not aligned themselves with the central narrative of the Greek state.

In her recent engagement with Cavafy, Hala Halim has refashioned this observation in the form of a provocative question, asking, "Is a Hellenophone necessarily a Philhellene?"[4] In other words, must someone who speaks Greek cultivate only adulation to the Greekness of the Greek state or the Hellenism of Western Europe? I hope that Ṣānī's poetry from the previous chapter might help answer this question in radically new ways, yet Cavafy pushes the envelope in a different sense, given the fact that the Greek national canon and certain strands of European modernism have drawn him into their spheres. Halim has gone to great lengths to recuperate Cavafy from both Greek nationalist and Eurocentric discursive frames, demonstrating his weak social contacts with Arabophone Egyptian poets—mediated through both local ephemeral print and oral conversations and recitations.[5] Foregrounding these interactions, Halim understands Alexandria's cosmopolitan network not as a peripheral creation of Europe but as a set of South-South coordinates— "Andalusia, the Maghreb, the Syro-Lebanese eastern Mediterranean and Baghdad"—that create their own imagined centers.[6] Halim's project is ambitious and helps reframe what has sometimes been a subtle colonial reading of Cavafy in the English-speaking world.[7] At the same time, however, it is important not to underplay Cavafy's deep engagement with British colonial historiographies and their unavoidably imperialist frameworks, as Takis Kayalis has demonstrated through careful investigation into the poet's library, sources, and milieu.[8] Cavafy may have offered qualified critiques of these frames, yet an honest reading of his historical position must acknowledge a deep ambivalence vis-à-vis the British colonial intelligentsia, some of whom were his interlocutors and indeed his readers.[9] Through his weak social connections, Cavafy was caught up in a number of competing and irreconcilable political discourses and intellectual networks.

Inevitably, political discourses and intellectual networks continued to entangle Cavafy's poetry after his death in 1933. None exemplify this later period more than George Savidis, the textual critic who most directly shaped the field of Cavafy studies as it has evolved today. Savidis was the first neither to examine Cavafy's archives nor to publish a collected edition of his poems, yet he was crucially the first to apply a philological method to those archives, a labor that led to the publishing of a series of new Cavafic poems and editions that, at least initially, advertised themselves as Complete (Άπαντα). Savidis's editions and the introductory essays with which he advertised them became standard-setting, and his choices have been followed by most subsequent editions.[10] Without overstating the case, one might say that Savidis assembled "Cavafy" as most readers know him today. Working through the scattered pieces of Cavafy's archive, he claimed to have created a singular, legible unity out of a multiplicity—even as his claims often hid ongoing (or newly created) multiplicities, errata, and variations. The contours and some of the taxonomies of the field of Cavafy studies today stem directly from Savidis.

Nonetheless, the theoretical claims in the service of which Savidis mobilized these sources have today proven deeply problematic. The importance of bibliographic research, he suggested in his groundbreaking Οἱ Καβαφικὲς ἐκδόσεις (*The Cavafy Editions*, 1966), lies "not only in the formation of a critical edition [...], but also in the interpretation of the text and the psychological portrait of the author."* Let me leave aside for the moment the issue of a critical edition and look only to Savidis's final goal: "psychological portraiture." With this bio-biblio-graphical criticism Savidis analyzed for example Cavafy's handwriting, his age, or his publishing practices to draw broader conclusions about the workings of his inner psyche.[11] Unavoidably, this was a psyche authored not by Cavafy but by Savidis, and it reflected the oftentimes deep biases of the latter, in no way more destructively than in his casual suppression of Cavafy's queer poetics.[12]

Even in the absence of such biases and suppressions, Savidis's method strikes me today as theoretically dated—to say nothing of its philological soundness.[13] More fundamentally, it is simply unproductive of the kinds of questions most in need of exploration now. Like others who have more recently waded into the messy textual history of Cavafy's poetry—primarily

---

* "Ἡ σημασία ποὺ μπορεῖ νὰ ἔχει ἡ βιβλιογραφικὴ μελέτη [βρίσκεται] ὄχι μόνο [...] [σ]τὸν καταρτισμὸ ἔκδοσης φιλολογικῆς [...] ἀλλὰ καὶ [...] [σ]τὴν ἑρμηνεία τοῦ κειμένου καὶ [...] τὴν ψυχογραφία τοῦ συγγραφέα" (Savidis, *καβαφικὲς ἐκδόσεις*, 20–21).

Anthony Hirst, Sara Ekdawi, and Karen Emmerich—my aims here depart significantly from those of Savidis. I want to disassemble and reassemble Cavafy in a new light, examining the printed objects and the print worlds in which they took shape, both during his lifetime and after. Yet rather than setting my argument in opposition to Savidis, I seek instead to treat him as a crucial historical agent in the textual development that I am tracing. That is to say, rather than reject his interpretations, we must understand them as part of the larger story that concerns us here: the multiple constructions and reconstructions of Cavafy's poems.

The first half of this chapter begins before Cavafy's death, retracing what (and where) these poems were in their initial years of circulation. I hope here to "disaggregate" the Cavafy corpus as most readers know it today, planting its many pieces again within their original print ecology.[14] I will wager here the claim that Cavafy's literary production emerged within a period of ongoing economic, social, and geographic disjunction in the world of Greek print—a disjunction that Cavafy's poetry productively engaged. Produced in Egypt and circulated across the Eastern Mediterranean and beyond, Cavafy's original poetic artifacts exceeded the orbit of Greece's national print culture, whose center of gravity supposedly lay in Athens. Through both its themes and textual history, Cavafy's poetry problematized contemporary national narratives of a cohesive or contiguous Greek identity—and, just as important, its concomitant textual apparatus: the complete edition. Instead, Cavafy's poetry embodied what one might call a "diasporic poetics"—and I mean this in its most literal sense, for by its very etymology *diaspora* points us back again to the action of a "scattering." As I show in the second half of this chapter, it was only after midcentury, in the wake of the forced population exchange between Greece and Turkey (1923–1925), Turkish state violence against and mass deportations of Greeks from Istanbul (1942; 1955; 1964), and the economic collapse and "voluntary emigration" of Greeks from Egypt (1937–1966), which cumulatively signaled the end of major Greek diasporas in the Eastern Mediterranean and their troubled absorption into the Greek state, that a more unified corpus and Greek-language readership of Cavafy finally emerged. The key bonding agent between this new readership and their texts was the Greek academy, which had institutionalized national philology departments over the same period. In the 1930s, just as the historical Mediterranean diasporas began to crumble, the most prominent philologist of Athens—Ioannis Sykoutris, whom we met briefly in the introduction to this book—began speaking of the need to shore up the scattered texts of modern Greek literature, and to put a stop to "the chaotic accumulation of variations."[15] It was this call for textual consolidation that, a generation later, Savidis attempted to implement with his own Cavafy.

Cavafy's Fluid Hellenism and His Fluid Books

In 1863, Cavafy was born into a diasporic merchant family. His father, an Ottoman subject from Istanbul, had acquired British citizenship during his long stay in Liverpool, where, like many other Greek merchants, the Cavafy family had opened a trading firm in 1849, specializing in Manchester textiles and Egyptian cotton. In 1855, his family moved to Alexandria, where the business thrived until the death of his father in 1870, soon after which the family lost most of its capital in the commodities market. Consequently, Cavafy spent his professional life as a civil servant in Egypt's Ministry of Public Works, in the Irrigation's Third Bureau. Earning a middling income by proofing and copying out official letters in English, Cavafy likely found the work tedious, yet it became a crucial sinecure for the developing poet.[16]

Although he later acquired a Greek passport and Greek citizenship, Cavafy's relation to the Greek state and its vision of Greekness was less than clear and has been a point of debate.[17] He allegedly eschewed "patriotic" poetry while nonetheless claiming a deep love for the Greek "race," announcing, "I too am Hellenic—but take note, I am not a Hellene [i.e., *Greek*], nor am I Hellenized; I am Hellenic."* This last term, *hellēnikos*, is an adjective by which one normally attributes a "Greek quality" to objects, ideas, and actions, but never humans, and it seems to place Cavafy in a category beyond the organic, not a person but a thing or an idea. Semantically capacious, this Hellenic idea stands in explicit contradistinction to the Hellene, the bounded subject of the modern Greek state. Born in Alexandria, schooled in England, spending four formative years of his young adulthood in Istanbul, and living out the rest of his life in the city of his birth, Cavafy's Hellenism is difficult to place—both geographically and ideologically. As Marios Vaianos once wrote, he was "a man who cannot stay put [...]. He is so multiform and manifold."† This slippage and multiformity permeated Cavafy's poetry on several levels, yet its most obvious

---

* "Εἶμαι κ' ἐγὼ ἑλληνικός. Προσοχή, ὄχι ἕλλην, οὔτε ἑλληνίζων, ἀλλὰ ἑλληνικός" (quoted in Malanos, *Περί Καβάφη*, 56).

† "Ἕνας ἄνθρωπος ποὺ ποτὲ δὲν μπορεῖ νὰ σταθῆ σ' ἕνα μέρος [...]. Εἶνε τόσο πολύμορφος καὶ πολυσχιδής" (Vaianos, "Κ.Π. Καβάφης," n.p.).

effect for readers today lies on the level of content. Across his oeuvre, Cavafy's "inability to stay put" productively complicated contemporary understandings of Greekness, bringing to the fore the failure of Helladic Greekness to overlap neatly with Hellenism and the tensions that were thus generated in a world of shifting borders, powers, and languages.

As one might expect, Cavafy's "Hellenic multiformity" has generated a number of scholarly responses. E. M. Forster observed that Cavafy's Hellenism "was a bastardy in which the Greek strain prevailed, and into which, age after age, outsiders would push, to modify and be modified,"[18] while early Greek enthusiasts celebrated instead his supposed narrative of Greek continuity, or the diverse glories of the Greeks.[19] Both these readings of Cavafy's Hellenism however share a single assumed foundation: a preexisting *Hellene*, even if it may later affix itself to the foreign (or the foreign to it). Peter Jeffreys thus argues that "the Asian component of Cavafy's Hellenistic cosmos is nearly always refracted through a Greek prism."[20] As a result of this selective framing, he suggests, populations that lose all but the faintest signs of "Greekness" lose all but the faintest interest for Cavafy's poetry.[21] I understand this perspective, yet I am equally drawn to readings that inflect Cavafy's Hellenism in the other direction, shining light not only on how it transforms but how it is transformed by the poems' North African and Asian protagonists (or, in rare cases, how it is fully ecclipsed and abandoned by those protagonists, such as in the much-discussed poem "27 June 1906, 2 P.M."). In the first decades of the twentieth century, as the nature of the state was changing, demanding from subjects more rigid understandings of identity and territoriality, Cavafy's poems offered a space to complicate both terms. Reassessing Cavafy's work through the lens of postcolonial studies, Martin McKinsey makes a similar claim: the historical poems, he argues, speak to the violence of centralized cultural systems but also the agencies that various subjects along the periphery were able to negotiate within and through these cultures.[22] It is precisely through these complex encounters and subtly violent collisions that the actors of Cavafy's poems take up, refashion, or discard their hellenisms.

Cavafy's "multiformity" was by no means limited to the theme of Hellenism. This same refusal to "stay put" pervaded nearly every level of his work, from the ideological to the linguistic.[23] Indeed, Cavafy's multivalent "slippage" has led today to a series of thriving critical approaches, centered on the queer Cavafy, the historical Cavafy, the political Cavafy, etc.[24] In this chapter, I focus on the "inability to stay put" of the Cavafic corpus itself, which has helped clear the space for these interpretive struggles in the first place. Rather than speaking of these various levels as self-contained phenomena, one might productively view them as multiple manifestations of a poetic fluidity and adaptability: one that stretches from the thematic of Hellenism to the materials by which this Hellenism was assembled, disassembled, and reassembled.

To see how these levels inform one another, I turn briefly to one of Cavafy's more famous examples of Hellenism: "Ἐπάνοδος ἀπὸ τὴν Ἑλλάδα" (Return from Greece).[25] Set in the mid- to late Hellenistic period, the poem follows two young sophists as they depart from Athens for their homeland, either in Ptolomaic Egypt or Seleucid Syria. Standing aboard the ship, leaving behind them the Greek peninsula and looking out upon the littoral waters of West Asia and North Africa, the speaker of the poem addresses his companion:

Ὥστε κοντεύουμε νὰ φθάσουμ' Ἕρμιππε.	Well, we're nearly there, Hermippos.
Μεθαύριο, θαρρῶ· ἔτσ' εἶπε ὁ πλοίαρχος.	In two days' time, I wager; so said the ship's captain.
Τουλάχιστον στὴν θάλασσά μας πλέουμε·	At least we're sailing now in our own sea;
νερὰ τῆς Κύπρου, τῆς Συρίας, καὶ τῆς Αἰγύπτου,	waters of Cyprus, Syria, and Egypt,
ἀγαπημένα τῶν πατρίδων μας νερά.	beloved waters of our homelands.
Γιατὶ ἔτσι σιωπηλός; Ῥώτησε τὴν καρδιά σου	Why so silent? Ask your heart:
ὅσο ποῦ ἀπ' τὴν Ἑλλάδα μακρυνόμεθαν	the farther we moved away from Greece
δὲν χαίρουσουν καὶ σύ; Ἀξίζει νὰ γελοιούμαστε;—	were you not gladdened too? Why fool ourselves?—
αὐτὸ δὲν θάταν βέβαια ἑλληνοπρεπές.	such a thing would not be Greek.
Ἂς τὴν παραδεχθοῦμε τὴν ἀλήθεια πιά·	Let's admit the truth at last:
Εἴμεθα Ἕλληνες κ' ἐμεῖς—τί ἄλλο εἴμεθα;—	We too are Greek—what else could we be?—
ἀλλὰ μὲ ἀγάπες καὶ μὲ συγκινήσεις τῆς Ἀσίας,	but with loves and passions of Asia,
ἀλλὰ μὲ ἀγάπες καὶ μὲ συγκινήσεις	but with loves and passions
Ποῦ κάποτε ξενίζουν τὸν ἑλληνισμό.	that at times put off one's Greekness.
Δὲν μᾶς ταιριάζει, Ἕρμιππε, ἐμᾶς τοὺς φιλοσόφους	It's unbecoming of philosophers like us, Hermippos,
νὰ μοιάζουμε σὰν κάτι μικροβασιλεῖς μας	to stoop to the level of our petty kings

(θυμᾶσαι πῶς γελούσαμε μὲ δαύτους	(do you remember how we laughed at them
σὰν ἐπισκέπτονταν τὰ σπουδαστήριά μας)	when they visited our classrooms):
ποῦ κάτω ἀπ' τὸ ἐξωτερικό τους τὸ ἐπιδεικτικὰ	beneath the ostentations of their Hellenified
ἑλληνοποιημένο, καὶ (τὶ λόγος!) μακεδονικό,	or (imagine!) Macedonian exteriors,
καμιὰ Ἀραβία ξεμυτίζει κάθε τόσο	a little bit of Arabia would show its face now and then,
καμιὰ Μηδία ποῦ δὲν περιμαζεύεται,	a little bit of Media that they couldn't hold back,
καὶ μὲ τὶ κωμικὰ τεχνάσματα οἱ καημένοι	and with what silly ploys the poor fellows
πασχίζουν νὰ μὴ παρατηρηθεῖ.	strive to keep it under wraps.
Ἄ ὄχι δὲν ταιριάζουνε σ' ἐμᾶς αὐτά.	Ah, no, such things do not become us.
Σ' ἕλληνας σὰν κ' ἐμᾶς δὲν κάνουν τέτοιες μικροπρέπειες	For Greeks like us, this pettiness won't do.
Τὸ αἷμα τῆς Συρίας καὶ τῆς Αἰγύπτου	The blood of Syria and Egypt
ποῦ ῥέει μὲς στὲς φλέβες μας νὰ μὴ ντραπούμε,	that flows within our veins—without shame,
Νὰ τὸ τιμήσουμε καὶ νὰ τὸ καυχηθοῦμε.	let us honor it, let us boast of it.
(1914)	

Whereas the petty vassal kings of Anatolia strive to mask the complex patchwork of their identities, thrusting it behind a supposed official standard of Greek exteriority, the speaker chooses instead to flaunt his "Greco-Asian" alloy. Yet there is another level of oppositions not to be overlooked, one that we might begin to explore in the speaker's silent companion, Hermippos, sulking on the prow of the boat. The latter's silence stands in stark contrast to the former, who quite literally *publishes* (i.e., makes public) his not-quite-Greek Greekness to those around him. In other words, the tension of this poem lies not simply in the tug and pull of "mainland Greek" and "diasporic Greek" identities, but also in the speech and silences, the porous boundaries of the public and private spheres in which the tug and pull take place.

It is therefore significant that "Return from Greece" numbers among Cavafy's many unpublished manuscript poems—those he kept within his workshop and archive but never printed or circulated in the "collections." The poem itself enacted a public performance of diasporic Hellenism but from within a manuscript that never made its way to press or periodical. When viewed as both aesthetic conceit and material object (what Jerome McGann has called, respectively, linguistic and bibliographic codes), "Return from Greece" ultimately leaves these tensions unresolved. While its text embraces the buoyant optimism of the speaker, its material history might also incorporate something of the silence of Hermippos. Or rather, perhaps we might best qualify this poetic object as navigating a liminal space between the two poles, seeking out an ideal community of readers somewhere between the private and public.

Similar tensions run throughout Cavafy's publication strategies. Most visibly, he published individual poems frequently and widely (first in almanacs, later in literary journals, newspapers, and even popular magazines) in Alexandria, Cairo, Athens, Crete, Salonica, and elsewhere, a practice that he continued throughout his life and one that has received less scholarly attention than it deserves. Simultaneous with these ephemeral publications, he also gave his poems to local printers for his own uses: after circulating broadsheets of poems for more than a decade (1891–1904), in 1905, Cavafy printed and assembled a thin book of fourteen selected poems arranged thematically, followed by a second in 1910, with additional poems interspersed. These were printed en masse and bound with two staples to the spine of a cardboard cover. Two years later, in 1912, these books evolved into the final and by far the most intriguing phase of Cavafy's personal publications. Here, Cavafy again assembled multiple poems into collections, yet the assemblages now began to bifurcate into two separate types—the one arranged from earliest composition to latest and the other arranged according to perceived thematic affinities between poems—each one circulating and evolving in successive forms (with varying chains of content) until his death in 1933. These collections bore multiple and manifest signs of their handmade construction, from retrimmed pages to pen-mark emendations on the verses to glue-strips that tipped single broadsheets into the binding. Such intimate signs of Cavafy's handiwork invited the intervention of readers' hands as well, who sometimes participated in the revision and reformulation of their book. Indeed, one of the scraps of paper featured on the cover of *Literature's Refuge* is drawn from a collection of Cavafy, bearing emendations penned in by the reader. The creative dialogue between Cavafy and his readers is an important backdrop to this chapter, but I have already told that story in detail elsewhere,[26] so I will refer you there rather than belabor the point here. Suffice it to say that all of his collections, upon closer inspection of their materials, betray a story of bricolage and multiplicity that extends beyond Cavafy himself.

Rather than a liability, however, the fluid logic of his books proved a central strength to the larger poetic project. As Cavafy wrote in 1922 to Napoleon Lapathiotis, a young Athenian poet, "How can I say anything about the future? [/] Perhaps, suddenly, I'll want to make a compound partition of only historical poems.—If we look at the entire corpus of poems, not divided up into Particular Collections, then with each new poem, the proper arrangement, the one according to theme, would change."* The ruptures, disjunctions, and tensions that one witnesses within Cavafy's poetic narratives of Hellenism extend to the broader material project of constructing—or, rather, indefinitely deferring the construction of—a unified poetic corpus. Rather than pursue the public project of a mass-produced and widely circulating *Poems*, Cavafy chose instead to embrace the unstable, shifting nature of a semi-public, semi-private publication strategy. It was a strategy that saw him one day mailing off a poem for publication to a literary journal in Macedonia, another day mailing off a new poem to the owners of his collections, asking them to slip it into their dossiers and attach it to an ever-shifting stack of works,[27] and a third day tucking yet another poem into his archive.

Hellenism's Fluid Geographies

What were Cavafy's motives for such a publication strategy? The question, with its explicit focus on authorial intention, has understandably driven much of the philological and bibliographical research within Cavafy studies.[28] Despite their difference of opinion, what such interpretations share is a prioritization of Cavafy's person itself, offering inner psychology as a tool for uncovering the "truth" of the Cavafic oeuvre. As Timos Malanos wrote, his primary goal was "to provide *the keys* to the Cavafy corpus, to show its secrets, to help in every way possible to decode it. For this reason, I gave particular importance to his life."† Stratis Tsirkas, in what later became a very public and increasingly bitter debate with Malanos, accused the latter of several misinterpretations, concluding that Malanos "cannot and does not want to accept that another

---

* "Πῶς μπορῶ νὰ πῶ γιὰ τὸ μέλλον; [/] Μπορεῖ νὰ θέλω νὰ κάμω μιὰ διαίρεσιν συγκειμένην ἀπὸ μόνον ἱστορικά, αἴφνης.—[/] Στέκοντας ὅπου τὸ ὅλον σῶμα τῶν ποιημάτων δὲν χωρίζεται εἰς Συλλογὲς Ἰδιαίτερες, μὲ κάθε νέον ποίημα, ἡ κατάταξις ἡ σωστή, ἡ κατὰ θέματα, θὰ ἄλλαζε." Quoted in Savidis, *Καβαφικὲς ἐκδόσεις*, 63.

† "Ὁ κύριος σκοπός μου ἦταν νὰ δώσω τὰ κλειδιὰ τοῦ Καβαφικοῦ ἔργου, νὰ δείξω τὰ μυστικά του, νὰ βοηθήσω μὲ κάθε τρόπο στὴν ἀποκρυπτογράφησή του. Γι' αὐτὸ καὶ γράφοντάς την ἔδωκα σημασία ἰδιαίτερη στὴ ζωή του" (Malanos, *Ποιητής*, 198).

way of viewing Cavafy and his work exists."* To his vast credit, Tsirkas expanded the field to take in the larger world of British-occupied Alexandria, with its enduring political and economic tensions—a logical focus of his marxist materialism and anticolonial framework—yet the recuperation of Cavafy's personal ideology remained a central cornerstone for his study.[29]

Rather than searching out Cavafy's publishing motives in his person or ideology, I want to turn my gaze outward, toward the broader world of Greek-language print in which these publications operated. If Cavafy's tight control of nearly every phase of his production seems on many levels to justify previous scholarship's focus on authorial intent, this intent was nonetheless embedded in a larger field. That is to say, Cavafy's poetic practice was not the isolated product of a mind "entrenched [...] within an asylum uncontaminated and deep,"† but a series of tactical trajectories traced along a larger social plane.[30] The conditions of Greek print, I argue, strikingly mirrored and ideally accommodated Cavafy's multiform publishing, constituting the field in which—and the mediums by which—the Cavafic corpora moved, morphed, and proliferated.

At the risk of hyperbole, one might say that Greek publishing was in pieces. In the early twentieth century, several "centers" of Greek publishing dotted the Eastern Mediterranean (and, to an increasingly lesser extent, central Europe), a manifestation of the diasporic world that still defined Greek life. To a degree, these centers were bound together by a common alphabet and set of cultural and aesthetic debates—thanks in large part to the leading monthly journals of each city. Yet these bonds were nonetheless shot through by important regional tensions, both economic and ideological, a point to which I will return in the next section. Here, it's worth emphasizing that beyond the narrow readerships that consumed this medium, there was little hope of unifying the larger masses of Greek readers that were emerging. The creation of a truly mass literary market for a language that was read in various pockets of the Mediterranean, the Black Sea, continental Europe and beyond seemed unattainable. Even in Athens itself (the supposed heart of Greek publishing), broader readerships proved elusive. Writing in his journal at the turn of the century, Cavafy noted:

---

* "Ὁ κ. Μαλάνος δὲν μπορεῖ καὶ δὲ θέλει νὰ παραδεχτεῖ πὼς ὑπάρχει κι ἄλλος τρόπος θεώρησης τοῦ Καβάφη καὶ τοῦ ἔργου του" (Tsirkas, *Πολιτικός Καβάφης*, 179).

† "Ζεῖ ἀποξενωμένος ἀπὸ τὴ ζῶσα πραγματικότητα, περιχαρακωμένος μέσα στὴν ἀφηρημένη διανόησι, σ' ἕνα ἄσυλο ἄχαντο καὶ βαθύ" (Takis Barlas, *Nea Techne*, nos. 7–10, 1924, p. 102).

Στις 3 μ.μ. μ' επεσκέφθηκε ο Τσοκόπουλος. Έμεινε μαζί μου μέχρι τις 3.40. Κουβεντιάσαμε, την περισσότερη ώρα, για φιλολογία και για τις υπέρογκες δυσκολίες που συναντούν οι συγγραφείς για να πουλήσουν μιαν έκδοση. Ο Τσοκόπουλος λέει ότι θεωρείται μεγάλη επιτυχία το να κατορθωθεί η έκδοση, χωρίς να πραγματοποιήσει κέρδος, μονάχα να μην έχει ζημιά.[31]

At 3 p.m. Tsokopoulos [an Athenian journalist, writer, and playwright] visited. He stayed with me until 3:40. For most of the time, we chatted about literature and the massive difficulties that authors face in selling an edition. Tsokopoulos says that it's considered a large success for an edition to see the light of day not with a profit but simply without going into debt.

Such problems would continue to plague Athenian publishers in the ensuing decades. There was simply no capital, meaning that periodicals were short-lived and book publishers were averse to risk, producing for the most part translations of European fiction.[32] Money was also scarce among consumers. Well into the century, books continued to be relatively costly commodities in Greece. In the 1920s, at the peak of Cavafy's career, one continued to read advertisements in periodicals and newspapers for a "monthly payment plan" for single books, as if buying porcelains or furniture![33]

In his *Cavafy Editions*, Savidis cites the same "Tsokopoulos" passage above from Cavafy's diary, ultimately positing the same claim: "Cavafy prints his poems on his own because he has no publisher, and he gives them as gifts to whomever asks them of him because he has the certainty that they wouldn't buy them and the hope that they'll value them more, for being non-commercial."[34] Savidis's insight crucially turns the debate from questions of aesthetics and ideology to the market conditions beyond Cavafy's studio, yet rather than stop here I want to return again to the geography of Greek print to address the larger question upon which this insight hinges: *why* was there no mass market, and how might this speak to Cavafy's diasporic poetics? Although several factors came to bear here, an important component of any answer must lie in political geography. So long as the Greek world spilled beyond the bounds of the Greek state on such a spectacular scale, readerships were perforce scattered.

To be sure, earlier market structures had accommodated these scattered Greek readerships well enough—when they were smaller and literacy was more limited. From the late fifteenth and early sixteenth century onward, Venice had served as the central node of Greek printing, with other centers emerging only later in central and Eastern Europe and Istanbul. Producing primarily religious books (in particular, liturgical books), printing firms such as those of the Ioulianoi, Glykides, or Saroi shipped them to merchants or agents scattered across multiple continents.[35] Unwilling however to risk capital investment, these firms printed and shipped only on demand, which is to say, upon receiving the requests of the regional merchants and agents themselves,[36] a process that likely retarded the trafficking of books significantly. By the mid-eighteenth century, in the decades leading up to the Greek Enlightenment, more and more printers began to supplement this unreliable network with a subscription system. The subscription system was in large part targeted to a scattered diasporic network of readers who identified as *φιλόμουσοι* ("friends of the muses"—i.e., highly literate), posting their remittances in advance to fund a book's print run.[37] Given such a readership, this system facilitated a gradual shift in content away from liturgies toward Ancient Greek philosophies, grammars, tragedies, and Modern Greek philosophical, scientific, and political tracts. Between 1749 and the start of the Greek War of Independence in 1821, more than 140 titles had been circulating by subscription, with approximately 23,000 subscribers spread across the Greek world.[38]

While such numbers may at first impress, one should bear in mind the large temporal window and the vast breadth of the Greek world in which they fall. Precisely because literacy was relatively limited and the production of print was funded more or less through diasporic remittance, the fact that Greek books were published in Venice, Vienna, Munich, Budapest, Odessa, or Istanbul, for example, presented few problems to their thinly spread network of select and devoted readers. Yet as mass readerships began to emerge at the end of the nineteenth century, this system proved less and less viable for such a scale. Grigorios Xenopoulos, one of the most prolific and popular prose writers of the early twentieth century, characteristically complained in 1906, "The eight millions of Greeks are scattered across the ends of the earth, and the means of communication and advertisement are in a most sorry state of deficiency,—even the means of sending money [for a subscription to a periodical or book] are deficient, thanks to the primitive state of our postal services."* More than a decade later, as Cavafy's poetic production reached its

---

*"Τὰ 8 ἑκατομμύρια τῶν Ἑλλήνων εἶνε διασκορπισμένα εἰς τὰ πέρατα τῆς γῆς, τὰ μέσα τῆς ἐπικοινωνίας καὶ τῆς διαφημίσεως εἶνε ἀτελέστατα,—ἀκόμη καὶ τὰ μέσα τῆς ἀποστολῆς χρημάτων, χάρις εἰς τὴν πρωτόγονον κατάστασιν τοῦ ταχυδρομείου μας" (Xenopoulos, *Παναθήναια*, nos. 141–142, 1906, p. 229).

apex, similar complaints appeared in the editorials and correspondence of leading Athenian literary journals. Sampling just one issue of Βωμός (*Altar*, no. 19, August 1, 1919), we read the following: "To M. S. in Chios [Crete]—Yes, we are sending [our issues] to you. But the postal service makes a mess of everything. [...] To D. Mil. In Smyrna—It would seem that our letter was lost along the way. [...] To D. Del., V. Ast., V. Ser.—Since [the issues] were lost, we'll send them again. [...] To Phyl. Nik. P.O. 901—It would seem that [the issues] were getting lost; we'll send them again. [...] V.Z. in Irakleio [Crete]—We're sorry that you did not receive our letter." As for regional booksellers, it was not unheard of for hidden costs to raise the sales price—even *within* Greece, in one case by 25 percent.[39] Spread across a webwork of nations, kingdoms, empires, colonies, and protectorates, readers of Greek in the early twentieth century could rely upon no unified apparatus for the distribution and consumption of their literature. Admittedly, much was changing in those first decades; by 1920, leading journals were boasting of sales representatives in nearly all the major ports of the Eastern Mediterranean. Yet with so many typographic centers and publications beyond Athens, the decentralization of Greek print remained a fact. How much the more so, indeed, when one turns to daily newsprint.

When compared to Western Europe, the Greek-language newspaper (i.e., daily print) was late in developing, taking hold only well after the establishment of the Greek state.[40] When it did, however, it was clear that a very different print ecology was taking shape. The newspaper, in contradistinction to the book or journal, was incapable of accommodating a scattered readership. The daily paper, owing to its ephemeral nature, survived poorly across seas or over continents. If it did survive, it became not a newspaper but an artifact. Its natural environment was the urban center. Until the rise of advanced distribution systems later in the twentieth century, the daily paper remained the foundation of a decisively local (and, for the first time, mass) readership. The Greeks of Istanbul, Smyrna, Alexandria, or elsewhere were turning in larger numbers to their own ephemeral print materials (to say nothing of their own journals and publishing houses[41]). Day by day, they were cobbling together a variegated, fragmented mass of poems, stories, gossip, local news, international events, advertisements, and editorials. As Hristos Hristovasilis, a Demotic prose writer and journalist, suggested,

Ὁ κόσμος ρίχνεται στὴς ἐφημερίδες, ὅπου βρίσκει λίγ' ἀπ' ὅλα, εὐχαριστιέται, περνάει τὴν ὥρα του... Ἡ ἐφημερίδα σκότωσε τὸ βιβλίο καὶ τὸ περιοδικό! Βιβλίο, ποὺ δὲ μπορεῖ κανεὶς νὰ τὸ τελειώση μεταξὺ ἑνὸς τσιγάρου κι ἑνὸς καφέ... Περιοδικὸ ποὺ βγαίνει στὴς δέκα πέντε καὶ στὸ μῆνα μιὰ φορά... εἶναι πλήξη μπορστὰ στὴν ἐφημερίδα, ποὺ βγαίνει κάθε μέρα, ποὺ σοῦ δίνει καὶ τὸ βιβλίο καὶ τὸ περιοδικὸ κατὰ δόσεις.[42]

People are turning to the newspaper, which has a little of everything. They enjoy it, they pass the time... The newspaper killed the book and the journal! The book, which no one can finish between a cigarette and a coffee... The journal, which only comes out on the 15th and the end of the month... it's sheer boredom compared to the newspaper, which comes out every day, and it gives you the book and the journal in doses.

Nonetheless, if local daily print was by far the most economically viable medium, it was not the only one. As I suggested earlier, literary connections *did* bind these regional publishing centers together, at least provisionally, thanks to the vital yet fragile medium of the literary journal and the little magazine. Many editors of non-Helladic journals, from Egypt to Istanbul, developed a rhetoric simultaneously local and Panhellenic, each holding their own publication up as a beacon of light, its rays reaching far-flung editors and readers across the sea. In *Ἀλεξανδρινὴ τέχνη* (*Alexandrian Art*), for example, whose editor Rika Singopoulou was one of Cavafy's warmest supporters in Egypt, the sentiment was always global. In the journal's first issue, published in December 1926, one reads the following: "ALEXANDRIAN ART sends a warm greeting to Greek writers, artists, and intellectuals. [/] [Our magazine] nurtures but one and only ambition: to contribute in its own way, and with all its power, to the formation of a purely *Modern Greek Culture* of ours."* As a sign of this, the editors astonishingly single out *Eleftheria* (*Freedom*), a journal from Larissa, a small city more than 350 kilometers north of Athens, annexed from the Ottomans in 1881. By all appearances, *Alexandrian Art* was part of a thriving interhellenic network that extended from the diasporic margins to the Greek Metropolis, and thence into the most remote corners of the Greek state.[43]

Yet such a network, while immensely important, was more precarious and thinly distributed than might at first appear. Much of *Alexandrian Art*'s Pan-

---

*"Η ΑΛΕΞΑΝΔΡΙΝΗ ΤΕΧΝΗ στέλνει θερμὸ χαιρετισμὸ στοὺς Ἕλληνας λογοτέχνες, καλλιτέχνες καὶ διανοούμενους. [/] Δὲν τρέφει παρὰ μιὰ καὶ μόνο φιλοδοξία: νὰ συμβάλλει κι αὐτὴ μ' ὅλες τὶς δυνάμεις της στὴ διαμόρφωση τοῦ καθαρὰ *νεοελληνικοῦ πολιτισμοῦ μας*" (*Ἀλεξανδρινὴ τέχνη* 1, no. 1, 1926, p. 21).

hellenism lay within the rhetorical gestures of the periodical itself, rather than the stability or longevity of any real material network.[44] Careful attention to the print runs and life spans of Greek-language literary periodicals in the twentieth-century Mediterranean reveals a sharp discrepancy between rhetoric and reality. The large majority of these small monthly magazines had miniscule circulations among intellectuals and artists; indeed, most journals survived little more than a handful of months or, less often, years. And of the few that did survive, most went into debt to do so. To be sure, the causes of financial strain were many, such as the regional spike in paper costs following World War I or (for periodicals in the Greek state) the successive raises in the wages of printers in the early 1920s,[45] yet the fundamental problem lay in circulation.[46] While evidence of sales numbers has not survived, even the leading journals wrote frequently of chronic problems. *Τὰ γράμματα* (*Letters*), the leading Alexandrian journal of its time,[47] published by Cavafy's friend Stephanos Pargas, complained in 1921 that "our budget is by no means healthy [...]. Our plea for [monetary] contributions remains as always. [...] We print 1,000 copies each time, of which we supply about 700 to our subscribers, the booksellers and the exchange. How many of those are sold? We don't have solid numbers yet. We can calculate that our subscribers and buyers keep up to 300."* Selling less than half its print run, *Letters* nonetheless found cause to celebrate what was an improved performance from earlier years, and perhaps one of the more remarkable success stories among Greek literary journals. Indeed, when one compares *Letters*'s print runs with those of most contemporary Athenian journals, one wonders why exactly we should be calling Athens "the center" of Greek print at the time. As for other, less popular journals, their print runs were lower—likely five hundred copies—with corresponding drops in sales. *Μακεδονικὰ γράμματα* (*Macedonian Letters*), published in Thessaloniki, was one such example. Changing editorial hands for a third time in as many years, the journal complained that "the driving force behind [our] failure must be sought [...] [in] the reading public [...], which accepted each wave of our attempts with indifference. The

---

* "Τὰ οἰκονομικά μας δὲν εἶναι καθόλου εὔρωστα.... Ἡ ἔκκλησίς μας γιὰ εἰσφορὲς παραμένει πάντα.... Τυπώνομε ὡς 1000 φυλλάδια κάθε φορά, ἀπὸ τὰ ὁποῖα διαθέτομε γιὰ τοὺς συνδρομητάς μας, τὰ βιβλιοπωλεῖα καὶ τὴν ἀνταλλαγὴ 700 περίπου. Πόσα πουλιοῦνται ἀπ' αὐτά; Δὲν ἔχομεν ἀκόμα ὁρισμένους ἀριθμούς. Μποροῦμε νὰ ὑπολογίσωμε ὅτι οἱ συνδρομηταί μας καὶ οἱ ἀγορασταί μας κρατοῦν ἕως 300 φυλλάδια" (*Τὰ γράμματα*, 1921, p. 269).

passive reaction of 'hoi polloi' has been the most important reason for the terrible fate of Greek literary journals."* If certain Greek journals of the early twentieth century spoke of a network of readers from Alexandria to Athens to Istanbul and beyond, closer examination proves this network was by no means as deep as it was supposedly wide, nor was it stable or sustainable. This is not to slight what was a massively important medium. I mean instead to suggest that the diasporic networks that these journals embodied—i.e., their "intellectual reciprocity" back and forth across the sea[48]—were difficult to construct and even more difficult to maintain, with the constant danger of any given node in the larger network coming undone. Greek print networks were in flux.

Hellenism Unhinged

The literary debates that occasionally spilled across the editorials of multiple journals (and, from there, into local newspapers) of Athens, Alexandria, and elsewhere were perhaps indicative of a certain connectivity, yet they simultaneously revealed at times just how decentered Greek identity was. Cavafy's poetry was particularly instructive in this, since the criticism that it met in Alexandrian and Athenian ephemeral print took a strikingly different tone in each city and demonstrated real geographic and cultural disconnects across the sea. Two seminal studies have already examined the early critical reception of Cavafy in Athens—namely, those of Moullas and Karaoglou—yet neither of them identifies the orientalist and at times racist geographic tropes to which Athenian critics resorted again and again in their attacks on Cavafy.[49] These tropes are important and I want to linger over them here, because they verbalize in real and tangible ways the racialized borderscape that was gaining discursive strength in the wake of the Population Exchange.

In the early months of 1924, Sokratis Lagoudakis, an eccentric doctor and essayist who had recently moved to Egypt,[50] began to publish *ad hominem* attacks against Cavafy, his poetry, and his circle—publications that in turn sparked reactions from pro-Cavafy Alexandrians, culminating in a violent demonstration against the doctor during a public lecture he gave in March of

---

*"Πρέπει τὰ ἐλατήρια τῆς ἀποτυχίας [μας] αὐτῆς νὰ τὰ ζητήσουμε [...] [σ]τὸ ἀναγνωστικὸ κοινό [...], ποὺ μ' ἀδιαφορία δεχότανε τὰ κύματα τῶν προσπαθειῶν [μας]. Ἡ παθητικὴ ἀντίδραση 'τῶν πολλῶν' στάθηκεν ἡ σπουδαιότερη αἰτία τῆς κακοδαιμονίας τῶν ἑλληνικῶν φιλολογικῶν περιοδι[κ]ῶν" (*Μακεδονικὰ γράμματα* 3, no. 1, 1924, p. 16).

that year. In hindsight, it was clear that such verbal and physical collisions offered Cavafy's poetry a golden PR opportunity, which soon took the form of an official letter of protest against Lagoudakis and support for Cavafy, signed by Egypt's leading Greek intellectuals and published in the newspapers of Alexandria that April. At the same time, a separate letter of protest was published in three Athenian newspapers, yet this was largely orchestrated by a single figure: Marios Vaianos, who was also busily preparing a "panegyric issue" of his journal *Νέα τέχνη* (*New Art*), devoted to Cavafy. As the feud shifted from a local affair to a transnational sensation, certain tensions came to the surface. Vaianos, born in Egypt, raised in Chios, and now studying in Athens, was a young and adamant proponent of Cavafy, and his ferocious insistence on the Alexandrian's poetry alienated not a few in the capital.

Kostis Bastias, who in 1927 would found and head the important journal *Ἑλληνικὰ γράμματα* (*Greek Letters*), devoted an entire column to Vaianos, whom he dubbed a "literary invader" (*φιλολογικὸς ἐπιδρομεύς*) from Egypt. He complained that Vaianos "lays forth with an onerously straight face his rosy dreams about the renaissance of Greek literature, delivered by means of a decisive and mandatory bath that all Greeks who write will take in the Delta of the Nile."* Other Athenians were less tactful in their attacks. Dimitris Tangopoulos, the influential editor of *Νουμᾶς* (*Noumas*), the oldest Demotic-language journal in Greece, wrote that same year, "The land of the Pharaos has been shaken by a terribly important matter today: Cavafism. You might characterize it as a kind of literary Pharaonism [...] But even after Egyptomania has come and gone, [...] Cavafism will reign supreme in the land of the Pharaohs. [...] Cavafism also has here in our city a few followers, which doesn't surprise me, since so many epidemics come to us *straight from Egypt*."† The repeated references to Pharaohs are self-explanatory and perhaps not too noxious on their own, but with his parting jibe about pestilence, Tangopoulos

---

* "Σᾶς ἐκθέτει μὲ σοβαρότητα χιλίων τόννων τὰ γλυκύτατα ὄνειρά του περὶ ἀναγεννήσεως τῆς Ἑλληνικῆς λογοτεχνίας δι' ἑνὸς μπάνιου τὸ ὁποῖον ὑποχρεωτικῶς καὶ ἀπροφασίστως θὰ λάβουν ὅλοι οἱ γράφοντες Ἕλληνες εἰς τὸ δέλτα τοῦ Νείλου" (Bastias, "Φιλολογικὸς ἐπιδρομεύς").

† "Τὴ γῆ τῶν Φαραῶ τὴν κατασυγκινεῖ ἕνα σπουδαιότατο ζήτημα σήμερα. Ὁ κ α β α φ ι σ μ ό ς. [...] Ἡμπορεῖ κι'αὐτὸ νὰ χαρακτηρισθῆ ὡς ἕνα εἶδος φιλολογικοῦ Φαραωνισμοῦ [...] Κι' ὅταν περάσῃ ἀκόμα ἡ Φαραωμανία [...] ὁ Καβαφισμὸς θὰ ζῆ καὶ θὰ βασιλεύῃ στῆ χώρα τῶν Φαραώ. [...] Ὁ Καβαφισμὸς ἔχει κ' ἐδῶ, στὴν πόλη μας, μερικοὺς ὀπαδούς του. Δὲ μοῦ κάμνει ἐντύπωσιν αὐτό, ἀφοῦ τόσες ἐπιδημίες μᾶς ἔρχονται, κατευθεῖαν ἀπὸ τὴν Αἴγυπτο" (Tangopoulos, "Καβαφισμός").

crosses a line: the insult derives from a centuries-old folk aetiology that, by the twentieth century, had acquired racist undertones and according to which many of the epidemics in Greece—the plague, scabies, and leprosy—were borne there from Africa, either through population movements and trade or through natural phenomena, such as the summer sirocco winds, blown across the Mediterranean Sea to Greece. Cavafy's poetry is thus naturalized as an Egyptian plague. Such language was offensive enough, yet in Tangopoulos's wake came even more caustic reactions, such as the satirical article "Higher Poetry," written by Spyros Melas:

> Ἐπάνω εἰς τὸ γραφεῖον μου εὑρῆκα τεῦχος μὲ τὸν μυστηριώδη τίτλον: "Ξεβάφης." Ὑπέθεσα κατ' ἀρχὰς ὅτι πρόκειται περὶ πραγματείας χρωματολογικῆς καθαπτομένης τοῦ κ. Μποτσαράκου. Πλάνη. Ὁ ὑπότιτλος ἐκφράζεται σαφέστατα: "Τεῦχος πανηγυρικὸ πρὸς τιμὴν τοῦ ὑπέροχου ποιητῆ!" Λαμπρὰ ἰδέα, νὰ σᾶς πῶ. Αὐτὸ τὸ ὄνομα δὲν μοῦ εἶνε καὶ τελείως ἄγνωστον. Ξεβάφης! . . . Βεβαίως! Ἐθορύβησε ἀρκετὰ τώρα τελευταίως. [. . .] Ἀλλά, νά, μόνον ποὺ εἶνε ἡ ποίησίς του ἐντελῶς ἄνγωστος! Τί σημαίνει ὅμως! . . . Εἰς τὸν αἰῶνα τοῦ "ἀγνώστου στρατιώτου" ἠμποροῦμεν, νομίζω, νὰ πανηγυρίσωμεν θαυμάσια καὶ μιὰν ἄγνωστον ποίησιν! Ἀνοίγω μετὰ κατανύξεως. Ἕνας πελώριος, στιβαρὸς φελάχος εἶνε ζωγραφισμένος εἰς τὸ πρῶτον φῦλλον. Τὸ ὅλον του προδίδει ἀγαθὸν μοάμπην, ἀλλὰ δὲν τολμῶ νὰ τὸ βεβαιώσω κατηγορηματικῶς. Μὲ τὰ πράγματα τῶν ποιητῶν—ὅλα κι' ὅλα! δὲν πρέπει ν' ἀστειεύεται κανείς. Πιθανὸν νὰ εἶνε καὶ ἡ Μοῦσα του. Ποιὸς ξέρει! Κάτωθεν του μαύρου, ἄλλωστε, διαβάζω [. . .] [πὼς] βούιξε ἡ ἀραπιὰ μὲ τὸν ταλέντο του. Ἀφοῦ πέντε κροκόδειλοι κατεβήκανε στὴν Ἀλεξάντρ[ει]α ἐπίτηδες γιὰ νὰ τὸν δοῦνε. Καὶ μάλιστα τοὺς ἄκουσα νὰ τραγουδοῦνε παθητικώτατα: "Θέλω νὰ πάω στὴν Ἀραπιά—μωρό μου!—Νὰ πιάσω ἕναν Ἀράπη! Νὰ τὸν ρωτήσω νὰ μοῦ πῆ ποὺ κάθεται ὁ Ξεβάφης!"[51]

On my desk I found a journal issue with the mysterious title "Xevafy" [*Paint-Remover*].[52] I assumed at first that it was a flier with the color samples of Mr. Botsarakos. Wrong. The subtitle was clear: "Panegyric issue in honor of the extraordinary poet!" A wonderful idea, let me tell you. That name is not entirely unknown to me. *Paint-Remover*! . . . Of course! He's been creating quite a lot of chatter recently. [. . .] But the thing is, see, his poetry is entirely unknown! What does it matter, though! . . . In the age of the "Unknown soldier" we can just as easily celebrate an unknown poetry,

I dare say! I start reading with rapture. On the first page I see a drawing: a massive hulk of a *fellah*. The entire portrait gives the sense of a simple Muslim peasant, but I wouldn't stake my life on it. With these poets, truth be told, there's no joking around. Perhaps this fellow is his muse. Who knows! Beneath this black man, moreover, I read [...] [that] all of *Arapia*[53] is a-chatter with his talent. Five crocodiles went down to Alexandria on purpose just to see him. And of course I heard them singing most plangently: I want to go to Arabia, baby, I want to grab myself an *Arapis*[54] and ask him where this *Paint-Remover* lives!

Melas was a prolific author and important figure in interbellum Greek publishing (he would later found with Giorgos Theotokas the journal *Idea*[55]), and his "Higher Poetry" speaks volumes. Central to this attack is the figure of the fellah, or the Arab Muslim peasant, who is explicitly marked as black. The racist vocabulary pounds away at the reader relentlessly with the clear aim of displacing Cavafy from Hellenism. But amidst the slurs it's important not to lose sight of the geographic tensions as well. Indeed, geographic difference lies at the heart of this attack; geography is racialized and weaponized in order to spatially distance and expel Cavafy, an "unknown poet" from somewhere "down there" in Africa, known only to the Muslim peasants who inspire him and the crocodiles who clamor to hear him. In short, Cavafy belongs not to Greece or Greeks but to African Islam and the Arabs, whom Melas later sexualizes in a mock poem of his own. It is important, again, to remember that such attacks were being written out and printed in the shadow of the Population Exchange. Just months earlier, hundreds of thousands of Muslims had been uprooted and deported from Greece, while hundreds of thousands of Greek Orthodox Christians from Turkey, many of whom bore rich traces of Islamicate culture in their speech, were still being disembarked into Greek ports. Across Athens and the Helladic hinterland, a rising tide of xenophobia had already begun to mark the incoming refugees as "Turkish spawn." It was from the context of these discourses that the responses to Cavafy outlined above drew their strength (and more such responses continued to do so in later years[56]). Admittedly, behind the geographic and racial slurs lay an equally deep unease over Cavafy's aesthetic program and sexuality—as Dimitris Papanikolaou has argued, Cavafy's modernist poetics are modernist precisely *because* they are queer[57]—yet whatever the source of their apprehension, a striking number of Helladic opponents situated their attacks within a discourse of geographic otherness.

Nevertheless, it is a well-documented fact that Cavafy had begun by the final decade of his life to make important inroads into Greece, thanks in no small part to a core of devoted allies—both young (e.g., Vaianos or Lapathiotis) and old (e.g., Xenopoulos). It's worth noting, though, that some of these allies reproduced similar geocultural stereotypes in their writing. Look back, for example, to Xenopoulos—Cavafy's first real ally in Greece and the first writer to introduce Cavafy to Athenian readers. Already in 1903, despite his overall sympathetic portrait of Cavafy, Xenopoulos was laying the foundations for later orientalist tropes: Cavafy here is "dark-skinned as an indigenous Egyptian [...]. His lively way of speaking, full of pomp and excess; his mannerisms, so very decorous; and those civilities and overwrought niceties of his—they all catch an Athenian off guard, accustomed as we are to modest simplicity."* Cavafy's speech, brimming with rhetorical surfeit, folding in on itself and spilling over like an arabesque; his decorum and social graces, belabored with artifice and excess—this description reads as a thinly veiled code for eastern or Islamicate decadence, juxtaposed against the homespun Hellenism of Greece. The Athenian poet Myrtiotissa, who was largely sympathetic to Cavafy, likewise wrote of him in stark orientalist terms: "He seems an exotic creature, living in an atmosphere different from ours, which you had to hear and see from afar [...]. Cavafy would not be able to fend for himself in today's Greece, and that is why he is wise to stay away from it."†

Other admirers eschewed orientalist tropes but nonetheless insisted on a stark geo-cultural difference between Athens and Alexandria. One anonymous supporter of Cavafy wrote, "Such a furious envy has surfaced recently among quite a few Athenian literary types and circles due to the large difference, to their detriment, between Alexandrian youth, educated systematically, with their trends well defined and channeled, and our own Athenian youth who are still blubbering and drooling all over themselves [...]. The Alexandrian youth have shown us clearly [...] that they want to bring today's modern literature

---

*"Βαθιὰ μελαχρινὸς ὡς γηγενῆς τῆς Αἰγύπτου [...]. Ἡ ὁμιλία του ἡ ζωηρά, ἡ σχεδὸν στομφώδης καὶ ὑπερβολική, καὶ οἱ τρόποι του οἱ πάρα πολὺ ἁβροί, καὶ ὅλες ἐκεῖνες οἱ εὐγένειές του καὶ οἱ τσιριμόνιες, ἐκπλήττουν κάπως ἕναν Ἀθηναῖον, συνειθισμένον μὲ τὴν σεμνὴν ἁπλότητα" (Xenopoulos, "'Ἕνας ποιητής," p. 97).

†"Ἔμοιαζε πλάσμα ἐξωτικό, ποὺ ζοῦσε σ' ἄλλη ἀπὸ μᾶς ἀτμόσφαιρα, ποὺ ἔπρεπε νὰ τ' ἀκοῦς καὶ νὰ τὸ βλέπεις ἀπὸ μακρυά [...] Ὁ Καβάφης δὲ θὰ μποροῦσε νὰ σταθεῖ στὴ σημερινὴ Ἑλλάδα, καὶ γι' αὐτὸ κάνει σοφὰ ποὺ μένει μακρυὰ της" (Myrtiotissa, Νέα τέχνη, nos. 7–10, 1924, p. 84).

into alignment with the new large intellectual currents of the West."* The editors of *Μοῦσα* (*Muse*) made a broader, generalized observation on the intellectual poverty of national print in comparison to its diasporic counterparts: "The single and incontrovertible fact is [...] the intellectual sterility of Athens, and at a moment when one sees a measure of more serious fermentation in Istanbul and in Alexandria." It was, the editors continued, a "deficiency so very detrimental to the Greek name."† Kostas Ouranis, an important poet and essayist of the period, later echoed and intensified this observation, writing that the Alexandrian journals *New Life* and *Letters* "became the mirror of Modern Greek Philology in an age when [Athens' leading journals such as] *Panathenian* had ossified and *Noumas* had outlived itself. [...] They introduced to Greek Letters the disinterested and objective criticism that Athens had no idea how to exercise. Foreign to the routines of Athens, to [its] personal friendships and passions, they set aside personalities in order to analyze works and give new life to ideas."‡ What becomes clear then, both here and in the rhetoric of Cavafy's opponents (who were by no means few or weak), are the geocultural tensions—sometimes subtle, sometimes glaring—that ran through this Panhellenic print network. It was a network of attractions and repulsions, of shifting and complex relations of power (economic, aesthetic, ideological) that my chapter can only gesture toward. To speak of a single center and a periphery is in fact misleading. Rather, one encountered multiple centers of print, each

---

* "Μιὰ ζηλιάρικη τέτοια ἐπιθυμιὰ γεννήθηκε τελευταῖα σὲ ἀρκετοὺς λογοτεχνικοὺς τύπους καὶ κύκλους γιὰ τὴ μεγάλη διαφορά, εἰς βάρος τους, μεταξὺ τῶν Ἀλεξανδρινῶν νέων μορφωμένων ἐπιστημονικά, μὲ τάσεις ὡρισμένες καὶ χαλιναγωημένες, καὶ τῶν δικῶν μας Ἀθηναίων νέων ποὺ ἀκόμα ξεσαλιάζονται καὶ σαλιαρίζουν. [...] Οἱ Ἀλεξανδρινοὶ νέοι μᾶς ἔδειξαν καθαρὰ [...] πῶς θέλησαν νὰ συγχρονίσουν τὴ σημερινή μας νεώτερη φιλολογία μὲ τὰ μεγάλα καινούργια ρεύματα τῆς Πνευματικῆς κίνησης τῆς Δύσης" (Κ.Th.Ρ., "Οἱ απουάνοι," *Βωμός* no. 7, February 7, 1919, p. 74).

† "Τὸ γεγονὸς τὸ μόνο, τὸ ἀδιαφιλονείκητο εἶναι [...] ἡ πνευματικὴ στείρωση τῆς Ἀθήνας, καὶ τὴ στιγμὴ ποὺ βλέπει κανεὶς νὰ γίνεται μιὰ κάποια σοβαρότερη ζύμωση στὴν Πόλη καὶ στὴν Ἀλεξάντρια"... "ἡ ἔλλειψη αὐτὴ [εἶναι] τόσο λίγο τιμητικὴ γιὰ τὸ ἑλληνικὸ ὄνομα" (*Μοῦσα*, vol. 2, no. 14, September 1921, p. 32).

‡ "Ἡ 'Νέα Ζωή' καὶ τὰ 'Γράμματα' ὑπῆρξαν ἀληθινὰ εὐρωπαϊκὰ περιοδικά. Ἔγιναν ὁ καθρέπτης τῆς Νεοελληνικῆς Φιλολογίας εἰς μιὰν ἐποχὴν ποὺ τὰ 'Παναθήναια' εἶχαν ἀποστεωθῆ καὶ ποὺ ὁ 'Νουμᾶς' εἶχεν ὑπερζήσει τοῦ ἑαυτοῦ του. [...] [Ε]ἰσήγαγον εἰς τὰ Ἑλληνικὰ Γράμματα τὴν ἀμερόληπτον καὶ ἀντικειμενικὴν κριτικὴν ποὺ αἱ Ἀθῆναι δὲν ἤξευραν νὰ κάμουν. Ξένοι πρὸς τὴν ἀθηναϊκὴν ρουτίναν, πρὸς προσωπικὰς φιλίας ἢ πάθη ἀφῆκαν τὰ πρόσωπα, διὰ νὰ ἀναλύσουν ἔργα ἢ νὰ ἀνακινήσουν ἰδέας" (quoted in Hatzifotis, *Ἀλεξανδρινὴ λογοτεχνία*, 82).

projecting outward its own image of "Hellenism," an articulation of topical, regional, and international Hellenisms that was subtly reassembled from one journal (or even issue) to the next.

Within Athens, many of Cavafy's opponents were defending what they saw as the national Greek standard—the poetry of Kostis Palamas—from Cavafy's "literary invasion" from Africa. Palamas himself was not averse to entering the fray, albeit with more measured attacks. While readers today may best remember his dismissal of Cavafy's poetry as mere "reportage" from the ancient world, Palamas also effected more subtle yet powerful critiques of the Cavafy corpus elsewhere. Writing in the final days of 1924 (just as Cavafy's name had begun to circulate in earnest in Athens), Palamas turned to the topic of meter and rhythm: "I know no verses more regular and immaculate, for example, than the fifteen-syllable lines of [Rigas Golfis'] *Hymns*, which maintain and enrich the grace of our vernacular poetry, from Cornaro to Markoras [...]. What a great difference they present in their handling of our eminently national verse from its insidious unhinging [ξεκάρφωμα] in the poems of Cavafy."* This quotation is a bit dense, so let me unpack it. Rigas Golfis was a contemporary Helladic poet and ally of Palamas; his poems, according to Palamas, preserved and enriched the "national" meter—which, incidentally, was the same meter as Şānī's Islamic poetry from the previous chapter: the *politikos stikhos*. This meter extended both temporally and ideologically beyond the Greek nation-state, as Şānī's *Gift* makes clear, yet it had been rebranded as the national standard just a generation earlier, conjoining the Cretan Renaissance of the sixteenth century (personified by "Cornaro" in the quotation above) to the recent national past (personified by "Markoras" in the quotation above) and, by extension, to Palamas himself. Cavafy's poetry, on the other hand, was deviously "unhinging" this meter and rhythm. The implications were clear: Cavafy's poetry did not belong in Greece; it was prying out nails where others were attempting to secure them. With its strange mixed language and lame rhythms, it threatened to break apart the national tradition.

Even certain neutral observers tended toward similar conclusions. The editors of *Macedonian Letters*, who not infrequently published Cavafy's work,

---

*"Δὲ γνωρίζω στίχους πιὸ κανονικὰ ἀλάθευτους ἀπὸ τοὺς δεκαπεντοσύλλαβους λ.χ. τῶν Ὕμνων, ἐκείνους ποὺ συνεχίζουν καὶ ποὺ συμπληρώνουν τῇ χάρῃ τοῦ στίχου τῶν δημοτικῶν τραγουδιῶν, τῶν Κορνάρων, τῶν Μαρκοράδων [...]. Πόση διαφορὰ στὸ μεταχείρισμα τοῦ κατεξοχὴν ἐθνικοῦ μας στίχου ἀπὸ τὸ ὕπουλο ξεκάρφωμά του στὰ ποιήματα τοῦ Καβάφη" (Palamas, "Στὸ γύρισμα τῆς ῥίμας").

nonetheless wrote in February 1924, after Cavafy had failed to secure a nomination for Greece's national literary medallion: "[His] work may be important, but it is unknown, a serious reason for [him] to remain beyond the margins of the circle of medal-holders. To win the medal, one's name must have been thoroughly kneaded into the history and tradition of the land."* Cavafy's poetry, as I hope to have shown, was anything but "kneaded into" the land of Greece: it was detached not just from the supposed rhythms of the national standard but from the geography of Greece itself—a detachment that was manifested in both the poems' content and material form(s). Rather than bind itself to a land or a book spine, Cavafy's poetry had unhinged itself. As if to reaffirm this, the editors of *Macedonian Letters* went on to add in the editorial of their following issue, "And how could you justify the awarding of the medal to [an artist] who has not published an edition of his work?"† How, indeed? Scattered across a series of fluid, unstable media—newsprint, popular magazines, short-lived literary journals, broadsheets pinned together inside a dossier or stitched into a cardboard cover, or finished manuscripts intentionally left unprinted—Cavafy's polymorphous poetry was entirely unfit for the national medallion.

The unstable nature of Greek print, stemming at least in part from the Greek world's dispersion across a vast political geography, had made the unification of any poetic corpus unprofitable. More than unprofitable, however, for Cavafy's poetics it was simultaneously unproductive of the fluidity at which his poems seemed to aim. Rather than despairing at its multiple readerships and scattered local markets, his poetry embraced them, cultivating what I've been calling a "diasporic poetics" in both its thematic engagements and its material apparatus. "Greekness," as his poems seemed to recite in their various locales, periods, and occasions, was most productive when left in pieces: reassembled by the writing (and the reading) of the poetry itself.

I conclude this section with one such poem, "Caesarion."[58] Not only in its idealized climax but also in the material and cultural props by which it is staged, "Caesarion" enacts much of what I have tried to argue here:

---

* "Τὸ ἔργο [του] μπορεῖ νὰ εἶναι σημαντικό, μὰ ἀγνοεῖται. Ἕνας πολὺ σπουδαῖος λόγος γιὰ νὰ μείν[ει] ἔξω ἀπὸ τὴν περιφέρεια τοῦ κύκλου τῶν ἀριστειούχων. Τὸ ὄνομα τοῦ ἀριστειούχου πρέπει νὰ εἶναι ζυμωμένο μὲ τὴν ἱστορία καὶ τὴν παράδοση τοῦ τόπου" (*Μακεδονικὰ γράμματα*, February 1924, p. 32).

† "Καὶ πῶς θὰ δικαιολογοῦνταν ἡ ἀπονομὴ ἀριστείου σὲ [...] καλλιτέχν[η], ποὺ δὲν ἔχ[ει] ἐκδώσει ἔργο" (*Μακεδονικὰ γράμματα*, March 1924, p. 48).

Ἐν μέρει γιὰ νὰ ἐξακριβώσω μιὰ ἐποχή,	In part, to clarify a certain period,
ἐν μέρει καὶ τὴν ὥρα νὰ περάσω,	in part, to pass the time,
τὴν νύχτα χθὲς πῆρα μιὰ συλλογὴ	last night I picked up a volume
ἐπιγραφῶν τῶν Πτολεμαίων νὰ διαβάσω.	of inscriptions about the Ptolemies to read.
Οἱ ἄφθονοι ἔπαινοι κ' ἡ κολακεῖες	The boundless praises and the flatteries
εἰς ὅλους μοιάζουν. Ὅλοι εἶναι λαμπροί,	resemble one another for each ruler. Each one
ἔνδοξοι, κραταιοί, ἀγαθοεργοί·	of them is brilliant, glorious, mighty, beneficent;
κάθ' ἐπιχείρησίς των σοφοτάτη.	all their projects full of wisdom.
Ἄν πεῖς γιὰ τὲς γυναῖκες τῆς γενιᾶς, κι αὐτές,	As for the women of their line, they too,
ὅλες ἡ Βερενίκες κ' ἡ Κλεοπάτρες θαυμαστές.	all the Berenices and Cleopatras, are marvelous.
Ὅταν κατόρθωσα τὴν ἐποχὴ νὰ ἐξακριβώσω	When I managed to clarify the period
θἄφινα τὸ βιβλίο ἂν μιὰ μνεία μικρή,	I would have put the book away had not a brief,
κι ἀσήμαντη, τοῦ βασιλέως Καισαρίωνος	a trifling reference to King Caesarion
δὲν εἵλκυε τὴν προσοχή μου ἀμέσως.....	suddenly caught my eye....
Ἄ, νά, ἤρθες σὺ μὲ τὴν ἀόριστη	And so you came to me, with your vague
γοητεία σου. Στὴν ἱστορία λίγες	charm. In history a few
γραμμὲς μονάχα βρίσκονται γιὰ σένα,	lines alone have survived about you,
κ' ἔτσι πιὸ ἐλεύθερα σ' ἔπλασα μὲς στὸν νοῦ μου.	and so I fashioned you more freely in my mind.
Σ' ἔπλασα ὡραῖο κ' αἰσθηματικό.	I fashioned you handsome and sensitive.
Ἡ τέχνη μου στὸ πρόσωπό σου δείνει	My art gives your face
μιὰν ὀνειρώδη συμπαθητικὴ ἐμορφιά.	a dreamy, sympathetic beauty.
Καὶ τόσο πλήρως σὲ φαντάσθηκα,	And so completely did I imagine you
ποῦ χθὲς τὴν νύχτα ἀργά, σὰν ἔσβυνεν	that late last night, as my lamp
ἡ λάμπα μου—ἄφισα ἐπίτηδες νὰ σβύνει—	went out—I let it go out on purpose—
ἐθάρρεψα ποῦ μπῆκες μὲς στὴν κάμαρά μου,	I fancied that you'd come into my room,
μὲ φάνηκε ποῦ ἐμπρός μου στάθηκες· ὡς θὰ ἤσουν	it seemed to me you stood there in front of me;
μὲς στὴν κατακτημένην Ἀλεξάνδρεια,	just as you were in conquered Alexandria,
χλωμὸς καὶ κουρασμένος, ἰδεώδης ἐν τῇ λύπῃ σου,	pale and tired, ideal in your sorrow,
ἐλπίζοντας ἀκόμη νὰ σὲ σπλαχνισθοῦν	still hoping they'd take pity on you,
οἱ φαῦλοι—ποῦ ψιθύριζαν τὸ "Πολυκαισαρίη."	those debased men—who whispered "Too many Caesars."
(1914–1918)	

Caesarion was the final Greek Ptolemy of Egypt. The son of Cleopatra and Julius Caesar, he was executed by Octavian upon the latter's entry into Alexandria, on the cusp of Roman conquest.[59] As Takis Kayalis has demonstrated, Caesarion may indeed have been largely absent in the ancient epigraphic records, yet in Cavafy's more contemporary milieu of the nineteenth and early twentieth centuries, Caesarion was a frequent literary figure and indeed an early symbol of homosexual desire and a site for its public ennoblement. This ranged from Elisar von Kupffer's *Lieblingminne und Freundesliebe in der Weltliteratur* (1900) to Edward Carpenter's *Anthology of Friendship* (1906), both of which marshaled Caesarion as a public champion of queer desire by drawing from a deeper index of eighteenth- and nineteenth-century publications.[60] Cavafy must have been aware of several examples of this popular print culture. Yet as Kayalis convincingly argues, the poem's most immediate inspiration came from yet another source, with a distinctly divergent genre and register: John Mahaffy's *The Empire of the Ptolemies* (1895). Mahaffy was an Anglo-Irish classicist and apologist for British empire, and he explicitly framed his historiography of the Hellenistic dynastic rule over Egypt as a prefiguration of British rule.[61] Mahaffy was Oscar Wilde's tutor, and the two had profound disagreements over the nature of Hellenism, empire, and homosexual desire.[62] As such, Cavafy's use of Mahaffy raises an important red flag: how did the former's poem synthesize or filter out the latter's political defense of empire and his conformity with the ruling homophobia of the age?

To answer this question, first we need a clear sense of what exactly Cavafy was taking from Mahaffy. The most important element from Mahaffy is his frustration over the lack of historical evidence and a desire for more physical descriptions of Caesarion.[63] This historiographical impasse is what seems to have inspired Cavafy. But there is a crucial difference between the two writers: for the colonial historian, such lacunae are a barrier and an intellectual dead end; for Cavafy's poem, they open a space of creative possibilities. And it is this difference that decouples the poem from the ideological framework of the colonial historian. While the poem begins its first two stanzas in the dry and elevated register and persona of the historian himself,[64] the third and final stanza (whose physical break is typographically augmented by an emphatic double space) subverts this figure into a queer aesthete and critical fabulist more akin to Saidiya Hartman. Indeed, what is Cavafy's "Caesarion" if not critical fabulation in the archives of Hellenism, drawing from imperial sources and filling in their gaps by recourse to the creative imagination of popular print cultures and homoerotic countercultures of the time, across whose print materials Cavafy the reader had free-ranged for decades? The poem begins in the voice of colonial historiography and its *translatio imperii* yet ends with an active reader's repurposing of that voice through the bricolage of other, countercultural sources and tropes. "Caesarion" assembles not a narrative of state but instead a sort of *ars poetica* on creative reading that repurposes the narratives of state. Meaningful engagement with Greek history (and Greekness), the poem suggests, blossoms not in the univocal narrative of imperial historiography but in textual recombination and assemblage that draws from a range of genres and countercultures. It is a history both consumed and produced by the reader, as they drift off to sleep one night in a world beset by colonial expansion.

And it is crucial that we tie this colonial framework explicitly not just to London but to Athens as well. The Greek state's ongoing project of territorial expansion lies quietly in the backdrop of this poem's composition and revision, first written in 1914, just a year after the Balkan Wars, when Greece had annexed a large swath of Ottoman territories in Epirus, Macedonia, and Thrace; published in 1918, it began to circulate just a year before the Greek Army occupied the Anatolian hinterland of the Ottoman Empire, setting in motion the events that led most immediately to the Population Exchange and its logic of partition. Greece's colonial apparatus during its occupation of Anatolia and its larger, decades-long project of irredentism often recycled rhetorical and ideological tropes of European classicism. Regardless of Cavafy's own ambiguous politics, therefore, we his readers could plausibly hear the tone and tenor of Greek nationalist historiography in the first two stanzas of "Caesarion," atop the deeper foundations of British imperial historiography. Yet the reimagining of Caesarion in the third stanza, where the creative powers of *the reader* take over from the historian, subtly eschews such colonial narratives. The poem's second half draws its creative energies neither from empire nor nation but from the incomplete remains of a peripheral Greek history, one whose gaps were speculatively reimagined by a series of popular publications and translations over the previous century—all of them read and recombined in Cavafy's poem "Caesarion."

Consolidating Greece

On July fourth, 1932, the Athens *Evening Post* published a short jocular poem under the title "Cavaf-arrivals" (*Kav-afixeis*), by Nikos Nikolaidis:

Καλῶς μᾶς ἦλθες, ποιητὰ Καβάφη,	We welcome you, Cavafy,
εἰς τὰ φιλόξενα τῶν Ἀθηνῶν ἐδάφη!	to Athens' hospitality!

Βοήθειά σου ἡ Ἀθηνᾶ—Ὑγεία	May Athena cure your cough,
κ' εἴθε, μὴ σὲ νικήσῃ ἡ νοσταλγία	and your nostalgia be warded off
διὰ τὴν Ἀλεξάνδρειαν π' ἀφίνεις.	for the Alexandria you leave behind.
Ἦλθες προσωρινῶς. Πολὺ νὰ μείνῃς...	You came for a quick stop. Stay for a long time ...

The day before, Cavafy had set foot upon Greek soil for the last time in his life. Diagnosed with terminal throat cancer, he'd come for surgery. And though the specialists ultimately failed to halt the cancer's fast metastasis, they succeeded in the far more symbolic task of destroying his trachea. He returned to Egypt some weeks later permanently mute, having lost his voice in Greece. The following spring—in fact, on the anniversary of his birth—he quietly died in Alexandria. Nikolaidis's jocular little poem would come to prove prophetic: in life, Cavafy's textual corpora had only ever come to Athens temporarily (and piecemeal); in the decades after his death, however, they came indeed to "stay for a long time." The poems' change of address was part of larger changes in the Greek geography of the Mediterranean, and the consolidation of the two fields—geography and texts—mirrored one another.

Two months after Cavafy's death, the Athenian poet and critic Tellos Agras published his assessment of the poet's corpus in the journal *Rythmos*, worth quoting at length here:

Ἐπιτρέψετέ μοῦ νὰ μεταχειρισθῶ μιὰ γραφικὴ ἀλληγορία. Πάνω στὸ γραφεῖο μου ἔχω μιὰ γυάλινη σφαῖρα, γιὰ νὰ πατᾷ τὰ φύλλα τῶν χαρτιῶν, μιὰ ἀπὸ τὶς γνωστὲς γυάλινες σφαῖρες, ποὺ ἔχουν σ' ἕνα τους τμῆμα τὴν ἐπιφάνεια ἐπίπεδη. Ὅσο δὲ βρίσκει κανεὶς τὴν ἐπίπεδη ἐπιφάνεια, ἡ σφαῖρα κυλᾷ,—ἕρμαια, ἔκθετη, ἀνισορρόπητη, πάνω στὸ τραπέζι. Μὰ ὅταν βρῇ κανεὶς τὴν ἐπίπεδη ἐπιφάνεια, ἡ σφαῖρα στέκεται ὀρθή, βασίζεται, δὲ σαλεύει. [...] Λοιπὸν αὐτὸ εἶναι: ἡ παρόμοια πλευρὰ τοῦ ἔργου τοῦ Καβάφη *δὲν ἔχει βρεθῆ*. [...] [Οἱ ἀντίπαλοι τοῦ Καβάφη] τὸ περιπαίζ[ουν]. Καὶ τὸ ἔργο, ἐλάχιστην ἀντίσταση παρουσιάζει... Γιατὶ ἡ βάσις του λείπει. Ὑπάρχει ὅμως. Κάποιος θὰ τὴν εὕρῃ. Θὰ τὴν εὕρῃ ὁ κριτικός.[65]

Allow me to make use of a visual allegory. Atop my desk I have a glass ball, which keeps my papers in place, one of those well-known glass balls, which have on one of their sections a flat surface. So long as one cannot find that flat surface, the ball rolls—adrift, exposed, unbalanced—atop the table. But when one finds the flat surface, the ball stands straight, it sets down a base, it does not stir. [...] So that's it: the corresponding side of Cavafy's work has *not been found*. [...] [Cavafy's opponents] insult it. And the work presents only the slightest resistance... Because its base is missing. It exists, however. Someone will find it. The critic will find it.

In the words of Agras, the Cavafic corpus lay adrift, unable yet to lay down its base. Such a project, he presciently concluded, was now the work of critics. While Agras likely meant *literary* critics like himself, the first phase of "base-building" was to fall perforce to *textual* critics, which is to say, the philologists or editors who undertook to publish a commercial edition of his poems. The first attempt appeared in 1935, brought to print by the Greek-Egyptian Rika Singopoulou, editor of *Alexandrian Art*. Consulting Cavafy's archive (bequeathed to her husband), she assembled what was Cavafy's first commercial book.

Another commercial edition did not appear again until near midcentury, in 1948, based on Singopoulou's first edition but published in Athens now (under the aegis of *Ikaros*). Tellingly, after 1935, Cavafy's words were never assembled again in Egypt. As for Singopoulou's editorial choices, she faced a difficult dilemma: how to arrange the poems? Choosing the logic of Cavafy's chronological dossiers, she necessarily omitted the parallel logic of his thematic collections, a decision that was later partially reversed by George Savidis in the 1960s. The latter's multiple editions—which included Cavafy's published (1963, two volumes) and unpublished poems (1968) and, much later, the "repudiated" juvenilia—were greeted as a breakthrough moment in the construction of the Cavafy corpus. To borrow Agras's term from above, it was within Savidis's editions that the Cavafic "base" was supposedly laid.

To build a context for Savidis's work, I must first turn to the larger shifts in the Greek world that preceded it. In 1919, after the capitulation of the Central Powers and the conclusion of the First World War, Britain, France, Italy, and Greece began a coordinated occupation of Anatolia, the heart of the Ottoman Empire. The Greek Army, launching its campaign in Smyrna, a coastal port city with a substantial Ottoman-Greek population, began to work its way inland, ultimately suffering a massive defeat and the physical destruction of the Greek world's oldest and largest diasporas (and their troubled absorption into the nation-state). Greek borders began now to solidify as Greece drew "Greekness" and "Greek citizenship" into closer alignment.

Admittedly, the Orthodox community of Istanbul was excepted from the Exchange (as was the Muslim community of Greek Thrace). Yet even the

Greeks who remained in Istanbul soon found themselves in dire straits once again. Due to increasing nationalist pressure from both the Turkish state and parastate actors, the Greek community of Istanbul declined and dwindled after a devastating pogrom in 1955. With shrinking numbers that totaled little more than 2,000 in recent census data, the community's once vibrant publishing life also withered (with the occasional help of state censorship[66]). Panayot Abacı (Παναγιώτης Αμπατζής), a violinist in the Istanbul City Orchestra, began publishing what would be the city's last Greek-language literary and art journal *Pyrsos* in 1954; it closed in 1962. Around the same time, the Greek Patriarchate's printing press also closed. For half a century thereafter, no Greek-language books or journals were produced in Istanbul.[67]

Meanwhile, the Greek community of Alexandria had also started to unravel. Since their arrival in the middle of the nineteenth century, the Greeks here had been closely knit and the nucleus of their community had always been its mercantile exporters and wealthy elite—among them, Cavafy's own father. They functioned as the economic lifeblood of a self-sustained and inward-looking micro-economy within the larger British protectorate. The Greek working class, who constituted the community's majority, shared a standard of living with indigenous Muslim Egyptians, yet for their employment and material survival they were largely dependent on the Greek elite. In 1937, however, Egypt began dismantling the foreign privileges that had sustained this system for generations, since those privileges had placed foreigners and foreign capital beyond the legal reach of Egyptian laws. From this point onward, an individual's fluency in Arabic, and Egyptian citizenship, were increasingly crucial to maintaining one's position. And while a twelve-year grace period had been baked into the 1937 agreement, the Greek elite made no real preparations for the new status quo. Greek schools, whose funding, pedagogical outlook, and curriculum were tied directly to the wealthy elite, failed to prepare students for integration into Egyptian society. Added complications, such as a shrinking postwar labor market for both blue- and white-collar professions, did not help. From the late 1930s to the early 1950s, the first major flight was that of the professional classes, but the death blow was delivered when financial elites and industrialists began to withdraw in fear of Nasser's Arab nationalization projects in the later 1950s. In the wake of the flight of both the professional and the elite classes, the entire micro-economy began to decay. The community schools, funded and shaped by elite Greek interests for decades, had failed to prepare the working-class base for the new, Arabophone realities of Nasser's Egypt. Most elements of this base—the unemployed, the lower- and middle-class laborers, shop owners and merchants—were thus forced to follow the growing waves of emigration.[68] The numbers speak for themselves: in 1949, Alexandria's Greek population was 42,835; just twelve years later, in 1961, it had dropped to 20,190; by 1967, it was approximately 8,000; by the end of the Cold War, the population numbered fewer than 800.[69]

This had obvious repercussions on the community's print production, on a similar scale to Istanbul. The bibliographer Eugenios Michailidis, writing in 1965 (just as the community was entering its most precipitous stage of collapse), was still able to boast, "Both the variety and abundance of these [Greek Egyptian] works bear witness in the most positive manner to the large attempt of the Greek Egyptian Intellectual to create a self-sufficient print culture."* It's worth noting that this "self-sufficient print culture" was largely ignored by mainland Greece and its bibliographers, who "remained unconvinced that there exists and has long existed a literary movement in Egypt."† Already in the 1930s, bibliographers and book historians in Athens seemed to have turned their back on diasporic publishing. Just three decades later, they would have found little remaining. Dinos Koutsoumis, the last editor of Ὁ ταχυδρόμος (*The Postman*, Egypt's oldest Greek-language newspaper), offered the following insight: "From 1930 to 1950, 487 books of literature (regardless of their quality) were published in Egypt, while from 1966 to 1980 only 15 books were published, most of which one could not call literary. Most of the writers left. The Greek printing operations were sold [...]. The Greek bookstores closed, nor did Athenian newspapers come for months."‡

Athens too was undergoing changes, in equal and opposite measure. After the end of the Greco-Turkish war and the ensuing Greco-Turkish Population

---

* "Ἡ ποικιλία ἀφ' ἑνὸς καὶ ἡ ἀφθονία ἀφ' ἑτέρου τῶν τοιούτων ἔργων, μαρτυροῦν μὲ τὸν πλέον θετικὸν τρόπον τὴν μεγάλην προσπάθειαν τοῦ Αἰγυπτιώτου Ἕλληνος Διανοουμένου πρὸς δημιουργίαν μιᾶς αὐτοτελοῦς βιβλιοθήκης" (Michailidis, *Βιβλιογραφία*, 10).

† "Εἶναι δὲ ἀκατανόητον, πῶς ἀκόμη δὲν ἔχουν πεισθῆ οἱ Ἕλληνες τῆς πατρίδος μας, ὅτι ὑπάρχει καὶ παραϋπάρχει φιλολογικὴ κίνησις εἰς τὴν Αἴγυπτον" (Michailidis, *Βιβλιογραφία*, 11).

‡ "Από το 1930 μέχρι το 1950 εξεδόθησαν στην Αίγυπτο 487 λογοτεχνικά βιβλία ανεξαρτήτου αξιολογήσεως και από το 1966 έως το 1980 εξεδόθησαν μόνον 15 βιβλία, τα περισσότερα από τα οποία δεν θα μπορεί κανείς να πει ότι είναι λογοτεχνικά. Οι περισσότεροι λογοτέχνες έφυγαν. Τα ελληνικά τυπογραφεία πωλήθηκαν [...]. Τα ελληνικά βιβλιοπωλεία έκλεισαν και επί μήνες ούτε Αθηναϊκές εφημερίδες πήγαιναν από την Αθήνα στην Αίγυπτο" (Koutsoumis, *Πώς και γιατί*, 14).

Exchange, Athens and Piraeus were awash in bodies: disembarking and distributing hundreds of thousands of refugees across the nation-state, the capital had become a massive site of reassembly. By necessity, it was also revising its national ideology and narrative of Greekness. Following the initial formulation of the *Grand Idea* in 1844, debates over Greekness had revolved around lands and human geographies beyond the Greek state. With the collapse of this project in the 1920s, however, many intellectuals were forced to redirect their visions of Greekness inward, toward the limited cultural geography of the Helladic state.[70] "Hellenism" became a project not of expansion but of consolidation and standardization. It was a markedly different breed of Hellenism from Cavafy's, no longer a process of acculturation but an institution of culture: a solid vessel of aesthetic nationalism to assimilate the incoming refugees and diasporic émigrés. The Nobel laureate George Seferis, himself a refugee from Anatolia, wrote quite lucidly on the consolidation of Greek space and Greek bodies:

> Στὸν καιρό μου οἱ περισσότεροι ἄνθρωποι τῶν γραμμάτων εἴχανε βγεῖ ἀπὸ τὴν περιφέρεια τοῦ Ἔθνους· εἴχανε γεννηθεῖ στὰ χρόνια ποὺ ὑπῆρχε μεγαλύτερη εὐρυχωρία γιὰ τὴν Ἑλλάδα, πρὶν ἀρχίσει αὐτὴ ἡ πόλωση τῶν ἑλληνικῶν πληθυσμῶν μέσα στὰ σύνορα τοῦ ἑλλαδικοῦ κράτους, αὐτὸς ὁ συνωστισμὸς ποὺ κάνει τοὺς σημερινοὺς νέους νὰ νιώθουν κάποτε στενόχωρα [...]. Ὁ ἑλληνισμὸς τῆς Μικρασίας ξεριζώθηκε· σὲ λίγο δὲ θὰ ἔχει μείνει τίποτε καὶ ἀπὸ τὸν ἑλληνισμὸ τῆς Αἰγύπτου. Σὲ λίγο θὰ καταταχτοῦν κι αὐτοὶ μαζὶ μὲ ἄλλες ἑλληνικὲς ἀρχαιολογίες, μαζὶ μὲ τὶς πολιτεῖες τῶν Πτολεμαίων καὶ τῶν Σελευκιδῶν ἢ μὲ τὰ πετροκομμένα μοναστήρια τῆς Καππαδοκίας. Καὶ οἱ ἑλληνικοὶ πληθυσμοί τους θὰ ἔχουν γίνει θρέμματα τῆς ὑδροκέφαλης Ἀθήνας.[71]

> In my time most people of letters had emerged from the margins of the Nation; they had been born in the years when Greece was more spacious, before this polarization of the Greek populations within the borders of the Helladic state, this cramming together that sometimes makes today's youth so constrained [...]. The Hellenism of Asia Minor was uprooted; soon there will be nothing left of Hellenism in Egypt. Soon they'll be arrayed with other Greek archeologies, together with the polities of the Ptolemies and the Seleucids or with the stone-carved monasteries of Cappadocia. And their Greek populations will have become fodder for hydrocephalic Athens.

The once fluid and vibrant Greek diasporic cultures of West Asia and North Africa, he ventured, were now bygone collections fit for a museum—a museum whose only likely home would be in Athens. And outside the museum, in the busy streets of the Greek capital, the surviving refugees and displaced remnants of these diasporas were scraping by as best they could, a mass of human "fodder" crammed into the maw of institutional Hellenism.

Consolidating the Text

As these scattered Hellenisms were gathered up in Greece, textual critics of mainland Greece had also been busily picking up the scattered pieces of Modern Greek literature's textual networks, with their ultimate goal the assemblage of complete editions. I will soon turn to the place of Cavafy's poetry within Helladic national philology, but first I need to set the stage and explore the primary philological stakes, starting with the initial project that philologists had assigned themselves in the early 1930s: the textual body of Greece's first "national poet," Dionysios Solomos.

Born in Napoleonic Zakynthos, raised with the Italian language and schooled in Italy, Solomos began (and concluded) his poetic career in that language, only turning to Greek shortly before the start of the Ottoman Greek insurgence of 1821. By the time he reverted to Italian, he had in toto published only two Greek poems ("Hymn to Liberty" and "Ode to the Nun"), a fragment from a third ("Maria's Prayer"), and a short epigram. Despite the immense popularity that the first poem had secured him, most readers beyond his inner circle knew little to nothing of his subsequent projects. After his death in 1857, he left in his wake a mass of incomplete works and notes. Immediately, his friend and soon-to-be editor Iakovos Polylas began assembling and collating the manuscript fragments, embracing an aggressive eclecticism to impose order and cohesion. Nonetheless, when this edition first circulated in 1859, the reaction in both the Ionian Islands and Greece (which Solomos had never visited) was one of unanimous disappointment. The dissatisfaction stemmed, interestingly, not from the fact that Polylas the editor had become silent coauthor; to the contrary, the implicit sentiment was that he had not done enough: Solomos remained in fragments. As the poet Aristotle Valaoritis wrote, the "nation's hopes had been dashed."[72]

Decades later, in the wake of the Population Exchange, a new hope was emerging: Modern Greek philology was taking its first steps toward institutionalization within the state academic system. The first chair in Modern

Greek Philology was established in 1926, and in less than a decade the Academy of Athens announced the foundation of a series of "complete editions" under the titular roof *Library of Modern Greek Literary Authors*. The flagship project for this series was to be the re-assemblage of Dionysios Solomos's poetic corpus and the production of a truly complete edition. As was perhaps inevitable, the critical edition never materialized, yet what did materialize (in Athens' leading literary journals) was nonetheless of great value in itself: a debate between two young scholars—Ioannis Sykoutris and Linos Politis—as to what precisely *was* a critical edition.

Linos Politis was a young Athenian, working at the time as a manuscript curator at the National Library of Athens, though in later decades he moved on to a university appointment at Aristotle University in Thessaloniki, where he supervised Savidis's dissertation on Cavafy in the 1960s. Due to his long tenure as chair of Modern Greek literature and his impressive teaching and research output, Politis is without doubt the most important figure in the institutionalization of Modern Greek philology throughout the second half of the twentieth century. Arguably almost as important to the trajectory of Modern Greek philology, however, was Ioannis Sykoutris, who had burst onto the scene in the late 1920s and early 1930s after completing his doctoral studies in Germany (where he worked under both Wilamowitz and Werner Jaeger). Sykoutris was a refugee of 1922, born and raised in Smyrna, a thriving center of Greek commerce and education. After 1922, when the city was recaptured by Turkish nationalists and the Greek and Armenian quarters were burned to the ground, Sykoutris disclosed in his personal correspondence that it had left a "wound" that "would never close."[73]

It could be stitched together, however, by philology. As he argued in the inaugural lecture at the University of Athens in 1931, the task of the philologist was to curate a society's "literary monuments" and revitalize them to make them speak to the needs of the contemporary moment.[74] Working in the wake of the Population Exchange and addressing himself to a new generation of philologists, Sykoutris was implicitly responding to the political, ideological, and sociostructural crises that had been gripping Greece for nearly a decade, as the Greek state was still working to integrate and assimilate more than a million refugees from Turkey.[75] To truly serve the needs of their society, Sykoutris argued that philologists would have to choose the "masterworks of big and powerful authors."[76] And while these works were supposedly "universal" and offered up new interpretations to every society and every period, terms like "universal" and "masterwork" in Sykoutris's worldview were ultimately stand-ins for something much more particular and exclusive: Western civilization and the European classical tradition. A century after Fallmerayer, Sykoutris explicitly called upon his fellow Greeks to apprentice themselves to Europe. He believed that modern Greeks—despite being the "natural descendants of the Ancients"—could achieve contact with Ancient Greek learning "not directly but only through the exigencies, the problems, and the values of contemporary European culture."* Modern Greeks, in his opinion, needed to submit themselves to the tutelage of Europe, just as Fallmerayer had suggested in 1835.

One important reason for this, Sykoutris implied, was that modern Greeks still needed to shore up Hellenism against lingering elements of Eastern "despotism" (δεσποτεία), which, he argued, "subjugates art and philosophy to any and every political expediency or religious dogmatism" and drowns individualism in "the endless ocean of the anonymous masses, which one finds among the Eastern peoples."† The supposed menace of the East is expressed in terms all too familiar to us today: a massive body of water that threatened to flood European individualism, subjugating aesthetic autonomy with Eastern dogmatism. After the ethnic cleansing of the Greco-Turkish Population Exchange, Sykoutris was now calling for a *textual* "cleansing"[77] on explicitly Eurocentric terms, in order to ensure the artistic autonomy and individualism of Greek authorship. Sykoutris committed suicide in 1937, a tragic and untimely end to a brilliant and promising human life, yet his intellectual rigor and his systematization of the discipline went on to mark several generations of philologists—including Savidis.[78]

The 1936 debate between Politis and Sykoutris was an important milestone in the development of Modern Greek philology. Despite their differences, both agreed that the philological edition should be "complete" (*πλήρης*), whether it contained a single work or a multi-volume set of the author's entire oeuvre. Sykoutris wrote, "The unswerving rule of every critical edition is *completeness* [. . .], the publisher must offer all that bears relation to the work and comes from the poet."‡ What defined the critical edition for Sykoutris was the systematic application of a scientific method to produce a text as close to the

---

* "Μόνον διὰ μέσου τῶν ἀναγκῶν καὶ τῶν προβλημάτων καὶ τῶν ἀξιῶν τοῦ συγχρόνου εὐρωπαϊκοῦ πολιτισμοῦ, ὄχι κατ᾽ εὐθεῖαν" (Sykoutris, Μελέται καὶ ἄρθρα, 516).

† "Ὑποτάσσει τὴν τέχνην π.χ. ἢ τὴν φιλοσοφίαν εἰς τὰς ἑκάστοτε πολιτικὰς σκοπιμότητας ἢ εἰς θρησκευτικοὺς δογματισμούς [. . .] τὸν ἀτέρμονα ὠκεανὸν τῆς ἀνωνύμου μάζης, ἡ ὁποία ἐμφανίζεται εἰς τοὺς ἀνατολικοὺς π.χ. λαούς" (Sykoutris, Μελέται καὶ ἄρθρα, 520; 524).

‡ "Κανὼν ἀπαρέγκλιτος κάθε κριτικῆς ἐκδόσεως εἶναι ἡ πληρότης [. . .] πρέπει νὰ προσφέρῃ ὁ ἐκδότης πᾶν ὅ,τι σχετίζεται μὲ τὸ ἔργον τοῦτο καὶ προέρχετ᾽ ἐκ τοῦ ποιητοῦ" (Sykoutris, Μελέται καὶ ἄρθρα, 422).

"original"—that is to say, the author's ideal text—as possible. Not just for Sykoutris but for all trained textual critics of the time, the critical edition was a textual homecoming by which the editor led their readers back to a pristine authorial ideal, cleansed from the "contaminations" of all the textual handlers producing, reproducing, and disseminating the work. Sykoutris spoke to this later in his article: "The rehabilitation of the text and its cleansing of all changes foreign to the intentions of the author constitute the most central and difficult portion of the critical edition."* Housed within a positivist, scientific language, Sykoutris's tenets seemed at the time unassailable.

It was not until the early 1980s, in the figures of Jerome McGann and D. F. McKenzie, that any concerted theoretical pressure was applied to this foundational assumption. Drawing from his practical work in the field, McGann argued that traditional textual criticism empties texts of the multiple social and institutional agencies that in fact produced them. Literary works, he complained, "lose their lives as they gain [their] critical identities [...] by being divorced from the social relationships which gave them their lives (including their 'textual' lives) in the first place."[79] It was precisely the recovery of these social relationships that interested McKenzie, who argued that rather than fetishizing authorial origin, textual critics might just as productively examine the cultural accretions of any given text as it proliferates across media and editions—i.e., rather than erasing variations as errata, one might engage them as significant sites of cultural production in and of themselves. The traditional philological concept of the book "and of an author's presence within it," McKenzie posited, "represents only one end of a bibliographical spectrum. The counter-tradition of textual transformations, of new forms in new editions for new markets, represents the other. A sociology of texts would comprehend both."[80]

The early philologists of Athens obviously had the opportunity neither to hear nor to read McKenzie's or McGann's insights. Yet even if there had been an opportunity, Greek philologists were busy with other concerns. In the interwar years following the Exchange, the very years that Greek space had begun to contract and solidify (partially under the dictatorship of Ioannis Metaxas, which successfully tied Greek nationalism to fascist political structures), it became clear to the emerging institutions of philology that past Greek texts must likewise be contracted and solidified, brought together and

---

* "Ἡ ἀποκατάστασις τοῦ κειμένου καὶ ἡ ἀποκάθαρσις αὐτοῦ ἀπὸ κάθε μεταβολὴν ἀλλοτρίαν τῶν προθέσεων τοῦ συγγραφέως ἀποτελεῖ τὸ κυριώτερον ἀλλὰ καὶ τὸ δυσκολώτερον μέρος τῆς κριτικῆς ἐκδόσεως" (Sykoutris, Μελέται καὶ ἄρθρα, 428).

rebuilt, with their central fundament planted in authorial intent, however that was to be interpreted by the editor. Sykoutris's metaphors were indicative in this sense, conflating the twin crises of population movements and textual migration. He likened previous Greek editions to "hastily pitched tents and sheds set up [...] without foundations and left to the mercy of the first strong wind. It's time to do away with this nomadism; it's time to build structures permanent and stable."* And as the plural form of "tents" and "sheds" suggests, this "nomadism" was endemic to the nation; Dionysios Solomos was only the tip of a massive iceberg.

The young Linos Politis voiced some initial skepticism. The Academy of Athens, he wrote, ought not to invest time and money in the construction of critical editions as a general rule, for "besides Solomos, Vilaras, perhaps Kalvos (and Rigas?—his interest is mainly historical), I don't see a need for a critical edition of any other literary author."† In the same issue, however, Sykoutris responded:

> Ἀναφέρω μερικὰ ὀνόματα λογοτεχνῶν ποὺ ὁ κ. Π. παρέλειψε: τοὺς πρὸ τῆς Ἐπαναστάσεως Φαναριῶτες ποιητάς, τῶν ὁποίων τὰ ποιήματα, θαμμένα πολλάκις ὑπὸ τὴν ἀνωνυμίαν, εἶναι τόσον ἐνδιαφέροντ' ἀπὸ γραμματολογικῆς ἀπόψεως καὶ εὑρίσκονται σήμερα κατεσπαρμένα εἰς δυσπρόσιτα βιβλία. Τὸν Ἀθανάσιον Χριστόπουλον [...] τὸν Γεώργιον Τερτσέτην [...]. Τὸν Ἰούλιον Τυπάλδον [...]. Τὸν Ἰάκωβον Πολυλᾶν [...]. Τὸν Λασκαράτον [...]. Ἔρχοντ' ἔπειτα οἱ ποιηταὶ τῆς καθαρευούσης [...]. Ἔρχονται ὁ Βιζυηνός, ὁ Κρυστάλλης, ὁ Παπαδιαμάντης, ποὺ δὲν ἔχει ἀκόμα γίνει ἔκδοσις τῶν Ἁπάντων του, καί, ὅταν γίνῃ, δὲν ἐπιτρέπεται βέβαια νὰ γίνῃ πρόχειρα καὶ ἀμέθοδα. Δὲν πιστεύω νὰ χρειάζεται καὶ ἄλλα ὀνόματα ὁ κ. Π.[81]

> I offer some names of authors that Politis has omitted: the pre-revolutionary Phanariot poets, whose poems, buried in anonymity, are so interesting from a grammatological perspective and are today scattered in books dif-

---

* "Ὁμοιάζουν ὅμως μὲ τὰ πρόχειρα τ' ἀντίσκηνα καὶ τὶς παράγκες, ποὺ στήνονται [...] χωρὶς θεμέλια καὶ εἶναι εἰς τὸ ἔλεος τοῦ πρώτου δυνατοῦ ἀνέμου. Εἶναι καιρὸς νὰ λείψῃ ὁ νομαδισμὸς αὐτός· εἶναι καιρὸς νὰ κτισθοῦν οἰκοδομήματα μόνιμα καὶ σταθερά" (Sykoutris, *Μελέται καὶ ἄρθρα*, 434).

† "Ἔξω ἀπὸ τὸ Σολωμό, τὸ Βηλαρά, ἴσως τὸν Κάλβο (τὸ Ρήγα;—τὸ ἐνδιαφέρο του περισσότερο ἱστορικό), δὲ βλέπω γιὰ κανέναν ἄλλο λογοτέχνη νὰ ὑπάρχει ἀνάγκη γιὰ μιὰ κριτικὴ ἔκδοση" (Politis, "Φιλολογικὰ θέματα," 344).

ficult to track down. Athanasios Christopoulos [...] Georgios Tertsetis [...] Ioulios Typaldos [...] Iakovos Polylas [...] Laskaratos [...]. Then come the Katharevousa poets [...]. Then come Vizyinos, Krystallis, Papadiamandis, whose complete edition has not yet been published, and, when it happens, it must not happen haphazardly or without method. I don't believe that Mr. Politis needs more names.

In short, Sykoutris spoke to the dawning realization that Greek philology needed first and foremost to shore up the bibliographically and geographically scattered national corpora. Until that moment, the production of complete editions had been the domain of commercial publishers and editors, a practice that had led to variations and textual multiplicity on an as yet uncalculated scale. Writing elsewhere, Sykoutris predicted that "for the near future [w]e will continue to use the old editions [of Solomos], reprinting them as per the initiative of booksellers, of which editions each will present a different text with a chaotic accumulation of variations. Booksellers, rather than philologists, likewise compiled nearly all the editions of other dead writers, and no one has yet felt the need to give us [...] their critical editions."* Textual multiplicity was everywhere, and only the institutional intervention of Greek philology could shore up the pieces, solidify and immobilize them.

A generation later, into this same atmosphere George Savidis entered with his Cavafy. The timing was perfect. He had first worked on the Cavafy corpus while studying philology at King's College in the early 1950s, continuing, expanding, and deepening his study through the end of the decade and into the 1960s, now in the form of a doctoral dissertation under the supervision of Linos Politis. Savidis was building his editorial project using the raw materials of Cavafy's diasporic papers. After Cavafy's death in 1933, the personal archives that he had meticulously amassed for decades were bequeathed to Alekos Singopoulos. Lending out certain pieces of the archive to scholars and friends of the deceased poet and perhaps selling parts of Cavafy's personal library,[82] Singopoulos unwittingly created yet another level of fragmentation within Cavafy's texts and books, dissolving the singular archive into multiple archives.

---

*"Εἰς προσεχὲς μέλλον [θ]ὰ ἐξακολουθοῦμεν ἀκόμη νὰ χρησιμοποιοῦμεν, ἀνατυπουμένας τῇ πρωτοβουλίᾳ τῶν βιβλιοπωλῶν, τὰς παλαιὰς [σολωμικὰς] ἐκδόσεις, ἐκ τῶν ὁποίων κάθε μιὰ παρέχει καὶ διαφορετικὸν κείμενον μὲ χαώδη συσσώρευσιν παραλλαγῶν. Βιβλιοπῶλαι ἐπίσης, ὄχι φιλόλογοι, κατήρτισαν καὶ ὅλας σχεδὸν τὰς ἐκδόσεις τῶν ἄλλων ἀποθανόντων λογοτεχνῶν, καὶ κανεὶς ἀκόμη δὲν αἰσθάνεται τὴν ἀνάγκην νὰ μᾶς δώσῃ [...] αὐτῶν τὴν κριτικὴν ἔκδοσιν" (Sykoutris, Μελέται καὶ ἄρθρα, 245).

Not until Savidis convinced Singopoulos to open the remaining archival collection to him did the situation begin to change. As Savidis wrote in 1963, "The whole of the Cavafy Archive must be published as soon as possible. Without this publication, we cannot have a true Complete Edition or a proper biography of the Poet."* It was through this archive that Savidis built his editions, yet after he purchased the former he never followed through on his own call to publish it or open up access. It is difficult to overstate the importance of these facts. Savidis arguably built his career on this archive, and around it he fortified the methods and aims of the larger field of Modern Greek philology for several generations to come, yet it was only with the purchase of the archive by the Onassis Foundation in 2012 that the material has been digitized and opened to the public.[83]

For decades, the reading public's main point of access to the poet's archive and his poems remained the several volumes of Cavafy's poetry and bibliography published by Savidis. Released on the centennial of Cavafy's birth (1963), the first two volumes of poetry in particular signaled a seismic shift and sparked new general interest in the poet, and they were enthusiastically if not encomiastically reviewed by a range of intellectuals, including Stratis Tsirkas. In the half-title pages of both volumes, Savidis introduced them as the "Complete Works" (Ἅπαντα), as seen in figure 5. This claim was dubious, though, and its motivations remain ambiguous to me. What exactly did Savidis mean by titling the two volumes "ΑΠΑΝΤΑ 1" and "ΑΠΑΝΤΑ 2"? Were these the first two volumes of a multi-volume complete edition?[84] Did Savidis consider his still unrealized edition *Hidden Poems* (1968) to be the third volume of the same edition? And what of Cavafy's juvenilia, his prose work, or his unfinished work, to name but three more?[85] Whatever Savidis had in mind, the title of "Complete Works" continued to appear in reprints of the first edition but was quietly dropped from subsequent editions, where other emendations and additions also began to appear. This bibliographic shift speaks in subtle ways to an important tension: despite Savidis's efforts to standardize and complete Cavafy—something that he signaled rhetorically and paratextually in the early years of his career—his own editions never actually did so and arguably multiplied further the endless multiformity of Cavafy's poems.[86]

---

*"Νὰ δημοσιευτεῖ τὸ ταχύτερο, στὸ σύνολό του, τὸ Ἀρχεῖο Καβάφη. Χωρὶς αὐτὴν τὴν δημοσίευση, δὲν θὰ μποροῦμε νὰ ἔχουμε οὔτε πραγματικὰ Ἅπαντα, οὔτε σωστὴ βιογραφία τοῦ Ποιητῆ" (Savidis, "Τὸ ἀρχεῖο").

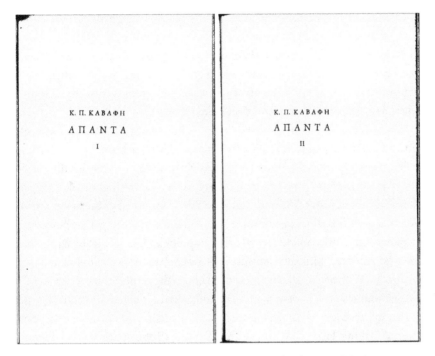

FIGURE 5. The half-title pages of the first and second volumes of George Savidis's 1963 edition, presented to readers here as "Complete Works 1" and "Complete Works 2." Copyright Ikaros Publishing.

I will return to this point soon, but I should also emphasize that, whatever their limits may have been, Savidis's editions were indeed revolutionary, playing an outsized role in public perceptions of the poet's work. If the poet's body remained in Egypt, continuing its process of decomposition beyond the borders of the nation-state, the body of his works was now undergoing a reversal in Athens, repackaged and advertised as "complete" to a new national readership. It was to Athens that Singopoulos had moved the archive as he abandoned Egypt. It was in Athens that Savidis produced and published his edition in 1963. And it was in Athens that he later bought the archive from Singopoulos's widow, from which in 1968 he published Cavafy's manuscript poems. These were not simply happy coincidences. The fact that both Cavafy's contemporary textual corpus and archive were now installed in Greece was a manifestation of the same consolidation—of bodies, geographies, and institutions—that I have been tracing here. Savidis emphasized the same process years later while teaching at Harvard: "It is important for me to return to Greece," he responded in an interview, "because I am needed there. Obviously, the real center of Modern Greek Studies is Greece."[87] As I have shown in the first half of this chapter, there was nothing obvious about such a claim just a generation earlier. Two generations earlier, during Cavafy's richest years of production, there had been no center at all of Modern Greekness. Cavafy's Greekness had thrived atop this decentered map.

To understand again just how the map had changed, let us look more closely at Savidis's edition of 1963. What precisely were these books? Savidis called them a "popular" edition (λαϊκὴ ἔκδοση), and in every sense they were just that, surrounding the poems with only a short introduction and a set of slim, laconic endnotes. The only dates provided were those of the first publication of a poem's final form, nor were any references made to earlier published versions. Savidis also made several orthographic changes. While he wrote that the first volume "faithfully reprints" the poems, he nonetheless added in a footnote, "With a very few typographical and orthographical modifications."* These modifications were in themselves indicative of a general, perceived need to tidy up, yet there was in fact more occurring behind the scenes. Forty years later, Anthony Hirst first noted that Savidis's interventions ran deeper. "Cavafy's quirks of punctuation and accentuation, and his occasional surprising spellings," Hirst wrote, "require no editorial 'correction'; his inconsistencies do not need to be standardized. We can be confident that they were in most cases deliberate and well considered."[88] Yet on multiple occasions it was precisely these orthographic "quirks" that Savidis emended and hence, as Hirst persuasively demonstrates, erased certain readings made possible by the original orthographic slippage. In effect, Savidis partially normalized Cavafy's "unhinged" orthography and brought it in line with the national standard of the Helladic core.

Despite Savidis's silent handiwork and interventions, his edition evinced in all its pages the stated goal of traditional textual criticism: salvaging and packaging original authorial intent. The clearest manifestation of this came in the ordering of the poems. Here, he had effected what was at the time a startling change, replacing the earlier, chronological Cavafy with a two-volume compromise: the first volume reproduced the arrangement of Cavafy's final two thematic collections (plus a small chronological aggregation of his earliest

---

*"Μὲ ἐλάχιστες τυπογραφικὲς καὶ ὀρθογραφικὲς προσαρμογές" (Cavafy, Ποιήματα, vol. 1, 12).

poems); the second volume reproduced the arrangement of his final chronological collection of those poems missing from the first volume.

As I have already noted, Savidis had made it clear that he aimed for a complete edition. Beyond the glaring half-page title shown in figure 5, his editor's introduction further expands and qualifies this claim. It was an edition, Savidis wrote, whose "goal [is] to render the whole of Cavafy's finished poetic work accessible to as many readers as possible."* Cavafy's long and meticulous process of assembling divergent poetic narratives within the collections and the ephemera press of the Mediterranean seemed to congeal here. For a brief moment in time, before Savidis himself reissued subsequent editions and emendations, Cavafy's poetry had become a singular, fixed, and finished product, multiplied and bound for the mass Greek readerships of the 1960s.

Precisely because the edition was popular, its four-page introductory note addressed itself not to a narrow field of scholars but to a national Greek readership. Its rhetoric thus provided ample evidence of the political and social realities that now governed Cavafy's poems.[89] Just as those poems forty years earlier had been informed and shaped by their time and space, so too was Savidis's edition shaped under the pressures of its own time and space. Describing the last day of Cavafy's life, Savidis began his introduction thus: "Mr. Kostis Petrou Photiadis Cavafy [...] the exiled lord of Greek Letters, closed, in the city of his birth, the seventieth circle of his earthly life and passed on to the circle of eternity: he became, once and for all, Cavafy."† There are at least two points worth pausing over here. First, Cavafy's name has become a central site of the editor's transformative project; both its multiplicity and mundane triviality have been cut down and crystallized to what seems to me almost a kind of postmortem trademark, like "Elvis." Second and more important, Savidis introduces a crucial paradox: Cavafy has been "exiled," yet he nonetheless lives in the city of his birth. He is both at home and not at home in Alexandria. Though Savidis is perhaps preparing his readers for "The City," the first poem of volume 1, the larger implications are clear. Living beyond the

---

* "Μιὰ ἔκοδση ποὺ ἔχει σκοπὸ νὰ καταστήσει προσιτό, σὲ ὅσο τὸ δυνατὸ περισσότερους ἀναγνῶστες, τὸ σύνολο τοῦ τελειωμένου ποιητικοῦ ἔργου τοῦ Καβάφη" (Cavafy, *Ποιήματα*, vol. 1, p. 11).

† "Ὁ κύριος Κωστῆς Πέτρου Φωτιάδης Καβάφης [...] ἐξόριστο[ς] ἄρχοντα[ς] τοῦ ἑλληνικοῦ λόγου, ἔκλεισε στὴν γενέτειρά του τὸν ἑβδομηντάχρονο κύκλο τῆς ἐπίγειας ζωῆς του, καὶ πέρασε στὸν κύκλο τῆς αἰωνιότητας: ἔγινε, ὁριστικά, ὁ Καβάφης" (Cavafy, *Ποιήματα*, vol. 1, p. 9).

borders of the Greek state, Cavafy has been exiled from his true home: the canon of Greek Letters. Savidis was now welcoming the exile back, and this edition was going to convey him there. To see just how, look to a final passage from the introduction on page 10:

> [Ὁ Καβάφης] μποροῦσε [...] νὰ ἔχει τὴν καθαρὴ συνείδηση τοῦ ἀγαθοῦ δούλου, ὁ ὁποῖος δὲν καταχώνιασε μήτε ἐπόρνευσε τὸ τάλαντό του στὴν κοσμοπολίτικη ἔρημο τῆς Ἀλεξάνδρειας ἢ στὴν βαλκανικὴ σκόνη τῆς Ἀθήνας, μὰ τὸ ἔσπειρε στὰ πιὸ παραμελημένα χώματα τοῦ Ἑλληνισμοῦ, καὶ τὸ πότισε καὶ τὸ ἀνάστησε μὲ ὅλα του τὰ δάκρυα καὶ μὲ ὅλο του τὸ αἷμα.

> [Cavafy] could [...] rest with the clean conscience of a faithful servant [*αγαθός δούλος*], who had neither hid away his talents nor prostituted them to the cosmopolitan deserts of Alexandria, nor to the Balkan dusts of Athens, but rather he cast them into the most neglected lands of Hellenism, and he watered them and he resurrected them with all his tears and all his blood.

Here too several points of concern warrant comment. First, Savidis unexpectedly fills Cavafy's poetry with *blood and tears*. I don't know about you, but this turn of phrase gives me pause. While mourning and memorializing indeed play an important part of Cavafy's queer poetics, they are never far removed from the complex irony—at times quite playful—that runs throughout his work. Indeed, I would argue that it is precisely in his poems centered on Hellenism that such irony becomes most playful. To my eye, there are few "blood and tears" sprinkled on the Hellenisms of Cavafy. Savidis's rhetorical frame here thus shifts the terms and affective bonds of belonging.

Crucially, Savidis also shifts the *geographic* terms of belonging. True, the passage casts its gaze beyond the "Balkan dusts" of the Modern Greek state, yet it simultaneously washes its hands of Cavafy's Alexandria and anchors its own geographic vision in no specific toponyms whatsoever, only "neglected lands" that are marked as Hellenic. Athenian critics of the early twentieth century, you'll recall, had racialized Cavafy's geography in subtle and not so subtle ways, at times tying his poetry explicitly to vulgar caricatures of Islam, to Orientalist stereotypes of Egypt and Africa, and to black and brown bodies. Now, with an equal and opposite force, Cavafy was being plucked out from that geography, divorced from Islamicate culture, and whitewashed for the Hellenic canon.[90] Make no mistake; what Savidis gives us here is a placeless, normative Hellenism. By the mid-1960s, as Artemis Leontis has shown, Hellenism had been transformed from a fluid process to a fixed Helladic Institution.[91] Readers of Savidis's introduction would by and large have understood their Cavafy as a "servant" (or more literally, "slave") of this second, institutionalized Hellenism, which was deeply entangled with the larger logic of the Population Exchange. Savidis himself later made this clear in a public lecture, arguing that "Cavafy's victory (in his battle to pass from the drama of the *Ego* to the catharsis of the *We*) becomes the victory also of the Greek conscience, in the years when the *Grand Idea* had shipwrecked and thus deprived the nation of its worldly brace."* If Cavafy's poems had once evinced a playful and idiosyncratic engagement with diasporic Hellenism, Savidis now swept them up into postwar Helladic politics, making Cavafy a bondservant of Hellenism as Institution. The poet had become a "brace" (ἀντιστύλι) that was shoring up the "We" of the nation in the wake of the Population Exchange.

It was with this logic that Savidis could write, "And nothing certainly would satisfy [Cavafy] more deeply than to know that we would celebrate the one hundred years since his birth and the thirty years since his death first and foremost with the first popular edition of his Poems, which also inaugurates the first edition of his Complete Works."†

Cavafy Unbound

Despite the performative power of those words, Savidis never actually completed Cavafy. As I have intimated several times throughout this chapter, Cavafy's multiformity never ceased its expansive recombinations, transformations, translations, and transmediations. And with the passage of the archive to the Onassis Foundation in 2012, the poet's own archive too has become more public, not only through an open-access digitization project but more importantly through public-facing initiatives that turn the archive into a communal

---

* "'Έτσι ἡ νίκη τοῦ Καβάφη (στὸν ἀγῶνα του γιὰ νὰ περάσει ἀπὸ τὸ δρᾶμα τοῦ Ἐγὼ στὴν κάθαρση τοῦ Ἐμεῖς) γίνεται καὶ νίκη τῆς ἑλληνικῆς συνείδησης, στὰ χρόνια ὅπου ὁ καταποντισμὸς τῆς Μεγάλης Ἰδέας ἔχει στερήσει τὸ ἔθνος ἀπὸ τὸ κοσμικό του ἀντιστύλι" (quoted in Tsirkas, *Πολιτικός Καβάφης*, 22).

† "Καὶ τίποτα, ἀσφαλῶς, δὲν θὰ τὸν ἱκανοποιοῦσε βαθύτερα, ἀπὸ τὴ γνώση ὅτι τὰ ἑκατόχρονα τῆς γέννησής του καὶ τὰ τριαντάχρονα τοῦ θανάτου του θὰ γιορτάζονταν, πρὶν ἀπὸ ὅλα, μὲ τὴν πρώτη λαϊκὴ ἔκδοση τῶν Ποιημάτων του, καὶ μὲ τὴν πρώτη ἔκδοση τῶν Ἀπάντων του" (Cavafy, *Ποιήματα*, vol. 1, 10).

project, spilling over into public schools, public universities, and public lectures and performances.

Amidst this important work, however, I don't want to lose sight of the larger diasporic print networks in which Cavafy's poetry moved and took shape beyond the confines of Cavafy's own immediate milieu. Because despite the important progress that we have made pushing beyond Savidis's reading of Cavafy, the fact remains that we are still often reading Cavafy's poems *through Cavafy*. The author himself and his inner circle still loom large over most discussions of the poems. As Karen Emmerich trenchantly notes, "The desire to present Cavafy's slippery oeuvre as a coherent, cohesive canon has plagued scholars and editors for decades—precisely because, one might argue, the instability of the texts feels so threatening to our conventional notions of authorship and literary meaning alike."[92] In other words, the desire to read Cavafy's poems through Cavafy is not entirely our fault. There's an entire critical history pulling us in this direction, one that began even during Cavafy's lifetime but was normalized by the early studies of the poet by Alithersis and Malanos and by the methods of early textual critics like Sykoutris. It was finally cemented by Savidis's influential bibliographical and philological analysis in 1966. Today, this author-centric approach has grown terribly claustrophobic. To my mind, the author-centric methods of Savidis, which helped shape both the field of Cavafy studies and more generally Modern Greek philology, have outlived their usefulness. Already in the 1980s, there were signs of impatience with the philological status quo,[93] and today, with the contributions of scholars such as Maria Boletsi, Karen Emmerich, Hala Halim, Dimitris Papanikolaou, and Takis Kayalis (to name just a few), the dam is at last breaking. What I have learned from these scholars is that to recover the true vitality of Cavafy's poems will require more than opening up Cavafy's archive; it will require a sustained engagement with the larger (and weaker) intellectual and print networks through which Cavafy's work was circulated, read, reviewed, and debated. The light that such readings and reviews and debates shed will fall not only on Cavafy's poems but on the larger tapestry of the Eastern Mediterranean, the Greek-speaking threads of which I have tried, with my own limited capacities, to trace in brief here.

How to make these larger reading publics of Cavafy available to contemporary reading publics a hundred years on? Would it be possible for example to collect the material traces of these Greek print networks, as well as their interactions with the Cavafy poems, in the form of an edited volume or—why not?—an *edition*? And just as importantly, how might such an edition embody the same logic of the poems and their ephemeral networks? A printed codex might simulate the experience, yet I fear that it would struggle to remain faithful to the spirit of the multiple and shifting Greek print networks. While a digital platform too holds its own possible pitfalls (none greater than the massive demands of coordination and maintenance), the MLA Committee on Scholarly Editions' 2015 White Paper, "Considering the Scholarly Edition in the Digital Age," offers hope for an emerging set of best practices. If coordinated properly, a digital format might promise not to bring forth a single text, buttressed by a critical apparatus, but to allow readers to explore, on their own terms, the poems' multiplicity of forms in newspapers, little magazines, and Cavafy's editions, as well as the reader and editorial responses and debates that they sparked. This might occur through a coordinated and collaborative digital archive—one that reaches well beyond the Cavafy Archive to incorporate a broader range of Cavafy's "collections" and ephemeral print—or, alternatively (or additionally), through a digital edition based on the standards of the Text Encoding Initiative. The 2015 White Paper posits that, using these standards, digital interfaces "can serve as environments for manipulation and exploration of the edition's textual space and also as environments within which the user can occupy the role of a contingent editor, examining less-traveled editorial paths and their interpretive consequences."[94] Ideally, such an edition of Cavafy's poems would grant us access to the multiple witnesses, inscriptions, and reactions that have been assembled, dispersed, circulated, and reassembled across the century—and, through the larger collaborative archive, to the networks of transnational Greek print that interlaced the Eastern Mediterranean and subtly shaped Cavafy's poems.

Chapter three, in which witnesses to war tell their truths

IN THE LATE MONTHS of 1943, as the German occupation of Greece neared its darkest nadir, the prominent literary critic I. M. Panagiotopoulos was preparing the second volume of his essays for publication under the title *Uneasy Years* (*Ανήσυχα χρόνια*). After nearly three decades of war, the upheaval of millions of refugees, and the collapse of several regimes, the book's title seemed fitting. "[T]he days we have lived through have their own particularity," Panagiotopoulos wrote, and as a consequence "the novelist, like a historian of the life that surrounds him, must transfer them onto his pages."* He saw an urgent need to document the epoch that had passed, to "transfer" it onto paper—and thence into the communal memory of a national readership. The medium of this transmission was literature, he argued, and it was to be carried out by the hand of the author.

This chapter will take issue with such a claim, yet it's important first to follow its logic closely to understand why. Surveying literary production since the 1920s, Panagiotopoulos located Greek prose's core strength in autobiography. Much of this literature, he admitted, was underdeveloped, incapable of "encompassing the greater whole, [...] of expressing collective ideals, of studying the age, of looking at the historical moment with the composure that so often befits the art of the novel writer, as an objective art."† Yet works

---

* "Οἱ ἐποχὲς ποὺ περάσαμε ἔχουν τὸ ἰδιαίτερο ὕφος τους καὶ πρέπει ὁ μυθιστοριογράφος, σὰν ἱστορικὸς τῆς ὁλόγυρά του ζωῆς, νὰ τὶς μεταφέρει στὶς σελίδες του" (Panagiotopoulos, *Ἀνήσυχα χρόνια*, 28).

† "Ν' ἀγκαλιάσει τὰ σύνολα... νὰ ἐκφράσει τὰ ὁμαδικὰ ἰδεώδη, νὰ σπουδάσει τὴν ἐποχή, νὰ κοιτάξει τὴν ἱστορικὴ στιγμή, μὲ τὴν ψυχραιμία ποὺ ταιριάζει τόσο συχνὰ στὴν

that succeeded, he claimed, did so precisely because they captured "the meaning and atmosphere of the epoch."* What was needed were authors who, by virtue of their objectivity, transformed their individual voice into collective history.

On the other side of the Aegean, in Turkey, one could read strikingly similar observations from İsmail Habib, the first literary critic of the Turkish Republic to treat contemporary literature. In describing the earliest modern Turkish novels to emerge from the war of 1919–1922, İsmail Habib's targeted commentary left little doubt that literature was being enlisted to bear witness to the historical moment. Writing of Halide Edib, who had herself participated in the Greco-Turkish War, he argued that "whether treating the Turkism movement, the victories of the National Struggle, or the tragedies of the occupation, her works stem from the fact that she has not only an individual but a collective conscience."† Or, as he wrote earlier, she had "the ability to feel the communal pulse within her own pulse."‡ The greatest boon of her novels, he continued, lay in "the sections devoted to detail, to life, to events. These are pieces of immediate realism. The novelist has taken all of them from the life that she herself lived."§ In his analysis of Halide Edib's fiction, İsmail Habib isolates and elevates the lived experience of the author, which has been directly (*doğrudan doğruya*) transferred to the pages we read. It is moreover an experience lived not only by the individual author but by the entire national community, a connection that is naturalized: our pulse is in her pulse. Across the Greco-Turkish borderscape, literature was being called on to testify.

Since the rise of Romanticism in Europe a hundred years prior, the historical novel had been a leading literary tool of nation-building. Now, it seemed, Greek and Turkish literature were busily inventing a new mode of national historiography, what has come to be called the testimonial.[1] The core logic

---

τέχνη τοῦ μυθιστοριογράφου σὰν τέχνη ἀντικειμενική" (Panagiotopoulos, *Ἀνήσυχα χρόνια*, 26).

* "Τὸ νόημα καὶ τὸ ὕφος τῆς ἐποχῆς" (Panagiotopoulos, *Ἀνήσυχα χρόνια*, 38).

† "Ya türkçülük cereyanına, ya Millî Mücadele zaferlerine; yahut ta işgal facialarına dair eserleri de onun yalnız ferdî değil maşerî bir vicdana dahi sahip oluşundan ileri geliyor" (İsmail Habib, *Edebî Yeniliğimiz*, 327).

‡ "Cemiyetin nabzını kendi nabzında duyan bir kabiliyet te vardı" (İsmail Habib, *Edebî Yeniliğimiz*, 326).

§ "Afakî kıymet ise romandaki teferruata, hayata, hâdiselere ait olan kısımdan ileri geliyor. Bunlar doğrudan doğruya realist parçalardır. Romancı onları bütün kendi yaşadığı hayattan almıştır" (İsmail Habib, *Edebî Yeniliğimiz*, 342).

separating the two genres is worth consideration. Many historical novels—perhaps most famously, Walter Scott's *Waverley* series—tended to embed the distant past within the textual artifacts of their fictional present. That is to say, readers accessed their national history not directly through the novel's narrator but through old letters, books, or journals that had supposedly been rediscovered and carefully compiled by the novel's editor-qua-narrator. Testimonial fiction, conversely, was said by its reviewers and readers to gesture toward an immediate and unmediated past, thanks to the direct experience of the witness-narrator. Testimonial fiction did not reconstruct history: it lived and breathed history. Such was the rhetoric in any case employed by authors and critics of testimonial works (a rhetoric that was, in part, replicated by some later proponents of Latin American *testimonio*, such as John Beverley). Yet to take such rhetoric at its word is to risk overlooking the fascinating collision, collusion, and contestation of several agents—witnesses, transcribers, writers, editors, printers, and others—each of whom has left a trace within the testimonial's text(s). To understand the genre's historical truth, this chapter will argue that we must treat testimonials not as disembodied discourses but as material networks. Historical truths are indeed articulated through these networks, but such a truth is by no means "authoritative"—i.e., a monopoly of the author. Careful examination of the testimonial and its several moving parts suggests that this truth is instead a kind of construction site. This is not to say that truth is a "social construct" or that testimonial fiction is a sham. On the contrary, to understand the genre as a construction site—to recover, in other words, the several hands through which it has passed before reaching ours—is to recognize its collective potential and to make the production of historical truth, in Bruno Latour's words, "*more* visible, *more* risky, *more* costly, *more* debatable, *more* interesting, and *more* publicly relevant."[2]

The two testimonials that I examine, Ἡ ἱστορία ἑνὸς αἰχμαλώτου (A Captive's Story) and *Ateşten Gömlek* (Shirt of Flame), one published in Greek and the other in Turkish, detail the events whose shadow has loomed large over both of the previous chapters: the Greco-Turkish War and subsequent Population Exchange. These events were definitive in the rupture and reconfiguration of the borderscape of the so-called Near East. Millions of bodies were destroyed or displaced, geopolitical borders were replaced, and a network of internal borders began to filter, immobilize, and remobilize linguistic and cultural elements within the new national body. Amidst this upheaval, national intellectuals and critics quickly perceived the need for a kind of "documentary bedrock" in which to solidify the national narrative. To achieve this bedrock, the critical reception of testimonial tended to cement together the narrating "I" and the phantasmagoric "we" of the nation for whom it spoke. Somewhere between the two extremes of author and nation, however, there existed a real if limited plurality of hands bound up in the production and reproduction of testimonial narratives—a range of disparate hands, from antiwar printers to nationalist publishers and editors. This small and polyphonic textual network was nonetheless rhetorically eclipsed and erased by the much larger community of the nation, which became the implicit subject of Greek and Turkish testimonials once they had been monumentalized and calcified through their critical reception.

This chapter, then, attempts to *decalcify* these texts, to break them down into their constituent parts, to view them not as monuments or finished products but as polyphonic and diachronic processes—processes that leave in their wake a material trail that spills across the borderscape of Greece and Turkey. In assembling these pieces, I want to restore the multiple hands and voices bound up in these testimonials and the mutual responsibility that they bear in the construction of historical truth. If readers and critics like I. M. Panagiotopoulos and İsmail Habib had isolated the word truth in the phrase "truth-telling," I argue that we can do it better justice by careful consideration of the second term—the telling—as an ongoing chain of communication, one that can occasionally bring together the most unexpected of hands, materials, and voices.

The Greco-Turkish War and Population Exchange

Writing in his diary during his military service in the Greco-Turkish War, a common soldier named Christos Karagiannis made repeated references to acts of violence against civilian populations, both Muslim and Christian. "Our superior officer," he wrote, "gives us the right to do whatever we please. Indeed, some soldiers have started doing many horrible things as reprisals [...]. Some soldiers do what the Turks do to our Greeks. An eye for an eye."* Hostilities had in fact begun earlier, during and in the wake of the First Balkan War of 1912, when the Greek, Serbian, and Bulgarian states attacked and annexed most

---

*"Ο διοικητής μας... μας δίνει το δικαίωμα να πράξουμε ό,τι βαστάει η ψυχή μας. Πράγματι, μερικοί φαντάροι άρχισαν να κάνουν πολλά έκτροπα σ' αντίποινα.... Μερικοί στρατιώτες κάνουν αυτό που κάνουν οι Τούρκοι στους δικούς μας τους Έλληνες. Οφθαλμόν αντί οφθαλμού" (Karagiannis, *Ημερολόγιον*, 134).

of Ottoman Europe. During this war, civilian populations were often the target of violence, leading to a surge of Muslim refugees into Istanbul and Anatolia from Europe. This traumatic event accelerated the radicalization of the ruling Ottoman regime, the Committee for Union and Progress (CUP), which had deposed Sultan Abdul Hamid and promised a new era of civil liberties.[3] Despite these promises, the nationalist radicalization of the regime was quick and brutal, leading to a series of policies against its own minority populations—primarily Armenians and Greeks—which reached a height during the First World War.[4] Things worsened even further with the Greek Army's occupation of Smyrna in 1919, soon expanding to the surrounding areas of Anatolia and concluding three years later with the army's irregular retreat as Kemalist forces pushed westward. These three years saw the looting of Muslim villages, the perpetration of physical and sexual violence against local Muslim populations, and several executions.[5] On the other side of the conflict, armed Muslims did much the same to local Christian populations of Anatolia, continuing and escalating systematic atrocities against Ottoman Greeks that had begun already in 1913.

The violence culminated in the final days of the conflict: as the Greek Army retreated in disarray toward the sea, it burned several Muslim villages and towns to the ground: more than 100,000 buildings were destroyed in a matter of days. As for human victims, only individual reports are available, yet the number is likely in the tens of thousands.[6] After the final withdrawal of the Greek Army, Kemalist forces entered the huge port city of Smyrna, which had been the headquarters of the Greek occupation forces and was moreover home to an immense population of Ottoman minorities. Less than five days after the Turkish entry into the city, the entire Greek and Armenian quarters were burned down, most likely by Turkish forces under Nureddin Pasha, the commander of the First Army.[7] The Muslim quarter remained untouched. Conservative estimates on the number of Greek and Armenian civilians murdered in Smyrna exceed ten thousand.[8]

Ultimately, both states agreed to the compulsory deportation and resettlement of their surviving minority populations, as described in the opening pages of this book. "Resettlement" was often an empty term, though; all too frequently, refugees were settled into nothing more than tents and shacks, some of which remained without running water or sewage for several years or even several decades, due both to limited state resources and to poor management, cronyism, and corruption.[9] Within a generation, however, the history of these displaced refugees was mobilized by nationalist discourses in Greek historiography, which created a narrative of homogenous historical loss, one that ultimately served the purpose of binding individual to nation, and nation to state. "Viewed in *retrospect*," Penelope Papailias writes, the traumatic ordeals of the refugees paradoxically became "instrumental to national redemption."[10] Borrowing heavily from the story of the Christian Passion, the discourse of suffering and redemption proved a powerful historiographic tool. Due to its ideological weight, this ordeal has remained a central locus in the national memory, narrated and re-narrated through a series of key histories, memoirs, testimonials, and novels.[11]

In Turkey, however, the Population Exchange met the opposite fate, buried beneath a semi-official silence since the founding of the Republic in 1923. Here, historical production focused its gaze on the war itself and the ultimate victory of the national army. In the wake of their victory, Kemalist loyalists quickly consolidated state power around a single-party system and within months began to implement a wave of institutional revolutions. Equally important, state entities such as the *Türk Dil Kurumu* (Turkish Language Foundation) and *Türk Tarih Kurumu* (Turkish History Foundation), as well as the vast state publishing industry, assured the state a central role in the linguistic, ideological, and material underpinnings of public discourse and national memory. These institutions paved the way for the secular Kemalist narrative that went on to dominate both historiography and literary production for decades to come. It was in every sense *year zero* of the modern Turkish narrative, in which the central motifs became victory, ethnic unity, and progress.

In this atmosphere, stories of trauma and linguistic and social difference among the Muslim refugees from Greece failed to gain access to the major media forms. While countless novels, memoirs, testimonials, histories, songs, and films over the next half century celebrated the victors of the war, the hundreds of thousands of refugees exchanged from Greece found virtually no audience for their narratives.[12] As one Exchanged Muslim from Greece confessed in an interview in 1995, "It's been over seventy years since we came here ... Until today not a single soul once came to ask us, 'How are you, what ails you?'"* Within such an atmosphere, the testimonials that found their way to print in Turkey until the end of the Cold War were almost without exception those of war heroes. Nonetheless, despite the drastically different tone between the testimonial fiction in Greek and Turkish—the one mournful, the other

---

*"Yetmiş yılı geçiyor geleli ... [Bugüne kadar] bir Allah'ın kulu gelip de 'Nasılsınız, derdiniz dermanınız var mı?' diye sormadı" (Yalçın, *Emanet Çeyiz*, 234).

celebratory—in both languages these printed books displayed a strikingly similar faith in the singular and broad representative nature of its authorial voice, in whose narrative national readers came to recognize their own as well.

A Simple, Sweet Monody

In 1929, a small Greek book under the title Ἰστορία ἑνὸς αἰχμαλώτου (A Captive's Story) was printed in Athens by the publisher Chrysostomos Giannaris. As the author Stratis Doukas admitted, the plot was simple and straightforward, narrated with equally simple and straightforward language: during the destruction of the Greek quarters of Smyrna in 1922, a Greek Orthodox Christian from Anatolia, named Nikolas Kozakoglou, is separated from his parents and imprisoned by Turkish soldiers. Along with thousands of other young Orthodox men, he is humiliated, beaten, and marched deep into the Anatolian interior in brutal "work brigades" (*amele taburları*). Escaping one night, the narrator and a friend spend many days wandering through the desolate countryside, where entire villages lie in waste. Nearing starvation, they decide to assume Muslim identities and enter Turkish society, seeking some means to make their way to the sea and secure a passage to Greece. They separate to avoid betraying one another through a slip of the tongue, but months later the narrator will hear of his friend's death by lynching, when the latter failed to perform his ablutions correctly, thereby revealing his Orthodox identity. The rest of the novella follows the adventures of the narrator, metamorphosed now into "Behçet," supposedly a Macedonian Muslim refugee from the Balkan Wars, working as a shepherd for a local landholder named Hacı Mehmet, who treats him with respect and paternal love. Indeed, Hacı Mehmet feels such a strong attachment to the narrator that he comes to offer his niece in marriage.

This marriage proposal triggers the dramatic crisis of the narrative. Though never stated outright, the proposal clearly portends "contamination," among the earliest instances of a generic trope that Vangelis Calotychos has shown to lie at the heart of most Greek-language narratives of Anatolia. "It is precisely at the moment when the protagonist is given the opportunity to marry into prosperity," Calotychos writes, "that he is obliged to defiantly resist and keep intact the integrities of family, race, country, and identity."[13] The operative word in this formula, I argue, is *integrity*, i.e., the quality of being "untouched" (*in+tangere*). Beneath the metamorphoses of the narrator there seems to lie an integral, uncontaminated core, never stated but implicitly understood by readers. In reality, though, identity is always and unavoidably "touched" by others. In building a series of social—and now, potentially familial—ties, the fictional figure of Behçet is quickly becoming a true social being, networked into a larger field of friendships and kinship alliances with their real connections and bonds. For *A Captive's Story* and its readers, the existence of more than one point of contact signals a dangerous anomaly. As Calotychos writes, "In Doukas's novel, the Greek reinstates himself because he understands the limits of 'passing' as the Other: he remains able to distinguish between sameness and difference."[14] In the latter half of this chapter, I'll return to this point and demonstrate that such borders are more difficult to determine than Doukas's story would have us believe. Here, however, I suggest that Calotychos perfectly captures the internal logic of the printed book's narrative: it raises the specter of national taboo in order to conduct its hero out of Turkey. After the marriage proposal, Behçet claims that before he can wed he must first travel to Bursa to find his own sister and bring her back. Through Hacı Mehmet's interventions, he obtains identity papers and sets out—not for Bursa but Izmir, where he boards a ship and disembarks at Mytilene. Here, after much disbelief on the part of the Greek authorities, the narrator slowly begins his second transformation, from "Behçet" to "Nikolas" again. The story ends here, and at the author's behest Nikolas places his signature in the final line of the book: "When he finished his story, I told him: Sign your name. And he wrote. *Nikolaos Kozakoglou*."*

It's important to note that up until this point the first-person voice of the book has belonged not to the author Stratis Doukas (the "I" of the quotation above) but to the captive himself, whose real name was in fact Nikolas Kazakoglou, with an "a." After some sixty pages of Nikolas's narrative voice, the intrusion of the author here in the final line is startling—an intrusion that forces moreover a third assumed identity onto the captive: neither Nikolas Kazakoglou nor Behçet Süleymanoğlu but Nikolas Kozakoglou—the literary invention of Doukas. Whose story is this, then? In his short prologue, Doukas had perhaps anticipated similar reader reactions, writing:

Ἡ ἱστορία τούτη εἶναι ἀπόχτημα μιᾶς βραδιᾶς ποὺ πέρασα σ' ἕνα χωριὸ Αἰχμαλώτων. Ἦταν μιὰν [sic] ἁπλὴ καὶ γλυκειὰ μονωδία ποὺ κυριαρχοῦσε, γιατὶ ὅλα σιωποῦσαν καὶ γι'αὐτὸ δὲ θὰ ταίριαζε οὔτε σήμερα νὰ τὴ συνοδέψω μὲ προλόγους. Ἂν ὅμως τέλος ἀποφάσισα νὰ

---

* "Ὅταν τέλειωσε, τοῦπα: Βάλε τὴν ὑπογραφή σου. Κ' ἐκεῖνος ἔγραψε. *Νικόλαος Κοζάκογλου*."

προτάξω δυὸ λόγια εἶναι νὰ διασαφηνίσω τὸ σκοπὸ ὅπου προσφέρω δημόσια καὶ καὶ [sic] μὲ τὄνομά μου τὸ ὡραῖο αὐτὸ λαϊκὸ λουλούδι τοῦ Λόγου.

This story is an acquisition from a night I spent in a village of Captives [i.e., refugees from Turkey].[15] It was a simple and sweet monody that dominated, because everything was silent and for this reason today as well it would be unbecoming to attach a prologue to this story. If, however, I've decided at last to add a few words here, it's in order to make clear my goal in offering, under my name, this beautiful folk flower of speech to the public.

We are told here that the story is "an acquisition" from a single night that the author spent in a refugee village; it's difficult, though, for me to parse out from this introduction how (or in what language) it was narrated, recorded, and reproduced, or whose story it is. Doukas's introduction transforms this story into a "monody"—i.e., a solo sung by a single voice—that dominates an environment otherwise sunk in silence. Positioning himself as nothing more than a recording device, Doukas seems to accede creative agency to the narrator Nikolas (although the word "acquisition" suggests that the story may in fact now belong to Doukas). This was the limited window that readers had into the history of the text's production for nearly half a century.

Yet is it really so simple? Drawing our attention to the parallel between narrator and author, Dimitris Tziovas has remarked that the latter "pretends to be a phonograph just as his hero pretends to be Muslim."[16] Tziovas further claims that the narrative does not represent a faithful recording but rather a reworking and reformulation at the hands of the author, "who Hellenizes and cleans the spoken word of the Turcophone protagonist." While I take issue with Tziovas's uncomplicated categorization of the witness as a Turcophone (more on this later), it's important to stress that his larger observation is groundbreaking. Doukas had indeed recreated his own version of the narrator's identity game, this time played out not in Anatolia but in the pages of a book. Just as the narrator eventually leaves his forged identity behind, reverting to "Nikolas," so too does the author set aside his mask in the final sentence, tacitly reminding readers of his mediating presence throughout the book. Juxtaposed with this authorial intervention, the introductory note's apparent cession of creative agency to the refugee Nikolas left an unresolved tension planted in the text. Who indeed was speaking here? Who was writing and rewriting? To whom did this story belong?

Critics ignored or dismissed this tension, choosing without exception to celebrate Doukas's artistry as the true creative force of the text. Yiorgos Vafopoulos, an important critic in northern Greece, wrote in 1929 that Doukas had offered "his talents in the service of a new genre that was unknown to us. Is this just a narrative? Something more. It is a wondrous model of language and style. Because, despite the cooperation of the protagonist [i.e., Nikolas Kazakoglou], the form belongs exclusively to the author. From beginning to end one perceives the hand of the artist, which invisibly carves out the riverbed in which runs the simple and crystal clear water of this folk narrative."* The form, Vafopoulos insisted, "belongs" to Doukas, for it was his hand and pen that had shaped the spoken word, directing its flow. Fotos Politis, a founding figure of modern Greek theater and prolific critic (and brother of Linos Politis, whom we met in the previous chapter), went even further:

> Τὴν ἱστορία αὐτὴ τὴν ἀληθινὴ διηγεῖται ὁ κ. Δούκας. Καὶ τὴ γράφει σὰ νὰ τὴν ἔζησε ὁ ἴδιος. . . . Δὲν πιστεύω νὰ κάθησε ὁ Νικόλας Καζάκογλου καὶ νὰ ὑπαγόρευσε, λέξη πρὸς λέξη τὴν ὀδύσσειά του στὸν κ. Δούκα. Τοῦ τὸ εἶπε κάποτε. Κι ὁ κ. Δούκας ἐπειδὴ εἶχε τὸν πόθο νὰ μπεῖ στὴν ψυχὴ τοῦ ἀφηγουμένου, ποὺ εἶναι τὸ κυριώτερο σημάδι βαθύτερου πολιτισμοῦ, . . . ἔγραψε ἔπειτα τὴν ἱστορία αὐτὴ μὲ τὴν ἴδια ψυχὴ τοῦ Καζάκογλου . . . Καὶ τοῦτος πῶς νὰ μὴν τὴν ὑπογράψει στὸ τέλος, ἀφοῦ ἔβλεπε τὸν ἑαυτό του ἀτόφιον μέσα ἐκεῖ.[17]

> This story—a true story—is narrated by Mr. Doukas. And he writes it as if he himself experienced it [. . .]. I don't believe that Nikolaos Kazakoglou sat down and dictated, word for word, his odyssey to Mr. Doukas. He told it to him once. And Mr. Doukas, because he had the craving to enter the soul of the one narrating the events, which is the main sign of a deeper culture, [. . .] later wrote this story with the very soul of Kazakoglou [. . .]. And how could he [Nikolas] not sign the story in the end, since he saw himself pure and natural within it there.

---

*"Προσφέρει τὸ ταλέντο του στὴν ὑπηρεσία ἑνὸς νέου εἴδους, ποὺ μᾶς ἦταν ἄγνωστο. Εἶναι αὐτὸ ἁπλῶς μιὰ ἀφήγηση; κάτι παραπάνου. Εἶναι ἕνα θαυμαστὸ ὑπόδειγμα γλώσσας καὶ ὕφους. Γιατὶ μ' ὅλη τὴ συνεργασία τοῦ ἥρωος, ἡ μορφὴ ἀνήκει ἀποκλειστικὰ στὸ συγγραφέα. Ἀπὸ τὴν ἀρχὴ μέχρι τέλους διακρίνει κανεὶς τὸ χέρι τοῦ λογοτέχνη, ποὺ χαράζει ἀόρατα τὴν κοίτη μέσα στὴν ὁποία τρέχει τὸ ἁπλὸ αὐτὸ καὶ γάργαρο νερὸ τῆς λαϊκῆς ἀφηγήσεως" (Vafopoulos, "Review").

In Politis's understanding, the author had in fact entered the soul of Kazakoglou and made it speak. Bearing the signs of a deeper culture, the author came to claim the story's truth as his own. Doukas "became" Kazakoglou, assuming a mask so lifelike that in fact the real Nikolas had no choice but to sign the document before his eyes. It was a document, as all critics agreed, that "pulsed with life."[18] Strangely, the more that *its* life pulsed, the fainter Kazakoglou's own pulse seemed to most readers. Indeed, at least one important fellow refugee author, Fotis Kontoglou, implicitly doubted whether Kazakoglou even had the power to read the document, calling him an "illiterate man."[19] Struggling to develop a vocabulary and critical frame for the never-before-seen genre of testimonial, critics had constructed an acute paradox: on the one hand, they reduced the agency of the witness-narrator to nothing more than the inert primary materials of an oral culture; they then went on to praise the author-artist for his skill in honing and reshaping these materials. On the other hand, the very vocabulary used to describe and laud such artistry reached back again to the original, unmediated world of the witness and his narrative: "bare and unrefined language" that was "pulsing with life," indicative of an authentic folk voice.

Even more paradoxically, as the author figure gained a monopolistic hold on the text and its production, to many readers it seemed that within his solitary voice was hiding the collective experience of millions. Writing after the release of the third edition in 1959, the prominent national literary critic Dimitris Raftopoulos crystallized this line of thought:

Ὁ ἥρωας εἶναι τόσο ἁπλός, ποὺ μοιάζει ἀπόλυτα μὲ τὸ μεγάλο ἥρωα: τὸν *ἀνώνυμο*. (Ὑπογραμμίζω αὐτὴ τὴ λέξη, γιὰ νὰ σημειώσω, μ[ὲ] τὴν εὐκαιρία, ὅτι ἕνας τέτοιος τύπος ἥρωα εἶναι καὶ πρόσωπο ποὺ ἀναγνωρίζεται εὔκολα στὴν καθημερινὴ ζωὴ καὶ σύμβολο καὶ, ἄρα, μὲ τέτοιους ἥρωες—ἔστω καὶ ἐλάχιστους ἢ μὲ μόνο ἕναν—γίνεται *λογοτεχνία μαζῶν*).[20]

The hero [Kozakoglou] is so simple that he attains an absolute resemblance to that great hero: the *anonymous hero*. (I've italicized this to note that such a type of hero is both an easily recognizable figure in daily life and also a symbol, and hence with such heroes—even just a few or just one—is created a *literature of the masses*).

Anonymized into the symbolic order, the book's narrator sublimates the experience of the nation's masses. Perhaps you'll ask: do "masses" necessarily mean the same thing as "nation"? While I can't answer decisively, the larger frame of the review implies as much. Raftopoulos writes of the national institutions whose task it should be—but, he bemoans, have failed—to form and shape the masses into a national body: "The entire superstructure of Modern Greek life—Education, public discourse, cultural institutions, Law—suffers from fragmentation, inconsistency, belatedness. If not for these chronic maladies [...], a mature literature would take root and blossom, aligned with the most vital powers of the nation."* Doukas's book, he claims, enters this barren landscape and, dramatizing "a moment of our national experience," lays down a new "law and form."† His book is able to do all of this thanks in large part to the genius of the author, who

> ἔστησε μπροστά του τὴν ἀφήγηση τοῦ ἀγράμματου μὰ τόσο ζωντανοῦ Νικόλα Κοζάκογλου, ὅπως τοποθετεῖ τὸ μοντέλλο ὁ γλύπτης ... Στὸ τέλος τὸ γλυπτὸ, ἱστορημένο πάνω σὲ σκληρὴ πέτρα, βγῆκε τελειότερο ἀπὸ τὸ φθαρτὸ πρωτότυπο.... Ὁ [συγγραφέας] βρῆκε τῆ δύναμη νὰ ἐξαφανίσει κάθε ἐγωϊστικὸ ἴχνος τοῦ φιλολογικοῦ ἑαυτοῦ του [ἀλλὰ καὶ] φθάνοντας στὸν ἀνώτερο βαθμὸ αὐτοεξαφάνισης κάθε ἄλλο παρὰ ἐξαφανίστηκε.[21]

mounted the narrative of the illiterate but lively Nikolas Kozakoglou before him, as a sculptor positions a model [...]. Ultimately, the sculpture, inscribed upon the hard stone, turned out more perfect than the perishable original [...]. [The author] found the strength to efface every egoistic trace of his philological self, [yet] by reaching the higher plane of self-effacement, he did just the opposite of efface himself.

In other words, by sculpting an anonymous story of the masses into permanent stone, Doukas had simultaneously immortalized his own name. And it was only through this name and authorship, which Raftopoulos tied to an almost nirvana-like ecstasy of self-effacement and transcendence, that the book's message was nationalized and codified. It gained a single authorial voice

---

* "Ὁλόκληρο τὸ ὑπεροικοδόμημα τῆς νεοελληνικῆς ζωῆς—Παιδεία, γλῶσσα τοῦ δημόσιου βίου, πολιτιστικοὶ θεσμοί, Δίκαιο—πάσχει ἀπὸ κατακερματισμό, ἀσυνέπεια, καθυστέρηση. Χωρὶς αὐτὲς τὶς χρόνιες ἀρρώστιες [...] θὰ μέστωνε μιὰ λογοτεχνία μὲ γερὲς ρίζες καὶ ψηλὰ βλαστάρια, στοιχημένη μὲ τὶς ζωντανότερες δυνάμεις τοῦ ἔθνους" (Raftopoulos, [Review], 70).

† "Ὁ Δούκας ἀπὸ μιὰ στιγμὴ τοῦ ἐθνικοῦ μας βίου ἔκανε ἕνα μῦθο ποὺ ... εἶναι καὶ μορφὴ καὶ νόμος" (Raftopoulos, [Review], 70).

precisely by effacing that voice (but also not effacing it) in the anonymous masses of the nation, on behalf of whom it spoke.

Product or Process?

At the end of this chapter I will provide a closer textual history of *A Captive's Story*, crafting what I hope is a compelling and inviting alternative to the "national-monument" frame developed above. Before this, however, in order to refine my tools I need to turn first to the other edge of the Aegean, looking to Halide Edib's *Ateşten Gömlek* (Shirt of Flame), the earliest and arguably most famous Turkish-language work of "testimonial fiction" from the war.

Halide Edib's oeuvre occupies a prominent position in the Turkish canon. She was a prolific writer, whose novels explored a range of fields from the domestic and social themes of her early work to the explicitly nationalist ideology of her later novels (most notably, *Shirt of Flame*) and, finally, the complex sociopolitical urban tableaux of her final period. While she was not the first woman to publish fiction in Turkish, her international distinction as a public intellectual was unprecedented for Ottoman women. And if some scholars have come to question the problematic gender norms embedded in much of her creative writing,[22] one cannot dispute that Halide Edib pushed for substantive policies like women's suffrage and educational reforms. She likewise made public declarations against the Armenian massacres in 1909 and the Armenian deportations that began the genocide in 1915, but her stance here was compromised and irreparably blemished by her participation in the forced Turkification of Armenian orphans at an Ottoman state orphanage in 1916 and her ongoing dissemination of anti-Armenian propaganda from Britain at the start of the next decade. To say the least, Halide Edib was a complicated and controversial figure.[23] In the wake of Turkish victory in 1923, she quickly pivoted to an open critique of the new Kemalist regime, which led to self-imposed exile in 1925. Within Turkey's state-dominated media landscape, her public image only partially recovered from this clash decades later, when she fully adopted the rhetorical stances of Turkish nationalism. Nonetheless, throughout her tumultuous career, her novel *Shirt of Flame* remained a cornerstone of the national literary canon, still taught today to tens of thousands of secondary-school students across Turkey—just as *A Captive's Story* is taught in secondary schools across Greece.

Like Doukas's work, *Shirt of Flame* has been enshrined as a first-hand testimonial of the war. Written by Halide Edib just days after returning from the front line and serialized before the war's conclusion, *Shirt of Flame* reads like a heated, hastily written chronicle. This haste is conveyed primarily by the pacing but also by the language, which generally favors one- or two-clause sentences. These elements have functioned for many readers as a marker of immediacy, yet the slapdash style also implies a heightened tendency toward error or omission. This feeling of haste is further encouraged by the text's supposed material form: a journal kept by the fictional narrator, Peyami, who is feverishly scribbling out a sort of last will and testament as he awaits brain surgery in a military hospital, after a wound to the head and the loss of both legs in the battle of Sakarya. Peyami had spent his youth as a Westernized Istanbul aristocrat. Capitalizing on his knowledge of foreign languages, he went on to serve as a civil servant in the Ottoman Foreign Ministry. His only contact with the world of action comes via his camaraderie with his distant relative Cemal and friend İhsan, two young officers in the military academy. Following the Greek occupation of Smyrna, Cemal's sister Ayshe flees that city, having witnessed the murder of her young son and husband by Greek soldiers. In Istanbul, her impassioned rhetoric against the occupation and in support of resistance, together with her strange beauty, draws both İhsan and Peyami into a love triangle and, eventually, the national resistance movement, set against the backdrop of the chaotic civil wars raging in Anatolia. They all flee Istanbul for the Anatolian interior, joining first guerrilla forces and, later, the Kemalist army. The remainder of the novel follows Peyami's transformation from Westernized dandy to nationalist Turk, driven by his feverish fixation (i.e., his "shirt of flame") on Ayshe, who comes to symbolize not only Smyrna but the nation. Both Ihsan and Peyami vow to win her love through an act of heroism on the field of battle, pledging to be the first to set foot in Smyrna and reclaim the city.

The implicit paradox, however, remains unspoken throughout Peyami's journal: the possession of a city is by necessity a collective enterprise, not a footrace between individual contestants. And despite his obsession with battlefield action, Peyami spends most of the war engaged in the grueling, behind-the-scenes collective labor of translation. Working in the translation and intelligence bureau—primarily, it would seem, on Greek texts—his days pass amidst print material, ink and paper. In the final months of the war, both İhsan and Ayshe are killed in the battle of Sakarya. Peyami, having heard of his friends' death and throwing himself at last into direct combat, is gravely wounded and transferred to the hospital from which he begins writing his testament in a fever, eventually dying during surgery. After his death, the novel's one-page epilogue details a conversation between the surgeons, who verify that Peyami had no friends named İhsan or Ayshe:

—O hâlde?
—Kurşunun dimâğındaki te'sîri.
İki doktor çok uzun ve fennî bir münâkaşadan sonra beyninden kurşun çıkarken ölen Peyâmi'nin ateşden gömleğine çetin ve Latince bir isim koydular.[24]

—And so?
—It was all an effect from the bullet in his brain.
The two doctors, after a very long medical debate over Peyami, who had died while the bullet was being removed from his brain, applied a harsh Latin name to his *Shirt of Flame*.

With this, the novel abruptly ends. I'll return to these unexpected final lines later, yet it's worth noting here that throughout the book's publishing history, readers often turned a blind eye to the ending and its shocking implications. Instead, they emphasized the work's supposedly direct, testimonial nature, which was planted firmly in the authorial "I" of one of Turkey's most famous writers at the time (who had, moreover, been serving at the front).

Earlier I gestured briefly to İsmail Habib's assessment of the novel in what was the first systemic survey of post–Ottoman Turkish fiction, yet even before İsmail Habib—indeed, *before the novel's release*—it was already being touted as a national monument. The editors of the newspaper *İkdam*, where Halide Edib's manuscript was first serialized, devoted a front-page ad to the work, praising it as an "exhilarating chronicle":

Güzîde muharriremiz Hâlide Edîb Hanım'ın "Ateşden Gömlek" 'ünvânı altında yazdığı ve Sakarya Ordusuna ithâf etdiği millî bir romanı yarın tefrikaya başlayacağız. Büyük edîbenin en kuvvetli eserlerinden biri olduğuna hiç şübhe etmediğimiz bu roman 'ayn-ı zamânda mütârekeden beri başımızdan geçen millî hâilelerin müheyyic bir târîhçesidir. [/] Anadolu mücâhedesinin dêstânı tam henüz yazılmadı diye üzülenler bu eserde bütün heyecân ihtiyâçlarının â'zamî bir sûretde tatmîn edildiğini göreceklerdir. [/] Hâlide Edîb Hanım'ın (Ateşden Gömleği) Anadolu şehîd ve gâzîleri nâmına edebiyât 'âlemine dikilmiş 'ulvî bir âbidedir.[25]

Tomorrow we'll begin serializing the national novel written by our prized writer Ms. Halide Edib under the name "Shirt of Flame," which she has dedicated to the army of Sakarya. This novel, which we do not doubt is one of the strongest of the great writer, is also an exhilarating chronicle of the national tragedies that have befallen us since the Armistice. [/] Those who sorrow over the fact that the epic of the Anatolian struggle has not yet been written will see all their needs for excitement satisfied in the grandest way with this work. [/] Ms. Halide Edib's *Shirt of Flame* is a sublime monument erected before the literary world in the name of the Anatolian martyrs and veterans.

For the editors of *İkdam*, Halide Edib's novel was both an "epic" (*destan*) and "chronicle" (*tarihçe*) of the immediate past and present. The choice of the two generic categories is worth brief consideration. It seems likely that the editors were using the term *destan* as a calque for the *epic* or *épopée* of the West, with its popular meaning of an adventure on the scale of the Homeric epics, but the Turkish word also has its own local genealogy whose continued resonance should be emphasized. The genre of *destan* was a medieval popular ballad of Persianate origin, which blended oral performance and written textuality. Within the Ottoman Empire, the genre survived into the twentieth century, through both handwritten commonplace books (more on this in the next chapter) and cheap printed chapbooks. To call *Shirt of Flame* a *destan*, therefore, is to locate it within a culture of collective folk narration. Yet to tie it simultaneously to the more elite genre of chronicle, which was a product of the Ottoman court, is to bind it to a regime of author-centric historiography, which the editor of *İkdam* further aggrandizes, in his final line, as an actual "monument." Tied to both these genres, the work had one foot in the realm of a monumentalized authority and another in that of an anonymous textual collective.

This duality remained invisible in critical reactions to the novel, which prioritized the author's hand as the formative force. What's more, popular critics celebrated in growing numbers the novel's supposed testimonial immediacy. The influential literary critic Fethi Naci, in a summary of twentieth-century Turkish literature, wrote of the work: "Most novels whose subject is the Liberation War have been written based upon the research of those who did not experience it. Halide Edib however is an author who participated in the war; who lived the war with all its pain and sorrow and in 1922, still in the heat of the moment, wrote *Shirt of Flame*. *Shirt of Flame* is Halide Edib's testimonial; its success and strength come from this testimonial."* Written "in the heat of

---

* "Kurtuluş Savaşı üzerine yazılan romanların çoğu, bu savaşı yaşamayanların araştımalara dayanarak yazdıkları romanlardır. Oysa Halide Edib Adıvar, Kurtuluş Savaşı'na katılmış bir yazar; savaşı bütün acısıyla, üzüntüsüyle yaşamış ve *Ateşten Gömlek'i*, 1922 yılında, sıcağı sıcağına

the moment," Naci tells us, the novel is inseparable from direct lived experience. The eminent novelist Selim İleri has more recently reinforced this rhetoric. In his afterword to the novel's most recent edition, he avers that the work functions as an internal witness (*içten tanıktır*) to the war. Azade Seyhan has likewise remarked that "it is the documentary and journalistic aspects of the novel [...] that lend the story its enduring power. [...] This novel succeeds not only in terms of journalistic observation but also as a poetic biography of a nation."[26] That is to say, not only does Halide Edib's novel collapse literature and the documentary into one another; in doing so, Seyhan argues, it simultaneously collapses the individual and the national collective into one.

There is much in the plot that corroborates this rhetoric, paralleling Halide Edib's own lived experience. In 1920, she had escaped English-occupied Istanbul and passed into the Anatolian interior, serving first as director of the Anatolian Agency, later as an interim nurse (June 1921), and finally (August 1921 to the end of the war) as an enlisted soldier behind the front lines, where she worked translating foreign-language print material that was circulating in Turkey. Her novel appeared in the Istanbul paper *İkdam* as a daily serial from June to August 1922, just as the Greek front broke. It's not unlikely that these close parallels between life and text encouraged the novel's first urban readers to treat the work as an immediate window into the distant, confused events in Anatolia.

In an interview with Ruşen Eşref Ünaydın a year before the war, Halide Edib had already claimed for her novels a similarly immediate power. They were, she said, as unmediated as her spoken word—if not more so:

—[Yazarken kelimelerimi] hiç aramam. Konuştuğumdan daha kolay yazarım.
　—Tabii sonra tekrâr gözden geçirir ve düzeltirsiniz; kelimelerinize ve cümlelerinize son, kat'î bir şekil verirsiniz!
　—Pek az okur, pek de az düzeltirim, 'aşk efsâneleri gibi yazılarım arasında en düzgün olanlarını bile bir daha okumam.[27]

—[While writing] I don't search at all for words. I write more easily than I speak.
　—Of course, afterwards, you look it over and you correct it, right? You give a final, definite form to your words and sentences!
　—I read my writing very little, I correct it very little; as for the smoothest pieces of my writing, like the romances, I don't look them over ever again.

---

yazmış. *Ateşten Gömlek*, Halide Edib'in tanıklığı; başarısı ve gücü bu tanıklıktan geliyor" (Naci, *Yüz Yıl*, xviii).

Ünaydın editorialized this confession in a rather blunt and unflattering way, writing that "Miss Halide has no concern to give her readers chic, pretty sentences, sentences that have finished putting on their makeup and fixed their clothes! [...] Given her inadequacy with words, she's not about to go carving diamonds."* This complaint, that Halide Edib's desertion of her editorial duties led to sloppy, broken sentences, would be repeated by subsequent critics. Yet Halide Edib had distanced herself from editorial labor with a certain sense of pride. Moreover, she claimed that, like Peyami, she entered into a sort of "passionate fever" when writing.† Once the manuscript had been sent to the printer, her finished works became useless to the author: "From the moment that I write and finish my works, in my view they have no value. Because once that spiritual passion within me materializes it has lost its significance. Like a snake that sheds its skin, I don't look at my previous work. I really want to remain foreign to them. Quite a large portion of my writings have in this way been lost to me."‡ What did it mean for Halide Edib to "lose" those pieces of writing that had been published? Her inner passion, once materialized on the printed page, was cemented and immobilized. To lose it meant not to destroy it but to abandon the work to readers. Foregoing the labor of editing and revision, Halide Edib treated her writing much like the spoken word: immediate, irreversible, and fleeting. But inevitably it *didn't* flee; it was printed, bound and circulated, reprinted and recirculated. And in never returning to her past writing, Halide Edib was not abandoning it solely to readers, but to editors, printers, publishers, and anthologists, who may have proved less reluctant to edit the text. To get a sense of this, we need look no further than the novel's first edition, serialized in the paper *İkdam*. As the paper was produced in occupied Istanbul, it was not infrequent that sentences or even entire paragraphs were censored by the Ottoman and British authorities (see figures 6 and 7).

The question then arises: why would Halide Edib, who was herself in Ankara, choose to serialize the work in occupied Istanbul, surrendering it to the scissors of the censors? While her primary motive must have been *İkdam*'s

---

* "Hâlide Hanım da biz kâri'lere, öyle tuvaletlerini bitirmiş, kıyâfetlerini düzeltmiş süslü, şık cümleler vermek merâkında değil! [...] kelimeler özründe koyumculuk etmeyor" (Ünaydın, *Diyorlar ki*, 173).

† "Rûhumda [yazdığım] eser ihtirâslı bir hummâ olur" (Ünaydın, *Diyorlar ki*, 175).

‡ "Eserlerimi de yazup bitirdiğim andan 'itibâren artık onlar bence kıymeti hâ'iz değildir. Çünki içimdeki rûhânî ihtirâs mâddîleşince artık ehemmiyeti kalmayor. Kabuğunu değişdiren bir yılan gibi eskisine bakmayorum bile. O kadar onlara yabancı kalmak isterim. Yazılarımın epey bir kısmı böyle gayb olup gitmişdir" (Ünaydın, *Diyorlar ki*, 177).

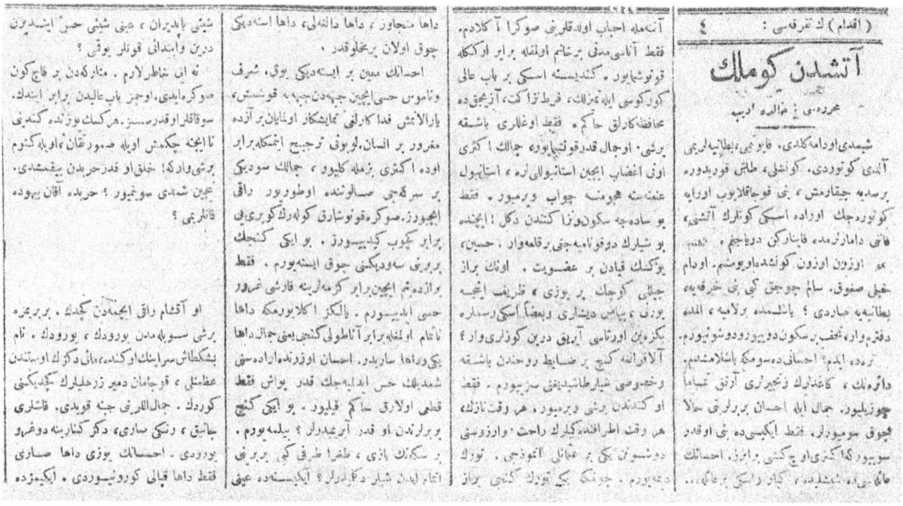

(اقدام) ك تفرقه‌سی : ٤

آتشدن کوملك

FIGURE 6. A sample (the fourth installment) of *Ateşten Gömlek*'s serialization in the newspaper *İkdam*. Copyright Can Publishing House; digital facsimile courtesy of Atatürk Kitaplığı and the İstanbul Büyükşehir Belediyesi Library and Museum Directorate. Notice the large gap in the fourth column, indicative of censorship. The lines immediately above the censored space read: “Halk o kadar harbden bıkmışdı. Niçin şimdi sevinmiyor? Harbde akan bîhûde kanları mı?” (*The people had grown so tired of war. Why aren't they happy [now that the Armistice has been signed]? Is it their blood, spilled in vain during the war [that saddens them]?*). Compare this with the passage in figure 7, taken from the bound book, published a year later (after the British occupation had been dissolved).

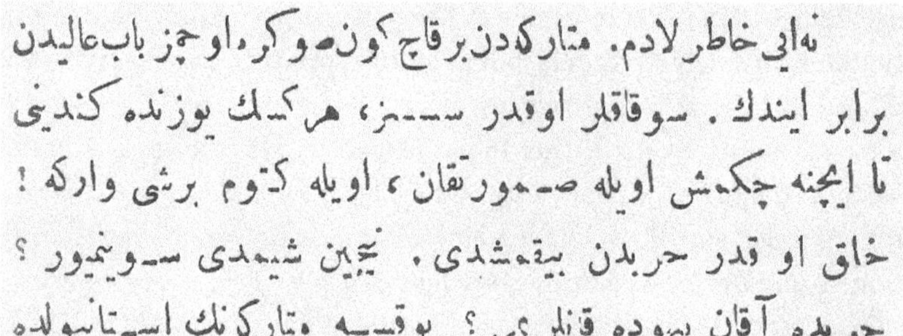

نه ایی خاطرلادم. متارکه‌دن برقاچ کون صوکره اوچز باب عالیدن
برابر ایندك . سوقاقلر اوقدر سسسز، هرکسك یوزنده کندینی
تا ایچنه چکمش اوبله صمورتقان، اوبله کتوم برشی وارکه !
خلق او قدر حربدن بیقمشدی . نیچین شیمدی سوینمیور ؟
حربده آقان بیهوده قانلری ؟ یوقسه متارکه‌نك استانبولده
قاریشدیراجغی، صاچه‌جغی داخلی چیرکفی ، دشیله‌جك اسكی،
قوقمش یارالرك آقیداجغی جراحتیمی دوشونیور ؟

FIGURE 7. As we see here, the passage quoted in figure 6 in fact continues as follows: “yoksa Mütârekenin İstanbul'da karışdıracağı, saçacağı dâhilî çîrkefi, deşilecek eski, kokmuş yaraların akıdacağı cerâhati mi düşünüyor?” (*Or are they thinking of the inner filth that the Armistice is going to mix up and spread across Istanbul, the puss that is to spill from old, fetid wounds, about to be re-opened?*). The sentence, missing from the serial, luridly attacks the postwar British occupation, and was removed by state censors. Similar redactions are present throughout the serialized edition. Copyright Can Publishing House; digital facsimile courtesy of University of Toronto Libraries.

massive print run and the promise of reaching the city's large readerships, one might also be tempted to imagine that such a newspaper was the only available venue, i.e., that beyond Istanbul there was a general material dearth of print. Such an assumption, however, would do a disservice to the region's rich and complex wartime print ecology. It was an ecology in which a small but vastly important body of anti-imperialist print material was in fact circulating in the language that Peyami was translating within the novel: *Greek*. This Greek material, which I'll detail in the next section, is the only reference within *Shirt of Flame* to the vast and multiform anti-imperialist print circulating in Anatolia. Halide Edib's decision to bypass the geographically dispersed print networks of Anatolia for the centralized but censored newsprint of occupied Istanbul likely reflected a desire for both a mainstream audience and textual fixity, yet lurking in the margins of her story was a surprisingly multilingual landscape of antiwar print.

Antiwar Print Networks

In the early stages of the conflict, central Anatolia's main newspaper and printing apparatus was *Öğüd*, which was produced in Konya.[28] Italian authorities made a half-hearted raid on the printing house, yet they simultaneously sent word the previous day to the editor in chief, allowing the printers to load a small pedal press and three boxes of typeset onto a car and relocate.[29] The next day, the main press was seized by the Italians. Working clandestinely with the most primitive means, the staff now changed the paper's name to *Nasihat* (meaning more or less the same thing as "öğüd": *admonition*) but maintained the same issue numbering. As Mehmet Önder writes, "Because its press was pedal-operated, the publication's length had shrunk. The paper was of poor quality. Packaging paper, sometimes white, sometimes yellow or green, which had been gathered from the halva stores in the market, was trimmed and used as newspaper."* Nonetheless, despite the lack of material and the inadequate hand press that produced it, the paper remained wildly popular. After the Italians were forced to evacuate, *Nasihat* returned to Konya and reverted to *Öğüd*. By the summer of 1921, its press had relocated to Ankara, whose material resources allowed newsprint

---

* "Ne var ki, pedalla basıldığı için boyu küçülmüştü. Kağıt iyi değildi. Konya çarşısındaki helvacı dükkânlarından kimi beyaz, kimi sarı veya yeşil ambalaj kağıtları toplanmış, bunlar kesilmiş, gazete kağıdı olarak kullanılmıştı" (Önder, *Milli mücadelenin yanında*, 14).

(such as *Hakimiyet-i Milliye*) to reach a run of 2,000 to 3,000 copies. From here, *Öğüd* quickly made inroads in Istanbul as well, where it established a clandestine circulation.[30] To meet the large demand of this new reading public, as the editor in chief recalled, "sometimes we worked the press twenty-four hours nonstop—even we the staff writers—turning it with our hand breathlessly, bathed in blood and sweat."* Moreover, as the struggle wore on, it was joined by other titles, printed in other centers of Anatolia; and despite their outdated materials and means of production, many of them reached a run of several hundreds.[31]

Virtually unknown outside of specialist research today, a small number of Greek-language presses were also producing materials in opposition to the occupying Greek Army. Working from within occupied Istanbul, Ahmet Hilali, a Cretan Muslim whose first language was Greek, translated Turkish texts into Greek. He also entered into contact with a local Greek-language press—again, within Istanbul—and arranged for the printing of his manuscripts. During each print run, he edited the proofs before passing them along to be smuggled to Ankara. Hilali's colleague Ahmet Cemaleddin Saraçoğlu, writing after the war, asks a pointed question: "I wonder whether those who make fun of Ahmet Hilali's glaring Cretan accent are aware of the incalculable service, at risk of his life, that this Turkish newsman, who may speak Turkish a little tortuously but writes it very cleanly, rendered to the national struggle, all thanks to his language knowledge."† Saraçoğlu's final phrase—"language knowledge"—is a euphemism for Hilali's mother tongue, Greek, which the former goes out of his way to avoid stating explicitly.

Hilali was only one point in a larger network—one that reached in fact to Athens. For in addition to his translations from Turkish, Hilali also excerpted texts from the Athenian newspaper Ριζοσπάστης (*Rizospastis*, i.e., Radical), a socialist periodical that by 1920 had adopted an openly antiwar position. As early as October 1919, its editor Yannis Petsopoulos was already calling for the

---

*"Baskı makinasını bazı zamanlar hiç durmaksızın 24 saat aralıksız ve bizzat kendimiz, kanter içinde, soluk soluğa kol çevirmek suretiyle çalıştırırdık" (quoted in Önder, *Milli mücadelenin yanında*, 24).

†"Onun pek bariz Giritli aksanını vesile ederek kendisine takılanlar acaba Türkçeyi biraz çetrefil konuşan, lâkin çok temiz bir Türkçe yazan bu pek kıymetli Türk gazetecisinin bu lisan bilgisi sayesinde Millî Mücadelede millî davaya yaptığı (hayatı pahasına) kıymet bilçilmez hizmetlerin farkında mıdırlar?" (Saraçoğlu, *Gazeteler*, 165).

Greek state to abrogate martial law and its asphyxiating censorship regime, writing that "the wartime has for Greece long since come to an end. The Turkish question is not among those that Greece can solve by force of arms."* The paper's antiwar position grew more pronounced over the following two years (by war's end, Petsopoulos had been imprisoned *thirteen* times for the antiwar contents of his publication). The paper's criticisms often came with a heavy dose of satire. On New Year's Day of 1921, the paper "celebrated" the fact that the Greek Army had advanced to the Baghdad railway:

> Τὸ χθεσινὸν πολεμικὸν ἀνακοινωθὲν ἀναγγέλλει ὅτι μία πτέρυξ τῶν ἑλληνικῶν στρατευμάτων ἔφτασε μέχρι τῆς σιδηροδρομικῆς γραμμῆς τῆς Βαγδάτης. Δὲν πρέπει μὲ κανένα τρόπον νὰ σταματήση, κ. Ράλλη! Νὰ προχωρήση ἐμπρός. Πρὸς... τὴν Βαγδάτην! Αὐτὸ ἐπιβάλλει ἡ ἔνδοξος ἱστορία τοῦ ἑλληνικοῦ ἔθνους. Κατοικεῖ δὲ ἐκεῖ καὶ κάποιος [δυσανάγνωστο] Ἕλλην, τὸν ὁποῖον ἔχομεν ἐθνικὴν ὑποχρέωσιν νὰ ἀπελευθερώσωμεν!³²

> Yesterday's announcement from the war department makes known that a wing of the Greek forces reached the Baghdad railway. It should by no means stop here, Mr. Prime Minister! It should keep moving forward to... Baghdad! Such is the mandate of the glorious history of the Greek nation. There is also some Greek guy in residence there, whom we have a national obligation to liberate!

Two weeks later, the journal continued its satire, writing that the Prime Minister "seeks a measure for the annexation of Baghdad to the Kingdom of Greece, on the grounds that one enslaved Greek family has been residing there since the dawn of time."† The newspaper's stance was remarkable, particularly when compared with the Socialist Labor Party of Greece (SEKE) and the relative silence it maintained until almost the final phase of the war. This silence stemmed in part from what Philip Carabott describes as "the government's campaign of terror and intimidation. Leading members were

---

*"Ἡ ἐμπόλεμος κατάστασις ἔληξε καὶ διὰ τὴν Ἑλλάδα πρὸ πολλοῦ... [Τὸ] τουρκικὸν ζήτημα δὲν εἶνε ἀπὸ ἐκεῖνα, τὰ ὁποῖα ἡ Ἑλλὰς θὰ λύση διὰ τῶν ὅπλων" (*Ριζοσπάστης*, October 6, 1919; cited in Carabott, "Greek 'Communists,'" 106).

†"Ζητεῖ ὅπως ληφθῆ μέτρον καὶ ἡ Βαγδάτη περιληφθῆ εἰς τὸ Ἑλληνικὸν Βασίλειον, διότι κατοικεῖ ἐκεῖ ἀπὸ παλαιοτάτων χρόνων μιὰ ὑπόδουλος ἑλληνικὴ οἰκογένεια" (*Ριζοσπάστης*, January 15, 1921).

imprisoned or exiled and militant trade unionists ruthlessly crushed."[33] Ironically, the entire party leadership was imprisoned and charged with treason in July 1922—not for anything the party itself had undertaken but for articles printed in *Rizospastis*. In every sense, it was not the political organ of the Greek left per se but rather its print apparatus, and the local strikes and protests that this print helped coordinate, that served as the antiwar engine in Greece. Supposedly a mere mouthpiece of the party, print had in fact moved to the vanguard.

Already in 1919, the Greek Army in Anatolia had proscribed the newspaper and was strictly policing its circulation among soldiers at the front. At the same time, conscripted soldiers at the front made their own weekly "trench newspapers," twenty or so in number, which they reproduced by mimeograph. The papers were then circulated within the particular corps in which they had been produced, serving as a medium for gossip, satire, and complaints. To be sure, censorship was omnipresent at the front and the "trench newspapers" generally maintained a relatively apolitical stance, though some did veer too far to the left and were quickly censored—and their editors were court-martialed.[34] One such case was Yiorgis Nikolis, who produced *Φούντα* (*Tuft*). Having grown up in poverty, Nikolis had early embraced Marxist revolution and used the trench paper as a means, as much as was possible under the oversight of his commanders, to spread antiwar sentiment.[35]

Another, more direct wing of Greek antiwar print material, however, were the internationalist pamphlets and papers printed and copied by embedded Greek communists.[36] They had infiltrated the army itself, both among the rank-and-file soldiers at the front (such as Nikolis) and at key telegraph operation centers (such as Pantelis Pouliopoulos). These decentralized cells used their positions "to enlighten the soldiers as to the true nature of the war and to distribute anti-war material to the front [...] [attacking] the imperialist nature of the campaign and prepar[ing] the people for the imminent 'revolution.'"[37] In addition to their own materials, communists also distributed illicit copies of *Rizospastis* from Athens and the even more radical *Φωνή του εργάτη* (*The Worker's Voice*) from Salonica, printed by a united front of Greek Orthodox and Jewish trade unionists.[38] The historian Mete Tunçay has recognized the important contribution of these leftists, writing:

> Türk ve Müslüman olmayan bu Yunan Komünistlerinin Türk işçilerine, fakir halkına, Harb-i Umumî içinde, zavallı halka ekmek yerine çamur yedirerek karınlarını ve kasalarını şişiren Türk ve Müslüman tüccar mebuslar-

dan ve bütün harp zenginlerinden ve ordu müteahhitlerinden elbet daha çok faydası dokunmuştur.[39]

These Greek communists, who were neither Turkish nor Muslim, benefited Turkish workers and the poor much more than the Turkish and Muslim bourgeoisie politicians, black marketeers and military contractors, who made the poor eat mud instead of bread, filling their coffers.

The material that these conscripted communists circulated ranged from printed pamphlets to journals to newsprint,[40] much of it produced not in Greece but in the occupied territories of Anatolia. One such case was the Κόκκινος Φρουρός (*Red Guard*), produced illegally in Smyrna by Greek leftists embedded in the telegraph corps (they reproduced the paper clandestinely through the corps' own mimeograph). But they were not alone; they were also in direct contact with the Ottoman Greek and Turkish socialists of Smyrna.[41]

The anti-imperialist print of the Greek left proved extremely effective. Considering that many of the conscripted Greek soldiers had been mobilized and at war since 1912, it reached a highly receptive audience, leading to a series of "strikes" at the front and a growing wave of desertions, which precipitated the general collapse of the front. One officer in the censorship bureau complained of the widespread effectiveness of "a certain booklet circulating among the conscripts [that] was full of [...] seemingly reasonable but anti-nationalist exhortations," such as, "What do you expect in this inhospitable country of Afyon, where there's no trace of Hellenism? Think of your fatherless family. Turn your rifles not against the Turk, who is defending his hearth, but against him who has been coercing you to fight for ten years now."* Historians caution that outright calls for physical violence were rare; the core mode of resistance being advocated was work stoppage or desertion.[42] Even so, some of my readers may balk at such print material. Did it not in fact aid the Kemalist war effort, responsible for its own share of attrocities? Did it not indirectly contribute to the mass refugee crisis? I think that the answer is complicated but unavoidably yes. I am not untroubled by this fact and, more generally, by this war, in which

---

* "Βιβλιάριόν τι κυκλοφοροῦν μεταξὺ τῶν ἐφέδρων [τὸ ὁποῖο] ἦτο πλῆρες ... εὐλογοφανῶν καὶ ἀντεθνικῶν παρακινήσεων" ... "Τί περιμένεις εἰς τὴν ἄξενον αὐτὴν χώραν τοῦ Ἀφιόν ὅπου δὲν ὑπάρχει ἴχνος Ἑλληνισμοῦ; Σκέψου τὴν ὀρφανεμένην φαμίλλα σου. Στρέψε τὰ ὅπλα σου ὄχι κατὰ τοῦ Τούρκου, ὁ ὁποῖος ἀμύνεται ὑπέρ τῆς ἑστίας του, ἀλλὰ κατ' ἐκείνου, ὅστις σὲ ἐκβιάζει νὰ πολεμᾶς ἐπὶ 10 χρόνια" (Spyridonos, Πόλεμος, 224; cited in Carabott, "Greek 'Communists,'" 112).

all belligerent parties were ethically compromised in some way and few or no civilians were untouched by violence. Perhaps, though, withholding one's labor from the war effort of both sides may have been the least worst option. Regardless of our judgment, though, it remains a fact that the print landscape of Anatolia was a complex battleground—one where the alphabet and language of any given press or mimeograph by no means determined the political alignment of its impressions.

That brings me back to *Shirt of Flame*, and I hope you haven't lost sight of Peyami in the crowd. As I already mentioned, his job for much of the novel is that of a translator, sifting through print material, and indeed he makes a passing reference to the Greek-language paper *Rizospastis*. In fact, Peyami confesses that he *habitually spends all his daylight hours working on it*, even as he immediately drops the reference and leaves it uncontextualized.[43] The entire network that I've sketched out above, reaching from Athens to Anatolia, lies condensed in a single sentence within the novel. Striving for an act of individual heroism that will win the love of Ayshe, Peyami scorns the collective (and polyglot) labor that lies behind the production, reading, analysis, translation, and reproduction of this print material, rarely deigning to write of the work in his testament. If the work of Greek leftists has today been entirely forgotten by the Turkish state narrative, the primary cause of such amnesia can be understood easily enough by a glance at Peyami's testimonial, where collectivist socialism is edited out and replaced with ethno-nationalism.

Textual Pluralities in *Shirt of Flame*

Peyami's own narrative, though, was pulling in different directions, fraying at the seams. He repeatedly questions the cohesion and reliability of his own individual voice. His doubts begin to surface as early as the first chapter:

> Doktor ne dedi? Başımdaki kurşun bende hayâlât yapıyormuş. 'Çıkarınız!' diyorum. Beyâz gömleğinin kollarına ciddî ciddî bakıyor. Bacaklarımı keseli daha kaç ay oldu? Yatağımın alt tarafı gülünç bir sûretde boş. Kurşun çıkarsa kafam da boşalır diye mi çıkarmıyorlar, ne bileyim? Belke başımdakileri çıkarup beni yalnız bırakmamak için kafamdaki kurşuna dokunmayorlar. [. . .] başımdan geçenlerin hepsi doğru. Belke de ba'zıları değil; fakat ne zararı var?[44]

> What did the doctor say? The bullet in my head is giving me illusions. "Well, take it out then!" I say. He looks solemnly at the arms of his white

shirt. How many months has it been since they cut off my legs? The bottom half of my bed is ridiculously empty. Is it the fear that, if the bullet comes out, my head too will empty out that keeps them from removing it? Who knows. Perhaps they don't dare lay a finger on the bullet so as not to take out all those who are in my head, leaving me all alone. [...] Everything that I've experienced is true. Well, perhaps some of it isn't true; but what's the harm in that?

The bullet, functioning both literally and figuratively as a cork, secures and shores up Peyami's entire cosmos inside his head. Confined to the stifling limits of this "I," however, Peyami's world has likely become corrupted by brain fever. The passage deftly plays "inside" against "outside," individual against collective, yet something seems to gnaw at these binaries from within. A rising wave of doubt suggests that the shared experiences of Peyami and his comrades are but so many phantasms of the former's febrile ego.

In the final two sentences of the excerpt, Peyami both asserts and immediately retracts the factual correctness of his text, and he will return to this doubt with growing urgency in later portions of the testament. From time to time Peyami pauses, revisiting his manuscript notes or his memory in the increasingly dim hope of uniting the multiple threads. "I tried to read my last notes," he confesses. "At first I couldn't understand a thing, but slowly a lukewarm memory awoke."* The text itself appears foreign, awaking only tepid memories after the reader's extended engagement. At another point, Peyami uses his manuscript as a metaphor for memory, suggesting that "in my story [...] there's a burnt page"—a lacuna that often seems in danger of expanding. In the face of this possibility he can only write, "I don't want to believe such a thing, for then I must doubt the other things, even myself."† This self is slowly unraveling into an uneasy plurality, as the early excerpt above had already foreshadowed. Preparing for the final section of his narrative, Peyami writes, "That thing called 'I' is composed of a number of people in my head and their remembrances. The more I narrate these, the more my head empties out and I slowly bring myself to its end."‡ Much of Peyami's story remains, as he writes

---

* "Son notlarımı okumağa çalışdım. Evvelâ bir şey anlamadım, fakat yavaş yavaş içimde ılık bir hâtıra uyandı" (Halide Edib, *Ateşden Gömlek*, 101).

† "Hikâyemde bir [...] yanık sahîfe var. [...] Böyle bir şeye inanmak istemem, sonra ötekilerden, hatta kendimden şübhe ederim" (Halide Edib, *Ateşden Gömlek*, 158).

‡ "Ben denilen şey başımdaki birkaç sîmâ ve onların hâtıralarından 'ibâret. Bunları anlatdıkça boşalup yavaş yavaş bitiyorum" (Halide Edib, *Ateşden Gömlek*, 169).

later, "behind curtains." And what little we do see is performed piecemeal by a multitude of actors, the sum of whom composes the "I" that in turn composes the pages. But rather than gaining flesh and blood, this multitude remains mere phantoms. The testimonial "I" is not borne up by its national "we"; rather, the national "we" is sinking down into a quickly deteriorating "I." Ultimately, it dies and cedes the stage to the two surgeons, whose dialogue is in fact the only one within the book to take place in real time, beyond the margins of the testament.

This returns us, then, to the question of the ending. How to understand its powerful reversal? Erdağ Göknar provides one possible reading: Peyami's feverish hallucination represents "a struggle of intellect, imagination, and authorship in the construction of the national self/subject."[45] That Peyami has imagined all of this, Göknar argues, should not trouble us: it's a model of the national imagining that all readers are now invited to conduct. This reading has several virtues, not the least of which is its diffusion of the narrative tensions that build throughout the text. It allows us, in other words, to read the novel as a uniform, unproblematic endorsement of the nation-state— something that Halide Edib herself likely intended. I readily acknowledge *Shirt of Flame*'s deeply problematic position vis-à-vis the nation-state, as Göknar argues, yet I don't want to lose sight of the novel's unresolved tensions and their potentially productive value. Rather than disarming the conclusion's reversal, my own preference would be to understand it as a kind of "deauthorization" of the testimonial: the testimonial's claim to unmediated and authorial truth-telling collapses under the pressure of the text.

Having lost this authoritative center, readers are left, on the one hand, with an immediate, fiery material that, as İnci Enginün has written, was "truly experienced" (*gerçekten yaşanılmış*)[46] and, on the other hand, a series of intermediary media that reassemble, reprocess, and convey that experience, from the bullet and fever in Peyami's brain to the doctors who diagnose it, from the pen and paper in his hands to the printed book that readers hold in theirs. And between these two poles lie the multiple hands that hypothetically recover his manuscript and remediate it. This chain of remediation renders the experience into a different kind of collective experience, one that belongs not to an entire nation but to a specific network of readers, editors, translators, and printers.

Unfortunately, Peyami never speaks at length of the intricacy and complexity of the media and fellow translators with whom he works for most of the war. Reading, translation, and remediation take up most of his days yet find almost no space in his testimonial, perhaps because they stand in opposition to the individual heroism toward which he strives. Peyami repeatedly complains of the "bundles of yellow paper in [his] office," which impede him from direct action. Writing of his appointment to the Kemalist defense ministry and his ongoing work as a pen-pusher, he bemoans the "paper, paper, paper! [...] There's a thick curtain between real life and me; and behind that curtain are [those at the warfront]!"* It is the physical paper through which Peyami makes his living that seems to keep him from living his dream of heroism. His attempts to write his way into heroism prove a constant frustration, so much the more so for his first readers, who were even further distanced by the "thick curtain" of Istanbul newsprint, which was indiscreetly passed through the hands of state censors before it reached publication each day.

And while later editions (and their readers) escaped the censor's scissors, they did not escape the pens of editors, who implemented a series of important alterations over successive decades. The most obvious change in the second edition of 1937 was that of the alphabet, shifting from Ottoman script to the new Latin-based script. The novel's third edition, which coincided with its eighth printing and was published in 1968, after Halide Edib's death, was drastically revised by its editor, Baha Dürder. Now all vocabulary deemed excessively "non-Turkish" (i.e., Arabic or Persian) was replaced with Turkish equivalents—which were, however, only rough equivalents. The narrator's voice was thus further Turkified and, in the process, blunted and distorted.

This was in fact common editorial practice during the period and, moreover, marked the effects of the final and most destructive phase of the Turkish Language Reforms. The Reforms had begun in 1928 with the script revolution, i.e., the prohibition of the Ottoman alphabet and the transition to the Latinized script. But they did not end here; they continued from the level of the alphabet to the word. With the radicalized agenda of the First Language Congress of 1932, the regime finalized its declaration of war against what Mustafa Kemal Atatürk himself identified as "the yoke of foreign languages."[47] Embarking on a project of purification, the central committee of the Language Congress set about collecting words from ordinary people. Nonetheless, the project's collection process was unsurprisingly top-down and regimented by regime officials.[48] The result was the *Osmanlıcadan Türkçeye Söz Karşılıkları: Tarama Dergisi* (*The Survey Journal: Word Equivalents from Ottoman to Turkish*). The journal functioned as a kind of ad hoc thesaurus, by which some 7,000 words

---

*"Kâğıd, kâğıd, kâğıd!. [...] Benimle hakîkî hayât arasında kalın bir perde var ve o perdenin arkasında onlar [cephedekiler]!" (Halide Edib, *Ateşden Gömlek*, 173).

of Arabic and Persian origin were sentenced to death by drowning in a deluge of 30,000 purist Turkish words, aligned in often arbitrary categories. And it bears noting that the "death" was hardly metaphorical, as newspapers had been forbidden to use Arabic or Persian words for which substitutes had been supplied. The excesses of the project did not take long to reveal themselves, and the speed and depth of the reforms were diminished after 1935.[49] Yet they were never reversed. And as editors in subsequent decades returned to Ottoman or early Republican texts, preparing them as Latinized "reprints," they often effected their own purification of the text at hand.

Halide Edib's novel was not simply shedding Persian and Arabic words, though. In both the 1937 and 1968 editions, editorial changes reached deeper, effecting basic semantic and ideological alterations, a practice that gained common currency in Turkey.[50] Already in 1937, the word "Greek" vanished from the text, now replaced with a vague "enemy." For example, where the 1923 edition had printed, "Come on, Nurse Ayshe, let's kick those Greek bastards out of Anatolia together!,"* the 1937 edition now printed instead "those enemy bastards" (*düşman keratalarını*). Similar "enemies" could now be found throughout the text, in spaces once occupied by the now-displaced "Greeks."

Who made the emendations? Halide Edib had been in exile since 1926 and was not present during the printing of the 1937 edition. For the duration of Atatürk's life, Halide Edib remained abroad, continuing her career (now primarily in English) in England and then France, with lecture trips to the United States and India. She returned to Turkish-language publications only in 1935, near the end of Atatürk's life, when she translated her English-language novel *The Clown's Daughter* into Turkish (as *Sinekli Bakkal*), which was serialized in Turkey and published in book-bound form the following year. It became a great success and likely instigated the reprint of *Shirt of Flame* the following year (1937). This latter was printed by the schoolteacher-turned-publisher Ahmet Halit Yaşaroğlu, most of whose works had been alphabet primers and children's books. How did Ahmet Halit come upon Halide Edib's novel? Did he base his edition on a revised manuscript or the 1923 printed edition? Who made the emendations and removed, among other things, all Greeks from the text? To what extent did Halide Edib herself have a hand? Given the fact that she was in communication with Turkish publishers for *Sinekli Bakkal*, it is certainly possible that Halide Edib herself made the emendations and mailed the manuscript to Turkey, where it was transcribed into the new script. None-

---

Haydi bakalım Hemşire 'Âyşe, bu Yunan keratalarını beraber atmayacak mıyuz!

theless, in the absence of definitive evidence, the answers to these questions—by no means idle, when one takes into account that they pertain to the novel's first Latin-alphabet edition, which went on to constitute a pseudo-*Urtext* for subsequent editions—remain for the moment unanswered, if not unanswerable.

Whoever made the changes, they reflect a broader trend in the early Kemalist regime: whitewashing or silencing historical differences with Greeks rather than openly discussing them.[51] The policy was largely abandoned after mid-century as tensions over Cyprus and the Greek minority of Istanbul became increasingly politicized. By 1968, almost five years after Halide Edib's death, Greco-Turkish tensions were immense. It seems likely therefore that if the editor and publishers of the third edition that year had bothered to consult the first edition of 1923, they would have gladly reverted back to the "Greek bastards" patiently waiting there in the Ottoman script. The fact that the changes of the second edition remained in place suggests that each editor simply consulted the novel's previous printing without digging further into its deeper textual strata. In any case, the central point I aim to make is this: decade by decade, the novel was being subtly rewritten by a chain of hands, from writer to editor to publisher to printer.

In 2007, as if sensing a looming abyss at the end of this chain, the publisher Can Yayınları produced a new edition that aimed to put a halt to the work's transformations. After at least sixty years of successive editorial interventions, the latest *Shirt of Flame* announced its return to textual roots. In a brief editorial introductory note, the Ottoman literary historian Mehmet Kalpaklı remarked,

> Zamanın gazetecilik ve matbaacılık teknikleri nedeniyle bu ilk basımlarda pek çok basım hataları oluşmuştur [...] Son yıllara kadar yapılmış yeni harfli, sadeleştirilmiş baskılar, eski harfli baskıların hatalarını sürdürmüşler, dahası bu hata ve eksikliklere yenilerini de eklemişlerdir. [...] Biz, Halide Edib Adıvar'ın okuyucuya yeniden sunulan metinlerini ilk basımından başlayarak bu hatalardan kurtarmaya, aynı zamanda yazarın özgün dilini ve üslubunu korumaya çalıştık. Bu nedenle sadeleştirmedik.[52]

> Due to the techniques of newsprint and publishing of the period, there appeared within these first impressions [of 1922 and 1923] quite a few typographical errors.... Up until recently, editions with the new [Latin] script and simplified language have continued the errors of the editions in the old [Ottoman] script, and they've added more of their own to these errors and

excisions.... In presenting Halide Edib's texts again to readers, we have started from their first edition in an attempt to free them from these errors and, at the same time, to protect the author's unique language and style. For this reason we did not simplify the language.

Given the realities of textual production, which nearly always enlist a multitude of hands, Kalpaklı's use of the first-person plural is refreshing. More important, the new edition closely mirrors that of 1923 and provides readers an until-now widely unavailable approximation of the text's early state. On the other hand, this early state has the inevitable outcome of withholding from the text certain historically important emendations from the 1937 edition. Given the possibility that Halide Edib herself had a hand in the production of the 1937 edition, such emendations and changes might possibly reflect not only important changes in Kemalist society at large but also the author's own final intentions for the text. Perhaps, though, the editorial aims of the new edition are not Halide Edib's final intentions but rather a return to the text's supposed origin. Here too, however, the editors are faced with a difficult choice: what and where is that origin? Does it lie in the 1923 edition or in the 1922 serial of *İkdam*? How to capture the entire print ecology within which the text moved, grew, and shed or accrued meaning for decades?

To understand the text's diachronic history, students of *Shirt of Flame* can, of course, consult multiple editions. Yet as I have argued here, they might reach similar conclusions from a sensitive close reading of Peyami's own story and its decomposing ego. Indeed, it's this aspect of the novel that renders the work so important for readerships today. Read within the larger context of its evolving textual history, the novel's final scene makes perfect sense; it seems in fact eerily prophetic. Peyami's death and the sudden foregrounding of his notebook open the manuscript up to a larger series of hands, belying the narrative integrity (*in + tangere*) of the authorial "I" and spurring its readers to look for a broader network of textual handlers. Extending this network outward, we do not undermine but in fact *strengthen* the historical truth of the testimonial genre. We make it thicker, denser, and more complex. It becomes not a sweet and simple monody but a political assembly of many voices: embedded Greek leftists, Cretan Muslims, Turkish nationalist editors, and exiled writers with a complicated past.

Critics of Turkish nationalism and the Kemalist project have dismissed *Shirt of Flame* as a mouthpiece of the emerging state's nationalist rhetoric.

Taking into account the novel's overt message of Turkish triumphalism and its subordination of females to patriarchal symbolism, such interpretations carry much weight. Nonetheless, when we read the novel with an eye toward its complex material and textual history, we hear it speaking quite candidly of the testimonial paradox that I've been wrestling with here. It reminds one, in other words, that the imagined national collectives personified by the "I" *in* the book rarely correspond to the smaller though much more interesting collectives *of* the book, who shape and reshape it.[53]

The Story of a Captive's Stories

With an eye toward the recovery of this "collective *of* the book," I'd like to return finally to Stratis Doukas's *A Captive's Story*, starting with its own revisions across editions. Something was changing as the story moved through later editions, particularly the third edition of 1958. First, as Angela Kastrinaki has demonstrated, a handful of isolated and subtle emendations in the third edition heightened the nationalist element of the testimonial, priming readers and critics in turn to further strengthen their own framing of the text as a national monument—something we've already seen in Raftopoulos's review of the third edition in 1959.[54] Besides the subtle, ideological alterations of single words or phrases here and there, however, the third edition also significantly "thickened" the narrative at key junctures throughout the book. Entire new episodes blossomed up from between the cracks, some as small as a sentence, some filling paragraphs or even pages, but all of them enriching the narrative and drawing out the human element. One saw this as early as the first page, in fact, when a contingent of Turkish soldiers now bursts into the barracks where the captives have been locked for the evening; they beat them indiscriminately with clubs and with boots and finally take a handful of men out to be executed. The episode continues with the appearance of a sympathetic Muslim scribe next door whose advice proves vital for the captive to avoid death during the ensuing nights. All this material—just one example among several others—was new to the third edition. Where did such episodes come from? How did Doukas come to incorporate them?

In an interview two years before his death, Doukas observed that "it was difficult for [readers] to understand the alchemy from which *A Captive's Story* emerged. Many worked on it. It's not just my work. It is a work of the people. Hand in hand I worked with the people."[55] At first glance, Doukas might seem here only to repeat the claims he'd put forth over half a century earlier in his introduction to the first edition. Yet I sense an important shift in rhetoric: rather than a single voice or a "solo song," Doukas was now writing of "alchemies" and collaborations. Why, though, did he fault readers for failing to understand these collaborations? After all, Doukas himself had kept them in absolute obscurity since the first edition's publication in 1929. His original, three-paragraph introduction had done little to enlighten readers, and even this introductory note was removed in the fifth edition of 1969, never to appear again.

Only in 1976, in an article fittingly titled "How the Captive Was Written" ("Πώς γράφτηκε ο αιχμάλωτος"), did Doukas at last afford readers a clearer window into the book's textual history. Because of its importance, I quote the article at length:

Στὸ τέλος τῆς πρώτης περιοδείας μου (Σεπτέμβρης - Δεκέμβρης 1928), εἶχα πέσει σὲ κάτι προσφυγοχώρια τῆς περιφέρειας Αἰκατερίνης. Στὶς σημειώσεις μου γράφω: ". . . βρέχει, βρέχει, βρέχει· λίγο ἀκόμα καὶ θά'μαι στὴν πολιτεία· πρέπει νὰ τελειώσω καλά. Εἶμαι πρὸς τὸ τέλος ἀλλὰ καὶ σ' ἕνα σπουδαῖο μέρος τῆς ἀποστολῆς μου· πρόκειται νὰ μιλήσω γιὰ πολὺ πονεμένους καὶ δυστυχισμένους ἀνθρώπους. Ὁ Θεὸς ἂς εἶναι μαζί μου κι ἂς μὲ βοηθάει."

Σταματῶ ἐδῶ τὶς σημειώσεις μου καὶ κατεβαίνω στὸ καφενεῖο τοῦ προσφυγοχωριοῦ Στουπί (Σπι), γιὰ νὰ δῶ τοὺς ἀνθρώπους του καὶ ν' ἀκούσω τους πόνους τους. Τὸ καφενεῖο γεμάτο. . . . Χτυπᾶ τὸ μάνταλο τῆς πόρτας καὶ μπαίνει κάποιος. . . . Κι ὅλοι τότε μὲ μιὰ φωνή: "Νά, ἕνας ποὺ ἔκαμε τὸν Τοῦρκο γιὰ νὰ γλιτώσει." Τὸν Τοῦρκο γιὰ νὰ γλιτώσει; Στυλώνω τ' αὐτιά μου σὰν ἄλογο στρατιωτικὸ ποὺ ἀκούει σάλπιγγα. Ἑτοιμάζομαι ν' ἀκούσω τ' ἀνάκουστο· μ' αὐτός, ντροπαλὸς ἀνατολίτης, κοκκινίζει, κάθεται σὲ μιὰ γωνιὰ καὶ δε μιλεῖ. Σὲ λίγο μὲ τὸ οὖζο, μὲ τὴν κουβέντα, ζεστάθηκε. Κι ἄρχισε τὴν ἱστορία του· τουρκόφωνος, ὅπως ὅλοι τους, μὰ ἀνατολίτης ἀφηγητής. Ἐγὼ θαρροῦσα πὼς μοῦ ἔπαιζε ἕνα βιολὶ σόλο. Ὅλοι ἀφοσιωμένοι, σωπαίναμε. Ἀπὸ τὰ μισά, εἶδα πὼς ἔπρεπε αὐτὴ τὴν ἱστορία νὰ τὴν κρατήσω· κι ἄρχισα πάλι τὶς σημειώσεις. Εἶχα πάρει πιὰ τὸ ρυθμό του. Σὰν τουρκόφωνος, ἔβαζε τὰ ρήματα στὸ τέλος. "Καλός, εἶπα, εἶναι." Αὐτὴ ἡ ξενικὴ καὶ παρατακτὴ σύνταξη μὲ τὰ πολλὰ συνδετικά "καὶ" μοῦ ἔφερνε στὸ νοῦ τὸ ὕφος τῆς Παλαιᾶς Διαθήκης· μέσα σὲ μιὰ ὑπερένταση, ποὺ μοῦ τὴν ὄξυνε ἡ βιασύνη, κρατοῦσα, παρέλειπα καὶ μετάλλαζα τὰ λόγια καὶ τὸν κάπως παραφθαρμένο ρυθμό τους, φέρνοντάς τον στὸν κλασικὰ ἐπικὸ λόγο καὶ ρυθμό. Ὅταν τέλειωσε τὴν ἀφήγησή του, πραγματικὰ τοῦ 'πα: "βάλε τὴν ὑπογραφή σου" καὶ ἐκεῖνος ἔγραψε "Νικόλαος Καζάκογλου" (τὸ Κοζάκογλου εἶναι δικό μου, σὰν πιὸ ἐντυπωσιακό).

Τὸ ἄλλο πρωὶ πῆγα στὸ σπίτι του [...] [καὶ] τὸν ἔβαλα τότε κι ἔγραψε στὰ τούρκικα ἕνα γράμμα στὸν Χατζη-Μεμέτη, ὑπέροχο γιὰ τὴ λαϊκή του εὐγένεια, ὅπου ἀφοῦ τοῦ ἐξιστοροῦσε ὅτι ὁ Μπεχτσὲτ ποὺ εἶχε κάποτε στὴ δούλεψή του ἦταν Ρωμιὸς καὶ βρίσκεται τώρα ἐδῶ στὴν καινούρια πατρίδα του, καὶ τὸν εὐχαριστεῖ γιὰ τὴν καλοσύνη ποὺ τοῦ 'δειξε, τελειώνει πὼς "ὅσοι γνωρίζουν ἀπὸ κόσμο, ξέρουν πὼς αὐτὰ ὅλα εἶναι ἀπὸ τὸ Θεό."

Ὅταν ἔβγαινα ἀπὸ τὸ χωριὸ τραβῶντας γιὰ τὴν Αἰκατερίνη, θαρροῦσα κιόλας πὼς κρατοῦσα στὴ φούχτα μου ἕνα κομμάτι χρυσάφι. Σὲ μιὰ στιγμὴ ἔνιωσα μιὰ πελώρια παλάμη νὰ μὲ χτυπᾶ φιλικὰ στὴν πλάτη σὰν ὁ ἴδιος ὁ Θεὸς νὰ μοῦ χάριζε μιὰ παρηγοριὰ καὶ ἕνα στήριγμα γιὰ τὶς ὑπόλοιπες μέρες τῆς ζωῆς μου. Χριστούγεννα ἔκανα στὸ Κίτρος καὶ παραμονὴ τῆς Πρωτοχρονιᾶς γύρισα στὴ Θεσσαλονίκη. Κάθισα ἀμέσως κι ἔγραψα ὑπαγορεύοντας τὴν ἱστορία μου μέσα σὲ μιὰ βδομάδα. [*Σημείωση τῶν συντακτῶν: Ὅπως μας πληροφόρησε ὁ κ. Δούκας, προκειμένου νὰ κρατήσει τὴν ποιότητα τοῦ προφορικοῦ λόγου στὸ κείμενο, δὲν ἔγραψε ὁ ἴδιος τὴν ἱστορία, ἀλλὰ τὴν ὑπαγόρευσε στὸν ξάδελφό του Ἀντρέα Χατζηδημητρίου, χρησιμοποιῶντας ὡς πρώτη ὕλη τὶς σημειώσεις του*] ... Τὸν ἄλλο χρόνο (1929), βγαίνοντας γιὰ τὴ δεύτερη περιοδεία μου ... πέρασα πάλι ἀπὸ τὸ Σπι καὶ πῆγα τοῦ Νικόλα καὶ τοῦ συντρόφου του ἕνα ἀντίτυπο τῆς ἱστορίας του ποὺ εἶχε πιὰ τυπωθεῖ. Ὁ Νικόλας ὅσο τὴ διάβαζε χαμογελοῦσε εὐχαριστημένος κι ἀπορημένος μαζί, ποὺ ἦταν γραμμένη ἀπαράλλαχτα ὅπως μοῦ τὴν εἶπε. ... Φεύγοντας ἄφησα ἀρκετὸ χαρτὶ τοῦ Νικόλα γιὰ νὰ γράψει τὴν ἱστορία του ὁ ἴδιος· κάθισε καὶ τὴν ἔγραψε καὶ μοῦ τὴν ἔφερε ὕστερ' ἀπὸ χρόνια στὴν Ἀθήνα. ... Μὰ δὲν τὰ κατάφερε στὸ γράψιμο ὅσο στὴν προφορικὴ ἀφήγησή του· τὰ καλύτερα κομμάτια εἶναι ὅσα ἀντέγραψε λέξη μὲ λέξη ἀπὸ τὸ βιβλίο· ὅμως πρόσθεσε μερικὰ ἐπεισόδια, ποὺ τὰ χρησιμοποίησα σὲ τρίτη μου ἔκδοση. Τὴ χειρόγραφη ἱστορία τοῦ Νικόλα τὴν κατέθεσα στὴ βιβλιοθήκη τῆς Κερκύρας. Ἐλπίζω νὰ βρίσκεται.

Δὲν ἐπιχειρῶ περαιτέρω ἀνάλυση τῶν προθέσεων καὶ ἐπιτεύξεων τῆς *Ἱστορίας* μου. Ἐλπίζω καὶ γὼ μαζὶ μὲ τοὺς φίλους της ὅτι θὰ ἐπιζήσει.

At the end of my first tour (September–December 1928), I'd come upon some refugee villages in the countryside around Katerini. In my notes, I write: "... Rain, rain, and more rain; just a little more and I'll be in the town; I need to finish well. I'm near the end, but also an important point, of my mission; I'm going to speak about people in deep pain and sorrow. May God be with me and help me."

I stop my notes here and go down to the coffeehouse in the refugee village of Stoupi (Spi), to see its people and to hear their pain. The shop is full . . . The latch on the door bangs and someone enters [. . .]. And then everyone with one voice tells me: "Here's a guy who pretended to be a Turk to escape." A Turk to escape? I perk my ears like a military horse at the sound of the bugle. I ready myself to hear the unheard of. But he, a bashful oriental, grows red, he sits down in a corner and doesn't speak. Soon, with the ouzo, with the conversation, he warmed up. And he started his history; Turcophone, like all of them, but a [talented] oriental narrator. It seemed to me like he was playing a violin solo. All of us, giving him our full attention, grew quiet. After he'd made it halfway through, I saw that I needed to keep this story; and I started my notes again. I'd finally got ahold of his rhythm. Like a Turcophone, he put the verbs at the end. "Good, I said, he is." That foreign and paratactic syntax with the several conjunctive "and"s brought to mind the style of the Old Testament; in a tense tumult that was sharpened by my haste [to keep up my writing with his speaking], I maintained, removed, modified his words and their somewhat corrupted rhythm, bringing it closer to the classical epic *logos* and rhythm. When he finished his story, I really did tell him: "Sign your name," and he wrote "Nikolaos Kazakoglou" ("Kozakoglou" is mine; it's more striking).

The next morning I went to his house [. . .] and I asked him and he wrote out, in Turkish, a letter to Hacı Mehmet [i.e., Ali Bey], superb in its folk-like generosity, where, after he had told him that the Behçet whom he had once employed was a Greek and that he is now in his new homeland, and he thanks him [Ali Bey] for the kindness that he showed him, he finishes, "those who know this world, understand that all these things are the work of God."

As I left the village and headed for Katerini, I felt as if I were holding in my hand a piece of gold. In a moment I felt a giant hand patting me kindly on the back as if God himself were bestowing on me a consolation and a support for all the subsequent days of my life. I passed Christmas in Kitros and for New Year's Eve I returned to Thessaloniki. I sat down immediately and wrote my story by dictation in a week. (*Editors' Note: As Mr. Doukas informed us, in order to maintain the quality of the spoken word in the text, he did not write the story himself, but rather he dictated it to his cousin Andreas Hatzidimitriou, using his notes [from Kazakoglou's oral story] as his raw material...*) [...] . The following year, setting out on my second tour [...] I passed by Spi again and brought copies of the book, which had by then been printed, to Nikolas and his comrade.[56] As Nikolas read it he smiled, in both pleasure and wonder that it was written unchanged just as he had told it to me. [...] On my way out, I left enough blank paper for Nikolas to write his story himself; he sat and wrote it and brought it to me some years later in Athens. [...]. But he couldn't manage it as well in writing as in his spoken narrative; the best pieces were those he'd copied word for word from the book; nonetheless he added some episodes, which I used in my third edition. I donated Nikolas' manuscript to the library of Corfu. I hope it's still there. [...]

I won't attempt further analysis of the intentions and successes of my *Story*. I hope, together with its friends, that it will survive. (*Tomes*, no. 6, November 1976)

Again, the question arises: whose story is this? Throughout the article, Doukas himself can't quite make up his mind. We see this already in the article's title— "How the captive was written"—which subtly confuses the human (captive) and the book (*Captive*), which came to rewrite and replace him. This duality of writing and overwriting becomes immediately clear in the ensuing scene inside the coffeehouse. While taking notes from Kazakoglou's oral story, Doukas tells us that he eventually "got ahold of"—literally, *took*—his rhythm, a verb choice that already begins to suggest a transfer of property. As if to justify himself, Doukas immediately adds that the spoken rhythm of Kazakoglou was, in any case, "somewhat corrupted" (*κάπως παραφθαρμένος*), and that only Doukas's written intervention (which at times left Kazakoglou's words in place, at other times removed them, and at other times modified them) could restore its "classical" form. Classicism and corruption—a key binary that we first encountered in the introduction to this book—rear their head again here as Doukas's studied writing steps in and restores the epic rhythms of Kazakoglou's supposedly contaminated speech.

These "restorations" seem to blur the property rights to the story. The next day, while leaving the village, Doukas wrote of the "gold" he had acquired, which would offer him "support" for the rest of his life. Both here and in his descriptions of the emendations that he brought to bear on Kazakoglou's voice, therefore, the article reinforces the arguments of earlier critics: that this story ultimately belongs to Doukas. Indeed, in the final line he says as much himself, referring to it as "my *Story.*" Be that as it may, other details in the article complicate this interpretation: first, Doukas paradoxically suggests that the first edition reproduced Kazakoglou's narrative "unchanged" (απαράλλαχτα), a preposterous claim when taken literally, yet it unsettles the question of narrative agency. More importantly, the article introduces yet another intermediary into the process of textual production: his cousin, who, as it turns out, had functioned as amanuensis. In effect, Doukas appears to have treated his notes from Kazakoglou's oral story as a sort of rudimentary stage script, donning not only the textual mask of Nikolas Kozakoglou but his *oral* mask as well, performing the part of the storyteller. In turn, he asked his cousin to play the part of "Stratis Doukas" and write his speech down, introducing a second layer and a third human hand of transcription from orality to writing.

And what of Nikolas himself? The article reveals several startling details. First, it seems to confirm, as readers had already assumed, that he was Turcophone. How else, after all, could he have "played the Turk" for over a year? Doukas attempts to prove this using Kazakoglou's oral syntax, with its verbs placed at the end of sentences. Doukas's observation is, in general terms, correct, yet it deserves a caveat here. Greek syntax is extremely flexible: since the language is heavily inflected, word order is of less importance for unpacking meaning. Even in the case of longer, more complex sentences, it's possible, though less customary, to place verbs in the ultimate position. To be sure, we have no evidence of how Kazakoglou himself spoke with Doukas. The single example that Doukas provides—*good, I said, he is*—sounds strange in both Greek and Turkish. While the Greek phrase that Doukas writes (*Καλός, είπα, είναι*) is awkward, the Turkish equivalent (*iyi, dedim, dir*) is simply incorrect. Even looser translations, such as *iyi, dedim, adam*[*dır*], strike one as awkward. Both Greek and Turkish would form this sentence in the same way: "καλός είναι, είπα" and "iyi adam[dır], dedim." This instance is likely an invention of Doukas rather than an actual utterance of Kazakoglou. Doukas is not only taking words out of his mouth; he is putting words in.

Rather than categorizing Kazakoglou as "Turcophone"—a trope that scholars, even those as sharp as Dimitris Tziovas, have uncritically repeated since Doukas—one might more productively describe him as bilingual. Or, even more accurately, I propose the term *interlingual,* thereby alluding to Kazakoglou's position *between* the linguistic borderscape. As I'll demonstrate shortly, Kazakoglou appears to have never felt himself at home in the standardized form of either Turkish or Greek. But to call him an "oriental narrator" or Turcophone, as Doukas does, obscures at least one important detail: his narration to Doukas *was in Greek*. He clearly knew both languages.

More critically, we learn from Doukas's article above that Kazakoglou was by no means "illiterate," as critics had long assumed. He was able not only to read Stratis Doukas's novel after its publication but to write a Turkish letter as well as an entire Greek manuscript story narrating his adventures. Unfortunately, Doukas rejected this last piece of writing as weak, but it was apparently strong enough for Doukas to "borrow" pieces of it, cannibalizing the manuscript for his revisions. As readers now learned, *it was Kazakoglou's manuscript* that had provided the numerous episodes inserted into the third edition in 1958. The "thickening" of the narrative structure was a direct result of Kazakoglou's *writing*. What does this mean? The witness's story by no means proceeded linearly from the oral interview to the printed book; it moved back and forth and between several hands, voices, and media: the supposedly illiterate witness at times took up the pen and wrote—at great length, in fact—while the writer, at other times, set down his pen and passed over into orality. These moments of intermediality occurred without a linear progression or hierarchy, as the oral and the written and the printed fed upon each other in a complicated circuit.

Once Doukas had finished with Kazakoglou's manuscript, he passed it along to the library of Corfu. This library was destroyed in 1943 when Nazi Germany bombed the island, and it seems unlikely that the manuscript survived (a conclusion that Kechagia-Lypourli reaches as well). Despite this loss, there are a few surviving witnesses to Kazakoglou's written literacy elsewhere: his letter to Ali Bey—or rather *two* letters, one written in Ottoman Turkish and one in Greek-script Turkish—in addition to a short Greek letter he later sent to Doukas. All three are preserved by the care of the staff at the Modern Greek Studies Archive, in the Department of Medieval and Modern Greek Studies at Aristotle University.

What these letters suggest to varying degrees is that Kazakoglou did not entirely "belong" to any of their languages, as his usage constantly confounds "sameness and difference" (to use the terms of Calotychos from earlier) in an intriguing indeterminacy. Employing a mixture of formal and informal codes, betraying several orthographic and syntactic deviations from standard norms, the letters house the remnants of a voice that belongs to no national tradition.

It's a voice more or less hidden by the printed copies of *A Captive's Story*. I transcribe and translate the two Turkish-language letters below—one in Ottoman script, one in Greek script:

[1 Ottoman Turkish]
Efendim ve Ağam ʿAlî Bey,

Kemâl Paşanıñ İzmir'e indi[ğ]i senesi yanıñıza çoban gelen Velî isminde ve soñra Süleymân oğlu Bekset Çirkince karyesinden Kazakoğlu Niko isminde rum idi. Siziñ yanıñızdan kız kardaşımı almak içün Bursa'ya kaçdığımda İstanbul vâsıtasıyla Yunanistan'a geçmeye fikir ediyor idim ve de İzmir'e indi[ğ]imde İstanbul'a gitmek içün bir İngiliz vapuruna girdim vapur da Midilli adasına geldi[ğ]inde çaresini buldum. Oraya indim. Pederimi vâlidemi ve umum familiyamı buldum.

ʿAlî Bey, Allah çok çok ömürler versiñ. Seniñ baña karşı rum olduğumu bilmiyerek fakat her bir insâna karşı iyi vizdânıñ olduğunu öğrendim ve de çok şeyler geçirdim ve de bir gün oldu bütün familiyamı gördük onuñ içü[n] ṭarâfıñızdan çok memnûn kalarak gece ve gündüz isminizi söyleyerek sağlığıñıza duʿ[a]cıyım. Ṭarâfıñızdan çok memnûn kalarak size bu mektûbu yazıyorum. Siziñ de benim ṭarâfımdan memnûniyetlığıñız var ise idi elimden baña karşılığını yazasıñız şunki ben sizi pederim yerine dutuyorum

My Lord and Master Ali Bey,

The year that Kemal Pasha entered Smyrna, the shepherd who came to you first by the name of Veli and afftterwards Behset son of Süleyman, was a Greek by the name of Nikos Kazakoğlu from the village of Çirkince. When I left you to get my sister in Bursa I was scheming to pass to Greece by meens of Istanbul and when I entered Smyrna I got on an English steamship for Istanbul and when the steamship came to the island of Mytilene I seized the chance and got off there. I found my father my mother and my toatal family.

Ali Bey, may Allah give much life to you. In your dealings with me, not knowing that I was Greek, but also in your dealings with every person, I learned that you have a good soul and I

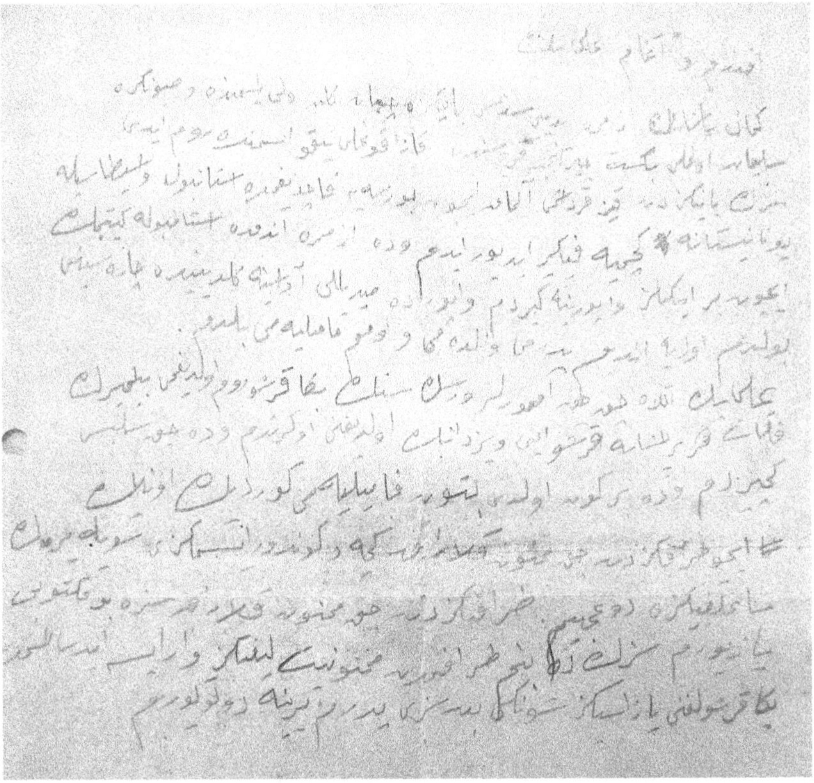

FIGURE 8. Nikolaos Kazakoglou's letter to Ali Bey (Turkish in the Ottoman alphabet). Courtesy of the Modern Greek Literature Archive, Department of Modern Greek and Comparative Studies, Aristotle University of Thessaloniki.

experienced many things and one day at last I finally saw my family. For that reason, being very thankful for you, I praiy for your helth day and night, saying your name. Being very thankful for you I am writing this letter to you. If you have thankfulness too for me and for the work I did, please write a response to me. Because I consider you a father to me.

[2 Greek-script Turkish]
Σεβκιλί ~~τοστούμ~~ αγάμ Αλή-βέη

Μαχσούς σελάμ ιντέριμ. Χαλινί Χατιρινί σορούπ σουβάλ εντέριμ σέντα μπενί σουρατζάκ ολούρσαν σούκιουρ μπασιμίζ σελαμέτ-τιρ. Κεμαλίν ισχάλ ιτιγί σενε

[ ] συζτεκί μπουλουναν τσομπαν βελιτιρ. σόνρα αλντιγίμ νοφούς Μπεχτσέτ ογλου Σουϊλεμαντιρ. Ονου μπιλεσιν χριστιάν τσιρκιντζέ κιοουντέν Νίκο Καζάκογλου ισμιντέ μπουνου μπίλεσιν σενίν γιανιντάν κατσιτζαγίμ [okunaksız] ντιγέν μπαχανά εττίμ άτζαμπα ιζμιρέ μη τσαρεσινι μπουλουπτα γκεσμιγέ Ιουνανιστανά βε μπασιμί κουρταρμαγά. Άμα Αλάχ εμουρλερ βερσίν σανά εττιγίν ελιγέ καρσί[,] βιζτανινιν ιτσούν τσανιμιζί κουρταρντίμ. Τσοκ εχλιγέ αντάμμισιν νασίλ μπενί σενίν γιανιντέ ικέν σοϊλεμ ιθίν ουρουμλάρ ιτσούν χεμντέ ταστικλεριμ οϊλε αντάμ ολτουγουνά ιτσούντεν εκμεγιντέν οργεντίμ σενίν βιζτανί ολτουγουνου—

Αλή Μπέη νε απαλούμ που κοτουλουκ κεντινι κιμ μπιλίρσε Αλαχτάν-τιρ. Μπίζιμ ντιγί που κισμέτ-τιρ. Αργιτζα σελάμ εντέριμ κεντινέ βε φαμιλινέ βε, πεντερίν βε βαλιντινέ βεντε ουμούμ μπενί μπιλέν ντοστλαρά. μπεν σιζτέν μεμνούν καλίομ σίζτε μπεντέν μεμνούν καλίορσ[α]νιζ, ιστερσενιζ καρσιλιγινί γιορλάρσινιζ.

My dear ~~friend~~ lord Ali Bey

I send warm greetings. I ask and enquire after your health and if you too ask about me thank heavens I'm in good health. This is the shepherd Veli who was with you the year that Kemal occupied [Smyrna]. [Or, according to] the identity papers I got afterward, son of Behçet Süleyman. Know this it is Niko Kazakoglou in the Christian village of Çirkince[.] Know this [illegible] [I went] to Smyrna, where I'd made an excuse saying I need to leave you, to find a way out and pass over to Greece and save myself. But may Allah give much life to you for the goodness you showed me. I saved my soul for [*i.e., because of*] your good conscience. You are a very worth[y] man, when I was with you how you would speak to me for [*i.e. 'about'*] the Greeks and also I give my verifications that you were such a man. From your drink and from your bread I learned that you have a good conscience.

Ali Bey what can we do? This evil [*i.e., the war*]—whoever knows himself will realize it's from Allah. It's not our fault, it's

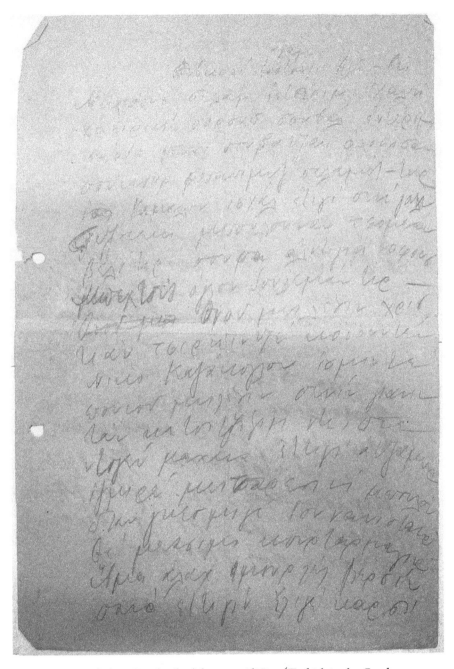

FIGURE 9. Nikolaos Kazakoglou's letter to Ali Bey (Turkish in the Greek alphabet). Courtesy of the Modern Greek Literature Archive, Department of Modern Greek and Comparative Studies, Aristotle University of Thessaloniki.

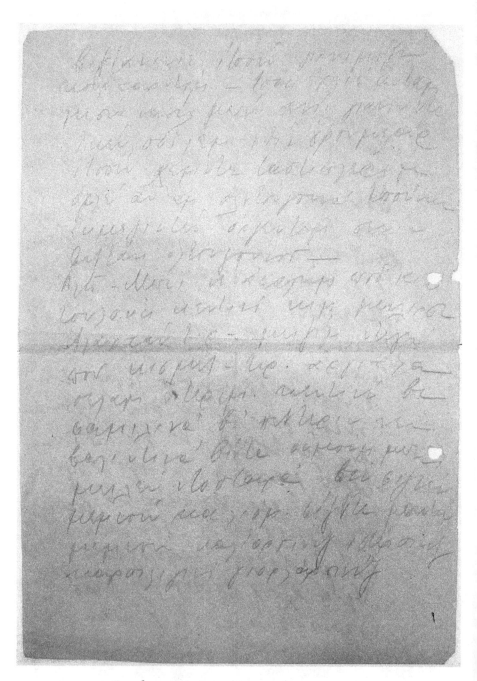

FIGURE 9. continued

fate's. I give particular greetings to yourself and to your family and to your father and mother and also to all my friends who know me. I am thankful for you, if you too are thankful for me, send me a reply if you want.

What can we say of these two epistles? Like Kazakoglou himself, their indeterminacy rendered them incompatible with Greek and Turkish grammatology. The Greek-script epistle bore the national alphabet of Greece but was unintelligible to most of that country's citizens. As for the Ottoman Turkish, it was written in December 1928, less than a month after the Turkish state had abandoned the Ottoman script, rendering the document equally illegible to most Turkish citizens today. In short, Kazakoglou's words were doomed to fall between the cracks of both Greek and Turkish.

A close reading of the letters themselves demonstrates at least two prominent points. First, those who characterize Kazakoglou as "Turcophone" might consider the many irregularities of his Turkish. In the very first sentence of his Ottoman-script epistle, he writes "indiği sene*si*," applying a possessive suffix where standard Turkish would have none. Remarkably, when writing his Greek-script letter, he instead chose the standard "işgal ettiği sene," suggesting that at least occasionally his Greek-script idiom was in fact closer to standard Turkish than his Ottoman script. Continuing in the Ottoman epistle, we see that he also makes multiple orthographic errors in his Arabic, which was understandable. More interestingly, to my mind, Kazakoglou writes his Turkish name as *Bekset* rather than *Behçet*—i.e., using a *kef-sin* rather than the standard *he-çim*. He makes a similar choice later when he renders the word *vicdan* (*conscience*) as *vizdan*, choosing a *ze* (ز) rather than a *cim* (ج). These two unorthodox spellings, which would certainly puzzle a Turkish reader, would give little pause to a Greek speaker, who would in fact pronounce the words this way by default. In short, despite the fact that the alphabet and language were perfectly equipped to produce the words "Behçet" and "vicdan," Kazakoglou wrote them instead with a Greek inflection. At nearly every other point in the letter, Kazakoglou represents "dj" and "ch" with standard Ottoman *cim* (ج) and *çim* (چ): *gece, duacı, kaçmak, çoban, Çirkince*, etc. This suggests that *Bekset* and *vizdan* were not the rule but rather the exception. My point, however, is precisely this. Kazakoglou was poised somewhere between the rule and the exception—between the two languages, that is, in a kind of linguistic borderscape that ranged freely across the standard rules of both. At times, the choices of his Greek-script epistle are more Turkish than his epistle in official Ottoman. At other times the choices of his Ottoman epistle seem oddly Greek.

This linguistic borderscape likely reflects the educational policies of his village's school, which had been built by the Smyrna-based organization "Omiros" in 1885. Despite the fact that the residents of his village had for generations spoken Turkish, the Bishop of the metropole who oversaw education had set as his primary goal the eradication of that language and its replacement with Greek. Urban Greek-speaking philanthropists who had built and staffed the school shared this vision and they hired a *παιδονόμος* (a class monitor), who "saw to it that the prohibition [of speaking Turkish] was enforced." In other words, it was not enough for the school administration to conduct all lessons in Greek; they paid a Greek-speaking adult to monitor the students' conversations and to slap them on the wrist as often as was necessary if they spoke Turkish.[57] Such policies of overt Hellenization were not exceptional to Kazakoglou's village; they could be found across Greek Orthodox Anatolia and were indicative of the nationalist bent that education had taken in the final decades of the empire.[58] Given his age, Nikolas Kazakoglou was no doubt among the children raised within this short-lived system: speaking Turkish at home and in his village but policed and punished for speaking it in school, he grew up in a linguistic no-man's-land. Wandering between scripts and official standards, Kazakoglou's documents spoke to a confluence of dialects, languages, and written training—a confluence that was however doomed to near oblivion after the Exchange.

Turn again to the contents of the epistles one last time. You soon realize that they are not mirror transcriptions of each other but rather two separate narratives, each with its own points of rhetorical emphasis. Look at the names for example: the Ottoman letter tells us that Nikolas's Turkish name was Süleyman oğlu Behçet (i.e., Behçet, son of Süleyman), yet the Greek script tells us just the opposite: Behçet oğlu Süleyman (i.e., Süleyman, son of Behçet). In both letters, we also learn that Kazakoglou went not only by the name Behçet (or Süleyman) but also, at some point, by "Veli"—a strange detail that Doukas had elided in his own story.

Generally, the two texts are written in a stilted, largely unsuccessful imitation of official formality. This wooden language is softened only at isolated instances in the epistles, when the writer offers short, condensed bursts of emotional energy. Interestingly, these brief moments of touching intimacy occur at different points and in different ways in each letter. In the Greek script, we see that Kazakoglou had first begun his letter by addressing Ali Bey as "my friend" (*dostum*), yet he later crossed this out and reverted to the more formal "my lord" (*ağam*). At the start of the final paragraph, however, he breaks off his previous thought and suddenly begins a disarmingly intimate direct address to Ali Bey: "Ali Bey, what can we do, this evil, whoever knows himself will realize it's from Allah. It's not our fault, it's fate's" (*Αλή Μπέη νε απαλούμ που κοτουλούκ κεντινί κιμ μπιλίρσε Αλαχτάν-τιρ. Μπιζίμ ντιγί που κισμέτ-τιρ*). In a gesture that extends beyond the two men's personal history, Kazakoglou seems to be opening here a reconciliatory window for all the populations of the entire region. The evil unleashed on so many civilians, he seems to say, was not their own doing; it was the work of fate. This was the sentence that had so captivated Stratis Doukas, as he wrote in 1976.

Such a gesture, however, is missing in the Ottoman-script epistle. Here, Kazakoglou transitioned directly from his praise of Ali Bey's personal generosity to the greetings he extended to family and friends. Nonetheless, the most touching moment of this document—and, crucially, a moment that is missing from the Greek script—comes in the final line, as Kazakoglou confesses to Ali Bey, "I consider you a father to me" (*ben sizi pederim yerine duyuyorum*). More literally: *I hold you in the place of my father*. Having waded through this strange, idiosyncratic letter, with its several irregularities and poor script, the reader stumbles upon the final words like an oasis, a moment of sharp emotional clarity that brings the entire story into focus. Indeed, returning to Calotychos's reading of Doukas's novel from the earlier section of this chapter, one sees now in this final sentence that, despite the failed marriage to Ali Bey's niece, the familial bond between the refugee and his protector remained solidly in place, at least as witnessed here in Kazakoglou's own letter. Setting Ali Bey in the place of his father, Kazakoglou eloquently demonstrates how the friendships and indeed *kinships* of Nikolas's past continue to touch his present. Both in its linguistic structures and its contents, Kazakoglou's writing was a space of confluence, dialogue, and kinship that even the Exchange could not partition in two.

Curating the Testimonial

Let me conclude with a final clarification: my intent is not to romanticize Kazakaglou as the lost voice of the original witness. As my study of *Shirt of Flame* suggested earlier, such an "original voice" is often inaccessible and never very helpful in understanding a text's complicated journeys. Instead, what I want to show is this: Kazakoglou's strangely pluralistic voice, which arose from a dense sociopolitical web and was likewise spread across a dense patchwork of media (oral speech, personal letters, and a book-length manuscript narrative), when read alongside Doukas's own strangely pluralistic interventions—to say nothing of his cousin, his publisher, the ensuing editions' successive visual artists, or others—illustrate the confluence of multiple creative forces that convey, transmit, and transform the printed testimonial. Kazakoglou's letters are but a small sample of the multiple voices and perspectives that have been unduly sidelined and circumscribed. If his texts have attained a prominence here, it is by virtue of their chance survival in an otherwise decimated archive. My analysis of Kazakoglou and his materials should be viewed therefore not as a return to an origin but rather as a model methodology of "reassembling the connections." This method should ideally extend to a number of actors and materials, however faint their traces in the archive today.

The philologist's job ought not to be to single out and canonize any single voice but to recover the trace of each within and beyond the page, to recover likewise the spaces of collaboration and struggle that play out as the text evolves and changes. By monumentalizing the testimonial text, many twentieth-century Greek and Turkish critics privileged truth as an end product. I have tried here to reassemble, to thicken, and ultimately to strengthen that truth through a careful examination of its tellings. My aim is not to critique in any absolute sense the testimonial and the very real historical truths that it articulates; instead, I want to better curate them. And this begins by understanding the testimonial as an assembly of voices and of hands. By pluralizing the agents within this assembly, it is my hope that we might also begin to pluralize the national histories in whose shadows they often operate.

Chapter four, in which displaced books make a place

CAN A WRITTEN LANGUAGE survive its own displacement from writing? In the second half of the 1920s, this was the question facing the Turkish-speaking Greek Orthodox Christian refugees of the Population Exchange. After they had been torn root and branch from Turkey, the only trace to be found of them there were the inscriptions left on their buildings and tombs: Turkish written in the Greek alphabet. Words now bereft of an audience. But even more striking than this was the scene across the sea in Greece, where the survivors had been relocated: for, despite the fact that tens if not hundreds of thousands of these refugees—the so-called Karamanli Christians—continued to live and speak in Turkish, their written language was even harder to find here, uprooted out of print.

In the decades before the Exchange, Karamanli print was thriving. Under the auspices of the prolific publisher and writer Evangelinos Misailidis, it had begun during the second half of the nineteenth century to circulate newsprint, educational materials, and a sizeable corpus of short stories, poetry, and novels.[1] Yet with the collapse of the Ottoman state and the mass deportation of this population to Greece, their formerly robust print apparatus crumbled almost immediately. Soon after the Exchange, Evangelia Balta writes, "no Karamanlidika printed matter would circulate, since the Greek State's policy of linguistic homogenization as well as the Turcophones' need to integrate as rapidly as possible into the new *status quo*, imposed the monolingual culture."[2]

The fate of their newspaper *Muhacir Sedası* (*Voice of the Refugee*) is particularly telling. As Balta has documented elsewhere, the paper was attacked by the mainstream outlet *Eleftheron Vima* in the summer of 1925, just over a year after the former had begun circulating. The editor of *Eleftheron Vima* insisted on the "inappropriateness" of the Turkish language and its use "in the streets of Athens." He continued:

> *Efendiler!*[3] Do not pollute the Greek-speaking refugees, allowing them the desire to learn the daily news from a newspaper published in Turkish. We recommend that you cease to publish the newspaper in this non-existent language. Replace the language of your newspaper with Greek. Because, alas, regardless of the freedom of the Press, it would be right for the Government to take action.[4]

Harsh and painful words. Apparently, when the larger media establishment of Greece was not ignoring the Karamanli Christians, it ostracized them for speaking a "pollution" that was, in any case, "nonexistent," going so far as to legally threaten them. Given such a toxic environment, it is not surprising that the newspaper folded within two years.

Yet while I recognize the devastation that such a closure must have meant to the Karamanli refugees, I wonder whether, from the 1930s onward, it's right to close the book on Karamanli literature entirely. I readily admit the hard and unavoidable facts at hand: with the exception of a few political tracts and a couple of chapbooks of poetry,[5] Karamanli literature would never again be printed (to our knowledge, at least). But does this necessarily mean that no literature was produced and circulated through other means besides print? Such an assumption is problematic. It derives from an implicit consensus that only the major media of the centralized nation-state (i.e., standardized, bound books, printed in bulk) qualify as literature and only commercial sales qualify as indices of circulation. Stated in the obverse, it overlooks the possibility that Karamanli literature might in fact have continued to find a material outlet elsewhere—not only in private media, such as personal correspondence, but in nonstandardized mixed-media formats, a small sample of which I explore in this chapter in the form of handmade manuscript and composite codices. The books that you will encounter in this chapter recycled, repurposed, and recombined source materials, sometimes mixing together print and manuscript, sometimes confusing the categories of original, adaptation, and copy, sometimes rebinding and remixing multiple texts together. Given their makeshift nature, they never achieved industrial reproduction; each traced out a singular trajectory. Nevertheless, I will argue that even as singular objects they achieved a degree of public circulation, moving from hand to hand beyond the bounds of the nation-state and its authorial regimes. Despite their singularity, these books were startlingly mobile. During and following the Population Exchange, pieces of their contents were produced successively in Turkey, Greece, and the United States, and they were in turn passed from hand to hand by multiple users who, as the decades wore on, moved them again across this geography. Weaving across a gridwork of borderscapes, these books were holding together a supposedly lost literature and, in doing so, the scattered community of its refugee handlers.

Books Behaving Badly

In the small village of Zografou, a few kilometers inland and uphill from the shores of Halkidiki in the northern Aegean, if you know the right person you can find an old copy of the Alexander Romance, written in Turkish and printed in Istanbul in 1871: *Alexandros Makedonialı Meşhur Padişah* (Alexander of Macedon, the Famous Sultan).[6] The Alexander Romance narrates the mythical exploits of Alexander the Great and is among the oldest and most widely diffused novels on our planet, spanning dozens of languages and several religious traditions (including Judaism, Christianity, and Islam), and actively and continuously evolving from at least the third century CE to the end of the nineteenth.[7] Precisely because of this wild diffusion, however, Alexander's story is impossible to pinpoint; it was continually reshaped by those who told it, heard it, and passed it along, subtly or extensively incorporating into it their individual and communal histories. Within the story of Alexander hide the stories of his many handlers.

The Alexander Romance in Zografou is no exception. Open the book and you find in its flyleaf a short manuscript poem, inscribed in a meticulous hand by the owner of the book. It tells the story not of "Alexander the Famous Sultan" but of a common soldier, wasting away in protracted military service far from his home. Conscripted into the Ottoman army, he writes to his own Sultan and demands permission to return to his village amidst a growing wave of bitter complaints. "If you knew how I've been debased, my Sultan, you too would be weeping," he writes at the end of the second stanza. The poem poignantly if subtly complicates the entire narrative of the Alexander Romance before it has even begun, demonstrating the human cost of an imperial military apparatus and the displacements and uprootings that it produces. It asks the reader, if nothing else, to compare the two narratives and join them in dialogue: the story of an emperor breathlessly expanding his territory; and the story of a common soldier, displaced from his home and kin. The poem, as it appears in figure 10, reads as follows:

Ἐφέντιμ πὶρ ναζὰρ ἔγλε	Please, my Sultan, cast your eye this way
ἀρζουχὰλ βὰρ σικαγέττε	at my petition and my complaints;
Τουνγιαλὰρ τουρτούκτσα τουρσούν	may your kingdom and your throne stand tall
ταχτήν ἤλε σαταρέττε	as long as this world stands in place.
γιάρην μεβλὰμ γιαρτὲμ ἐτέρ	Help me now and my Lord Allah's help
σανὰ ρουζὶ κηγιαμεττέ	be yours henceforth in the end of days.
γιαληνήζαμ χασρετὶμ βὰρ	I'm forlorn and I long for home,
νιγιὰζ ἐτὲρ βιλαγέττε	and my whole village begs your grace:
γιαρατὰν μέβλα ἀσκηνά	for the love of the Lord who created us
κόιμα πενὶ σου κουρπεττέ	don't cast me off in this foreign place.
κιταπήμ τιουριουλιοῦ καλτή	My book has been closed, unread is each page;[8]
τιλιμτὲ κορανὴμ ἀγλέρ	on my tongue my Quran keeps on weeping.
πιουλπουλιοὺμ καφεστὲ καλτή	My nightingale stays closed in its cage;
σιλατὰ κιουλσάνημ ἄγλερ	in my homeland my Gülşan is weeping.
κερὲκ ἐβλὰτ κερὲκ ἀγιάλ	Our children too weep with her;
σαπὶτ σουπχανὴμ ἀγλέρ	even Allah the Exulted is weeping.
ιουφτατὲ ὀλτούγουμ πιλσέ	If you knew how I've been debased,
Ἀπτοὺλ ἀζὶζ χανὶμ ἀγλέρ	Abdülaziz,[9] you too would be weeping.

Gülşan is of course the speaker's wife, while his nightingale (as you'll recall from our time with Şānī in chapter one) is a symbol for the soul. Yet more striking than the speaker's wife or soul is the image of his "closed book" with which the second stanza begins. As I've signaled in an endnote, the original Turkish phrase suggests a metaphorical understanding of "book" as life itself, which, for the speaker, has been prematurely "closed" far away from his native soil. On a more literal level, however, the closed book of this poem ironically raises another question: will the actual, physical book that we hold in our hands also remain shut, foreclosed from a chance at life? Whose book was this? Where has it been, where was its own homeland? Was it "closed" before its time?

While the next line provides no immediate answers, it does offer hope. We read that despite the closure of one book, another remains open: the Quran, which seemingly weeps on the tongue of the speaker. If the "book of life" remains shut to him, the speaker nonetheless maintains access to his holy book

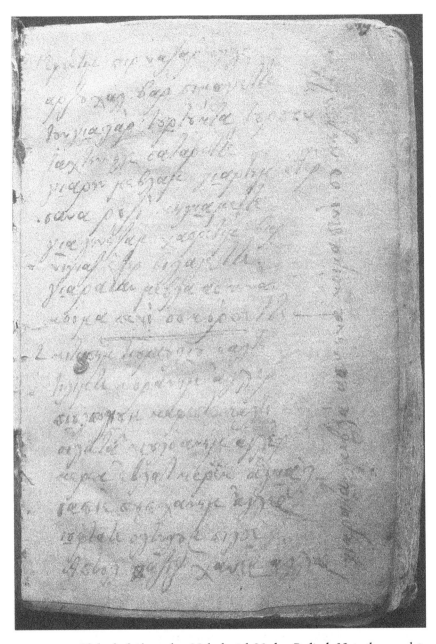

FIGURE 10. Flyleaf of *Alexandros Makedonialı Meşhur Padişah*. Note the couplet in the fore-edge margin. Courtesy of Giorgos Kallinikidis.

of faith, whose recitation he continues in exile even as he adapts it to his own needs, i.e., lamentation. Yet there is another, meta-textual irony here: the owner of this book—not to be confused with the fictional speaker of the poem—the man, in other words, who inscribed the weeping Quran onto the first page of his Alexander Romance, is not a Muslim. He is a Karamanli Christian, as one can deduce both from his name, Ἀγαθάγγελος (Agathangelos), and through the Greek alphabet of the poem itself.

Despite their difference of religion, Agathangelos and the fictionalized soldier of the poem share something deeper: they are both exiled in foreign lands, one an unwilling conscript and the other a refugee. This is further reinforced by another couplet, the last two lines of the first stanza, which Agathangelos has written twice, repeating it vertically in the fore-edge margin (see figure 10):

| γιαρατὰν μεβλὰ ασκηνὰ | for the love of the Lord who created us |
| κόιμα πενὶ σου κούρπεττε | don't cast me off in this foreign place |

The emphatic repetition of this couplet in the margins, I suggest, bears witness to just how deeply Agathangelos identified with the poem's speaker and his plight. Despite his own Orthodox faith (indeed, he was a cleric!), what ultimately leads him to assume the performative mask of a Muslim soldier here, weeping through the Quran, is their shared experience of exile and displacement.

Like Nikolas Kazakoglou from the previous chapter, Agathangelos was forced in the aftermath of the Greco-Turkish War and Population Exchange to abandon his native village—in this case, Andaval in Cappadocia. Carted, marched, and shipped across approximately one thousand kilometers of hinterland and sea, he eventually found himself in Greek Macedonia, where he stayed for two years. Unlike Kazakoglou, however, Agathangelos left again, setting out for the United States in 1927 at the request of his two sons, who had already settled there. He spent the rest of his life in Michigan, as evidenced by the *ex libris* stamped on the obverse of the same leaf (see figure 11).

But more than just geography, there is something else that renders Agathangelos distinct from Kazakoglou and other refugees whose stories would eventually find a voice in the mainstream media and hence national memory of Greece: he kept his stories in Turkish, and he intermixed them freely with Anatolian Turkish culture. Such intermixtures provide an important contrast to nationalist images of an essentially and eternally Hellenic Anatolia—images that seem at times to color the memoirs and narratives of mainstream authors,

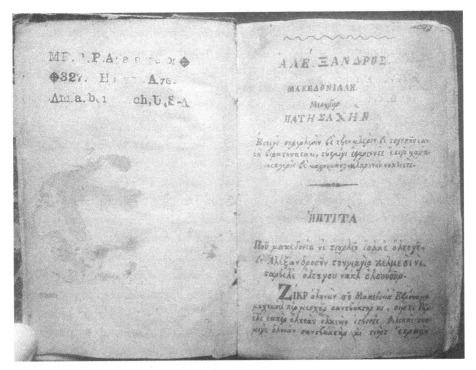

FIGURE 11. Verso of flyleaf and first page of *Alexandros Makedonialı Meşhur Padişah*. Note both the *ex libris* on the verso and the manuscript *incipit* on the recto, which Agathangelos has carefully written in imitation of the now-lost print original. Courtesy of Giorgos Kallinikidis.

such as Fotis Kondoglou's *Aivali: My Homeland* and Venezis's *Aiolian Land*. Despite the discrimination and gatekeeping of Greece's mainstream media, many Turkish-speaking refugees like Agathangelos quietly continued sharing their rich mix of stories across several generations. Today, a hundred years on, these stories are difficult but not impossible to recover. The difficulty lies not only in the now-obscure combination of language and script but often in the material medium and format. With their print apparatus in Turkey destroyed and an indifferent or openly hostile Greek publishing world awaiting them abroad, many Karamanli poets turned to manuscript media, scrawling their poems by hand. Their doubly displaced stories of displacement should give us pause as we continue to debate the contours of world literature. What kind of a world literature would be able to account for the stories of lost worlds like those of the Karamanli Christians? Basic formal and material assumptions regarding our objects of study in modern language departments have forced certain literary border crossings underground. To recover and to honor these crossings, scholars of literature have already posed some important questions: what modes of storytelling and what modes of reading get lost in the melting pot of world literature?[10] To these I would add: before the story has been read, before it's even told, how is it manufactured? What are the means of production of world literature, and how is access to those means regulated? From at least the early twentieth century onward, the fact is that some minor literatures, displaced from mass production, have been forced to cross the borders of world literature beneath our radar, their forms and formats unsung and undocumented by philologists. Careful consideration of alternative media assemblages, such as manuscript codices and oral performance, can expand our vision to even the most marginalized literary networks.

For his part, Agathangelos continued to assemble books, stories, readers, and listeners for twenty years after the Population Exchange, working creatively into the 1940s. Physically poaching printed books and a startling variety of paper sources, inscribing poems into the blank leaves of printed codices, adapting entire Greek novels into his own Turkish versions, and composing original poetry in a commonplace book that he also filled with, among other things, popular Ottoman songs, Agathangelos was building a narrative just as culturally complex, historically valuable, and aesthetically vibrant as what might be found in Greek-language narratives like *A Captive's Story*. In naming this section "books behaving badly," therefore, I refer not to illicit subject matter but quite literally to books that stop behaving as a modern reader would expect. Books that accrue both media and meanings, that come apart and are re-assembled in unexpected ways, bringing together multiple modes of inscription, contents, geographies, handlers, and readers. This last point is crucial: Agathangelos made these books not only for himself but for his wider community of Turkish-speaking readers, at least some of whom have, in turn, left their own marginalia and notes in his books, which continued to circulate and be read well after his death.

In the following sections of this chapter, I will turn to a more careful consideration of these books, but before I transition there I want to emphasize that similar complexities could be observed in the larger Karamanli community and their narrative of self well before the war's upheaval. In other words, Agathangelos was not telling his story in a vacuum but was building on a complex communal process of self-definition that had been drawing from both

Greek and Turkish cultural systems for decades. It had long lived on the margins of these systems, yet through the second half of the nineteenth century the Karamanli community was increasingly targeted for standardization and codification by multiple, often conflicting parties. Writing in 1899, the Turkish nationalist Şemseddin Sami claimed,

> It is almost proven that the more than half a million Orthodox population which lives in Anatolia, having absolutely no relationship with the Greeks, and speaking nothing but Turkish, have arisen from the mixture of the ancient inhabitants of Anatolia with the Turkmens. [...] They should therefore not be regarded as Greeks. Just as every Muslim is not a Turk, an Orthodox Christian is not necessarily a Greek. Faith stands on belief, and nationality on language.[11]

The entire debate was, as can already be sensed here, grounded upon the question of origin. Greek nationalists, in turn, countered that the Karamanlis derived from Byzantine Greek settlements that had begun speaking Turkish after centuries of "isolation."[12] To bring them back into the fold, so to speak, three separate actors began formalizing Greek-language instruction through the formation of schools, syllabi, and faculty: first, philanthropic societies of Greek-speaking Orthodox Christians in Istanbul and Smyrna; second, metropolitan bishops representing the Orthodox Church in the provinces; and third, the Greek state. (Recall from the previous chapter what effect these schools had on Nikolas Kazakoglou and his fellow villagers in Çirkince.) Balta writes, "Schools ceased to be treated only as an instrument of education and socialization, and acquired an additional mission, as a means of nationalization and nation-formation." Thus, Greek "was called on to take the place of the existing mother tongue, Turkish, and to oust it."[13]

Amidst these ideological maneuvers, what did the Karamanlis themselves say? As Balta has helpfully noted, we might best set aside questions of origin to instead "investigate the consciousness of the Turcophones themselves in their historical place and time."[14] Interestingly, the major media outlet of the Karamanli language during the nineteenth century, the ephemeral paper *Anatoli*, was at least partially complicit in the ideological project of Greek-speaking nationalists. For while it celebrated the distinct and localized culture of the Turkish-speaking Orthodox Christians of Cappadocia, it nonetheless advertised itself as a bilingual primer for helping its readers "reacquire" Greek.[15] On the other hand, other voices both within the paper and beyond it indicate that

Turkish continued to be a vital part of the community's identity—voices such as Yannis Gavrilidis, who wrote in the same paper of the principal importance of teaching their children good Turkish in schools (to be prioritized over both science and theology!),[16] or the collective Orthodox community of Nevşehir, who withheld their support from a philanthropic educational society at least in part for its insistence on keeping minutes only in Greek.[17] Taking in a broader range of voices, one soon understands that the web of attachments by which the Karamanlis defined themselves was far more complex and fluid than either Greek or Turkish nationalism was prepared to recognize. Looking at an aggregate body of forewords to printed books in the late nineteenth century, Balta notes that "'our fatherland, Anatolia' is often mentioned, which rules out any confusion with the other fatherland across the sea, Greece. Also, however hard we search for the ethnic prosonym 'Greeks,' we shall not find it anywhere. Whenever they are declared 'ethnically,' they are always declared as Rum, which alludes to the *Rum millet* [i.e., Ottoman Orthodox Christian], and wherever the word 'Greek' and its derivatives occur, they denote the language."[18] Some Greek-speakers, in turn, continued to remark on the resistance of Karamanlis to Greek identity. Ioakeim Valavanis, a celebrated scholar from Cappadocia, wrote in 1888:

> Today, if you ask any [Cappadocian] Christian, even if he speaks this corrupted Greek language,
> —What are you?
> —Christian, he will reply without hesitation.
> —Well, there are many other Christians, the Armenians, the Franks, the Russians.
> —I don't know, he will say. Yes, they believe in Christ, but I am Christian.
> —Maybe you are Greek?
> —No, I am nothing! I have already told you that I am Christian, and I repeat that I am Christian, he will say impatiently.[19]

Like Odysseus cornered in a cave, some Karamanlis declared in the face of Greek and Turkish nationalisms: "I am nothing." To find the something hiding behind these nothings, more recent scholarship has begun to look beyond the mainstream media of those final decades, whether to footnotes, forewords, or archival records: "cries and whispers," to borrow an evocative phrase from Balta and Kappler. Like the manuscript poem of an exiled Muslim soldier, fronting and framing Agathangelos's copy of the *Alexander Romance*, it is in such textual assemblages that we can hear more clearly the multiple and complicated stories that Karamanlis told about themselves. And these textual stories, I insist, did not stop with the Population Exchange.

Assembling Agathangelos's Commonplace Book

It's unknown when Agathangelos was born, yet by 1902 he was already acting as a priest at the church of Saint Nikolaos in Andaval. This was the village that he identified as his home and, as becomes clear from his poetry, it was the apple of his eye.[20] Nevertheless, he was by no means tied down to Andaval; as you might recall from the introduction to this book, he served as an itinerant confessor to the Christians of the surrounding region as well. This comfortably regional mobility of course could not prepare him for the mass uprooting that would mark his life at some point in 1924, when he and his fellow villagers were deported to Greek Macedonia, arriving in early 1925. While I have no textual evidence to confirm this, it was likely here in Macedonia that Agathangelos began composing the poems now found in his *mecmua*, or commonplace book.

The *mecmua* begins with a printed text, the Greek-language pamphlet Βίος τῆς Ὁσιομάρτυρος Παρασκευῆς (Life of the Holy Martyr Paraskevi), printed in Istanbul in 1894. After fifteen pages detailing the life and martyrdom of Paraskevi, the pamphlet abruptly ends and gives way to a lengthy manuscript poem in Turkish, titled "Ἀνδαβὰλ καριεσὶ ἰτζοὺν διουζιουλὲν δεσδάν" (The Ballad of Andaval), which might be understood easily enough as its own kind of martyrology: it's a long poem describing the final days of Agathangelos and his community in Andaval, as they await the Kemalist bureaucrats and oxcarts that will uproot them forever. Modeled on the *destan* form (i.e., ballad) of Anatolian minstrel poets, the work maintains a strict meter and rhyme scheme: quatrains (*koşma*) of hendecasyllabics in AAAB. The final word in each stanza is invariably the same: a fatalistic *n'eyleyim* ("what can I do?" / "what's to be done?").

Much of the poem is devoted to documenting and amassing the details of the village. It's a kind of epic catalogue, an aggregation of objects—murals, relics, heirlooms, buildings, rivers, crops—that is driven, I think, by a desperate impulse in the poet to record a life and a world that were about to vanish. As such, in what might have otherwise become the driest of historical records, one can sense a raw tragedy bubbling up just beneath the surface. It makes itself felt, if nowhere else, in the ineluctable "what's to be done?" that closes each stanza like the tolling of a bell, as seen already from the introduction:

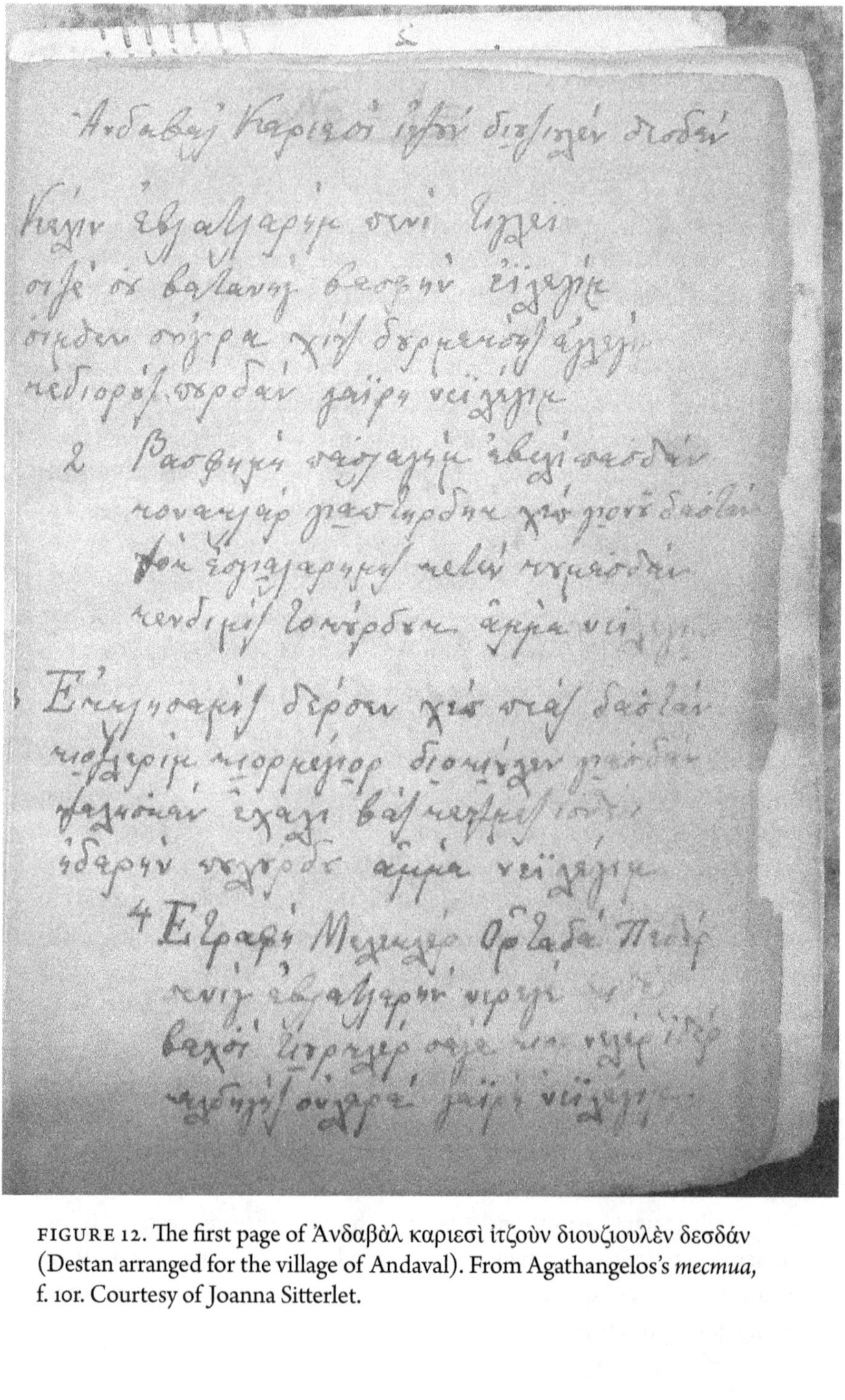

FIGURE 12. The first page of Ἀνδαβὰλ καριεσὶ ἰτζοὺν διουζιουλὲν δεσδάν (Destan arranged for the village of Andaval). From Agathangelos's *mecmua*, f. 10r. Courtesy of Joanna Sitterlet.

Κέλιν ἐβλατλαρὶμ πενὶ τιγλεγί	Gather round, my children, listen to me now:
σιζὲ ὁου βατανὴγ βασφὴν ἐϊλεγίμ	let me sing this homeland's story to you all,
ὁίμδεν σόγρα χὶτζ δουρμακσὴζ ἀγλεγίμ	let me weep black tears with every word I tell,
κεδιορούζ πουρδὰν γαϊρη νεϊλέγιμ	for we're leaving this place, what else can be done?
Βασφημὴ παὁλαγὴμ ἐβελὶ παὁδάν	Let me start from the beginning, in our homes,
κονακλὰρ γιαπτηρδὴκ χὲπ γιονοῦ δαὁτάν	which without fail we built from soft freestone
τζὸκ ἐὁγιαλαρημὴζ κετὲν κουμαὁδάν	and adorned with the linens that we wove
κενδιμὶζ τοκουρδοῦκ ἄμμα νεϊλεγιμ	with our own hands, but now what can be done?

At other moments, this subtle emotional charge spreads out from the final refrain and contaminates entire lines or even stanzas. In such cases, the poem's historical project of assembling objects and documenting their stories is interrupted as the impending deportation violently pulls the frame into the present (or even future) tense. We see this, for example, in a lengthy portion of the poem narrating the church's construction, which I excerpt here:

Πὶγ σεκὶζ γιοὺζ κὴρκ ἰκὶ ταριχὶ ἰσέ	In the year of eighteen forty two, then,
κοϊμουὁλὰρ τεμελιν πὶρ παὁδάν παὁά	they laid the fundaments from end to end.
καρὴ τζολοὺκ τζοτζοὺκ κοὁμουὁλὰρ ἰσέ	Everyone set to work, women and children.
γιεργὲτ ἐδὶπ γιαπτηρμηὁλὰρ νεϊλέγιμ	Their efforts built the church, but now what can be done?
Κιμὶ τοπρὰκ κιμὶ δαὁηνὴ δαὁήρ	Some bore soil on their backs, some bore stones.
σάνκι ἰουστλερινδὲ βάρδηρ μουπαὁήρ	as if there were a foreman looking over them;
πιλμεδιλὲρ κελσὶν πιογλὲ πὶρ ἀσήρ	they had no idea a century like this would come.
πρακδηλὰρ περκουζὰρ ἄμμα νεϊλεγιμ	They left us this gift, but now what can be done?
Γαϊρέτλε γιαπτηρμὴζ ἀταλαρημὴζ	With much effort our ancestors saw this church get built.
Ράππιμ ἀφ ἔγλεσιν χαταλαρημὴζ	But my God please forgive us now our guilt:
τζαμὴζ ἀραπαλὰρ κοὁάρλαρημής	they tell me that the ox-carts run full tilt
τζινκιδὲν διρεκλὲρ κελσὶν νεϊλεγιμ	to put us on the ships, what now can be done?
Παντωκρατωρουνοὺγ τζεβρεσὶ Μελέκ	Christ sits in the vault, the angels round the rim.[21]
μερδιβὲν κουρούπδα γιανηγὰ βαράκ	We'll set up a ladder, climb up next to him

νούρλου σουφατηγὰ γιουζιουμιοὺζ σιουρέκ	and rub our face against his bright countenance;
σὸγ σελαμὴ βερὶπ κιδὲκ νεΐλέγιμ	we'll say our last goodbye and leave, what can be done?

The longer description of the church, only part of which I've excerpted here, mostly uses past tense forms to stage the history of the village's collective struggle—at one point even selling their individual chattel property to pool a common fund (*eşyaların*[*ı*] *satıp borcu verdiler*). Yet in the second stanza quoted above, the present begins to pry its way into the narrative, in a dark and ironic act of foreshadowing: "they had no idea a century like this would come." And come it does, filling all four lines in the final stanza, with the heartbreaking image of an entire village ascending a ladder, one by one, to bid farewell to the murals in their place of worship.

The poem goes on for more than forty stanzas and can be read in full elsewhere,[22] but more important for this chapter is the larger sense of the codex as a whole. It's a patchwork of texts, some of them poetic creations by Agathangelos (for the most part, *destans*), while others are popular or anonymous songs that he has transcribed. When brought into dialogue, these various texts reveal the complicated identity suturing the Karamanli together. Look, for example, to his transcription of the still-popular Sevastopol Battle (what he calls "A Soldier's Song from the Russian War"). While it is today performed as a nationalist and indeed militarist march ("Sevastapol March"), the version that Agathangelos arranges is notably darker and anti-militarist. Not only that, but it is again sung from the explicit perspective of a Muslim conscript, decrying the needless death of "the Muslim community"—details that today's versions have excised. While there are many variations to this song, all that I know maintain the following refrain:

Aman padişahım izin ver bize	My Sultan, give us permission
vermez isen dök bizi denize	If you don't, then throw us into the sea

The meaning of the refrain is admittedly ambiguous. The "permission" (*izin*) here might be understood as "leave" or indeed permission to flee the battle, yet some versions include other lines that make the meaning clear: "permission to attack."[23] Many likewise include the gung-ho line: "If we die, we'll be martyrs; if we live we'll be heroes" (*ölürsek şehidiz, kalırsak gazi*). No matter how one interprets this refrain, however, in Agathangelos's version it is irrelevant, for the simple reason that he supplies an entirely different variation, which I have been unable to locate elsewhere—one that leaves no ambiguity whatsoever:

| Ἀμὰν Πατισαχὴμ βαζ κὲλ ποῦ ἰόδέν | My Sultan, abandon this war |
| ἰουμέτι μουσλιουμὰν κετζδὶ κηληνδζδάν | The community of Muslims has been put to the sword |

Driving him to this refrain are the atrocities of the war, such as "the brooks [that] run over with blood instead of the spring flood" (δερελερδὲν σὲλ γερινὲ κὰν ἄκαρ) or the more mundane if devastating agents of death, such as hunger and disease:

Καρσὴγ καλασήνδα μουχασάρ ὀλδούκ	In the tower of Kars we were surrounded
καπανδὴκ καλεγιὲ ἀτζληκδὰν ἰολδιουκ	shut up in the tower we died of hunger
σεκσὲν πὶγ κισίδὲν σεκὶζ πὶγ καλδὴκ	from eighty thousand eight thousand we became

And after every such atrocity, Agathangelos supplies the same refrain, crying out against the senseless slaughter of the Muslim faithful. The fact that he planted such a song in the *mecmua*—that he consciously chose this variation, if he did not indeed invent pieces of it himself—again demonstrates his unproblematic and frequent identification with Ottoman Turkish Muslims, while at the same time he never severed his ties to the Greek Orthodox tradition. This is clear, for example, in the next song of the codex, the "Dance of Zalongo," a Greek piece on the Souliote War at the start of the nineteenth century. This is in turn followed by a Turkish song from the Black Sea, praising Turkish sailors and in Agathangelos's variation their brave resistance to the imperialist encroachments of Russia (an Orthodox Christian state). Despite his own Orthodox faith, Agathangelos identified closely enough with the Muslim Turkish sailors not only to place their song of praise within his *mecmua* but indeed to notate the song for live performance. His notation, however, is in the form he knew best: not Ottoman but Byzantine. Such notation recurs in many of the songs—even those most deeply rooted in the Muslim Turkish tradition—a subtle indication of the complicated amalgam of the Karamanli identity.

Taken together, what do these poems and songs indicate? They stitch together a patchwork of displaced worlds that were neither entirely local nor global; they were regional. Most of Agathangelos's original *destans* narrated the acutely local stories and myths of Andaval, a village that he deeply loved,

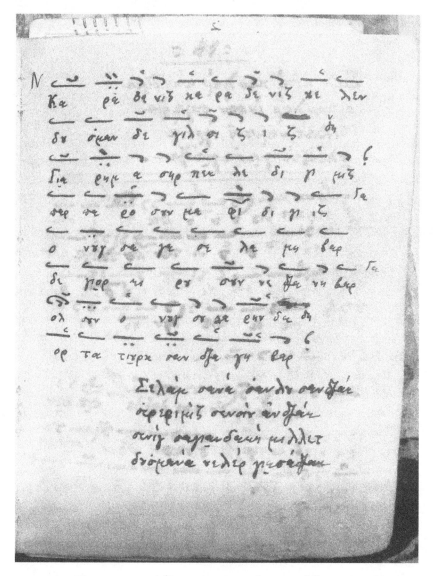

FIGURE 13. Παρασημαντική (Byzantine musical notation) for a song of Turkish sailors in the Black Sea. From Agathangelos's *mecmua*, f. 30r. Courtesy of Joanna Sitterlet.

yet some of them were devoted to other cities and villages in the surrounding area (Niğde, Kayabaşı, Semendre, Matala). Later sections of the *mecmua*, those that contain the popular songs, expand this geography further, drawing from cultural traditions across the Aegean in mainland Greece or from the north, along the coast of the Black Sea. In other words, the *mecmua* pieces together a localized yet regional, complicated and composite world that fit into neither Greek nor Turkish nationalism, both of which had been busily partitioning this same cultural geography for decades. The book ushers us moreover into the broader textual logic of Agathangelos's entire collection: drawing together, assembling, reworking, and adapting pieces of a world that were being or had been displaced.

In doing so, he was also drawing together the refugees of that displaced world, for there are strong indications that he used his commonplace book for live musical performance before an audience of fellow refugees. Beyond the allusions in the ballad to assembling a community of listeners, the musical notation above many of the poems indicates that they were to be sung aloud. Ultimately settling in Michigan, Agathangelos found himself amidst a more scattered but by no means numerically negligible constellation of Turcophone Christian émigrés in Detroit and the larger region. From what remains of his personal papers and the oral interviews that I have conducted, it appears that he stayed quite mobile, traveling to communities as far north as Pontiac, Michigan, and at least as far south as Warren, Ohio, performing his poetry and music for fellow refugees. His work provided an important platform for the displaced communities of Turkish-speaking Orthodox Christians in the region, who were linguistic outcasts on two fronts: not only from mainstream anglophone America but from the dominant Greek language of the Greek Orthodox community as well. Facing indifference or open condescension from these two dominant groups, Turcophone Christians were in sore need of a sense of community.

Reassembling a Commons

When Agathangelos arrived in Ann Arbor, Michigan, in 1927, he had come for a specific purpose: to fulfill the spiritual and sacramental needs of the city's Greek Orthodox community, which lacked not only a priest but even a building in which to house one. Agathangelos's two sons had volunteered their father. One of them, Konstantinos, volunteered his garage as well, converting it into a makeshift church, and it was here that Agathangelos, after his arrival, began performing the first Orthodox liturgies of Ann Arbor, as well as the sacraments of baptism and marriage; he was paid only through the collective donations of the community.[24] Problems quickly arose. While he was beloved by many, there were others who did not warm to him, creating a rift within the community that played out primarily along linguistic lines.[25] The Turcophone Orthodox immigrants—not just in Ann Arbor but across the region, reaching north to at least Pontiac and south to Ohio—felt a great attachment to the man.[26] Yet many of the Greek-speaking Orthodox of Ann Arbor may have felt differently. For although he could read Greek (and write his own, albeit grammatically erratic poems and epistles in Greek), he was reportedly unable to speak it, save for recitations of the liturgy. When the Archbishop brought the community together six years later, in 1933, to plan for the construction of their first official church, one of the agreements reached in their meeting maintained:

> Ἡ θεία λειτουργία μέχρις ἀποκτήσεως ἰδιοκτήτου Ναοῦ θὰ γίνηται εἰς αἴθουσαν τὴν ὁποίαν θὰ ἐξεύρη τὸ Διοικητικὸν Συμβούλιον τῆς Κοινότητος τὸ ὁποῖον ἐν συνεννοήσει μετὰ τῆς Ἀρχιεπισκοπῆς θὰ φέρη εἰς τὴν Κοινότητα τὸν κατάλληλον Ἱερέα.

> The divine liturgy, until the acquisition of a private Temple, will occur in a space to be located by the Administrative Council of the Community, which will also confer with the Archbishopric to bring a proper priest.[27]

Implicitly, then, Agathangelos was not a "proper priest" in their eyes. The archbishop's visit had admittedly mended important political schisms within the Greek community (between Venizelists and Royalists) yet it perhaps came at the cost of marginalizing other, non-Greek voices. By 1935, with the construction of the new church (if not sooner), Agathangelos found himself again displaced. Michael Konteleon, a Greek-speaking priest, was hired to lead the parish and officiated at the building's first liturgy in December of that year.

Having failed to integrate himself into a predominantly Greek-speaking community of Orthodox Christians in Ann Arbor, Agathangelos would have to find a way to connect with other Turcophones elsewhere. He did so by turning to, among other outlets, hundreds of pages of literary adaptation, which he wrote, bound, and circulated along with his other printed books to a network whose size and scale it is difficult to determine. His two manuscript novels, *Monte Cristo in Marseille* and *Theodora*, are dated 1939, as seen in figure 14 (though other later novels may remain as yet unknown to me). As indicated by the phrases "translated from the Greek" (ἔλληνος λισάνηνδαν [...] τερδζουμὲ ὀλουνμουστούρ) and "interpreted from the Greek" (ἑρμηνεύθη ἀπὸ τὴν ἑλληνικὴν γλῶσσαν) that center the title pages of both novels, he adapted them from Greek sources, one of which was itself undoubtedly a translation/adaptation from Dumas's famous French serial *Le Comte de Monte-Cristo*, although I have been unable to determine the precise title and

FIGURE 14. The title pages of *Monte Cristo* and *Theodora*. Courtesy of Giorgos Kallinikidis.

edition.[28] The other novel is a fictional account of the Byzantine heroine Theodora, who began her life as an impoverished orphan, later becoming an actress and sex worker, and eventually assuming the title of empress and carving out an important political role for women within the regime. This novel, as I've established, was adapted into Turkish from the Greek-language novel *Theodora* by Aristeidis Kyriakos (1906). Through a comparison of the language and style of the Greek and Turkish *Theodora*, I'll suggest that the major differences between the two arise primarily from the corresponding differences in their target audiences. Aimed not at a mass commercial readership but a relatively small and spread-out network of handlers, Agathangelos's Turkish-language novels were yet another tool, like the ballads in his *mecmua*, by which to assemble Karamanli refugees together in the wake of their displacement and their exclusion from mainstream print. His books and their users were, in other words, creating a literary "commons"—i.e., a collective cultural resource.

Before I proceed to the language of *Theodora*, however, I want to look first at its material medium, which was subtly assembling its own network of displaced persons. As you'll note from the title page (reproduced in figure 14), Agathangelos wrote his novel atop leaves that already bore impressions in a language and script distinct from his own: Chinese characters. These leaves derived from a student planner (自由日記 / "Freedom Diary") that was likely printed and sold by the Commercial Press (商務印書館), the largest publisher in Shanghai at the time. Printed in the second half of the 1930s, this student planner must have made its way to Ann Arbor just a couple of years before Agathangelos unbound its pages and turned them into a Karamanli novel.[29]

What to make of these leaves? First, it's important to emphasize that Agathangelos was deeply invested in visual aesthetics. You might have guessed this already from the touching farewell that he offered to his church's murals in the ballad of the previous section, yet the fact is that he himself was a painter and a visual artist, as witnessed through the half dozen or so icons that he painted and gave to friends and that today you might find in the Church of Saint Nicholas in Ann Arbor or in private homes across and beyond Michigan. Alongside these large-scale creations, he also spent hours poking small, needle-sized holes into paper to create hidden images that the reader could only discover upon holding them up to light. Consider, finally, the floral-patterned wallpaper with which he lined the binding of his *Monte Cristo* novel. Given the preponderance of examples, each of which bears witness to the

FIGURE 15. Icon of John the Baptist, painted by Agathangelos. Courtesy of Joanna Sitterlet.

meticulous care that he invested in the visual impact of his materials, it therefore seems probable to me that his use of the leaves bearing Chinese characters was intentional. These pages were meaningful to him.

But how did Agathangelos get his hands on them? What was their own story? Unfortunately, I have found no textual evidence by which to answer this

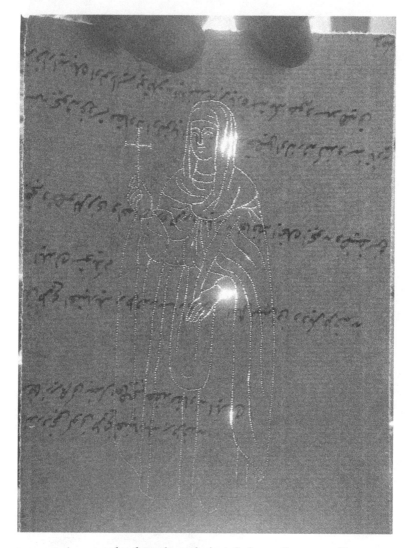

FIGURE 16. An example of Agathangelos's pinhole art. Courtesy of Joanna Sitterlet.

question in the particular, yet it's important to remember that while Agathangelos had been forced out of his role in the Orthodox parish, he was nonetheless living in a thriving university city that offered him access to several other networks. In particular, the university had been funding female students from East Asia to study on its campus since 1917, through the Barbour Scholarship. Funded by Levi Barbour, it was a program that aimed to give women from the

"Orient" access to the University of Michigan's faculty and research. By the time of Barbour's death in 1925, more than sixty women had already studied at the university through his fellowship, a number that would triple by the time that Agathangelos was creating *Theodora* in 1939.[30] Despite Barbour's overly ambitious vision that the program might lead to cultural understanding and avoid war—"We certainly would never have any war with Japan," he wrote in 1917[31]—the woman who had brought this student planner with her from Shanghai, likely in 1936 or 1937, would become a sort of displaced person herself as the Japanese military invaded mainland China. I don't know whether she remained stranded in the United States or returned to occupied China, yet if the latter is true she might likely have found herself displaced again, in even more acute circumstances. As the program's secretary, W. Carl Rufus, noted in 1942, "A few of our Barbour Scholars, accustomed to luxurious surroundings, have been bombed into refugee treks and camps."[32] One such example was Katherine Yu Tseng, among the possible owners of the book: after finishing her master's degree in library science, she returned to China and began working at the university library in Wuhan. The university was bombed and the library was displaced at the start of 1939. As of February of that year, her parents were still unable to locate or communicate with her.[33] In the pages of *Theodora*, therefore, we can just begin to make out two displaced stories from two separate wars at the two ends of Asia, whose strands and whose book connected in the middle of North America. Such was the twentieth century. As Agathangelos had written in his commonplace book, πιλμεδιλὲρ κελσὶν πιογλὲ πὶρ ἀσὴρ (they had no idea a century like this would come).

Following the title page, Agathangelos continued to use these Chinese leaves for the majority of his novel. As the story wore on, the impressions made in Shanghai came to shape his own inscriptions. He had begun inscribing his text horizontally, against the lines (and logic) of the vertically ruled Chinese codex, yet he eventually shifted to vertical inscription, adapting his novel and his orientation to that of his materials (see figure 17). This shift occurs on page 171 and continues until the end of the novel, on page 343. Like a carpenter or craftsman, Agathangelos developed a close relationship with his materials, adapting the content of his novel to the pre-histories of the papers he had salvaged, reaching out for unexpected connections and striving for mutual integration.

For Agathengelos, it seems that bookmaking was less an act of authorship than craftsmanship. In fact, his novels had no author. Recall that in the title pages of both *Theodora* and *Monte Cristo* Agathangelos neglected to name a

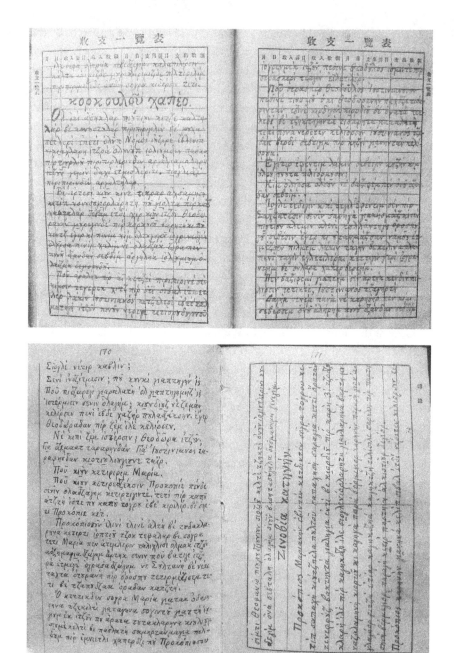

FIGURE 17. *Theodora*, f. 2b and 3a (above); f. 92b and 93a (below). Courtesy of Giorgos Kallinikidis.

source or an author, including only his own name as "translator" beneath the title. To my mind, what we witness here is not a transference of authorial power from writer to translator but a general abolition of it. Of course, removing the author from the title page doesn't abolish the existence of the work's first writer. Instead, what it signals is that the writer is a *writer*, not an *author*. Put another way, it signals a different approach to translation, neither as a process of linear filiation (author-centric) nor as a revolutionary sundering or break (translator-centric) but rather as a transmission network, one that draws from multiple nodes and connections rather than a single source. Traditionally, Karamanli translations had worked in just such a manner, drawing not only from a Greek source text but mixing into it the cultural repertoires of Ottoman Anatolia as well.

Anthi Karra provides an excellent case study of the creative power of Karamanli translation, and I commend it to my readers.[34] Particularly useful for me here, however, is her focus on language. Most of the source texts used by Karamanli translations were in Katharevousa Greek, an artificially high register that drew on Ancient Greek vocabulary and morphology.[35] The Karamanli Turkish into which these texts were translated, however, dispatched with such a register and generally preferred a much more colloquial Turkish. This was because, as Karra writes, the Karamanli novel "has a very strong oral character. It was written in order to be read out loud to a wider, probably illiterate public."[36] Karamanli translation, in other words, was not just articulating a different message from its source text; it was doing so in a different register to a different audience through what was likely a different combination of media: written texts performed orally.

In Agathangelos's refugee novels from 1939, the linguistic transformations of his Turkish continue and expand on this tradition. We see this clearly in *Theodora*, which Agathangelos adapted from Kyriakos's Greek novel of the same name. Although Kyriakos's use of Katharevousa was simpler and less brittle than the highest registers of Greek from the nineteenth century, his elevated language is impossible to ignore. In Agathangelos's novel, however, any notion of a higher register is dissolved in what has become a droll and colloquial Turkish. It would not be too much of a stretch, in fact, to argue that his Turkish codex resembles the base text of an Ottoman *meddah* (oral storyteller), who performed to large audiences in coffeehouses and elsewhere.[37] Part of this oral tradition was a focus not on overextended description but dramatic action. As such, Agathangelos cut out the lengthy descriptions of scenery and surroundings that Kyriakos had front-loaded into many chapters.

Compare, for example, the opening of the two works, beginning with Kyriakos's Greek:

> Ἀντικρὺ τοῦ Βυζαντίου, ἐπὶ τῆς Ἀσιατικῆς ἀκτῆς, ἐν μέσῳ κήπου θαλεροῦ, κισσοστεφής, κομψὴ καὶ χαρίεσσα ἠγείρετο λαμπρὰ ἔπαυλις. Ὑπερύψηλα δένδρα ἐξέτεινον τοὺς καταπρασίνους κλάδους των, ὑπὲρ τῆς ἐπαύλεως τὴν ὀροφήν, καὶ τῶν ἀνθέων τὸ ἄρωμα, ἄφθονον ἀναδιδόμενον ἀπὸ κάθε τοῦ κήπου γωνίαν, περιέβαλε τὴν ὡραίαν ἔπαυλιν μὲ τὰ λευκά της μάρμαρα, τὰ μεγάλα της παράθυρα, τὰ κομψὰ προπύλαιά της, πρὸ τῶν ὁποίων μεγαλοπρεπεῖς φοίνικες ἐσκίαζον μὲ τοὺς κλάδους αὐτῶν μαρμάρινα ἀγαλμάτια, ἕκαστον τῶν ὁποίων ἀντεπροσώπευε καὶ ἕναν τύπον τῆς γυναικείας καλλονῆς, ὅπως ὀνειρεύονται αὐτὴν οἱ ποιηταὶ καὶ οἱ καλλιτέχναι. Τὸν ἀπέραντον δὲ τῆς ὡραίας ἐπαύλεως κῆπον διέσχιζον κατὰ μῆκος καὶ πλάτος σκιεροὶ ἀμμόστρωτοι δρομίσκοι, εἷς τῶν ὁποίων ὡδήγει πρὸς τὴν ἀπωτάτην τοῦ ἐξοχικοῦ ἐκείνου παραδείσου γωνίαν, τὴν ὁποίαν τοῖχος ὑψηλὸς ἐχώριζεν ἀπὸ τῆς ἀκτῆς, εἰς τὴν ὁποίαν ἁπαλά, ἤρεμα, φιλοπαίγμονα ἤρχοντο τοῦ Βοσπόρου τὰ κύματα, διὰ νὰ ἐκπνεύσουν διαλυόμενα εἰς γλυκεῖς ψιθύρους καὶ λευκοὺς ἀφρούς. Ἡ ἔπαυλις ἐκείνη, τὰς περισσοτέρας ἡμέρας τῆς ἑβδομάδος, ἔμενεν ἀκατοίκητος. Ἀλλὰ κατὰ πᾶσαν Τετάρτην, Παρασκευὴν καὶ Κυριακήν, ὀλίγον μετὰ τὴν δύσιν τοῦ ἡλίου, περίκομψον ἀκάτιον, ἰσχυρῶς ὑπὸ ρωμαλέων ἀνδρῶν κωπηλατούμενον, ἐξώρμα ἀπό τινος τοῦ Βυζαντίου γωνίας, διέσχιζεν ἐν ἀσυλλήπτῳ ταχύτητι τοῦ Βοσπόρου τὰ γαλανὰ νερά, καὶ φθάνον πρὸ τῆς ὡραίας ἐπαύλεως, ἀπεβίβαζεν εἰς ξυλίνην πρὸ αὐτῆς ἀποβάθραν ὡραίαν μικρόσωμον γυναῖκα, πολυτελῶς ἐνδεδυμένην καὶ ἀκολουθουμένην ὑπὸ θεραπαινῶν καὶ θεραπόντων ἀποτελούντων τὴν συνοδείαν αὐτῆς [...]

Opposite Byzantium, on the Asian shore, in the midst of a flowery garden, crowned with ivy, graceful and charming ariseth a bright manor. Towering trees extend their deep green boughs above the roof of the manor, and the aroma of the blossoms, transfused abundantly from every corner of the garden, surroundeth the lovely manor, with its white marbles, its large windows, its graceful archways, before which grandiose palm trees shade with their boughs marble statuettes, each of which representeth one of the types of female beauty, as poets and artists dream it. The endless garden of the beautiful manor is crossed in length and breadth by shadowy, sand-strewn pathways, one of which leadeth to the furthest corner of that paradisiacal country house, which a tall wall divideth from the shore, upon which fall the waves of the Bosporus softly, peacefully, playfully, in order to exhale as they dissolve into sweet whispers and white spume. That manor, for the most days of the week, remaineth uninhabited. But each Wednesday, Friday and Sunday, a little after the setting of the sun, a most graceful barque, briskly rowed by powerful men, emergeth from some corner of Byzantium, crosseth the peaceful waters of the Bosporus with inconceivable speed, and arriveth before the lovely manor[.] [I]t disembarketh upon a wooden platform a lovely woman of small figure, dressed luxuriously and followed by female and male attendants constituting her train [...][38]

And here is the introduction to Agathangelos's novel:

Ἰουστίνος Βυζαντὶν ἰμπερατωρουνοῦν ζεβδζεσὶ Ἐφιμία Βυζαντὴν ἐχαλισινὶν πουτπερεστλικτὲν καλμὰ πὶρ φενὰ ἀτετλερινὶν μαχβηνὰ ὀγραστηγὴ βακητλαρδὰ. Γεγενὶ Ἰουστινιανὸς πὶρ κιοῦν Ἐκήβολος νὰμ πὶρ ζαπίτλε περαπὲρ κεζέρκεν πὶρ χανεγὲ κελιρλὲρ. Ὀλ Χανὲ ἰσὲ Κομήτω ναμηντὰ πὶρ οροσπου[για] ἐγίτ, πουνοῦν κιουτζδζιουγιοῦκ πὶρ Θεοδώρα ἰσμιντὲ κὴς καρτασὴ δαχὶ γάγετ μενδοῦρ κοζελ ὀλοὺπ ταχα ἄνδζακ σεκὶζ γιὰ τοκοῦζ γιαδήνδα ἠτῆ. Ἰουστινιανὸς ποὺ κηζὴ κιορδιουγιουνδὲ ποῦ κὴζ Βυζαντινὶν σουλτανὴ ὀλατζὰκ τεμίσιτι. Λάκιν ποῦ κηζ[ην] ἰουτς καρδὰσ[ι] ὀλοῦπ ἀταλαρὴ ἀγητζη σοκακλαρδα ἀγὴ μαϊμουν οἰνατῆρ πὶρ φακὶρ κιμσελὲρ ἰσὲ δὲ ἀζ ἐβελ βεφὰτ ἐτμιδλὲρ [...]

We're in the time of Justin the Emperor of Byzantium, whose wife Euphemia was struggling to wipe out some unpleasant customs—remnants from paganism—of the Byzantine people. One day, their nephew Justinian was taking a walk with an officer named Ekivolos when they came to a house. That house belonged to a prostitute named Komito. She had a younger sister named Theodora, who was quite famous for her beauty already, although she was only eight or nine years old. When Justinian saw her, he said, this girl will be the Sultana of Byzantium. But her father, who had been a street performer who made bears and monkeys dance, had been killed a little while ago by some vagrants [...]

Some of my readers might protest that there is in fact no relation between these two texts. There must be some mistake! But I assure you; there's no mistake. Only after lengthy and meticulous comparison, in fact, do traces of the two novel's connections arise, primarily through their shared dialogues.

The difficulties are due, first of all, to the fact that Agathangelos's narrative leaves no trace of Kyriakos's higher register in his Turkish, a sense of which I've tried to convey in my English translations of both texts. Just as important as the linguistic registers, however, are the stylistic priorities of each novel, which were often vastly divergent: while the Greek text unfolds slowly across a chain of baroque descriptions, Agathangelos's Turkish cuts to the chase—it often does so quite literally, cutting hundreds of pages and coming in at under half the size of its source text.[39] Kyriakos's Greek *Theodora* was a serial novel, which meant that it was *long*. Just as important as the story, for Kyriakos, was its elongation by any means necessary. He had no major authorial pretensions but was a prolific writer of serial fiction, who, by his death in 1919, had published approximately 120 novels in less than twenty years![40]

As becomes clear in the excerpt above, he often luxuriated in long and overripe descriptions and details, perhaps in an attempt to fill space but just as likely to provide the distinct feel of a European (which is to say Romantic or Realist) work of fiction—a *written* work, that is. Kyriakos was cultivating a style that called out for silent reading. Agathangelos's novel, on the other hand, gives the sense that it was intended to be read aloud, to a room full of listeners. It was a novel whose style at least had traditionally borne the aim of building a community through performance, rather than an intimate dialogue (between author and reader) through silent perusal. It was an object that was supposed to bring bodies together.

To what extent were Agathangelos's Turkish-language novels able to pack a coffeehouse in the United States? To be honest, it seems unlikely that they would have drawn large audiences, given the mass media forms (almost invariably in English) that were replacing public storytelling for many of the second- and third-generation refugee families in the United States. Nonetheless, these books did not remain idle; they moved from handler to handler for decades and were read by second- and third-generation refugees. Just as Agathangelos had created his icons expressly to share them and to see them in the hands of others,[41] I am certain that many of his books were made to move—and move they did, as readers' notes and the current locations of the books indicate.

Of course, Karamanli literature had always lived or died by its readers. In multiple senses, readers were the most vital agents in the lives of Karamanli books. Had not the large bulk of Karamanli literature been created by readers-turned-translators, whose readings and recombinations of other texts were then published and shared with other readers? Did not some of these other readers go on to write to the editors of the newspaper *Anatoli*, telling them their frank opinions of the stories and serial novels? Speaking of the period before the Population Exchange, Balta asserts, "I do not see the relationship between publishers and readers of Karamanli books simply as a relationship of production-consumption, for the simple reason that there is no radical distinction between them."[42] How much the more so does this hold true for the period *after* the Population Exchange, when publishing collapsed and left the remaining textual agents to their own devices? Unfortunately, for obvious reasons, I cannot map out where, how, and when Agathangelos's books reached their multiple readers and joined them together. If Balta writes that "[k]nowledge of the radius of circulation is also one of the desiderata of research on the Karamanlidika press,"[43] then it is doubly true for the refugee codices that I am tracing out here.

Before the Population Exchange, subscriber lists were printed in the backs of books and noted the names of readers and the numbers of books ordered for each city within the empire; ephemeral print likewise published letters to the editor written by readers from Adana, Adapazarı, Bafra, Samsun, Ürgüp, Unye, and Konya.[44] Such clues can help historians of the book trace, however rudimentarily, a map of Karamanli print networks. Yet after the Population Exchange, such data are of course lacking for the networks whose strands I am attempting to follow here. As such, I cannot hope to plot the journeys of Agathangelos's books in any great detail. What I can do, however, is map out their current locations, which to my knowledge range from the US midwest (Michigan) to the east coast (Delaware) and, across the ocean, to Greece (Zografou). It was here that his fellow villagers, after their deportation from Andaval, settled in 1925 and to which, at some point in the second half of the twentieth century, at least half a dozen of Agathangelos's books made their own pilgrimage, where they continued to be read by others. Indeed, the current caretaker of the books in Zografou, Giorgos Kallinikidis, tells me that just a few years ago he lent Agathangelos's novel *Monte Cristo* to a fellow villager who, upon returning it to him, remarked, "It was really good." He was not the only one to think so. In the margins of some of Agathangelos's books one finds the approbations and thanks of other readers, invariably left with a name and even, in one particularly moving case, a date and a wish:

ποῦ κυταπη όκουτου Μαρικα Τσίνογλου 1972	Marika Tsinoglou read this book in 1972
γιαζανην τσανη κοκ γ[ι]ουζουντε σεβηνσην	may the soul of him who wrote it take joy in heaven[45]

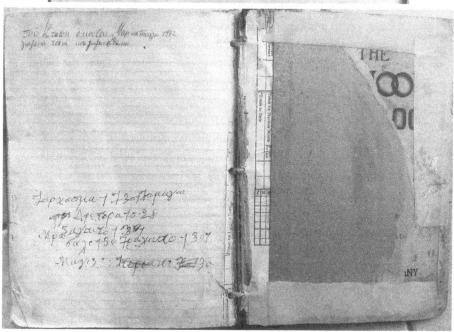

FIGURE 18. Sample reader's note in *Monte Cristo*. Courtesy of Giorgos Kallinikidis.

Where was Marika Tsinoglou when she read *Monte Cristo*? Where was she when she wrote this note? On what side of the ocean? These questions remain open, yet it seems likely that, given her spelling of certain words, Marika was a second- or third-generation refugee: rather than spelling the word "book" as κιταπ (kitap), she wrote κυταπ (kytap), suggesting a certain distance from Karamanli Turkish. Marika was likely reading *Monte Cristo* not only for pleasure (although aesthetic pleasure was doubtless an important motive as well) but also to hold on to a heritage language that she deeply loved but that she had learned outside of Anatolia, after the deportation of her grandparents or parents. In any case, this much is clear: passed from hand to hand across a wide geography, uncharted and uncontrolled by the mainstream market, these books were creating in their own small way a commons of the displaced—one that would exist only so long as their handlers continued to move these books, to read them (perhaps aloud and to one another), and to write in them. Only in this way could Karamanlidika survive. And as the marginalia of readers and the testimony of my friend Mr. Kallinikidis document, it continued to survive well after the last block of type had been pressed into the last copy of the last printed book of Karamanli literature.

The Refugee Undercommons

In August 1956, Eugene Dalleggio was on his way out of Athens, bound for the island of Evoia. As his name might suggest, Dalleggio belonged to the Greek-speaking Catholics of Syros; at some point in the nineteenth century, however, his family had relocated to Istanbul, where he had been born and raised. He was thus fluent in both Turkish and Greek, as well as French. Now in his sixties, he was collaborating with the Centre for Asia Minor Studies in Athens to document the books and manuscript archives of the Karamanli refugees across Greece. It was for this reason that he now found himself on the island of Evoia, where many Anatolian refugees had been settled after 1923. He was on a fact-finding mission of sorts, to document and, ultimately, to purchase and/or collect as many Karamanli books as possible for their relocation and safekeeping in the Centre's archives in Athens.[46] The day-to-day notes and report that he amassed over his weeklong journey offer an important window into the state of Karamanli literature at midcentury.[47]

While he returned to Athens with many Karamanli titles that would enrich both the holdings of the Centre and the soon-to-be-published bibliography,[48] one also cannot help but linger over the repeated and multiple instances of destruction and loss that he records. "I ask my hosts whether they have any manuscripts," he writes on Thursday, the first day of his arrival in Evoia. "Mr. Eleftheriadis tells me that after a disagreement with one of his relatives on their day of spring cleaning, he set the archives of his father, which had been carefully classified in a crate, on fire."* The story is repeated, with only minor variations, in another village four days later, on Monday. On Wednesday, again,

---

* "Je demande à mes hôtes s'ils n'ont pas des manuscrits. M. Eleftériadis me raconte qu'à la suite d'un différend avec une de ses parentes, il mit au feu, un jour de grande lessive, les archives de son père soigneusement classées dans une caisse" (published in Balta, *Beyond*, 95).

Dalleggio remarks of another village, Makrimalli: "Two fires during the last war destroyed almost everything that the refugees had brought here from their homelands."* Such stories are a sobering reminder of the very real precarity in which Karamanli literature now found itself. Excluded from print, some might suggest that it was dying a slow death, hastened by the intermittent fires and, above all, the Nazi occupation and Greek Civil War that had scarred the country at midcentury.[49] If I have celebrated the continued vitality of Karamanli-Turkish refugee books in this chapter, I do so in full knowledge of the dangerous conditions in which they operated—conditions that were only exacerbated by the singularity of their material forms.

Yet precisely because of these conditions, the survival of so many Karamanli texts—and the ongoing production, recombination, and circulation of new Karamanli texts—bears witness to the value that they held for their communities. Bookmaking and storytelling, I have argued, were important tools by which the geographically uprooted and displaced Karamanlis could continue to seek and suture connections to one another amidst their geographic and social displacement, and they continued well after the Population Exchange. Blurring the lines between print and manuscript, between Greek and Turkish (and Chinese), the Karamanli codices that I have featured in this chapter disassembled and reassembled the codex format in order to assemble their readers—not within any specific nation-state or territorial space but in an undercommons of the displaced, one that was to be assembled over and over by the handlers of the books themselves.

This refugee medium has not gained the prominence it deserves. In particular, the question of media access—whether, for example, refugee story-telling has access to industrial print and commercial publishing—deserves more prominence and discussion. To make assumptions about such media access is to engage in what Trish Loughran has called a violent act of "absorption and erasure." Loughran argues that "[w]hile book historians have chipped away at the facts and figures behind [the Gutenberg] master narrative, they continue to ignore the ways in which print capitalism is accepted not just as a regional history but as universal history."[50] The challenge before us, she suggests, is in how we might instead attend to "the edges of systems, the limits of premises, the boundaries of our historical imagination."[51] The Karamanli refugees lead us up to and beyond just such a boundary. Locked out of mainstream media

---

*"Deux incendies durant la dernière guerre ont détruit à peu près tout ce que les réfugiés apportèrent ici de leur pays" (published in Balta, *Beyond*, 100).

by the institutional partitions of commercial publishing in Turkey, Greece, and the United States, Karamanli refugees assembled their stories and communities across that same geography only by decentralizing and democratizing the means of production. By providing a new platform and amplified audience to these refugees today, a hundred years on, we chart new ground not only within the literary geographies of the past century; we simultaneously chart new ground across the lingering blind spots and invisible partitions that institutional philology has bequeathed to contemporary literary studies. Rather than fossils of a dead and lost literary culture, in other words, this refugee undercommons might in fact help us see the living literary landscape of today in a new light. Just what we might find there is the subject of the next chapter.

Chapter five, in which the script is rewritten

THE LEGACY of the Population Exchange far exceeded the borders that it built. Long after the treaty had been signed and sealed, long after the final refugees had been uprooted from their homes and consigned to historical oblivion, the Exchange continued to multiply and export its border logic abroad. For an entire generation of intellectuals and statesmen in Europe, West Asia, and North America, the massive, bilateral, and diplomatically legitimized ethnic cleansing carried out by Greece and Turkey marked the beginning of a new era of geopolitical possibilities. From Zionists like Ze'ev Jabotinsky to liberal democrats like Franklin Roosevelt, from Fascist Italy and Nazi Germany to postwar Czechoslovakia and Palestine-Israel, the Greco-Turkish Population Exchange offered nothing less than the ideological and institutional blueprint for a brave new world of partition and displacement.[1] A hundred years on, even as the general publics outside of Greece and Turkey have largely forgotten the Exchange, we are all still tangled up in the borders that it helped create.

In this my final chapter, then, I want to pivot to contemporary borders beyond Greece and Turkey, albeit through a case study especially close to both states: Cyprus. Not only did the Greek and Turkish Compulsory Exchange of Populations lay the groundwork for plans of population transfer and partition far afield in Europe and Asia; ironically but perhaps not unexpectedly, it also washed up closer to home on the shores of Cyprus in the late 1950s and became an increasingly common template for viewing the island's future. Actors as diverse as the Adnan Menderes Government in Turkey and the Central Intelligence Agency in the United States returned to the *locus classicus* of the Population Exchange and superimposed it onto their vision of post-independence Cyprus, a vision that became reality after the 1974 invasion and de facto partition.²

But the Exchange was not the only paradigm that Greece and Turkey imposed on Cyprus. The subsequent language politics of the Greek and Turkish states were also of critical importance and impacted the ideaological formations of Cyprus. It will thus be necessary here to keep a close eye on the parallel developments in the language policies of post–Exchange Greece and Turkey. In the minds of nationalists, the Population Exchange had by no means neutralized the perceived threat of ethno-linguistic contamination; indeed, several linguistic minorities, such as Slavophone Orthodox Christians in northern Greece or Sunni Kurds in eastern Turkey, had escaped the mechanisms of the Exchange, which was based on religion, while other linguistic minorities had been newly introduced into the national body *by* the Exchange itself, as previous chapters of this book have detailed. While state actors continued rummaging through their populations, categorizing, systematizing, and red-flagging this or that group, national philologists and linguists likewise rummaged through the wayward words of these same populations. The aim was to immobilize what Nergis Ertürk has called the "threat of indeterminacy," behind which lies the menace of linguistic and therefore social others.³ In Cyprus, as I will outline in the next section, nationalist actors began even before independence to import, modify, and intensify similar language engineering and language policing projects from Greece and Turkey.

Against this backdrop of Greek and Turkish nationalism, however, Cyprus was bound up in a wider web of colonial entanglements, due to decades of direct British rule over the island, first as a protectorate and then as a colony (1878–1960). Sorting out these tangles of colonization and nationalism, Bahriye Kemal uses the apt term "layers of invention"; that is, layers of competing Ottoman, Greek, British, and Cypriot discourses that unwrite, overwrite, or rewrite the island's cultural geography.⁴ Cyprus is not alone, of course, in its colonial ordeal—nor, I would add, in the impact that European colonial tongues like English have had on local language politics. From the nineteenth to the middle of the twentieth century, the European protectorates, mandates, and colonies lining the Mediterranean littoral shaped and often overdetermined many forms of linguistic contact and exchange between confessions and cultures. Perhaps it was in response to this kind of colonial footprint that Abdelfattah Kilito, writing from Morocco, commanded his foreign readers: *Thou Shalt Not Speak My Language*. And if he wrote with his tongue somewhat in cheek,⁵ the larger power dynamics spurring his interdiction are clear and have been challenged by others, such as Gayatri Spivak, Emily Apter, and Aamir Mufti.

Beset by both linguistic nationalism and extractive globalization, what is literature to do? This chapter explores that question through Mehmet Yashin's Cypriot novel *Sınırdışı Saatler / Σηνηρδηση̃ι Σαατλερ* (*The Deported Hours*[6]). Printed and distributed by a major Istanbul publisher, the novel nonetheless maintains large portions of its typeface in the Greek alphabet, a kind of neo-Karamanli Turkish that is refashioned and redeployed across divided Cyprus. Yashin himself has no personal or familial claim to Karamanli Turkish; unlike the literature treated in each of my earlier chapters, Yashin's novel is a postmodern reappropriation. The question thus arises: why Karamanli Turkish? What can this language teach Cyprus or the broader region today? As a refugee literature that was quite literally *un-authorized* out of print by the philological borderscape, I believe that Karamanli Turkish offers Yashin a working proxy model to sort through the ongoing violence of the literary borderscape in the current century—and the dynamics of authorship, authority, and authorization that underpin it.

With its admixture of scripts and languages, *The Deported Hours* bends its pliant tongue this way and that across standard Turkish and standard Greek, across Cypriot Turkish and Cypriot Greek, even across physical formats (a printed novel and a manuscript *Book of Hours*). Besieged not only by Turkish and Greek nationalists but by Anglophone globalists, Yashin's novel turns its back on them all and addresses itself instead to those readers, however small in number, who are willing to apprentice themselves to its several dialects and scripts, drawn from the rich history of linguistic contact in Cyprus and the larger Greco-Turkish borderscape. Weaving the supposedly incompatible scriptworlds of Greek and Turkish together, *The Deported Hours* seeks out an alternative regional mode of textual production and promulgation distinct from that of Cyprus's de facto partition and the nationalist literary systems that maintain this larger border logic.

In the pages that follow I too will apprentice myself to this textual underground, tracing its twists and turns of script and voice. The novel's success derives from at least two strategic departures from the modern literary system: by incorporating the logic not only of the region's supposedly premodern scriptworlds but of their material media as well—i.e., manuscript codices—and the human agencies assembling and reassembling them across linguistic and confessional divides: readers, copyists, commentators, and translators. Their several voices and scripts, displaced from national canon formation,

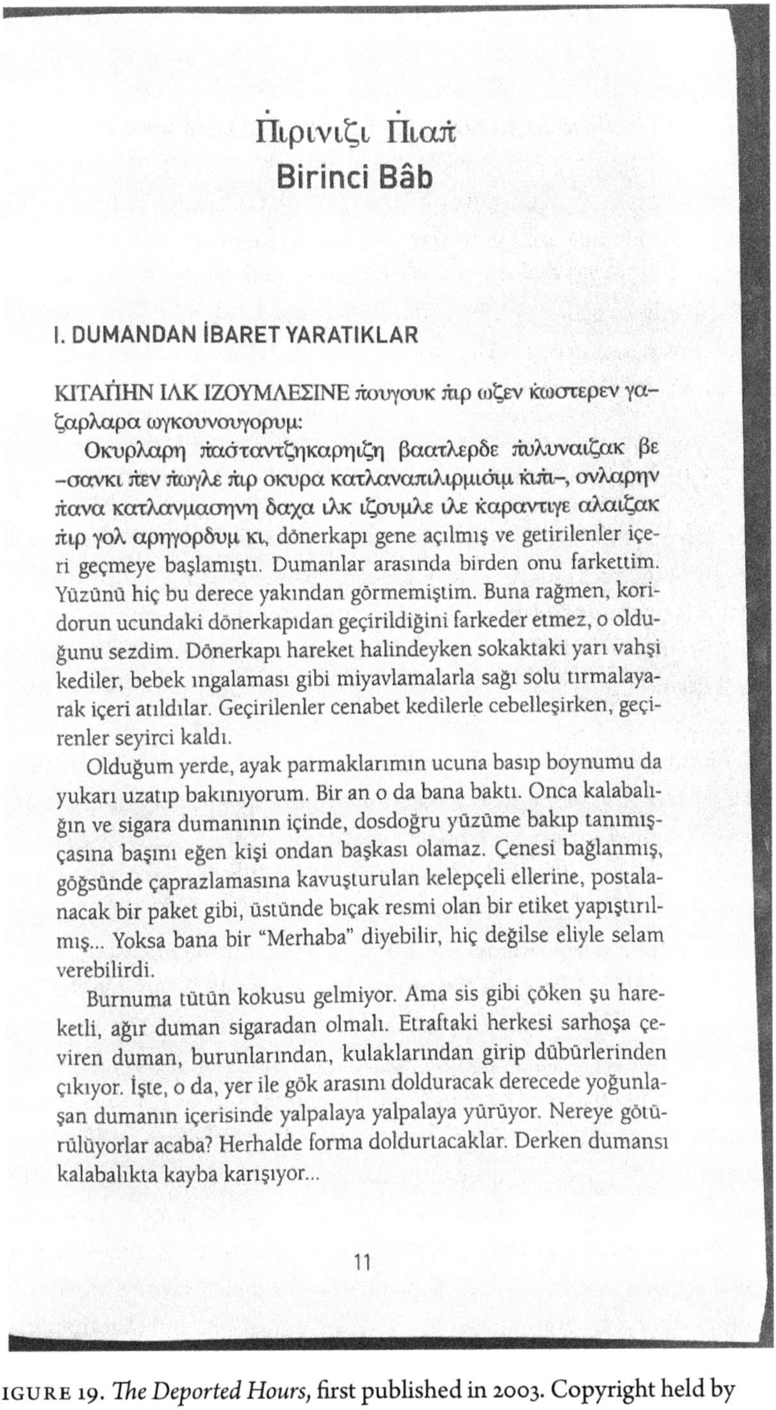

Πιρινιζι Πιαπ
Birinci Bâb

I. DUMANDAN İBARET YARATIKLAR

ΚΙΤΑΓΙΗΝ ΙΛΚ ΙΖΟΥΜΛΕΣΙΝΕ πουγουκ πιρ ωζεν κωστερεν γα–
ζαρλαρα ωγκουνουγορυμ:
 Οκυρλαρη παστάντζηκαρηιζη βαατλερδε πυλυναιζακ βε
–σανκι πεν πωγλε πιρ οκυρα κατλαναπιλιρμιωιμ κιπι–, ονλαρην
πανα κατλανμασηνη δαχα ιλκ ιζουμλε ιλε καραντιγε αλαιζακ
πιρ γολ αρηγορδυμ κι, dönerkapı gene açılmış ve getirilenler içeri geçmeye başlamıştı. Dumanlar arasında birden onu farkettim. Yüzünü hiç bu derece yakından görmemiştim. Buna rağmen, koridorun ucundaki dönerkapıdan geçirildiğini farkeder etmez, o olduğunu sezdim. Dönerkapı hareket halindeyken sokaktaki yarı vahşi kediler, bebek ıngalaması gibi miyavlamalarla sağı solu tırmalayarak içeri atıldılar. Geçirilenler cenabet kedilerle cebelleşirken, geçirenler seyirci kaldı.
 Olduğum yerde, ayak parmaklarımın ucuna basıp boynumu da yukarı uzatıp bakınıyorum. Bir an o da bana baktı. Onca kalabalığın ve sigara dumanının içinde, dosdoğru yüzüme bakıp tanımışçasına başını eğen kişi ondan başkası olamaz. Çenesi bağlanmış, göğsünde çaprazlamasına kavuşturulan kelepçeli ellerine, postalanacak bir paket gibi, üstünde bıçak resmi olan bir etiket yapıştırılmış... Yoksa bana bir "Merhaba" diyebilir, hiç değilse eliyle selam verebilirdi.
 Burnuma tütün kokusu gelmiyor. Ama sis gibi çöken şu hareketli, ağır duman sigaradan olmalı. Etraftaki herkesi sarhoşa çeviren duman, burunlarından, kulaklarından girip dübürlerinden çıkıyor. İşte, o da, yer ile gök arasını dolduracak derecede yoğunlaşan dumanın içerisinde yalpalaya yalpalaya yürüyor. Nereye götürülüyorlar acaba? Herhalde forma doldurtacaklar. Derken dumansı kalabalıkta kayba karışıyor...

FIGURE 19. *The Deported Hours*, first published in 2003. Copyright held by Mehmet Yashin.

form a kind of textual underground in *The Deported Hours*. They rewrite the script not only of the words on the page but of the stories we tell ourselves about linguistic and cultural contact in the twenty-first century.

Before taking up the novel itself, my first task will be to survey the nationalization and standardization projects driving Greek and Turkish linguistic modernity, touching on the devastating effects that they have had not only on the languages in question but the larger human geography of the region. This is particularly clear in Cyprus, whose geopolitical and linguistic borderscape I subsequently consider. Having laid this groundwork, I can then transition to a closer consideration of *The Deported Hours*, which I analyze in turns on structural, formal, linguistic, and theoretical levels.

Linguistic Pluralism Before and After the Exchange

"To modern eyes," Sharon Kinoshita writes, the interlocking languages and alphabets of the premodern Mediterranean "remain puzzling curiosities."[7] Yet the truth is that modernity and premodernity are relative terms. In the Eastern Mediterranean, linguistic modernity arrived quite late; it did not plant its feet solidly on the ground until, perhaps, the third decade of the twentieth century. Through the end of the nineteenth century and into the twentieth, the Sephardim of Salonica and Istanbul continued printing Judeo-Spanish in the Hebrew script, while Romaniote Jews to the west in Ioannina used the same alphabet for their Greek poetry. As I have detailed in my first chapter, it was likewise in Ioannina, as well as Crete and elsewhere, that Greek-speaking Muslims wrote poetry in their local Greek dialects using the Ottoman-Arabic script. Across the sea in Smyrna, meanwhile, some Levantine Catholics used Greek catechisms and prayer books printed in the Latin script; a few hundred kilometers north in Istanbul, various publishers circulated (with an ever greater intensity as the century neared its end) Turkish newsprint and fiction not only in the Ottoman script but in the Greek and Armenian alphabets of Karamanli and Armeno-Turkish, respectively—to say nothing of the Kurdish language of Armenians living, for example, to the east in Diyarbakır.[8] Up to and into the twentieth century, the threads of this massive tapestry continued weaving themselves across the warp and woof of the Eastern Mediterranean—not infrequently crossing confessional divides.[9] It was only after each community's deportation or assimilation that their literatures were quietly swept under the rug of the emerging national philologies, where they have often remained until recently. Out of sight, out of mind.

Nevertheless, as the previous chapter demonstrated, some of these scriptworlds survived decades after their displacement. While research into each of these textual communities exists and in some cases is growing quickly, the focus usually lies in the nineteenth century or earlier and there remains much work to be done on their twentieth-century afterlives.[10] I am hopeful that a larger, coordinated exploration of alternative archives, such as family collections, might reveal a broader range of scriptworlds that continued to operate across the century.

Here, however, my aims are quite the opposite: I need to document not the survival of these scriptworlds but the nationalist language reforms that attempted to erase them. In Greece, I have already documented in brief the discrimination that linguistic chauvinists leveled against Turcophone Christians, yet it was not limited to this. Already in the nineteenth century, Greek nationalists began to turn with suspicion in all directions, such as the Greek-speaking Catholic Levantines. In 1841, less than a decade after the establishment of the Kingdom of Greece, an anonymous correspondent from Smyrna wrote the following scathing report to the Athens-based paper *Athena*:

> Ἡ δυτικὴ Ἀσία ἔτεινε χεῖρα εἰς τὴν δυτικὴν Εὐρώπην, ἀμφότεραι προσῆλθον, συνεστάλησαν, καὶ ἐσταμάτησαν ἐπὶ τῆς δυστυχοῦς Μικρᾶς Ἀσίας... καὶ αἱ γαῖαι μας ἐπλήθησαν ἀπὸ νόθα Ἀρμενο-Φραγκικοῦ τινος Δευκαλίωνος τέκνα... [Ἔχουν] πνεῦμα τὸ Ἑλληνικόν, καὶ οἱ ἀπόγονοι αὐτῶν δὲν ἤθελον παραλλάσσειν ἀπὸ τοὺς Ἕλληνες ἂν εἶχον καὶ καρδίαν Ἑλληνικήν. Ἀλλὰ δὲν φθονοῦν τὸν τίτλον, προτιμοῦν νὰ μὴν ἔχουν ἔθνος κανὲν παρὰ νὰ ὀνομάζωνται Ἕλληνες.... Εἰς τὴν Σμύρνην τοὺς ὀνομάζομεν Κατωλύκους καὶ μεταχειρίζονται μὲν τὴν ἰδικήν μας διάλεκτον, ἀχρεῖα ὅμως τὴν ὁμιλοῦν.... Τὸ περίεργον εἶναι ὅτι πολλάκις μεταχειρίζονται εἰς τὰς ἐκκλησίας των εὐχολόγια Λατινικοὺς μὲν περιέχοντα χαρακτῆρας, Ἑλληνικὰς δὲ λέξεις ἀλλὰ τῆς ἀχρειεστάτης φράσεως.[11]

> Western Asia reached its hand out to Western Europe, and the two of them drew near and embraced over ill-fated Asia Minor... and the bastard children of some Armeno-Frankish Deucalion multiplied across our lands... [They have] a Greek spirit and their offspring would not differ from Greeks if they had a Greek heart. But they don't envy the title; they prefer to have no nationality rather than be called Greeks.... In Smyrna we call them *Katolykoi* and, yes, they make use of the same dialect as we, but they speak it brutishly.... The strange thing is that in their churches they

often use prayer books containing Latin characters but Greek words of the most brutish phrasing.

In the body of the Levantines, it seemed, heart and soul failed to meet, producing a nationless people. While it's unclear which prayer books the anonymous author of this editorial had surveyed, the truth is that the so-called Frangochiotika (Latin-script Greek) of the Catholic Levantines boasted a significant literary corpus beyond liturgical print. Frangochiotika had served as a crucial incubator for some of vernacular Greek's most treasured literary accomplishments during the Cretan Renaissance of the sixteenth century, as we see from some manuscript witnesses of both Vincenzo Cornaro and Georgios Hortatzis's work. In the mid-nineteenth century, however, much of the Greek-speaking intelligentsia (with important exceptions in the Ionian islands) had largely consigned vernacular to oblivion and was investing its energy instead in Katharevousa, a fabricated Greek language with several archaizing registers of varying austerity, all of which tended toward Ancient Greek vocabulary, morphology, and syntax.[12] The excerpt above, for example, is written in a middling register of Katharevousa. For its writer and those like him, aberrations from the Greek script were an easily diagnosed symptom of deeper linguistic degeneration, which in turn was a symptom of ethnic degeneration: "Διαφθείροντες τὴν διάλεκτόν μας βαθμηδὸν πλήττουσι καιρίως τὴν ἐθνικότητά μας" (corrupting our dialect by degrees [the users of Latin-script Greek] deal a deadly blow to our nationality).

Concepts like "corruption" and "degeneration," along with their counterpart "regeneration," were the cornerstones of linguistic nationalism in the region. I do not have the space to provide a detailed overview of Greece and Turkey's language reform projects,[13] but I do want to devote a few pages to comparing their key institutional mechanisms and discursive topoi, starting here with "degeneration." In the Greek sphere, the concept of linguistic degeneration found its most potent formulation in Adamantios Korais, who is remembered today as the founding father of Katharevousa. Constructing his linguistic system on moralist foundations, he proposed that "the barbarization of language, by perverting the true meaning of words, results in the perversion of morals."[14] To reverse the degeneration, he proposed not the wholesale replacement of vernacular dialects with Ancient Greek—a task he recognized as impossible—but rather the steady grafting of ancient words and forms onto the vernacular, pruning and purifying it. This grafting was to be carried out by διόρθωσις (correction) of not only "barbarous" vocabulary but morphological forms, replacing them with their supposedly genuine (i.e., ancient) forms. In the Turkish sphere, such notions of purification would eventually find their parallel in the early Kemalist *tasfiyeciler*, or purifiers, who threw themselves into a much more rapid eradication of Arabic and Persian vocabulary and syntax.[15] When it became clear that they had progressed too rapidly and radically, Atatürk decided on a general reprieve for words of Arabic and Persian origins—*but only so long as those origins were construed and sold to the public as Turkish*.[16]

To be fair, such obfuscation and misdirection were often accidental, given that the language reforms in both Greece and Turkey were frequently governed by happenstance rather than systematic method. Indeed, I need to make a crucial clarification here: despite the stated aims of the reformers—i.e., that they were rooting out hybridity and replacing it with pure forms—their own language was exceedingly hybrid. Katharevousa, for example, was "a hybrid consisting of lexical and grammatical features belonging to different historical stages of spoken Greek from Classical times to the present day, and writers of Katharevousa differed from each other (and were often inconsistent with themselves) in the proportions and the categories of the archaic features that they used."[17] And if Katharevousa was officially abrogated in 1976, much of its archaizing vocabulary and some of its morphological forms continue to live on in what is now known as Standard Modern Greek.[18] In Turkey, the often haphazard additions of "pure Turkish" words and suffixes were not infrequently drawn from obscure medieval texts, distant Anatolian dialects, or entirely different languages, such as Bashkurt and Kazakh or French,[19] and those that found a niche and survived often did so alongside Ottoman and Arabic counterparts that had been retained and rebranded. My aim in this chapter, and indeed this book, then, is not to naïvely celebrate hybridity as such. There are multiple, often conflicting forms of hybridity, many of them state-sponsored and violent by nature. As Murat Cankara writes in a different context, it is often the case that those navigating language within such a terrain necessarily "valorize[] one form of hybridity ... over another."[20] I do not want to establish a false dichotomy between some essentially premodern hybridity and the modern purism that purportedly destroyed it. At stake here is neither a battle to save hybridity from purism nor to recover a past now lost to temporal rupture. Instead, what I have found in my research is a continuum or spectrum, at both ends of which hybridities are generated and disseminated: toward the one end, we find localized nodes and interlocal contact points transmitting hybridity within a more or less decentralized field; toward the other end, we find the more or less centralized gears of state churning out its hybrid forms and imposing them, as its strength and reach allows, on the geographic and linguistic peripheries.

Throughout the nineteenth century, the strength and reach of the Greek and Turkish language reforms were small indeed. Greece's language reforms were largely dependent upon private initiatives and were limited to lecture halls and periodicals.[21] During the same period in Ottoman Istanbul, while several script reforms were proposed, none were taken seriously by the state, often for reasons of institutional inertia just as much as ideological resistance.[22] It was only in the wake of the First World War that language reformers managed to take the reins of power within the state apparatus, albeit to differing degrees and toward different ends in Greece and Turkey. In Greece, Demoticist linguists and pedagogues surged to power first in 1916 with Venizelos's provisional government, in whose Ministry of Education they swiftly removed Ancient Greek from primary schools and Katharevousa from the first four grades. And if they were soon displaced in the national elections of 1920, they had nonetheless established a strategic protocol for cultivating inroads with state officials to gradually achieve their aims, a protocol that would soon lead to Triandafyllidis's standard-setting grammar of Demotic Greek in the 1940s.[23] In Turkey again the process was much more abrupt. While the Young Turks had begun to debate language reform during the final years of the Ottoman regime, their authority remained entirely intellectual in nature. With the coming of the Kemalist state, however, this authority swiftly gained institutional weight and force. And unlike the situation in Greece, the early Turkish Republic had inherited a tradition of a centralized state, which smoothed the implementation of radical script and language reforms through widespread censorship, arrest, or exile. Dissent to the script reforms in 1928 was strangled in the cradle, while state-sponsored institutions like the Turkish Language Association (TDK) and the People's Houses (*Halk Evleri*) filled the void of autonomous social organization left by such prohibitions and purges.[24]

Everyone was affected by the state's turn to language reform, yet its most obvious victims were those identified as linguistic others. By the third decade of the twentieth century, many such "others" were subject to outright surveillance and punishment in both Greece and Turkey.[25] Starting in the 1920s, Greek authorities began to set up Greek-language night schools for speakers of languages other than Greek in the newly annexed territories of northern Greece. In the 1930s, with the rise of the Metaxas regime, state directives were issued prohibiting the use of non-Greek languages in public; those violating the directive were to be fined, arrested, or subjected to corporal punishment, while schools regularly turned students against one another in an atmosphere of surveillance and punishment.[26] During the same period in Turkey, one could witness similar restrictions on non-Turkish speech, albeit at a municipal rather than state level. This is not to say that the atmosphere was any less tense. So great was the pressure of linguistic fascism in Turkey, in fact, that even the liberal Ahmet Emin Yalman wrote in 1937:

> Türk vatandaşlığı dünyanın en yüksek sıfatıdır. Bun[a] ... kıymet vermeyen insanlara bizim ihtiyacımız yoktur. Bu yolu kendi arzu, sevgi ve menfaatlerinin sevki ile tutmak istemeyenleri neden zorla riyakârlığa sevk edelim? Türk vatandaşlığını benimsemediğini dilleriyle, hareketleriyle ispat edenler ... varsınlar kendilerini belli etsinler ve bir ecnebi cisim halinde kendi kendilerini bünyenin haricine düşürsünler. Ak koyunla, kara koyunu birbirinden ayırmaya imkân bulmak bir ihtiyaçtır.[27]

> Turkish citizenship is the loftiest designation in the world. We have no need of people who do not respect this. But why force such people, who are not moved by their own will, love, and interest to hold the course [of Turkishness], into a hypocritical posture [of speaking Turkish in public]? Let those who prove with their tongues and gestures that they do not adopt Turkish citizenship ... make themselves plain in public and let them expel themselves like a foreign body from the system. We need to find a way to separate the white sheep from the black sheep.

Just to be clear: Yalman, writing in the left-leaning paper *Tan*, is arguing here *against* public laws prohibiting foreign languages in public spaces. "If civil society comes to see itself justified in taking up the duty of policing [language]," he wrote earlier in the article, "it will certainly lead to extremist movements." Yet against the mounting forces of linguistic authoritarianism, he sees as the ultimate horizon of liberal accommodation ... *wait for it* ... casual discrimination and self-willed exclusion from the social body! For such unwarranted generosity toward linguistic others, he was viciously excoriated by the centrist paper *Cumhuriyet* and labeled a "crypto-Jew" (he was a dönme).[28] As was true elsewhere in 1937, so too in Turkey had the moral compass been lost.

But it had gone missing, off and on, for some time. A decade earlier, the Law School Students' Association of Istanbul University had devised a campaign to "encourage" minorities to speak Turkish, the "Citizen, Speak Turkish!" (*Vatandaş Türkçe Konuş!*) campaign. While it was approved and partially subsidized by the Ministry of the Interior, the campaign was carried out autonomously by the students of the Association, who quickly linked with other Associations, such as that of the Teachers College in Izmir or the Turkish Hearths across Western Turkey.[29] These parastate elements, who identified with but independently pursued the aims of the state on their own terms, began posting signs in restaurants, public transportation, movie houses, and elsewhere calling on "fellow citizens" to speak Turkish as a national duty. Soon, thanks to the intellectual networks of the Associations, major newspapers were editorializing on the campaign, stirring up a wider segment of the population. Threats, beatings, and citizens' arrests soon became a daily occurrence, culminating in a citywide campaign against the Jews in Edirne, which was only broken up by state intervention.[30] With this, the "Citizen, Speak Turkish!" campaign ground to a halt, only to be revived the following decade with the rise of the larger, quasi-fascist National Turkish Students' Union (MTTB). Several decades after this, as I will discuss shortly, the campaign was also resurrected in Cyprus to terrorize Greek-speaking Muslims.

And if these debates revolved around speech and vocabulary, rather than alphabet, this is largely a sign of the swift success by which both Greek- and Turkish-language reformers (thought themselves to have) shed the several scripts of their languages, along with the centrifugal communities who used those scripts. The state alphabet was the foundation of everything that was to be built atop it. It was a jealous god; the scripts of others, like brazen idols of a bygone era, were now consigned to popular oblivion, for not only did they encourage morphological waywardness; they also bore the unforgivable traces of racialized others from across the ethno-religious divide. The state-recognized alphabet, by contrast, elides traces. In a mundane but deeply problematic way, both the standard Greek and Turkish alphabets leave unrepresented certain features of peripheral dialects beyond the national center. The Greek alphabet, for example, cannot fully represent the phonemes of the Greek Cypriot dialect,[31] while the Turkish alphabet cannot represent certain aspects of Anatolian dialects for the simple reason that they didn't exist in, and were therefore irrelevant to, Istanbul Turkish.[32] Ertürk has explored this phenomenon as a kind of "phonocentrism," which locked language within the alphabetic imagination of a given elite. For despite their outward celebration of the vernacular, Ertürk suggests that nationalists feared nothing more than its centrifugal tendencies and attempted at all costs to contain it.[33] The standard alphabet, in other words, was codified and controlled by the linguistic centers in Athens and Istanbul, respectively, and was an important prerequisite for the broader project of shoring up the linguistic borderscape.

The reach of Athens and Istanbul across this borderscape would be tested most strenuously in Cyprus. Here, any attempts at centralization were complicated not only by the island's divergent networks of contact but by the presence of the British colonial administration (1878–1960) and its own linguistic agenda. To be sure, there had always been multiple linguistic centers pulling on Cyprus. In his fifteenth-century chronicle (Κρόνακα τούτέστιν Χρονικόν), for example, Leontios Machairas famously wrote that after the Lusignans took the island, French superseded Syriac, which had previously served as a second tongue to Greek, and people "started to learn the language of the Franks, and their Greek turned barbarous, [...] and so we write Frankish and Greek such that the whole world over can't tell in what language we're conversing."* A century later, French had largely vanished when Martin Crusius documented Greek, Chaldean, Armenian, Albanian, and Italian on the island, with Anatolian Turkish soon to be added.[34] By contrast, under British occupation English remained unknown to the majority of Cypriots and did not function as a lingua franca.[35] Indeed, until the large-scale 1931 uprisings of the Greek Cypriots, who called for unification with Greece, the approach of the British administration had been largely hands-off, preferring to leave in place the existing system by which the confessional communities funded and administered their own schools.[36] Because of this, much of the pedagogical material, such as textbooks, was supplied directly from the respective linguistic centers of Athens and Istanbul (a practice that would continue after independence). After 1931, however, British policy shifted. It pivoted quickly toward the centralization of schooling and language instruction, implementing a policy whose central goal was to reorient Cypriots away from their so-called ethnic centers, building instead a local middle class whose anglicized education would make them both culturally and politically dependent on the colonial regime.[37] Cypriots were to be awakened, as Governor Palmer himself stated, to "their responsibilities as Cypriots and the position of Cyprus as part of the British Empire."[38] Translation services were nullified and English became mandatory for all official communication, while elementary education was administered directly by the regime, which established a series of

---

*"Άρκέψαν νὰ μαθάνουν φράνγκικα, καὶ 'βαρβαρίσαν τὰ ῥωμαῖκα,... καὶ γράφομεν φράνγκικα καὶ ῥωμαῖκα, ὅτι εἰς τὸν κόσμον δὲν ἠξεύρουν ἴντα συντυχάνομεν" (Sathas, ed., Ἐξήγησις, 124).

inter-confessional English-language schools and introduced English into the later curricula of Greek- and Turkish-language elementary schools as well.[39] The ulterior aims of such policies should necessarily complicate any assessments of linguistic cosmopolitanism today.

Another lasting effect of the British colonial structure was the system of bicommunalism, whereby heterogeneity was packaged and contained in two ethnically homogenous categories of Greek and Turk. Other identities, such as Armenian, Maronite, Latin, or Roma, were ethnically and therefore legally invisible and, upon independence in 1960, were forced to choose a side, since the postcolonial period only saw the continuation and intensification of bicommunal administration.[40] Within the bicommunal model, language became increasingly politicized and dependent on the standards of their respective centers. In Cypriot-Greek print, standard Greek was catching up with Katharevousa by the 1940s, while Cypriot Greek was forced into an ever-narrowing field of niche genres. True, elevated and more standardized registers of Greek had always had a place in Cyprus (particularly in the spheres of the church), existing and leaving a footprint alongside local dialects.[41] But it was also true that, before the twentieth century, Cypriot Greek had also held a more prominent role in literary production, from Machairas's Chronicle, quoted above, to Konstantinos Diakonos's Ἄσμα τῶν Διερμηνέων (Song of the Dragomans; c. 1700), to Vasilis Michaelides's lyrical poetry during the first decades of British occupation. Now Cypriot Greek was being elbowed into folklore, as some writers eagerly anticipated "linguistic redemption" by the Greek state, which meant discarding local Cypriot Greek dialects for Standard Greek after the desired union with Greece.[42] Up through the end of the twentieth century, state policy in Cyprus reflected this view for the most part. In public schools, Cypriot Greek was deemed inadequate for most classroom settings and Standard Greek served as the only official index of literacy.[43]

Turkish largely followed in reaction to developments in Greek. Admittedly, Cypriot Turkish, in contrast to Cypriot Greek, had always left a weak mark in written literature. Throughout the Ottoman period, written literary works from Turcophone Cypriots generally avoided dialect and instead used the standard Ottoman Turkish of Istanbul,[44] yet such a practice assumed extra political weight in the twentieth century, as Turkish Cypriots observed with growing trepidation the rising nationalism among many Greek Cypriots, suffering from what Kızılyürek and Gautier-Kızılyürek call "the Crete syndrome"—i.e., fear of annexation to Greece and/or mass deportation. In the minds of a growing number of the Turkish Cypriot leadership, therefore, Turkey assumed the guise of a loving mother ready and willing to protect her "lonely children."[45]

But who were these supposed children? While Turkish had always been the first language of the Muslim elite, bilingualism in Cypriot Greek and Turkish was widespread among the wider Muslim population, and a sizeable minority of them spoke primarily or only Cypriot Greek.[46] During the final years of the nineteenth century, in fact, Muslim communities introduced Greek language into their middle school education and sought bilingual teachers for primary education where Greek was spoken; this was abolished in the 1930s, as Greek and Turkish nationalisms worked their way into more and more facets of Cypriot life.[47] But it was not until 1958 that the "Citizen, Speak Turkish!" campaign found its way to Cyprus, organized by the Turkish Cypriot nationalist leadership. Here, it took a more extreme form, engaging not simply in informal intimidation but in systematic punishment, meting out monetary fines for *every word* of Greek spoken. Not only speaking the Greek language but even using perceived Greek-origin words common to Cypriot Turkish was policed in coffeehouses, streets, and other public spaces.[48] Mustafa Gökçeoğlu recalls,

> Konuşma sırasında ağızdan çıkan her Rumca sözcük için para cezası uygulanmaktaydı. İşte bu dönemde Türkçe bilmeyen yurttaşlar çok büyük sıkıntılar yaşamışlar. Olabildiğince büyük yerleşim birimlerinden uzak durmuşlar. Gelmek zorunda kalanlar da olabildiğince ağızlarını açmamaya çalışmışlardı. Ceza uygulamaları büyük yerleşim birimlerinden uzaklaştıkça etkisini yitirmişti. Evlerde aile bireyleri en iyi bildikleri dili kullanmayı sürdürdüler. Kolaylarına gelen dili kullanmayı yeğlediler. Olay günümüze kadar uzanmaktadır. Günümüzde bile Baf, Karpas, Dillirga kökenli yurttaşlar bir araya geldiklerinde Rumca konuşmakta, içki masalarında çatışmalı maniler, türküler söylemektedirler.[49]

A monetary punishment was put into effect for every Greek word that came out of one's mouth in conversation. This was a time when our compatriots who didn't know Turkish suffered greatly. They stayed away from larger population centers. Those whom necessity brought to such places tried not to open their mouths as best they could. The further you got away from the large population centers the smaller the effect of the punitive measures. In their homes, they continued using the tongue they knew best with their family members, preferring the tongue that came easy to them. And they continue to this day. Even now, many of our compatriots from Baf/Paphos,

Karpas/Karpasia, Dillirga/Tillyria, still speak in Cypriot Greek when they get together; when they sit down to a feast they sing their *tsiattista* poems and folk songs.

This linguistic terrorism provoked strong reactions among some, yet any who publicly resisted were relentlessly abused.[50] In effect, the campaign forced entire communities underground, but as Gökçeoğlu attests in his final lines above, *it did not silence them*. Their Cypriot-Greek poetry survives even today, as do their manuscript collections, written out in the Latin alphabet.[51]

Nevertheless, the damage done by the campaign is obvious. It is no coincidence that it began in 1958, two years before the end of British rule: this was also the year that the newly organized Turkish nationalist guerrilla organization TMT began a broader series of attacks against "internal enemies"—primarily leftist Turkish Cypriots and workers associated with the Pancyprian Federation of Labour (PEO) or the Progressive Party of Working People (AKEL), the island's Marxist-Leninist party. The nationalists of TMT threatened and dehumanized leftist and left-leaning Turkish Cypriots, forcing them to make public apologies and renounce their commitments in Turkish newsprint, or they simply murdered them, as they did to Fazıl Önder, Ayhan Hikmet, Ahmet Muzaffer Gürkan, and Derviş Ali Kavazoğlu, for example. Ironically, the TMT was only mimicking the tactics of its Greek nationalist rivals in EOKA, who had not only been carrying out a systematic guerrilla campaign against the British authorities and local police but political assassinations of Greek Cypriot leftists as well.[52] In other words, before the interethnic violence, ethnic cleansings, and communal partitions that marked the period 1958–1974, both Greek and Turkish nationalists had first to put their own houses in order, removing from the field leftists and other so-called traitors. Linguistic violence was only a small piece of a much larger nationalist agenda, one with material and ideological ties to geopolitical centers outside Cyprus.[53]

Nevertheless, however small it may seem within the larger picture of political polarization and violence, language *was* an important factor. In its way, it embodied Cyprus's centripetal and centrifugal potentials, the second of which would come into greater focus following the de facto partition of 1974. In the wake of this, a significant number of Greek and Turkish Cypriots came to feel a sense of betrayal from what they had been told was their motherland.[54] In the realm of language, this sense of betrayal produced among some a growing investment in local dialects as opposed to standard Greek and Turkish. For Turkish Cypriots in particular, the local dialect has accrued an ever growing level of prestige in the face of a standing Turkish military apparatus and an influx of settlers from Turkey who, while we ought not to classify their culture or politics as a monolithic bloc, are generally viewed by many local Turkish Cypriots as religiously and politically conservative and a threat to indigenous culture. As such, "Turkish Cypriots use their dialect more and more," write Hadjioannou, Tsiplakou, and Kappler, "in order to differentiate themselves from non-Cypriots as a means of creating/defending identity."[55] In a sense, language became one of the last refuges of an island betrayed. You might hear this refuge, for example, in certain phonemes, intonations, or syntactical arrangements shared across the buffer zone. Or you might read it, for example, in Yashin's novel *The Deported Hours*.

The Deported Book

Believe it or not, one of the last Karamanli books ever printed came out of a press in Cyprus. It was an unassuming book of prayers, assembled by a refugee from *Syllê* (now Sille, near Konya) and published in 1935 in Paphos.[56] Printed more than ten years after the Greco-Turkish Population Exchange, the book is an indication that at least some refugees must have not only passed through Cyprus but remained on the island permanently—a community large enough to warrant a printed book of prayers. Perhaps, like the Armenian refugees who preceded them,[57] these Karamanli Christians settled in the Turkish-speaking neighborhoods of the Muslims, whose language was closer to their own. What happened to them, though, in the upheavals that would shake the island a generation later? What would happen to them today if their adventure were to be repeated? Would they be rendered stateless not once but twice, lost somewhere in the Cyprus Dead Zone?

Such questions constitute the starting point of *The Deported Hours*. The novel's protagonist is a Karamanli refugee named Misail Oskarus, brought back to life and tossed headlong into twenty-first-century Turkey, from which he is again deported and shunted off to Cyprus. The book is broken up into four chapters, the first three of which constitute a triptych collectively titled "The Book of Deportation" (*Sınırdışı Kitabı* / Σηνηρδηότ Κιταπι). It is within these initial three chapters that Misail's adventure runs its course, beginning in a detention center near Istanbul. This is no run-of-the-mill detention center, however. As the first chapter progresses, we descend deeper and deeper into a hellish, underground prison system whose guards transmogrify into unsettling *Zabaniyya*, monstrous demons tirelessly engaged in torturing and mutilating

Misail's fellow inmates, some of whom have become informants. As Misail quickly learns, he can trust no one here—not even the author who has brought him back to life, a Cypriot writer (and fellow prisoner) named "Mehmet Yashin."

Following a final interrogation, Misail is deported to an island, never named but clearly northern Cyprus, where the second chapter begins and our narrator can finally confirm with growing terror that he has been cast into someone else's story, someone else's home, and someone else's dialect: those of "Mehmet Yashin." The hellish demons of the first chapter continue their work here in northern Nicosia, prowling the walls of the Dead Zone, but they are now joined by a host of military personnel from the mainland whose torture centers threaten to divert the novel down a generic sidetrack, something close to Stalag fiction, replete with scatological rape and domination fantasies. These are dissolved as Misail finds his way beyond the military grounds and wanders the city's neighborhoods, now peopled by settlers from Turkey whom the novel describes alternatively as *koloniciler* (colonists) and *göçebe akıncılar* (nomadic raiders), mixing histories of contemporary settler-colonialism and early Ottoman conquest. Many of the houses are also haunted by the ghosts of local Greek Cypriots who had been raped, killed, and buried in the gardens, while a host of local Turkish Cypriots have been forced underground, transformed into fairytale creatures and hunted by the demons on the walls.

Misail is miraculously transported across those walls in the third chapter, to a place that turns out to be Heaven. Most immediately, "Heaven" is a stand-in for southern Cyprus (i.e., the Republic of Cyprus), yet later in the chapter we learn that it is also the name of a multinational Anglophone publisher ("Heaven Publishing House") with a branch office there. In Heaven too, however, something is amiss, as the angels parade in military formation armed to the teeth and Misail is again threatened with deportation if he fails to file his papers (now in Greek) correctly. *Heaven Publishing*, for its part, approaches his story only as an exciting escapist genre for their target audience of Western readers, curious to learn about the "Orient." Moreover, before Misail's story can even reach these readers (i.e., via English translation), the publishing house needs the Karamanli Turkish translated into standard Turkish. In Heaven too, Misail fails to find an outlet not only for his story but his language, which has been demoted to a dead dialect.

But is it really dead?

Despite the assimilationist threats or cold indifference that Misail finds in his Turkish-, Greek-, and English-speaking interlocutors on both sides of the de facto partition, his story and its language may yet still find a second chance at life. Even the "translator's preface" admits that "it's not yet clear whether Karamanli Turkish will die there [in Cyprus] too or whether it will be resurrected."* The question is, on what conditions do its ultimate death or resurrection depend? If the Turcophone, Hellenophone, and Anglophone authorities cannot be trusted to carry Misail's story forward in good faith, then who can? The answer can only be articulated in the novel's fourth and final chapter, which bears the title of a second book: "The Book of Hours" (*Saatler Kitabı* / Σαατλερ Κιταπι). Pivoting away from all that has preceded it, "The Book of Hours" methodically develops a strikingly different, decentered model of literary production and promulgation.

I will close my chapter by examining "The Book of Hours" in the following section, but first we need to explore the complex textual world of "The Book of Deportation" across the novel's initial three chapters. For readers approaching this triptych from within the framework of the Western canon, Misail's story is a nearly perfect calque of Dante's *Comedia*: Istanbul's underground prison network takes the place of hell, northern Nicosia that of purgatory, and southern Nicosia and its international Anglophone publishing networks that of heaven. What's more, Misail is accompanied in the first two chapters by a guide: the lawyer who has arranged his prison release and deportation; this guide is then replaced in the third chapter by Misail's girlfriend (and translator), Marjori. The parallels are clear and need no elaboration here, yet while Dante is certainly one inspiration for the triptych of the afterlife, he is not the only one. The eschatological nature of the story and many of its angels and monsters are just as deeply indebted to Islamic sources, none more so than Hibetullah bin Ibrahim's *Sâ'atnâme* (Book of Hours), which I'll examine in the following section. More important for us here, however, is one particular spatial departure from Dante's model: Misail's journey through the afterlife draws not from Christian purgatory but Islamic *a'raf*, with important implications for the larger narrative.

Purgatory arose in the late twelfth century, slowly differentiated and rearticulated as a separate domain from hell. Its first literary representations often placed it geographically within hell itself, as a kind of underground penal colony. By the end of the twelfth century, however, purgatory was moving up in the world, transferred out of hell and into a truly intermediary space.[58] It

---

*"Karamanlıca [...] orada [Kıbrıs'ta da] ölecek mi, dirilecek mi belli değil" (Yashin, *Sınırdışı*, 131).

eventually took the figure of a mountain, which would find its best-known form in Dante's *Comedia*. Purgatory became a lofty summit that, while austere in nature, is ultimately closer to heaven than hell. Most importantly, it represented a *space of transit*, one that encourages mobility through the soul's active penitence, by which it climbs upward toward heaven. By contrast, Islamic *a'raf* takes the form not of a mountain but a border wall—a partition whose geospatial function is not to facilitate movement but to *contain* it.[59] There is no vertical ascent here, since the wall is sheer; passage to heaven (which is not *above* but *across*) hinges not on the penitence or indeed any action of the souls themselves but on the intercession of divine authority. The souls can only sit and wait in anxious anticipation—either in hell at the base of the wall or, perhaps, atop it. There is some dispute regarding this last point, however, for while there are indeed beings stationed atop the wall (*ashab al a'raf*, "companions of the heights"), exegetes debate their precise identity. Among the foundational *tafsirs* (exegeses), most read these beings as human souls, whose fate will be determined by the intercession of the Prophet. A dissenting opinion, though, originating from Abu Mijlaz of Basra, suggests that these beings are not men but angels, stationed on the wall to survey the torment of those below in hell.[60]

The Deported Hours seems to draw its inspiration primarily from this latter tradition. Most obviously, the *a'raf* chapter takes place not atop the wall but beneath it, where all the characters are confined. One such character, a local Turkish Cypriot boy (who is slowly transforming into a giant rat), explicitly warns Misail against the soldiers in the watchtowers of the wall above them. Stationed at the heights like angelic demons, they torment the dead and dying below. The second chapter, therefore, can be said to take place not in a purgatorial space of transit, as with Dante, but at the very edge of hell, a horrific buffer zone of internment and torment hopelessly buried beneath the border of *a'raf*. The first and the second chapters are not separate domains; it is a difference of degrees, not kind, as hell has overrun and assimilated northern Cyprus.

This departure from Dante's model is crucial and cannot be overstated. Dante's purgatory, which was truly a space of passage, has been replaced by partition. It sets the tone for all three chapters and ripples outward to the larger fault lines of the region—not only the linguistic lines carving up dialects and scripts but, closely tied to these, the *literary and institutional* lines carving up the users of those dialects and scripts, some of whom the Turkish and Greek literary establishments authorize, rendering them "authors," while they unauthorize others and circumscribe them in the literary margins. If the actual physical partition of *a'raf* only comes into focus in the second chapter, we might say that it reverberates into and contaminates nearly every page of the larger triptych, a massive borderscape bearing the linguistic and literary traces of *a'raf*.

Let's examine these traces, starting with language. Despite the fact that Misail speaks Turkish, from the very first sentence of the novel (which is written, like much to come, in the Greek alphabet) we understand that both his script and his dialect set him apart from those around him—or rather, they prompt the authorities to set him apart in something like a quarantine, lest he contaminate others. Even the language of the authorities themselves is vulnerable, given that it is read, internalized, and remediated by Misail onto the pages of the book. For example, when he sees a sign posted by the authorities forbidding Turkish Cypriots from speaking Cypriot Greek, he conveys it to his readers, naturally enough, in his own script: Greek! What should read, in the eyes of the authorities, "Ecnebi Yerlilerin Lehçesiyle Konuşmak Tehlikeli ve Yasaktır" (Speaking in the Dialect of the Local Foreigners is Dangerous and Forbidden) becomes in the pages of *The Deported Hours*, "Ετζνεπι Γερλιλεριν Λεχτζεσιγλε Κονυσμακ Τεχλικελι βε γασακτηρ."

Many of the Cypriot characters follow Misail's lead and begin forcing their own dialectical voices into the text. On the most basic level, we see this in morphology, with both verbal formations (e.g., *bakan* for *bakıyorsun*; *açamayıyoruk* for *açamıyoruz*, etc.) and adverbial formations (e.g., *tabiyattynan* for *tabiyatıyla* or *bununnan* for *bununla*). More interestingly, the larger domain of syntax is contaminated by particle combinations like "o şu" and its several variations. "O şu" literally means "that-this" but is used in Cyprus to introduce right-branching clauses, whereas standard Turkish is left-branching. As Matthias Kappler has convincingly argued, these particle combinations and some of the larger syntactical arrangements that they govern (such as relative clauses) were adapted directly from entanglement with Greek (i.e., "ό,τι").[61] And while it is distinct to Cyprus, the *o şu* paradigm works its way into the speech of the novel's *non*-Cypriot characters as well, appearing as early as page 17: "Belli değil o şu bir soruya cevap aradığının dahi farkına varamadan cehennemi boylayıyor bu?" (Isn't it clear that [*o şu*] he's wound up in hell without even realizing that he's looking for an answer to a question?). In this same excerpt, we see another widespread dialectical feature of Cypriot Turkish: the lack of the interrogative particle *mi*, which in standard Turkish is a necessary component of any yes-no question. In Cypriot dialect, however, the particle drops out and its function is transferred to intonation, which the speaker raises as they approach the focus-word or the end of the sentence. This too is a direct adaptation from Greek, and it finds its way into the speech of many characters in the novel. Even more threatening than these *adaptations* from Greek, however, is the *adoption* of wholesale Greek or Greek Cypriot dialect, which occurs in the novel either via single words (e.g., *gutçimbi* [κουτσομπόλης], *gannavuri* [καννaβoύριν], *mavra yerimo* [μαυρογέρημον], etc.) or entire sentences (e.g., *lambron na se gabsi* [λαμπρόν να σε κάψει]). Drawing together all of these dialectical forms, some of the characters turn them directly against the authorities. The local Turkish Cypriot boy whom I mentioned above, for example, shouts out to Misail: "Get down! Get down! *sombre maramba tag.* [...] Steer clear from the soldjerkoffs in the watchtower [...] they pull the gold teeth from the dead and fuck-a-luck 'em while they warsh 'em! *Boner in the body bag*"* His words move playfully between Turkish, Cypriot Greek, and a poetic idiolect, culminating in an assonant chain of *sik* (dick; fuck) sounds, whose barbs are pointed against and indeed lodged within the soldiers (*a-sik-erler*).

The mainland authorities, for their part, want nothing more than to put an end to this contamination. They can't destroy Misail, as he is the novel's protagonist, but they can certainly attempt to redact and standardize his tongue and script. One fellow inmate, describing how the others are executed willy-nilly, tells him flatly, "You're bound up too tightly in this book, so your situation's different from ours. They can't take back your life; at most they'll change it. But someone looking on from outside won't understand that it's been changed. They'll still think you're you."† What will have been changed, I argue, is Misail's dialect and script. Mainland Turkish readers, "looking on from outside," would fail to notice any change, since they would see only a homoglot narrator, but it would devastate Misail himself. As the process of standardization begins, Misail bewilderingly confides:

> Kimseye meramımı anlatamıyordum. Yazarımın yetkililere itiraz maksadıyla bana sarfettirdiği her sözcük, güya yanlış bir şifreydi de kelime hazinemi kül edivermişti. Dilim bana ait değildi. Beni sokmak isteyen yılanla birdi. Ανα-πάπα διλιμ, ζεχιρ ζεμπερεκ κεσιλμιότι. Onun sinsice sokmasından

---

* "Aşağıya! Aşağıya! *Mavra ya maramba* [...] Nöbet kulesindeki asikerler [...] ölüyü yıkariken sike mike altın dişini söke[rler]! *İsikeleti ya muşamba*" (Yashin, *Sınırdışı*, 90).

† "Kitapla haşır neşirsin, durumun farklı. Ömrünü geri alamazlar, en fazlası hayatını değiştirecekler. Ama değiştirildiğini anlayamaz dışarıdan bakan. Seni hâlâ sen zanneder" (Yashin, *Sınırdışı*, 32).

sakınacağım derken, yazılıp konuşturulduğum dilin mantık silsilesinden büsbütün kopmuştum.[62]

I couldn't make myself understood to anyone. It was as if every word that my writer made me speak in objection to the authorities was an invalid code, demolishing all my vocabulary in the blink of an eye. My tongue didn't belong to me. It was one and the same with the snake that was trying to bite me. Μάι μόθερ-φάθερ τογκ χαδ πίκόμ α πίτερ πόιζον.* Attempting to avoid the treacherous bite of the tongue that I was written in and made to speak, I'd broken away entirely from its train of logic.

There are two pivotal points in this passage worth pausing over. First, while Misail has never stopped speaking Turkish, increasingly it seems no longer to be *his* Turkish. Infected by the language of Turkish nationalism, the "mother-father" tongue has turned to poison. To avoid it, Misail has no recourse but to tear himself out of language's most basic grammatical units (*dilin mantık silsilesi*) and cast himself into a communication void. The second point that I want to stress, however, is that behind this life and death struggle lie not only the authorities but the author: "Mehmet Yashin." Who is this man forcing words into Misail's mouth?

While he began his life in admiration of his author, Misail quickly grows to question the latter's motives and resist his authority. Yashin appears to be a fellow "foreign prisoner of war" (*ecnebi savaş eseri*), occasionally seen among the endless mass of prisoners marched forever downward into the catacombs of the first chapter, yet at some point Misail's doubts begin to multiply, culminating in the suspicion that Yashin might in fact be an informant cooperating with the mainland authorities. In Misail's final interrogation, they show him an affidavit supposedly signed by Yashin and tell him, "The novelist agrees that you must do what we say."† At other points, it appears that not only have the authorities brought Yashin under their control but that they in fact accuse Misail, not Yashin, of orchestrating everything: "Do they really think that I led my writer down this road—I mean, into this novel? God knows but it seems I'm being accused of having caused myself to be written! It turns out, they say, that he wanted to write a completely different character. And suddenly I—a fictional

---

* In my translations throughout this chapter, I use Greek-script English for passages translated from Greek-script Turkish. This passage reads: "My mother-father tongue had become a bitter poison."

† "Romanyazarı, dediklerimizi yapmana onay verdi" (Yashin, *Sınırdışı*, 47).

character!—seized hold of his pen! Just as Satan lays hold of a weak soul. Oh, if only such a thing were possible. Is it possible, I wonder?"* Indeed, is it possible that an author might lose control of his text? What we see unfolding in the hellish prison of the mainland is a struggle over nothing less than textual authority as the narrative's agents are divided and turned against one another. Who is in control of this text? Who shapes its language and authorizes its story? The narrator reading himself? The author writing him? The authorities pressing in against them both? Is Yashin writing against the state authorities or has his soul been "occupied" by them (*bir yazar olarak ruhu işgal edilmekte*)?

In fact, not only has the writer been occupied; he's been partitioned. In the second chapter, Misail finds his writer near the Dead Zone, caught up in the barbed wire of the wall. Yashin cries:

> Allah'ım, ben kendi bedenimin yanında bekleyen bir ruhum. İki parçaya bölündüm. Bundan böyle bana Mehmet Yaşın denemez. Çünkü doğrulup kendimle bir olamıyorum. Bir kısmım öbür kısmımı yiyor. Ruhum, dikenli telörgülere asılı kalmış bedenime dönemiyor. Hiçbir günahım yok. Ama soru melekleri bir türlü ruhumu temize çıkaracak soruyu sormaya gelemiyor. Çünkü devriyeler, melayikelere geçiş izni vermiyor.[63]

> My God, I'm a soul in limbo next to my own body. I've been partitioned in two. Henceforth my name is no longer Mehmet Yashin, since I can't rise up and become one with myself. One half of me is eating the other. My soul can't return to my body, hung up here on the barbed wire. I have no sin, but the questioning angels can't come and clear my soul, since the border guards won't let them pass.

How are we to interpret this partition of the writer? An obvious allegorical reading might envision him as the body of Cyprus itself, sundered in two, yet there is more at play here; there is a push and pull not simply between the two halves of the island but between the island itself and the so-called mainland. This push and pull has played out in real life over Yashin's career, since Istanbul's major publishers (Cem, YKY, İletişim) have in fact been publishing his poetry and essays since his debut there in the 1980s. If he has come to occupy

---

* "Yazarımı bu yola—bu romana demek istiyorum—benim sürüklediğimi mi zannediyorlar? Kendimi ona yazdırmakla suçlanıyorumdur Allah bilir! Yazmak istediği meğerse bambaşka bir karaktermiş. Derken ben—bir romankişisi—onun kalemini ele geçirmişim! Zayıf düşmüş bir ruhun bedenine iblis nasıl el atarsa. Ah, keşke mümkün olsaydı bu. Olabilir mi acaba?" (Yashin, *Sınırdışı*, 43).

a space in the Turkish canon, it is thanks to this media infrastructure in Turkey, yet part of him remains foreign to that center, which he has never ceased critiquing in his published essays. Cut off from his body, which hangs in awful stasis at the base of *a'raf*, his soul has gone off in search of a new paradigm distinct from Turkey—a paradigm that Turkey in fact once possessed but has expelled like a foreign body: Karamanli Turkish. In other words, the soul of "Mehmet" has transmigrated into "Misail," mixing the Karamanli Christian and the Cypriot Turkish literary worlds together in an uneasy coexistence. To be sure, while both Karamanli and Cypriot Turkish are minor tongues threatened by assimilation, they are by no means the same and have their own separate historical trajectories. That is why I write "uneasy"; we should be suspicious—as Misail himself is—of any attempt to reduce these tongues to interchangeable equivalence. But forces greater than himself are driving him into the life-world of Mehmet Yashin. As Misail wanders the island, he confesses that "the streets seem familiar. As if I've lived here, despite never having set foot here."*

Misail-Mehmet's reincarnation will remain in limbo, though, so long as the mainland's partitions stand in place. We see this most immediately in the physical and administrative mechanisms of the Buffer Zone, which in the block quotation above keep away the "questioning angels." Who are these angels? Traditionally named Munkar and Nakir in Islamic eschatology, their job is to ask souls in the grave to identify their faith. These angels are the key to unlocking your passage to the next life. Only after you have identified your faith correctly to Munkar and Nakir can you pass into heaven (or hell, if you answer incorrectly). But what if you can't answer either way, immobilized in static waiting? Indeed, in Ottoman lands where Islam's ranks were filled by substantial Christian converts, there was often a fear among converts that they would be unable to understand Munkar and Nakir, since they knew no Arabic.[64] Look back for example to Şānī's *Tuhfe*, whose story I explored in my first chapter. In his book, Şānī felt the need to reassure his fellow Greek-speaking Muslims:

اِذِيْوُ آنْكَلِي يُورْخُونْدَه كَتُونْ رُوتُونْ سِتُوْ مْنِمَا
تُوْ اَثْرُوپُوْ سِتِغْلُوصَا تُوْ لَي تُونْ رُوتُونْ قُوسْقرِيمَا
آفُونْدَاسْ مَسْتِنْ قِسْتَاقْشِي سِتِغْلُوصَا تُوْ تَلْقِين
كَسْتُونْ اَذِي آپُوفَاشِي سِتِغْلُوصَا تُوْ نَا ذِينِي

(f. 165b–166a)

---

*"Yollar tanıdık geliyor. Burada hiç yaşamadığım halde yaşamışım gibi" (Yashin, *Sınırdışı*, 81).

İ ðyo angeli pu'rhonde ke ton rotun sto mnima
tu athropu sti ġloṣa tu, leyi, ton rotun 'ḳus ḳrima
afondas mestin ḳsetaḳṣi sti ġloṣa tu telḳîni
ke ston Aði apofaṣi stiġloṣa tu na ðini

When two angels come interrogate you in the grave
they'll ask your confession in the tongue you spake,
because the questions in the grave and Hades's verdict
will be in whatever tongue the *talqîn* was worded.

The talqīn is the Islamic confession of the faith on one's deathbed, and Şānī assures his Greek-speaking readers that if they perform these last rites in Greek, the interrogating angels in "Hades" will likewise speak to them in Greek and allow them to respond in kind.

In *The Deported Hours*, however, no such assurances are forthcoming. Indeed, earlier in the novel Munkar and Nakir have already addressed themselves to the masses of the underworld, yet the only answers that anyone can give them are unintelligible murmurs: "With a rasping megaphone they ask everyone in the file:—*Man rabbuka?* .... *Ma dinuka?* ... The prisoners in the file, more dead than alive and looking for a place to lie down, give answer:—Hr, hm. Hr, hm ... Hr, hm. Hr, hm. ..."* The rasping and distorted voices of Munkar and Nakir over the megaphone, barely intelligible to the dead, trigger from the latter even more incoherent gibberish. On a symbolic level, this disconnect and incoherence result from the linguistic partitions set in motion by the Population Exchange a hundred years ago—partitions that have rendered heterogeneous speech into static nonsense and have foreclosed any definitive decision from the authorities. They are trapped in static waiting.

In the case of Mehmet Yashin, the angels themselves have been held up at the geographic checkpoint along Cyprus's Buffer Zone, leaving the writer's soul in dubious suspense. But the Buffer Zone is not the only problem; again, language itself proves another plane of partition, sundering "Yashin" in two. For even in the absence of Munkar and Nakir, the writer could at least call out to God for mercy if he were in command of his own tongue, but "not even my lips can pray to you, my God. I've become incapable of calling out with my inner voice. Because it's that cursed Satan who now speaks with my

---

*"Elindeki cızırtılı megafonla kuyruktaki herkese soruyorlar:—Men rabbûke?.. Mâ dinüke?.. Ölü gibi yatacak yer arayan kuyruktakiler cevaplıyor:—Ha, hı. Ha, hı ... Ha, hı ..." (Yashin, *Sınırdışı*, 21).

tongue."* His "inner" voice has no means of egress now that Satan has occupied his tongue. His own words sit immobilized inside him, besieged from above.

As for "Satan," I would understand it as a metaphor not simply for his Istanbul publishers but more centrally for the larger literary complex of critics and public intellectuals shaping and regulating published discourse. This literary complex stretches from the Kemalist-era language reformers and men and women of letters to their contemporary heirs, a chain that Yashin has identified and criticized in his influential collection of essays *Poeturka*. Across the many ideological and aesthetic differences and debates of these intellectuals, Yashin pinpoints a core consensus that unites them: the implicit understanding that their object of study is "Turkish" literature (*Türk edebiyatı*), which is marked as ethnically and racially Turkish. This consensus has necessarily excluded the messy plurality of textual handlers like those detailed here in *Literature's Refuge*. These handlers and their texts, Yashin notes, "are considered 'backward,' 'inadequate,' or 'lower' by the monist, centralizing men of letters in Turkey"† (and, I would add, Greece). If Yashin himself has managed to make a name for himself in Istanbul's literary scene, it is only to the degree that this name and its language are "authorized" and evaluated under the rubric of *Turkish* literature. Like the barbs atop the wall from which he hangs, Yashin the author seems incapable of extricating his corpus from such a rubric.

His only hope lies in Misail, whose script and vocabulary offer an underground escape route away from mainland authorship.[65] Yet this textual underground is by no means secure. It too is under siege, cordoned off from mainstream print and ghettoized. It is largely confined to manuscript and composite media, which fail even to register in the mainland: its words, "since they're not printed in a book, don't exist. [/] (my exist ence is un raveling he re in th is confine ment)."‡ Misail's words themselves have begun to come undone, left to fray outside the mainland's print media and national archives. And amidst such deprivation, the underground of which he is a part is bombarded not only with attacks and prohibitions but with propaganda, the sole aim of which is to lure out and assimilate pockets of resistance by promising them authorship.

---

* "Dudaklarım dua bile edemiyor sana ya Rabbim. İçimin sesiyle seslenemez oldum. Çünkü benim dilimle konuşuyor o lanet olası İblis" (Yashin, *Sınırdışı*, 68–69).

† "Farklılıklarından dolayı [...] tekçi, merkeziyetçi Türkiye edebiyat-adamları tarafından 'geri', 'yetersiz', 'düşük' sayılıyorlar" (Yashin, *Poeturka*, 49).

‡ "Bir kitapta basılmadığından yok. [/] (yok ol uyorum bu rada kapa lı)" (Yashin, *Sınırdışı*, 46).

In one of the final interrogations, the head *Zabaniyya* (demon) tells Misail that "they'll even acquiesce to a book in which they themselves are criticized to a reasonable degree. So long as the book is written in their alphabet, their dialect, and their vocabulary."* Like the soft diplomacy of many a colonizing state, the authorities liberally extend an olive branch and open themselves up to reasonable critique, inviting Misail to an exchange of ideas, but only so long as they themselves control the script of whatever dialogue emerges. When, in a moment of weakness, Misail seems close to accepting this olive branch, Yashin warns him: "Look, brother, you're a banished protagonist. You haven't the smallest speck of space in this language's collective story. Na to kafa na to mermer.[66] Did you really think you could butter them up and slip in from the margins—how to put it?—without them getting wise, and finagle your own story into some corner? Nothing doing! All the stories in this tongue have been *pre*determined."† Unless Misail forfeits his script and language to the demons of the so-called motherland, he will find no real accommodation there. Nor in northern Cyprus, for that matter, because here too the nationalists have infiltrated the local media[67] and carved up not only the island's physical space but its scriptworlds and linguistic pluralism. In doing so, they simultaneously draw a de facto partition through the field of literary production, "author-izing" certain writers and cordoning the other textual handlers into an ever-shrinking ghetto. Safe passage from this ghetto can only be negotiated on the terms of the authorities.

Failing all else—and it does indeed fail—the authorities can deploy their secret weapon: the parents of Misail-Mehmet, whose spirits he meets in the final moments of *a'raf*. It all begins in a dream. As they approach, they immediately start berating him: "That dead language in which you're written is a bottomless pit. Climb out of it, come back to life."‡ Ironically, even his own dead parents exhort him to abandon his supposedly dead tongue and promise him new life if he will only embrace the living tongue of Standard Turkish. His mother and father here function as the physical embodiment of his poisoned

---

* "Makul ölçüde eleştirilecekleri bir kitaba da razılar. Yeter ki onların alfabesi, lehçesi ve sözlüğü ile yazılsın kitap" (Yashin, *Sınırdışı*, 47).

† "Kardeşim, sen kovulmuş bir romankişisisin. Bu dilin ortak masalında zırnık dirhem yerin yok. Na to kafa na to mermer. Hâlâ alttan alıp, kenardan köşeden kayıp, efendime söyleyeyim, çaktırmadan kendi masalını da bir yerlere sokuşturabileceksin mi zannetiydin? Yağma yok! Bu dildeki bütün masallar belirlenmiş*tir*" (Yashin, *Sınırdışı*, 92).

‡ "Şu yazıldığın ölüdil dipsiz bir kuyu. Yukarı çık, hayata dön" (Yashin, *Sınırdışı*, 108).

"mother-father tongue." But they are not *his* tongue. The narrator answers with a question: "How? And where? I don't want to die. But how can one whose own written language can't find a place in the world live as himself in that world?"* Notice that we are speaking here of *written* language, i.e., with explicit focus on the techniques and technologies of inscription. How to live as oneself in a land whose alphabetic and typographic technologies have been centralized and turned against your tongue? To this, his parents deftly reply: *Then become someone else!* This is not categorically bad advice. To escape partition, after all, Mehmet has already tried to become Misail. Yet his parents want to push this transformation in a very different direction.

To understand the stakes here, we need to press pause for a moment and turn to Yashin's essay "Turkish-Cypriot Poetry" (Kıbrıslıtürk Şiiri), which performs a deep dive on the island's traditions of Turkish-language poetry across three successive generations: the "Ottoman identarians" (generation of 1914), the "Kemalist nationalists" (generation of 1943), and his own generation (of 1974). Regarding his father's generation, Yashin writes of their astounding ignorance in all things Greek and Levantine and, as a corollary, their nearly umbilical tie to mainland Turkish literature.[68] But take care: this critique is not limited to his father's generation; it is leveled specifically at his father too. Özker Yashin (note that the first name provides the root to Misail's last name, Oskarus) was among the most prominent poets of the Kemalist generation, celebrated for his nationalist verse while other, more heteroglot poets were marginalized. Mehmet Yashin writes, "In the 1950s when Özker Yashin was approved by Istanbul (the center) as the leading poet, Nicosia (the periphery) easily forgot about Taner Baybars."† Baybars was perhaps the one exceptionally polyglot poet of his generation, embedding in his work a knowledge of and dialogue with both the Greek and Levantine heritage of the island (which he left in 1956, never to return). In Mehmet Yashin's unflinching estimation, his own father could not but compare unfavorably with Baybars. As the years passed and communal tensions rose, Özker Yashin's early support for partition (*Taksim*) and the overt nationalism of his poems were only augmented and cemented. From the 1960s onward, with the renewed explosion of widespread ethnic violence, Özker Yashin felt he had little choice but to run into the

---

* "Nasıl? Hem nereye?.. Ölmek istemiyorum. Ama dünyada kendi yazılı dili bile bulunmayan biri, kendisi olarak nasıl yaşayabilir ki?" (Yashin, *Sınırdışı*, 108).
† "1950'lerde Özker Yaşın, İstanbul (merkez) tarafından bir numaralı şair olarak onaylanınca, Lefkoşa (çevre) Taner Baybars'ı kolayca gözden çıkarır" (Yashin, "3 kuşak," 44).

bosom of the motherland.[69] In *The Deported Hours*, then, when Misail-Mehmet's parents tell him, "become someone else!" they most likely mean: "become Turkish!"

The narrator, however, has another idea: why not become Marjori? As I noted earlier, Marjori is Misail's girlfriend and translator—and, as it turns out, his third alter ego. Bearing a Levantine name and a facility with the island's several languages, she embodies an identity unthinkable for and invisible to the nationalist and bicommunal paradigm. The Turkish authorities have no qualms in making public their hostility for translators, whose work "is more dangerous in these times. You can't easily tell what they are. The foreigners can translate a novel into their own language and use it against us."* The narrator's parents, for their part, shrilly object to Marjori and call her a "secret informant" and a "devil." As they allege, it was she who translated him into a dead language. This claim should give us pause, though. As we learn in the following chapter, Marjori in fact accuses *Mehmet* of translating the novel *out of* Karamanli Turkish (and into Standard Turkish). She seems actually to be the primary force holding the text back from total standardization, reintegrating the dialectical and scriptural patchwork back into the text. In any case, the false claims that the narrator's parents make against Marjori drive him, in a final fit of rage, to rebuke them, shouting, "Maybe it's you who's sold your souls to the devil."† With this, he suddenly awakens from his dream and finds himself miraculously passing through the walls of the Dead Zone toward his beloved Marjori—and, of course, toward Heaven.

Heaven is no paradise, however. As the narrator lies peacefully in bed with Marjori, a Greek Cypriot worm crawls up his flank and accosts him. Speaking in heavy Cypriot dialect, the worm avers that the two of them used to be classmates in elementary school and that he's come to give his old friend a few helpful warnings. Although the narrator attempts to shoo his supposed friend away, saying dismissively *But this is Heaven!*, the latter insists that if a slew of paperwork is not filled out soon he (the narrator) will again be deported. Besides the paperwork, he must also pass through another series of interrogations: "Turns out those speakin' the separate language [i.e., Turkish], εσπέσιαλι θοζ χου φλεδ θι ακιουπάιδ ζων, need to undergo an investigation, even if they're

---

* "Daha tehlikeli bu zamanda, daha tehlikeli. Ne olduğu anlaşılmıyor açıkça. Ecnebiler, bir romanı kendi dillerine çevirip kullanabilir" (Yashin, *Sınırdışı*, 54–55).

† "Ruhunu şeytana satan siz olmayasınız sakın" (Yashin, *Sınırdışı*, 108–109).

citizens of the Republic of Cyprus."* This was not an invention of the novel when it came out in 2003. As Olga Demetriou notes, until recently those identified as Turkish Cypriot could only obtain Cypriot passports after submitting themselves to a background check performed by the Central Intelligence Service, and their passports, if issued, lasted only two years instead of ten.[70] Such a process did not render them merely second-class citizens; it rendered them internal enemies and objects of suspicion. But this is not all. The worm warns our narrator that soon Heaven too will start constructing a smaller Hell within its own domain, an internal borderscape meant especially for the Turkish-speaking citizens who have remained, because "for an out-a-place protagonist like you, deported from his home, everywhere will always be a hell! *Comprende?*"† The worm then directs Mehmet-Misail's line of vision out the window to a contingent of angels flying in military formation, armed with pikes: these are God's Imperial Bodyguards, we're told. As the examples make painfully clear, passing into Heaven did not put an end to militarism, surveillance, and ghettoization; it simply put another face to it.

To top it all off, here too the borders and divisions are not limited to physical walls; they are linguistic as well. In addition to the other paperwork, the narrator must secure a letter of sponsorship from among the Greek-speaking intelligentsia of the Republic of Cyprus. But who would write such a letter for him here? Contrary to his expectations, his literature here is just as suspect as it was on the other side. The worm confides:

> Kalktım, yazdıklarını bizim dergiye verdim. Vermez olaydım. 'Re' dedi yayın yönetmeni, 'Barbarların diliyle roman mı olurmuş re! Delisin, yoksa zoli?' dedi. 'Bu hainnerin sebebine işgal edildiğimiz yetişmez, bir de onnarın yazdığı mı temsil edecek bizim yerimizi?' [...] Haa, zannettiydin ki, o tarafın dili bu tarafın alfabesiyle yazılsın diye müsaade çıkacak sana. Pü'üüh, çok beklen daha. Kalk oğlum, eziyetlendirme beni, hade kalk da doldur şu formaları. Bizim cennetimizde senin yazı ile ilişkin bundan ibarettir. Katalaves?[71]

---

* "Ayrı dili konuşannar, χελε δε ισκαλ πωλκεσινδεν κατζανλαρ, vatandaş olsaymış bile soruşturma lazımmış" (Yashin, *Sınırdışı*, 113). The Greek-script English reads: "especially those who fled the occupied zone."

† "Sınırdışı edilmiş senin gibi uygunuksuz bir romankişisi için her yer cehennem olmaya devam edecektir! Katalaves?" (Yashin, *Sınırdışı*, 114).

I went and gave your writing to our journal here. Wish I hadn't. "Bud," the director of publishing told me, "you can't make a novel out of the Barbarians' tongue! You nuts or just daft?" he said. "It's not enough that we get occupied cause'a these traitors, now it's *their* writing's gonna represent *our* country?" [. . .] Aah, you went and thought that you could get a permit by writing the other side's language in this side's alphabet? Pfft, don hol yer breath. Get up, man, you're killing me, come on, get up and start filling out these forms. Here in Heaven, your work as a writer will be limited to paperwork. *Comprende*?

In the Republic of Cyprus, not only is the narrator unwelcome, so too is his language and his story. The Greek Cypriot publisher makes this readily clear in his reductionist and jingoist logic, according to which the narrator's Karamanli Turkish, a unique dialect in its own right, is condescendingly reduced and *partitioned* to "one side's language" (Turkish) in "the other side's script" (Greek). This is of course inaccurate on both counts, given his dialectic variations and special characters, but it indicates the reductionist violence of the Greek nationalists. Any hope that passing into Heaven would somehow liberate this story, streamlining it for publication by an enlightened media apparatus, now seems in hindsight like misguided folly.

Rejected by Greek Cypriots, the narrator has one last hope: the Anglophone publishing world whose offices retain colonial-era connections to the island. In *Heaven Publishing House*, Mehmet-Misail is met with a warmer reception. The publisher manifests honest curiosity for the story, but here too something is amiss, because that curiosity hinges on another, broader partition: one between the global north and south. While the narrator waits to see the director, the receptionists inform him, "Heaven Publishing specializes in translation. A few writers from your side—after their deaths, of course—are chosen to represent the exotic trends of world literature."* When he asks what "trends" they mean exactly, they give him a catalogue titled *Written Trends from the Other Side of the Wall* whose contents include: *torture, military regimes, genocide, epidemics or starvation, occupation, mystical Eastern religions (on the condition that they are not well known), jihadist terrorism, migration, human trafficking, child abuse*, etc. As he peruses the list, the receptionists explain its logic, "Like we said, one or two writers are chosen from the other side of the wall. Heaven's readers, who grow

---

*"Cennet, çeviri üzerine uzmanlaşmış bir yer. Sizin taraflardan birkaç yazar, o da ölümlerinden sonra, dünya edebiyatındaki egzotik izlekleri temsilen seçiliyor" (Yashin, *Sınırdışı*, 138).

bored from their excessive peace of mind, need exciting stories. Even if we can't guarantee bestseller status, we always make sure our showcase has a few books from the lands beyond. They help secure Heaven's prestige."* The motives of the publisher are clear: combing through the fictions of the lands beyond *a'raf*, they're looking for disaster pornography to put it bluntly, disaster pornography peppered with some popular ethnographies. With these titles, they hope to open up new trends in an otherwise glutted market of liberal readers drowning in ennui. And even if a given title fails to secure real capital for the house, it is a net gain inasmuch as it shores up their prestige. Such an extreme depiction may appear mere caricature, yet critics of Anglophone World Literature would contend that behind the hyperbole there lies a subtle truth: the industry invents "diversity" only to homogenize and standardize it.[72]

The director of *Heaven Publishing*, John Sainthood, recognizes all of this and speaks openly of the need to package the book in Western-derived equivalences: "My real concern is the reaction of the Heaven crowd. As everybody knows, they're the old guard around here. When it comes to overseas books they place them within one of two things: a discourse that they already know or the dustbin."[†] Be that as it may, Sainthood is excited by Mehmet's prospects: writing a modern novel in a dead language is an innovation that no one has yet thought up![73] The only thing it needs is a "translator who can unlock the secret" of that language (*sırrını çözecek bir çevirmen*), rendering it accessible to *Heaven*'s readers. The first step is to translate it into Standard Turkish, a process that ultimately renders Misail's own story nearly illegible to him.[74] But this matters little to *Heaven*'s readers. Ultimately, Sainthood confesses, Karamanli Turkish and Standard Turkish are essentially the same thing to them, since "soon all languages will be as good as dead, obviously, except for our world's Most-Widely-Spoken-Language. [...] Look, my dear fellow, let me be frank, the languages written in the lands where you come from are as dead to us as those of lost peoples."[‡] Standard Turkish, Karamanli Turkish,

---

* "Dediğimiz gibi, bir iki yazar seçilecek duvarın öbür tarafından. Aşırı huzurdan içi sıkılan Cennet okuruna heyecanlı hikâyeler lazım. Çoksatışlı bir romanı garanti edemesek de, Cennet'in prestiji açısından öte diyarlardan birkaç kitabı vitrinde bulundururuz hep" (Yashin, *Sınırdışı*, 138).

† "Benim asıl endişem, Cennet camiasının tepkisi. Malum, onlar mahallenin eskisi. Ya kendi bildikleri bir diskura sokuştururlar denizaşırının kitabını ya da üzerine dosya lastiği geçirip doğruca bir sandığa" (Yashin, *Sınırdışı*, 140).

‡ "Yakında tüm diller ölü sayılacak, malum, dünyamızdaki En-yaygın-dil hariç. [...] Bakınız azizim, açıkça söyleyeyim, sizin geldiğiniz diyarlarda yazılan diller, bize göre kayıp halklarınki kadar ölüdü!" (Yashin, *Sınırdışı*, 141).

Cypriot Turkish ... ultimately, it makes little difference to the readers of *Heaven*, who approach them all as so many dead or dying languages "from the despotic southeastern borderlands of our continent."* What *does* matter, however, is how you market the book: advertising it as written in the dead language of Karamanli Turkish—whether it is actually Karamanli or has been standardized into mainland Turkish is irrelevant—would immediately draw the attention of Western readers by the force of its sheer novelty.

Here the narrator interjects, insisting that the novel is not written in a "dead" language: "Don't mix up this novel with notions of loss ... Because the people who spoke and wrote in this tongue didn't die; as if the earth swallowed them up whole, they simply vanished."† This point is crucial. If they didn't die, where did they go? I've already noted the answer earlier in passing, but I'd like to pivot now in earnest to this point: they went underground. They went underground and in doing so they took their literature with them, living in the margins and poaching whatever materials and technologies passed their way, like the refugee codices that I traced out in the previous chapter. Like the ancient temples built to one god and later converted to another,[75] the alphabets and books of this textual underground transform and shape shift as they move from hand to hand across the region's linguistic and confessional divides. That they do so to the total ignorance of the national literary system does not mean they're dead; it simply means they're off the grid. The problem though for Yashin, as I've already noted, is that so long as his story remains tied up in modern authorship, he cannot follow these "lost peoples" off the grid. When Sainthood asks him for the novel's ending, he can only shrug his shoulders and confess that it breaks off in a fragment.[76] Misail, like his ancestors before him, vanishes mid-sentence. Taking his story's conclusion with him, he leaves Mehmet without an alter ego.

But wait, that's not quite right: we still have Marjori. While her character flits in and out of the plot and is not always easy to pin down, Marjori's broader structural function seems clear to me: she is a translator, i.e., a transformative reader, whose identity escapes both the Greek and Turkish sides of bicommunalism. Drawing from this function, we can begin to discern the novel's true heroes: not Misail or Mehmet nor even Marjori herself per se, but the

---

*"Kıtamızın despotik güneydoğu sınırından" (Yashin, *Sınırdışı*, 140).

†"Kayba karışma romanı ... Ölmedi çünkü bu dilde konuşup yazan halk, yeryüzü onları yutmuşçasına ortadan kayboldular" (Yashin, *Sınırdışı*, 140).

larger underground network of transformative textual handlers. While we have until this point been cheering for Misail and hoping against hope that he will find a modern mainstream publisher to authorize his story, in the conclusion to the third chapter we understand that no such authorization is forthcoming, none that would not simultaneously erect a linguistic, literary, and geopolitical *a'raf* through the resulting text. The Turkish and Greek states, their nationalist media allies in Cyprus, even the liberal Anglophone publishers of *Heaven*—if left to their own devices, they all stand poised to build walls and hierarchies with and within Misail's story. His story depends instead on readers and textual handlers like Marjori. Even if his words ultimately *do* pass through a press (whichever press it ends up being), those to whom he must entrust the book are not only nor even chiefly the publishers themselves but the readers who will transformatively engage it with their own hands.

In a sense, though, if they really want to honor his story, such readers must also move beyond Misail himself. Readers who have come this far with Misail and who have internalized the logic of his words must lay Misail to rest. As its new handlers, they will transform his text through their marginalia, their transcriptions, their remediations or translations, each of which will ideally draw together disparate linguistic and cultural domains, as Misail did in his life. The aim is not to resurrect Karamanli Turkish circa 1930, as a kind of Frankenstein's monster, but to continue its work of assemblage with our own materials today: weaving together multiple dialects, multiple scriptworlds, multiple textual objects, and multiple cultural networks. And the driving engine of that project must be neither Misail (a past tradition) nor Mehmet (a modern author): it must be Marjori and those like her, the textual handlers of the Mediterranean borderscape as it stands today.

After a century or more of border-making and displacement, if traditions like Karamanli Turkish can survive, they will do so not as they once were, not *untouched* but, to the contrary, touched and transformed by those like Marjori. In joining one's hands to the handiwork of these texts and their past handlers, one does not attempt to turn back the clock to a reputedly pristine premodern hybridity that modernity destroyed (remember: hybridity itself is inextricably bound up in the modern project!). Instead, one openly recognizes such hybridity, which never ceased to exist, and engages it by seeking more lateral and horizontal networks of empowered readers. It is in the fourth and final chapter—i.e., "The Book of Hours" (*Saatler Kitabı* / Σαατλερ Κιταπι)—that such an opportunity explicitly emerges in *The Deported Hours*.

The Book of Hours

Turn to the fourth chapter of *The Deported Hours* and you're greeted with a long, free-verse poem. Gone is the prose fiction. Gone is Misail. Gone too is his individual story. In its place, "The Book of Hours" weaves together a collective, nearly four-centuries-long story of linguistic and script pluralism in the region. It casts multiple oblique glances at Latin Europe in the west and Istanbul in the east—i.e., the political centers to which Cyprus has historically been subject—yet it reassesses the power of those centers by inverting its focus to their margins, framing the region's broader literary history within the narrower, decentered textual networks of Cyprus itself.

The poem has been lifted and freely adapted from a single manuscript witness of a premodern book of prayers: the *Sâ'atnâme*, i.e., *Book of Hours*, ascribed to the otherwise unknown Hibetullah bin İbrahim. The work, which can be roughly dated to the sixteenth century, vividly dramatizes the End Times and lays out a series of prayers to be spoken at every hour of the day to obtain a place in heaven. The *Sâ'atnâme* was wildly popular across the Ottoman Empire, with well over two hundred extant witnesses today, copied at local sites that stretch from the empire's easternmost borders with Iran to North Africa in the west.[77] The copy that has inspired the final chapter of *The Deported Hours*, however, is unique among them all. Written down in early seventeenth-century Cyprus and passed from hand to hand across ten successive generations of Yashin's family, the Cypriot *Sâ'atnâme* accrues reader-inscribed passages, commentaries, and marginalia in at least three languages and just as many alphabets. The book is not a fictional conceit of Yashin's novel; it is real and continues to reside in his family library. But he doesn't offer readers a simple or transparent window into this text and its long transmission network; his final chapter continues the same work of creative adaptation by riffing its own poetic version, and it invites its new readers to do the same, transformatively reconfiguring its pages with their own hands, words, and scripts.

I will dig into the poetry soon enough with some close readings, but first I need to trace out the wider generic tradition of the *Sâ'atnâme*. What exactly is this book and where did it come from? Ahmet Buran, who has given us a recent best-text edition of the work, writes of its peculiar relationship to other so-called Islamic genres, such as *rûznâme* (almanac) or *yıldıznâme* (astrology). These other genres are primarily concerned with interpreting the hidden meanings of the days and hours according to the zodiac tradition. But Hibetullah's

FIGURE 20. A Christian illumination, transposed (via Photoshop) by the Ottoman Turkish of Hibetullah bin İbrahim's *Sâ'atnâme* and reproduced in *The Deported Hours*. Courtesy of Mehmet Yashin.

Sâ'atnâme gives little space to stars, signs, or zodiacs. Instead, dividing the day into five symbolic stations, it provides the particular prayers and rituals to be recited and performed during each. In this, Hibetullah's *Sâ'atnâme* differs considerably from its supposed cousin genres. Where did the inspiration for this innovation come from? The work's modern editor Ahmet Buran provides no answers, yet it is tempting to imagine (as Yashin explicitly does in *The Deported Hours*) that Hibetullah's *Sâ'atnâme* is at least partially the result of a cross-pollination with the Catholic book of hours.

The book of hours emerged in Western Europe during the thirteenth century. While it traced its origins to the monastic psalter, it soon found its way into the ranks of the laity as well, where it achieved a much wider audience and in fact became the most commonly owned book in Latin Europe for several centuries.[78] In essence, the book of hours took the form of an anthology of prayers and psalms intended to structure one's day around a devotional regimen. It was centered on the Hours of the Blessed Virgin Mary, yet the genre gradually accumulated a varying number of prayers whose arrangement and contents were never fully standardized. Indeed, not even the advent of print and the consolidation of publisher templates could truly codify the book of hours, since its users continued to modify it in subtle or far-reaching ways: within its margins they made annotations; onto blank leaves they inscribed their own prayers, wrote narratives of local legends, drew up medicinal recipes for intestinal disorders, kidney stones, sprains, etc., or crafted instructions for protective amulets to be worn during pregnancy; in the initial flyleaves they wrote intergenerational family histories (*livres de raison*) of varying length and detail; here and there they stitched keepsakes and badges directly onto the page; or they had the book bound or rebound alongside other devotional texts that they had separately procured.[79] These insertions and additions were often the work of several hands, since the book of hours was a multi-generational project, passed down within a single family or exchanged between friends. In short, the book of hours had no author; its authority was stitched together from (and maintained by) the users themselves as they kept it and passed it along.

The same can be said for the Cypriot *Sâ'atnâme* that has inspired Yashin. While it's unknown by what particular sources Hibetullah himself was influenced when drafting the work, it's clear that his copyist(s) and readers on Cyprus were well versed with the practices of their counterparts in Latin Europe. They treated their *Sâ'atnâme* much as Catholics elsewhere treated their books of hours. In the first pages of the codex, Yashin describes a brief family history, containing a quotation ascribed to "our dear departed ancestor Mehemed Michel." This is likely another persona of Yashin himself (*Mehemed* is an alternative form of Yashin's own first name, and *Michel* is the Latin form of Misail), but it is buttressed by other, genuine names of textual handlers bound up in the larger *livre de raison*, such as Molla İbrahim Hasan Efendi in 1833, who names another forefather, Ahmet Hulûsi Efendi, as the book's first owner. In later pages, we find a Western-style illumination copied from a French book of hours. Further on, lengthy passages are (Turkish) written in the Greek alphabet. Other passages are in the Greek language outright, while yet others—"particularly the descriptions pertaining to the rites after death"— are in Latin. Later in the codex, Yashin's aunt, i.e., the ninth generation of the book's handlers, inserts an English-language newspaper clipping from July 19, 1940, anxiously following developments in fascist Italy and Germany. When the book falls at last into the hands of Yashin himself, he rewrites the prayers and has them bound together with "The Book of Deportation."

What is truly astounding about this patchwork is not so much the long line of handlers that pass the book along—this was, after all, a common textual practice for the genre—but rather the plurality of scripts, tongues, and confessional practices that are thereby joined together: the Latin Office of the Dead, copied verbatim and bound into an Islamic book of prayers, alongside other passages in Greek, which in turn share the page with Greek-script Turkish. And Yashin wants us to understand this textual assemblage not as an unthinking or randomized accretion but as an explicitly political choice made by each of its handlers, in spite of the orthodoxies of whichever sovereign territory claimed Cyprus as its own. One can see this in an early inscription attributed to "our dear departed ancestor Mehemed Michel":

> Zannetmeyesin ki, sonumuzu getiren Osmanlının topu tüfengiydi.
> Hayır, hayır! Frengistan krallarımızın hasedi, ihanetiydi.
> Kendi adacığımızda Katolik kalıp
> başka çeşit bir Frenkçeyle dua etmemizden hazzetmezlerdi
> dilimize dil, alfabemize alfabe karıştırmamızı horgörürlerdi.
> Çünkü mühür kralın elindedir ve kral bir tanedir.[80]

> You mustn't think it was the shot and muskets
> of the Ottomans that brought about our end.
> No, no! It was the resentment and betrayal
> of our Latin lords in Frangistan.
> They relished not that here on our own little island

> we maintained our Catholic faith
> by praying in a different breed of Frankish;
> they disdained how we mixed new tongues
> into our tongue, new alphabets
> into our alphabet. Because the seal
> lies in the king's hand and there is but one king.

Reflecting on the Ottoman conquest of Cyprus in 1571, "Mehemed Michel" (whose dual name clearly marks him as a former Catholic, converted to the new state religion of Islam) neither celebrates the coming of the new regime nor mourns the passing of the old; he focuses instead on "us," meaning the local Cypriots, whom the mainland authorities had mercilessly castigated for their heretical mixing.[81] It was the center's intolerance of difference, he warns, that decimated the Cypriots of his generation. His meditation will fail to garner favor under the new regime as well, but it will wait patiently in Nicosia until "a child of our children will transmit our book again." Even then, however, he predicts that the mainland authorities will continue to "take no relish in how [future Cypriots] will speak and write a different form of the same tongue."* In this way, the note not only chronicles the fate of Mehemed Michel's own generation but joins it to future hands in the transmission network, which will be caught up in the same ongoing push and pull of center and de-center.

Yashin eagerly takes his place within this transmission network, yet he is careful neither to accede absolute authority to his predecessors (*benden önce gelenler*) nor demand it from those who will follow in his wake (*benden sonra gelenler*). In this, he is pushing back against the authorial agenda of Hibetullah himself, the original compiler of the *Sâ'atnâme*, who exerts a sometimes subtle but often overt pressure upon his readers and listeners to conform to his own standards:

> biz ẖod dünyâdan naḳl idüp ve bizden ṣoñra gelen 'azîz ümmetlere ve şeyẖlere ve 'âlimlere benden selâm olsun ben ża'îf ṭopraḳ oldum bende neş'e ḳalmadı bir du'âya muḥtâc ḥasret nedâmetde ḳaldum imdi her kim ki bu kitâbı ele aldukca bu ża'îf ve naḥîf ve bîçâre bir ẕerre ṭopraḳ bendenüñ sizden temennâsı oldur ... bu kitâbdan çoḳ kimse intifâ' ider eger vüs'ati olup iki üç yazdursa anuñ ṣevâbı ve 'ivażı tafṣil olmak muḥaldur bir ḳaç bu kitâb ḳadar tafṣîl olunur anuñ ṣevâbını ancaḳ Cenâb-i Bârî bilür ... anı

---

* "Evlatlarımızdan bir evlat, kitabımızı yeniden nakledecek [...]. Aynı dili başka çeşit konuşup yazmalarından hazzedilmeyecek" (Yashin, *Sınırdışı*, 179).

nesiḫî ḫaṭ ile yazalar 'abeş yazu ile yazmayalar ... tamâm başdan başa yazalar eksük ḳomayalar ve hikâyetlerine tamâm ri'ayet ideler 'abeş eylemeyeler her ḥâlde ri'âyet ideler bu kitâb ḥürmetine[82]

We ourselves have moved on from this world and send our greetings to the people and sheiks and intellectuals to come after us. I became a paltry piece of earth with no joy left, I am penitent and in need of your prayer. Whoever takes up this book, it is a greeting from me, this paltry, wretched patch of earth, to you. . . . Many people will benefit from this book if they have the capacity and copy it two or three times, [the person who does so] will have accrued such a store of good deeds and rewards in heaven that it is useless to describe here, if they copy this book several times only God knows how much their store of good deeds in heaven will be. . . . Let them copy it with Naskh script not a ridiculous hand ... Let them write it out whole and not leave any gaps and let them respect its stories completely, don't let them add any empty talk, in all let them show respect to the work's stature.

Hibetullah sends his greetings to future readers with a tongue that is endearing for its directness and humility, yet it soon becomes clear that behind his friendly greeting lies another motive. He wants not only to extend his work's life through his readers but to police those same readers and ensure their fidelity to the original. Authorial concerns for the errata or liberties of copyists were admittedly common enough in manuscript cultures—recall the similar if gentler concerns expressed by Şānī in chapter one—yet they take on an insidious form when read in the cruel light of the region's modern language politics. Yashin thus mimicks and twists Hibetullah's language, freeing his own future readers from his authority: "Those who come after me, free yourselves from what is written in the book, / free yourselves from what I'm writing here right now."* With this gesture, Yashin reminds us again why, if we are to remain faithful to Misail, we must lay Misail to rest and move on.

In the middle of the first station of prayers (Evening Hours), Yashin pauses to reflect, "They say that EVERY BOOK IS A TRUST."† That last word, *trust*, by which I translate *emanet*, functions here as a concrete rather than abstract noun: a physical object entrusted to the care of another, who, by accepting it, acknowledges their moral obligation to safeguard its integrity. Here again Yashin

---

* "Benden sonra gelenler, kitapta yazılandan serbest olunuz, [/] şu anda benim burada yazdıklarımdan serbest olunuz" (Yashin, *Sınırdışı*, 189).

† "Derler ki: HER KİTAP BİR EMANETTİR" (Yashin, *Sınırdışı*, 189).

is toying with the language of Hibetullah, who had likewise noted, "If a person leaving [this world] entrusts something to another person, the dues of that trust last forever,"* implicitly binding his readers to unending fidelity. Yashin, however, sees the dangers that inhere within such a model. He immediately retorts: "Is that so? [/] Look, I hereby free *The Book of Hours* from any dues of trust. [/] The time has long since come for us to free ourselves from books, [/] because the texts we write have ossified into legal fiat and have enslaved us."† The problem is clear: treating books as the trusts of our predecessors enslaves us rather than empowers us. But what is the alternative? What precisely does it mean to "free oneself from a book"? I could be wrong, but what I think Yashin is advocating here is not that we categorically renounce our books (or ancestors); instead, we should refuse them a priori authority. In other words, we should recognize authority not as some innate quality of an original author but as something that is generated and regenerated from the negotiations of the transmission network itself, as a work is passed from hand to hand.

Inevitably, such negotiations are bound to rewrite the script. And here I use "script" in the sense not only of an alphabetical system but as a code of protocols, like scripts of computer code. As both an alphabetic technology and a chain of commands, scripts can and should be sorted out and revised at regular intervals.[83] You can think of it as a kind of debugging or a systems check or recalibration. What is this book and how should I use it? Is it a sacred relic to be venerated? Is it a family keepsake to be marveled at? Is it a historical document to be analyzed and debated? Should we emend it? Should we transcribe it, translate it, interpolate it, or fill it with our commentary? Should we hold a workshop with a community of multigenerational refugees and parse its lines out together? Asking and debating these kinds of questions not only keeps our scripts pliant; it keeps them more democratic by allowing each textual handler to reassess, renegotiate, and ultimately reassemble the scripts that they've been given by both local and regional networks of transmission. It may be slow and tortuous to submit a text to this kind of pluralist deliberation—no: it *will* be slow and tortuous—but we can be sure that, in this way, texts will eventually find their way to where they need to go. In its ideal condition, therefore, textual transmission is a long and glorious process of "hobbling along."[84]

---

* "ḳaçan bir kişi bir kişiye emânet itse dâ'im ol emânet" (Buran, ed., *Sâ'atnâme*, folio 5a).

† "Dedim: Öyle mi [/] Bakınız, ben Saatler Kitabı'nı emanetlikten çıkarıyorum. [/] Kitaplardan kurtulmanın zamanı gelmiş de geçmiştir, [/] çünkü kendi yazdığımız yazı, yasa hükmüne çıkıp bizi esir etmiştir" (Yashin, *Sınırdışı*, 189).

To streamline this hobble into a sprint—i.e., to leave the job of textual transmission exclusively to philologists and textual authorities—is to make texts less democratic. And in a region like the Eastern Mediterranean, the stakes are high: it is not merely a question of reformulating your elders' book of prayers into fashionable poetry, as in the current example; it is a question of textual communities like those of Cyprus reclaiming for themselves again and again the stories that they tell and retell about themselves, in dialogue with several scripts but beholden to the higher authority of none. Not the authority of offshore publishers. Not of language institutes. Not even of local writers—including Yashin himself, whose "Book of Hours" beseeches us:

> Yazdığıma bakarak yeni şeyler yazası gelecek olanlar[...]
> yazı yoluyla bilmeden taşıdığım fenalıklardan özgür olalar.
> Çünkü fenalık yazının içindedir
> siz okurken yazılanı bozmadıkça, o vardır.[85]

> Those who look at my writing and are moved to write new things[...]
> let them free themselves from the evils that I carry unknowingly
>   by writing.
> Because evil is hidden in the text
> so long as you who read what is written do not muck it up.

Suddenly, the stakes of reading have changed. What enables "evil" (in this case, the evil of Yashin the author) is not a reader's particular intellectual or ideological disposition but rather our physical interaction with the textual object in front of us. To leave a book unmarked and untouched ossifies the text, ceding the power of witnessing, storytelling, and memorializing to an authority that is always prior and higher than our own. And through that authority it turns our books into our doom. This last point is not rhetorical hyperbole on my part but is hiding in the Turkish wording of the excerpt above.[86] In the final line, what I translated as "what is written" (*yazılan*) also means "fate."[87] When paired with the verb *bozmak* ("muck up"; "mess up"; "spoil"), it gives us the expression "to change fate," almost always articulated in the negative: *yazılan bozulmaz*. You can't change fate. But you *can*, in point of fact. If fate is "what is written," then it is as simple as taking up your pen, scissors, and needle and reforming the text. If we are to save ourselves from books, this book tells us, then we must save books from becoming fate. And we do so by "mucking up" the text, by disorganizing and reorganizing its scripts.

Even in its darkest hour, "The Book of Hours" triumphantly boasts: "And if the army of demons cries out and stands before you with maces of fire, [/] Let Satan leap forth and strike his tail like lightning, [/] Let him pluck you up and dash you down, [/] Let the earth open up, let the lava seep out and pull you underground." Even here, the text concludes, in this underground "there will always be a script φὸρ θὸζ λάικ ἄς."* The demons of the motherland may have partitioned much of the media landscape, they may have partitioned many of the scripts, but "those like us" will always find new media and scripts to patch together.

And as *The Deported Hours* itself bears witness, these scripts need not remain underground; they can and indeed must find their way back into mainstream print, where they can find new readers. Literature's refuge, in other words, does not reject the institutions and infrastructures of the mainstream but seeks out strategies to infiltrate them, opening them up and integrating more lateral textual networks into their technologies of reproduction. This book itself, I hope, is just such an example. Whether you're a published writer (γαζαρ), a schoolchild (ιλκοκυλ τζοτζυγυ), or a homemaker (εβκαδηνη), it makes no difference; "The Book of Hours" singles out and celebrates each of these explicitly as handlers of the text. "In the eyes of the angels," it affirms, "all are the scribes of the heavens and earths."†

This is a lofty claim, no doubt about it. The past hundred years of borderthink have worked themselves deeply into our heavens and earths, and in few landscapes are its scars more deeply felt than Cyprus, whose scriptworlds may seem worlds apart at times. Yet even here Misail's story can survive. It can survive displacement. It can survive de facto partition. It can survive even the publishers, editors, and taste-makers of Athens, Istanbul, divided Cyprus, and Anglophone publishing. But only if we its readers follow it along that journey, only if we its readers train ourselves to cross alphabets, languages, and confessions, mixing our own scripts into the scripts that we encounter.[88] Slowly but surely, this borderscape can be rewritten; we have only to become its scribes.

---

* "Varsın zebaniler orudsu haykırıp ateşten çomakla karşınıza dikilsin, [/] İblis, başının üstünden sıçrayıp, kuyruğunu da yıldırım gibi çarpıp, [/] sizi ayağınızdan tuttuğu gibi yere çalsın. [/] Yer yarılsın, içinden lavlar çıkıp sizi dibe çeksin. [/] πίζιμ κιπιλερε her zaman bir alfabe bulunur" Yashin, *Sınırdışı*, 231). The Greek-script English reads: "For those like us."

† "Meleklerin nazarında herkes yerler ile göklerin kâtibi, kâtibesidir" (Yashin, *Sınırdışı*, 206).

Afterword

A HUNDRED YEARS ON, whose stories have survived the Exchange? How did the story of the Exchange itself survive public scrutiny? How were its blunt edges softened over time for national and international audiences? I use the word "story" here intentionally, because the fact of the matter is that storytelling played an outsized role in the expansion of this border logic. Even before the Exchange itself, as I discussed in the introduction to this book, philology had long been sorting out what pieces of whose stories belonged where, and because philology was institutionally hardwired into many of the key domains of the nineteenth century—from national historiography to law to state administration[1]—these arguments about stories and texts mattered not just for the stories and texts themselves but for the communities whom they served; displacing a community's texts and voices from the historical record made it that much easier to justify the community's own geographical displacement in due time. And after such a time indeed came due in 1923, it was again storytelling that helped shape the standards-setting power of the Exchange across Europe and the Middle East in subsequent years. When narrating the Exchange to foreign policymakers and publics in the 1930s, whose perspectives were to be cited and whose were to be slighted? How closely were the post-Exchange realities on the ground to be reflected by international observers? What did it mean to be or to speak or to write—or to *not* be or to *not* speak or to *not* write—Greek or Turkish (or Albanian or Kurdish, to name just two other examples that exceed my language training), and whose answers to that question had the means and the media to make themselves heard? The Exchange was sold to world audiences as a success story in the interwar years, yet it was a story founded on the partial suppression of the experiences of the local populations themselves, on an ignorance of (or indifference toward) the ensuing Greek and Turkish state policies of forced cultural and linguistic homogenization, and on a preference instead for the sunny assessments of foreign technocrats. Put another way, the supposed success of the Exchange was narrated through a selective, largely Anglophone and Francophone diplomatic history of great men.[2]

Against this backdrop, what new stories can literature teach us? What coalitions can it help us build? The answer to that question depends in large part on what kinds of literature we invite into the conversation. *Literature's Refuge* has opened its doors wide (though I hope others after me will open them even wider), gathering stories and storytellers known and unknown, authorized and unauthorized. The refuge in my title places all of them on equal footing and belongs neither to Greek nor to Turkish nor indeed to Ottoman literary history but to the fugitive borderscape between them. In building such a refuge, I have tried to rethink and reassemble some of the core conceptual cogs and gears of this borderscape, such as Hellenism and Islam.

That word "reassemble" has been critical to my method and is worth pausing over here. On a fundamental level, "to reassemble" has meant to break down the objects of my study into their constituent parts—editions, drafts, emendations, bindings, reviews, reprints, reader marginalia and translations, etc.—and to put them back together with a stronger sense of unexpected intersections, chance crossings, and cross-pollinations within and among them. Starting from something as small as a single sentence, such as a Turkish novel's passing reference to the Greek-language newspaper *Rizospastis*, or from a large and integrated corpus, such as the Book of Hours in Mehmet Yashin's *Deported Hours*, I have sought to model a method of reading that crosses supposedly hard and fast divisions of language, alphabet, genre, and material media in order to shed light on the fascinating connections between texts and the networks through which they were moved.

Seeking out these connections across texts sometimes entails a second, more charged form of reassembling: gathering up disparate communities within the shared narrative frame of my book. It entails for example seating at the same table a Turkish-speaking Greek Orthodox priest like Agathangelos alongside a Greek-speaking Islamic scholar like Şānī; it entails integrating their communities' narratives across the national and civilizational partitions of mainstream memory, which is often selectively curated. And it therefore entails giving a platform not only to the authors themselves but to their subsequent readers—as best I can with what little material evidence remains—such as Marika Tsinoglou from chapter four or Hasanis from chapter one. The role of the reader here is important and brings me back to the broader concept of "textual handler" on which my book pivots. These handlers function as a hinge-point because they almost literally *are* the hinges on which literature moves and turns. For example, notwithstanding the different languages, genres, or registers that divide the poetry of Şānī, Cavafy, and Agathangelos, each eventually came to bind together a geographically wide—even if numerically small—community of handlers. These texts operated through a logic of accretion, assemblage, and reformulation, one that, while begun by Şānī, Cavafy, and Agathangelos, was reproduced in subtle but crucial ways by other handlers. Sometimes, these handlers effected radical transformations in the text, rebinding or reassembling the codex entirely; at other times, they left smaller but no less important traces, such as a note of thanks in the margins of the page or a pointed question mark above the text itself.[3] These marks were important; they transformed the text as they transmitted it forward in time and space, enriching it and framing it anew for its next handlers. The works of Şānī, Cavafy, and Agathangelos therefore shared more than just a language (in the case of the first two) or an alphabet (in the case of the latter two); in each case, their own existence and survival were inextricably bound up with the existence and survival of a small community of handlers, scattered across a shifting geography but loosely connected through the material texts themselves. These were not exactly the imagined communities that Benedict Anderson theorized as the nation.[4] They were not contained within a contiguous, national, or even civilizational space, nor were they bound together solely through their imagination. Read, transported, and reread across an uneven landscape, these books tied people together in real material ways. *Literature's Refuge* has sought out a host of such textual handlers across each chapter, joining them under a new vision for the region: a decentralized federation of languages, scripts, confessions, and stories whose many caretakers share a stake in the cultural past and future of this borderscape.

That leads me to another set of readers and a final act of reassembly that I have undertaken here: the readers of my own book, whom I have tried to draw together both from a range of academic fields and, perhaps even more importantly, from among the broader reading publics with a stake in the Mediterranean borderscapes that I have navigated. Dressing my narrative in an approachable and welcoming English, which I hope will inspire approachable and welcoming translations in relevant languages, I have tried to imbue this book with what Kathleen Fitzpatrick calls "generous thinking"—that is, a way of thinking out loud about literature that invites public collaboration, that listens just as much as it speaks, that works hard to build trust among complex and at times contentious communities. Fitzpatrick rightly emphasizes that "community is something that does not simply exist but instead must be built"; that it is "always complex, negotiated, multifarious"; and that there are explicit forces "arrayed against the formation of community."[5] This is particularly true in the Eastern Mediterranean, where a century of border-making and border-thinking has driven deep fissures between groups, many of whom have rightful claims to real trauma and hurt. If this book has accomplished anything, I hope it is to have provided avenues of "generous thought" to these different communities and, in doing so, opened bridges between them, empowering them not simply as passive readers of this or that national body but *as a joint community in progress.*

Have I succeeded in this? I honestly don't know, but I remain convinced that there is much to be gained by empowering disenfranchised or disaffected communities of readers, with whom scholars can and, I believe, must share the tools of their trade. While this book proper is now at its journey's end, it marks only the beginning of what I hope will be a larger curatorial project, integrating multiple publics through lectures, workshops, and collaborative works of documentation, translation, and exhibition, expanding literature's refuge beyond *Literature's Refuge* itself. To expand the borders of the book means, at some fundamental level, to extend to each of its handlers a voice in its curation; as such, it also means to assemble a decidedly large and diverse group of publics together to speak and to share and, perhaps, to debate with one another. If curated properly, literary objects can thus become an open platform, a kind of raucous commons whose protagonists are not simply the characters in its pages but all of those who have had a stake in its transmission and transformation. No one need agree completely with each of these voices—I ultimately disagreed, for example, with many of the editorial practices of George Savidis. But while I owe full agreement to none of a book's handlers (just as the handlers of this text owe none to me), I do owe them equal access to the public assembly that this book has built.

In such an assembly, therefore, it's important to "speak well,"[6] hoping that our words will move as many of a book's handlers as possible. If we fail at this, the risks are clear: the public space will empty of its publics and literature will lose something of its collective and combinatory power. This is not to say that all these stories will empty out entirely and remain unread (though a number of them, such as refugee poetry in Ottoman-script Greek and Greek-script Turkish, might indeed be in danger of disappearing within a generation if their texts are not curated); instead, it is to point out the very real likelihood that, as a book's handlers abandon the shared space of refuge that I've tried to facilitate here, they will return to their several partitions, reading and interpreting their national stories in isolation. Eleventh-grade high school students in Turkey, for example, will go on reading *Shirt of Flame* in their closed communities, while twelfth-grade high school students in Greece will do the same with *A Captive's Story*, both works framed by state textbooks, published and distributed nationally. However sensitive these textbooks might be to the multiple hermeneutic possibilities of the work itself (both of them are), they do not as yet offer a comparative window into the more complicated and polyphonic textual landscape that I've tried to curate here.

These, then, are the stakes. To curate literature's refuge at the Mediterranean borderscape is to assemble not only the multiple texts and variations of this or that work but, through them, to assemble one another. To listen and be listened to. To hear the richness of tongues, speaking once more across the divide:

קִינָא גְלוֹסָא נַמִילְיִיס	Kina glosa namiliyis	*Rise up, tongue, and speak*
תְיַמַזְמָאה נַמוֹלוֹיִיס	Thamazmah namoloyis	*tell the wonder that you keep*
קִימִימֶנוּס נַקְסִיפְנְיִיס	Kimimenus naksipniyis	*stir the sleepers from their sleep*
מֶקְרָסִי נָטוּס מֶתְיִיס	Mekrasi natus methiyis	*and make them drunk with drink.*[7]

NOTES

Preface

1. Millas, *Türk Romanı*; Lemos, "Early Literature."
2. Zeitlian Watenpaugh, *Missing Pages*, 40.
3. Rozakou, "Solidarians"; Grewal, "Obligation."
4. Bryant, *Post-Ottoman Coexistence*, especially the introduction, offers thoughtful insights into the pitfalls of Ottoman nostalgia and the complexities of writing about coexistence.
5. For a recent treatment of undocumentation in the American context, see Villavicencio, *Undocumented Americans*.
6. Ballinger, *World Refugees*, notes a similar problem in historiography: "Refugee histories often don't present themselves neatly as such in terms of the archival classifications common to state institutions [...]. Because the sites of refugee camps are usually transient, the literal infrastructures of many refugee histories were typically dismantled" (26).
7. Miéville, *City*. For an academic discussion of unseeing, see Pachirat, *Every Twelve Seconds*.
8. Miéville, *City*, 370.
9. Here I may be echoing Spivak, *Death of a Discipline*—especially pages 9–10—even as my focus on *borderland* language training charts a slightly different itinerary across her "hemispheric" fault lines.

Introduction

1. For an overview of the geopolitical climate at this moment, see Psomiades, "Fridtjof Nansen"; Hirschon's introduction to *Crossing the Aegean*; and Aktar, "Türk-Yunan." For general historiographies of the Exchange, see Yılmaz, *Diplomacy*; Hirschon (ed.), *Crossing the Aegean*; Özsoy, *İki Vatan*; Mazower, *City of Ghosts*, 293–420; Clark, *Twice a Stranger*; Tsitselikis (ed.), *Ελληνοτουρκική ανταλλαγή*; and Kostopoulos, *Πόλεμος*.
2. Nansen initiated the diplomatic back and forth before the convention but was aloof from the difficult daily grind of the negotiations themselves. Nonetheless, his mere presence at the convention and the symbolic status of his name and title lent crucial political capital to the idea of forced displacement. See Frank, *Making Minorities*, 49–72.
3. *Lausanne Conference*, 114–115.
4. For compelling readings on cultural and linguistic difference among the refugees and the social exclusion that awaited them, see Hirschon, *Heirs*; Yalçın, *Emanet Çeyiz*, 70, 107, 143, 199, 265–267; Balta, *Cries and Whispers*, 11–12; Clark, *Twice a Stranger*; and Janse, "Καππαδοκική διάλεκτος." On the homogenization projects in Greece and Turkey, Özkırımlı and Sofos, *Tormented*, provide solid comparative overviews, while Kostopoulos, *Απαγορευμένη*, and Ertürk, *Grammatology*, provide focused case studies of linguistic homogenization in Greece and Turkey, respectively.

5. Clark, *Twice a Stranger*, xi–xvii; Yıldırım, *Diplomacy*, 11–13; Frank, *Making Minorities*; Ther, *Outsiders*, 66–67.

6. Hamid Bey, representing the Turkish government, told Nansen "that his instructions were to negotiate on the basis of a complete exchange of the respective racial minorities in the whole of Turkey and Greece, thus also in Constantinople, and that this exchange should take place without regard to the wishes of the individuals. In other words, that his instructions foresaw a complete exchange of racial minorities by compulsory emigration" (United Nations Archives at Geneva, Folder R1761/48/24318). Nansen adopted this same language in the subsequent draft report to the League of Nations, referring to the entire endeavor as "The Reciprocal Exchange of Racial Minorities Between Greece and Turkey" (see figure 1). In the official treaty, however, the word race is substituted by religion.

7. Stroebel and Gedgaudaitė, "Borders," xv.

8. For the global legacies of the Exchange, readers can look ahead to the start of chapter five.

9. Torunoğlu, "Neo-Hellenes," sheds light on even earlier Ottoman state directives to deport Greeks in 1869, and notes that Turkish diplomats in 1922 consulted these directives (see page 67).

10. Pollock, *World Philologies*, has succinctly called this "the theory of textuality as well as the history of textualized meaning," providing an equally succinct survey of global philology's historical developments. Turner, *Philology*, and Güthenke, *Feeling*, provide lengthier surveys of Anglophone and German philology respectively, while Ahmed, *Archaeology*, explores philology's complicity in the British colonial project, reifying indigenous traditions and erasing their nontextual or text-adjacent voices. In the following section, I will map out similar power dynamics in the institutionalization of Greek philology in Greece.

11. On the nineteenth-century drive to bind philology to race, see Harpham, "Roots."

12. In 1922, just as all remaining traces of Greeks from Anatolia were vanishing, Fuad Köprülü dismissed any possibility of Greek or Armenian influence in Anatolian folk literature, where Turks were "numerically and politically superior" and hence, in his view, their civilization was "superior." See Köprülü, *Edebiyat Araştırmaları*, 268. Köprülü was the founding voice of modern Turkish philology, and later endeavors—from Ahmed Hamdi Tanpınar's survey of late Ottoman literature (see Mignon, *Ana Metne*, 133–149) to Sabahattin Eyüboğlu's assessment of ancient Greek Anatolia (see Sharpe, "Hellenism")—followed a similar pattern of dispossessing non-Turkish cultures. For a sweeping discussion of the larger entanglement of Turkish humanism with nationalism, see Kara, "National Literary Historiography"; and Oruç, "Rewriting."

13. For Modern Greek philology's crypto-colonial relationship to European Hellenism, see Gourgouris, *Dream Nation*, and Herzfeld, "Absent Presence." Apostolidou, *Λογοτεχνία*, shows how this relationship was replicated in the Greek academy, where Modern Greek was subordinated to Ancient Greek. Turkish literature also had a fraught relationship with European philology, since the former was increasingly informed and shaped by the latter over the last decades of the nineteenth century (Kara, "National Literary Historiography"; Dickinson, *DisOrientations*, 87–102), yet Europe had no immediate claims of its own on Turkish literary history. European appropriations of Greek literature and history, on the other hand, lay at the core of most Western European identity constructs.

14. Kurtz, "Philological Apparatus," 769; Vasunia, *Classics*.

15. For uses of the Greco-Roman tradition by proslavery advocates, see Malamud, *African Americans*, 128–146, and Lupher and Vandiver, "Yankee She-Men"; for the racecraft that has continued to shape the Greco-Roman tradition in the twentieth and twenty-first centuries, see Padilla Peralta, "Anti-Race"; for histories of gendered access to Classics, see Prins, *Ladies' Greek*; for the role of Classics in colonial India, see Vasunia, *Classics*, especially pages 193–235; for the Greco-Roman tradition in the Nazi imaginary, see Chapoutot, *Greeks, Romans, Germans*; and for the use of Classical Greek in justifying the ethnic cleansing of modern Greeks, see Mazower, *Inside Hitler's Greece*, 155–180.

16. On borderscape, see Perera, "Pacific Zone" and *Australia*; on contemporary Greece as a borderscape for asylum seekers, see Cabot, *On the Doorstep*.
17. For the heuristic of literary checkpoint, see Apter, *Against World Literature*, 104.
18. Konuk, *East-West Mimesis*, 13.
19. Filelfo, *Collected Letters*, 455.
20. One important exception to this rule is Martin Crusius and his *Turcograecia* (1584), which provides a more sympathetic view on Ottoman Greeks. Nonetheless, at the base of his project too lay a deep suspicion of Greek Orthodoxy. See Calis, "Reconstructing," 153.
21. Heinsius, *Poemata graeca*, 100.
22. See for example Zanou, *Transnational Patriotism*, 149–150. Attacks against Greeks also spilled over into the genre of travelogues, where philology was joined to ethnography. See Suzanne Said, "Mirage," 270–274, and Hanink, *Classical Debt*, 70–103.
23. Fallmerayer, *Geschichte der Halbinsel Morea*, iv.
24. Gourgouris, *Dream Nation*, 141, and Hanink, *Classical Debt*, 168, both point to Fallmerayer's marginal position in European historiography and his therefore remarkably outsized role in Greece, where he has largely set the tone and terms of debate around Modern Greek identity for almost two hundred years. Hanink likewise traces several more recent iterations of Fallmerayer's claims in the popular press of Western Europe (see pages 167–168; 199–201), which suggests that his theses are not as obscure to the contemporary West as one might think.
25. Herzfeld *Ours*, 77; Skopetea, *Πρότυπο βασίλειο*, 167; Gourgouris, *Dream Nation*, 142.
26. Here and in the next block quotation, I am working from Konstantinos Romanos's Greek translation of Fallmerayer's German, *Περί της καταγωγής*, 127–128.
27. See for example Herzfeld, *Ours*, 79.
28. See, for example, Hume, *Essays*, 213.
29. Fallmerayer, *Περί της καταγωγής*, 128–129.
30. On this point, see Lambropoulos, *Rise*, 170, or Gourgouris, *Dream Nation*, 132–134.
31. Gourgouris, *Dream Nation*, 122–140; Herzfeld, *Anthropology*, 19; Güthenke, *Placing Modern Greece*, 99–101; Mani, *Recoding World Literature*, 74.
32. Suzanne Said, "Mirage," 280, 288.
33. Zanou, *Transnational Patriotism*, 137–138; Grammatikos, *British Romantic*, 32–38. For exceptions to this rule, see Wallace, *Shelley and Greece*, 178–205. Grammatikos, *British Romantic*, also introduces several welcome wrinkles into the larger mainstream tropes of philhellenism.
34. Gourgouris, *Dream Nation*, 133–134.
35. For a detailed discussion of the responses to Fallmerayer, see Herzfeld, *Ours*, 88–90.
36. Admittedly, some Greek intellectuals attempted to shift the focus of the Helleno-Christian tradition away from Greek antiquity and center it outright on Byzantine Christianity. Academics and writers like Yannis Psyharis and Kostis Palamas anchored modern Greek identity in *Romiosyne*, a sense of Greekness rooted in the Roman (i.e., Byzantine) Empire and Orthodox Christianity. *Romiosyne* became for many Greeks a cultural domain capable of centering modern Greek heritage on its own terms. Nevertheless, proponents of *Romiosyne* rarely attacked the ancient origins of Greek culture, nor did they ultimately see *Romiosyne* as opposed to Hellenism. Instead, as Leontis, *Topographies*, has demonstrated, "they made the two equivalent titles of honor. And they kept both in circulation. Their reasoning was that both names had eminent origins; they each bore witness to the twin glory of being Greek" (191).
37. Paparrigopoulos, *Ἱστορία*, vol. 1, 877.
38. Moustoxidis, "Βιογραφικά," 94–95.
39. Sathas was building on the earlier vision of Andreas Moustoxidis, whose philological work however remained piecemeal. For an important intellectual biography of Moustoxidis, see Zanou, *Transnational Patriotism*, 165–186.
40. Sathas, *Ἱστορικαὶ Διατριβαί*, 123–336.

41. Tsitselikis, *Old and New Islam*, 8.

42. The Muslims of Western Thrace and the Cham Albanians of Epirus were excepted from the Exchange.

43. I draw the term "minor losses" from Demetriou, *Refugeehood*.

44. As cited in Dedes, "Was there a Greek Aljamiado Literature?," before the end of the Cold War only two brief articles had been published in Greece on Greek-language Islamic literature, both in provincial journals of Epirus by local amateur historians, Pyrsinellas and Salamangas. These studies were ignored by the intellectual elite in Greece's cultural centers.

45. Sykoutris, Μελέται καὶ ἄρθρα, 516–533. Güthenke, "Editing the Nation," provides an insightful English-language overview of Sykoutris's philological outlook. Sykoutris was from Anatolia and had passed through primary and secondary schooling in the post–Tanzimat Ottoman school system. He thus had knowledge of the Arabic script, a fact that is confirmed by his personal correspondence (see Sykoutris, Γράμματα, 31). He had the training, therefore, to incorporate Arabic-script Greek poetry into the philological project of the Greek literary canon. But such poetry had already been scattered to the winds by the time that Sykoutris was starting his career, and even if he had chanced upon it in some far-flung library, it did not hold a place in the Greek textual tradition as Sykoutris envisioned it.

46. For the use of racial vocabulary—e.g., "our race" (ἡ φυλή μας)—see Dimaras, Ἱστορία. Politis, Ἱστορία, chooses instead "our folk" (ὁ λαός μας), which is nonetheless circumscribed by the same implicitly ethno-religious borders of national consciousness, understood to have been triggered by the incursions of Islam (27; 47). Both histories (which ironically bear the same title: *History of Modern Greek Literature*) note to varying degrees the impact of the Italian Renaissance on Greek diasporas in Italy, but no similar explorations of hybrid Ottoman identities are pursued.

47. *Digenis Akritas* was excluded from Greek diasporic print in Europe, likely due to its archaic language and prosody, as well as its distant eastern provenance. See Kehagioglou, "Τύχες," 88. The work was not published until a manuscript was "rediscovered" and prepared by Konstantinos Sathas and Emile Legrand in 1875.

48. When Turks do enter the pages of Dimaras's *History*, they are almost always two-dimensional caricatures of despotism and greed, e.g.: "The Turk had a vested interest in not stamping out every Greek activity. Surrounded by Turkish military elements, the Greek populations of the Ottoman Empire secured the Empire's wealth and taxes. The Greeks had to be left alive, at least as long as they supplied their wealth to the depredations of the conquerer" ("Συμφέρον εἶχε ὁ Τοῦρκος νὰ μὴν πνίξει κάθε ἑλληνικὴ κίνηση. Οἱ ἑλληνικοὶ πληθυσμοὶ τῆς τουρκικῆς αὐτοκρατορίας, περικλεισμένοι μέσα στὶς μαχητικὲς τουρκικὲς ὁμάδες, εἶταν οἱ πληθυσμοὶ ποὺ ἐξασφάλιζαν τὸν πλοῦτο, τοὺς φόρους. Πρέπει νὰ ζοῦν τουλάχιστον ὅσο χρειάζεται γιὰ νὰ παρέχουν τὰ πλούτη τους στὴν ἁρπαγὴ τοῦ κατακτητῆ," 56).

49. I draw this term from Mezzadra and Neilson, *Border as Method*, 312.

50. Mezzadra and Neilson, *Border as Method*, 159.

51. For the economic inflection of borders, which traffic populations whose partial and hence precarious integration facilitates easier exploitation and value extraction, see Mezzadra and Neilson, *Border as Method*; Andersson, *Illegality, Inc.*; Milkman, *Immigrant Labor*; and Coddington, Conlon, and Martin, "Destitution Economies," among others.

52. For the mutual imbrication of the border regime and the labor market in Greece today, see Triandafyllidou and Ambrosini, "Irregular Immigration"; Mufti and Gourgouris, "Immigration and Neocolonialism"; and Papada, "Evolving Moral Economies." For the cultural dynamics and Islamophobia fueling this nexus, see Kirtsoglou and Tsimouris, "Migration, Crisis," and several contributions to Dalakoglou and Agelopoulos (eds.), *Critical Times*.

53. For a poetic litany of first-hand accounts of this exploitation, see Balta et al., *Muhacirnâme*—especially pages 44–47.

54. See for example Lambropoulos, *Literature as National* and *Rise of Eurocentrism*; Jusdanis, *Belated Modernity*; Leontis, *Topographies* and *Eva Palmer Sikelianos*; Gourgouris, *Dream Nation*; Dimiroulis, Ποιητής ως έθνος; Calotychos, *Modern Greece* and *Balkan Prospect*; Yannoulopoulos, Διαβάζοντας τον Μακρυγιάννη; Kolocotroni and Mitsi, *Women Writing*; Van Steen, *Theatre and Adoption*; Tziovas, Μύθος; Boletsi, *Barbarism*; Papanikolaou, Σαν κι εμένα; Hanink, *Classical Debt*; and Kayalis, *Cavafy's Hellenistic Antiquities*. Beyond the discipline of literary studies, the list would grow even larger, including titles such as Herzfeld, *Ours, Anthropology*, and "Absent Presence"; Hamilakis, *Nation*; Damaskos and Plantzos, *Singular Antiquity*; Anagnostou, *Contours*; Panourgia, *Dangerous Citizens*; Avdela et al., Φυλετικές θεωρίες; and the recent scholarly collective "dëcoloɴɪze hellás" (decolonizehellas.org).

55. Zanou, *Transnational Patriotism*, 7.

56. I do not find the concept of "postcritique"—see Anker and Felski (eds.), *Critique and Postcritique*—the most useful frame for the kinds of ideas and readerships that I want to articulate. I aim instead for what Kathleen Fitzpatrick calls *Generous Thinking*, which pinpoints the problem not in critique per se but in the zero-sum logic of eristic argumentation—i.e., "coming out on top" or "getting ahead" rather than collectively exploring and shaping one another's knowledge bases.

57. For what I mean by "diplomatic language," see Latour, *Inquiry*, 262–263. For a similar stance in my own field, see Gedgaudaitė, *Memories*, 28.

58. Many of these readerships likewise negotiate a complex and multigenerational memory regime, influenced and shaped by factors as diverse as family histories, oral history archives, and national historiographies and communal and public discourses that shift under the weight of political trends from decade to decade, as well as the effects of adaptation across media, including print and film and music. For influential work on memory regimes of the Exchange, see Hirschon, *Heirs*; Yalçın, *Emanet Çeyiz*; Papailias, *Genres*, 93–138; Salvanou, Συγκρότηση; Sjöberg, *Making*; Gedgaudaitė, *Memories*.

59. Levy, *Poetic Trespass*, 7.

60. Damrosch, *What Is World Literature*, provides an early and foundational vision of the field.

61. See, for example, Spivak, *Death of a Discipline*; Apter, *Against World Literature*; Slaughter, "World Literature as Property"; Mufti, *Forget English!*; Fisk, *Orhan Pamuk*; Goyal, *Runaway Genres*, 29; Mattar, *Specters of World Literature*, 21–27; and Dickinson, *DisOrientations*, 166–167.

62. See, for example, Halim, "Lotus"; Shih, "Race and Relation"; Mani, *Recoding World Literature*, 189–203; Elam, *World Literature*; Yoon, *China*; and Gvili, *Imagining India*. For a thoughtful study of the *disconnect* and *frictions* of south-to-south comparison, see Mangalagiri, *States of Disconnect*.

63. See, for example, Edward Said's depiction of Erich Auerbach as a scholar in exile (*The World, the Text, and the Critic*, 1–30) and Mufti's further theorization of "exilic" scholarship as a counter to world literature (*Forget English!*, 203–242).

64. See, for example, Apter, *Translation Zone*, 94–108, for a discussion of translation markets and the marginalization of particular national literatures within the "monoculture" of large-scale transnational publishing.

65. McGill, "Copyright and Intellectual Property," writes that "history offers numerous alternatives to tightening control over circulation in the name of the author, a process that was strengthening its grip in the mid-1990s. If authors' rights were from the start a legal fiction, a tactic used in a struggle between powerful political and economic interests, disclosing the author's fictive status does not promise to do much to dispel its power" (394).

66. Brouillette, *Postcolonial Writers*; Davis, *Creating Postcolonial Literature*.

67. Apter, *Against World Literature*, explores translation as one kind of non-authorial patchwork, which she describes as "deowned literature," a kind of literary commons built by "unalienated literary labor" (15; 289).

68. Here I am adapting my language from an astute observation in Mufti, *Enlightenment in the Colony*: "Whenever a population is *minoritized*—a process inherent in the nationalization of peoples and cultural practices—it is also rendered potentially *movable*" (13).

69. Mufti, *Forget English!*, 250. It is worth noting that at least two generations of book historians have been doing just what Mufti calls for, working hard to recover the stories of non-elite and anti-hegemonic actors from within the larger textual networks of colonial, imperial, patriarchal, and capitalist systems. It was perhaps D. F. McKenzie's 1985 Panizzi lectures (later collected and printed in *Bibliography and the Sociology of Texts*) that first demonstrated the potential of book history to shed light on non-elite agencies, but for representative examples of more recent research in this direction, see McHenry, *Forgotten Readers* and *To Make Negro Literature*; Joshi, *In Another Country*; Fraser, *Book History Through Postcolonial Eyes*; Ghosh, *Power in Print*; Round, *Removable Type*; Garvey, *Writing with Scissors*; LeGette, *Remaking Romanticism*; Cloutier, *Shadow Archives*; Fielder and Senchyne (eds.), *Against a Sharp White Background*. And while most such studies are limited to *textual* networks traditionally understood, other pioneering scholarship has developed methods that account for nontextual communication infrastructures as well, and the ways that they both elude and dovetail with the book format, as demonstrated by Cohen, *The Networked Wilderness*.

70. The notion of disassembling and reassembling one's object of study draws on Assemblage Theory and Actor Network Theory, which only occasionally surface explicitly in this book but, over the years of my initial doctoral research, have left an impact on my book's frame. For representative work, see Latour, *Reassembling* and *Inquiry*; DeLanda, *New Philosophy* and *Assemblage Theory*; and Deleuze and Guattari, *A Thousand Plateaus*. If I have applied a light touch with this theoretical apparatus, it is due to my overriding goal of keeping my book as broadly accessible as possible.

71. See for example Johns, *Nature of the Book*; McGann, *Critique of Modern Textual Criticism* and *Textual Condition*; John Bryant, *Fluid Text*; Piper, *Dreaming in Books*; Knight, *Bound to Read*; and Emmerich, *Literary Translation*.

72. For a thorough and thoughtful treatment of existing scholarship on copyright and intellectual property, see McGill, "Copyright and Intellectual Property."

73. Mani, *Recoding World Literature*, traces out the particular trajectories of books through the "way station" of libraries and collections, which serve a diverse range of networks, from imperialist colonial migrations northward, as in the case of Aloys Sprenger (see pages 116–121), to internationalist and socialist networks of editors, scholars, and translators, such as those who constituted the GDR's *Volk und Welt* (see pages 189–203).

74. Mani, *Recoding World Literature*, 34.

Chapter one, in which Şānī and his readers save the nightingale

1. The word *Tuhfe*, which translates literally to *Gift*, was a title used for a range of essayistic genres in Ottoman literature, from bilingual dictionaries to compendia—in each case conceived and composed as a "gift" for their readers.

2. The literature of Greek-speaking Muslims has until now fallen mostly to Ottomanists—primarily Yorgos Dedes and Phokion Kotzageorgis, whose excellent work has not found the reception it deserves in Greek philology or Modern Greek studies.

3. For the tallies of Golden Dawn hate crimes, see Smith, "Nobody knows"; for the use of Krypteia within Golden Dawn, see Baskakis, "Αυτή είναι η εντολή."

4. Park, "Introduction."

5. Charrière, "Translation, Transcription," 42. For a similar treatment of the medieval Mediterranean period, see Mallette, "Boustrophedon."

6. Damrosch, "Scriptworlds," 200.

7. Dedes, "Was There a Greek Aljamiado Literature?," 88, cites around a dozen surviving codices as of now, though more are likely yet hiding in private or state collections. More generally, Dedes, "The Eighteenth-Century Greek Aljamiado Mevlid," 334, points to the destructive or even epistemicidal effect of the Population Exchange on what was a predominantly manuscript tradition.

8. The Library of Congress Subject Headings (LCSH) are institutionally contiguous with the Library of Congress Classification System (LCC), which along with the Dewey Decimal Classification System (DDC) physically groups books together or sunders them on the shelves of college libraries in the United States.

9. The only marks of provenance are the inscription "a. 1819" on the pastedown endpaper of the cover and the letter "Z" on the spine of the current binding.

10. To my knowledge, the only published scholarship that mentions Şānī's *Tuhfe* are Theodoridis, "Über die griechische-aljamiadische Handschrift," which provides a brief bibliographic overview, and Dedes, "Was there a Greek Aljamiado Literature?," which mentions Şānī's *Tuhfe* in passing while engaging the larger corpus of Ottoman-script Greek as a whole.

11. As Şānī notes in his codex, many Muslims were participating in Greek Orthodox Christian ceremonies, such as singing and dancing at carnival, coloring Easter eggs and making Mayday wreaths, and even becoming blood brothers or godparents to their Christian neighbors (ff. 163b–164a).

12. Most famous is Yanyalı Esad Efendi (fl. early 1700s), who began his studies in Ioannina and completed them in Istanbul, where he built his career atop a number of intellectual connections with high-ranking Ottoman scholars, officials, and patrons (including Phanariot Greeks, whose critical place in Ottoman society has been meticulously reconstructed by Philliou, *Biography*). Esad Efendi's surviving work has served as an important touchstone for recent intellectual historians such as Küçük, "Natural Philosophy," and Greene, *Edinburgh History of the Greeks*, 192–215. Nonetheless, Esad Efendi's work is written almost exclusively in Arabic and is addressed to an elite audience at the imperial core and thus functions quite differently than the vernacular Greek literature about which I am writing here, as will become clear over the course of this chapter.

13. Galanti, *Vatandaş*, 13–14.

14. My Ottoman-script transcriptions faithfully reproduce the *kesra* diacritics sometimes inserted between two initial consonants—e.g., بِشْخِي (pişihi / πισυχή) instead of بْشْخِي (pşihi / ψυχή)—but I do not reproduce them in my Latin-script transcription. This feature, which occurs only irregularly, is a holdover from Turkish-language protocols rather than an actual aspect of Şānī's Greek. Another point worth noting here is the capacity of the Ottoman script to document and preserve the regional Epirus dialect, such as the "sh" phoneme, which cannot be represented with traditional Greek script.

15. Salutations to the Prophet, traditionally uttered (in Arabic) as part of ritual prayer.

16. For an excellent treatment of the Turkish-language catechism, see Terzioğlu, "Where ʿIlm-i ḥāl." Krstić, *Contested Conversions*, fills out the larger geopolitical backdrop in relation to conversion in the Balkans. Theodoridis, "Unbekanntes" and "Birgivī's Katechismus," mention another Greek-language catechism translated directly from Birgivi's Turkish-language catechism. Georgios Salakidis and Phokion Kotzageorgis are currenrly preparing an edition of this work.

17. In the final stages of my book's production, my colleague Samet Budak alerted me to the existence of a second surviving witness to Şānī's work at the Süleymaniye Library in Istanbul (Yazma Bağışlar ms. 3954, dated to the early eighteenth century), which offers a complete copy of the first volume of the BS cod. graec. 593 witness, although it lacks the latter's second volume. This exciting discovery unfortunately comes too late for me to make much of it here.

18. I have emended the copyist's dittography: نَه نَتْرُغُو (ne netroğo).

19. The preposition *oh* (οχ) is a dialectical alternative to *apo* (από).

252 NOTES TO CHAPTER 1

20. Turkish/Arabic term for "hell."

21. This line is replete with several key Arabic terms from Islamic theology: 'arş and kürsī are the Throne and footstool of God; the levḥ is the eternal tablet of God, on which He first composed the Quran with his ḳalem, or pen.

22. Turkish term for *keepsake*.

23. For this term and those in the next line, see the corresponding footnotes in the Latin-script transliteration above.

24. The passage was so beautiful, in fact, that it was later adapted into the opening lines of a Greek-language mi'rājnāmeh. See Kotzageorgis, *Το Ισλάμ στα Βαλκάνια*, 127–128.

25. E.g., surah 6, verse 103: "No vision can grasp Him, [/] But His grasp is over all vision." All my quotations of the Quran are drawn from the Yusuf Ali translation.

26. E.g., Sahih Muslim, Kitab al-Iman, no. 334: "he [the Holy Prophet] saw [Allah] with his heart."

27. Surah 13, verse 2: "God is He Who raised [/] The heavens without any pillars."

28. E.g., surah 35, verse 9: "It is God Who sends [/] Forth the Winds, so that [/] They raise up the Clouds, [/] And We drive them [/] To a land that is dead, [/] And revive the earth therewith [/] After its death: even so (will be) the Resurrection!"

29. Again, I am drawing from the Yusuf Ali translation.

30. Line 6 is likely drawing as well from the famous "throne verse" of the second surah.

31. Dedes, "The Eighteenth-Century Greek Aljamiado Mevlid," 328.

32. Arabic and Turkish traditions make no mention of "souls," referring to God's tablet instead as the "Well-Preserved Tablet" (*Lawh Mahfuz*) and marking it specifically as the book of the Quran. Şānī's innovation here is unique and seems to push the concept toward a broader "book of fate," containing God's foreknowledge of every human soul.

33. See the Persianate *izafet* (translated as "of") in the example here.

34. Lammer, *Elements*, 429–430, provides a helpful survey of existing scholarship on the topic, followed by a more extended discussion on the specific adaptations and innovations of Avicenna's *Physics*.

35. I have emended the copyist's بُوۡیِپی (puyipi). The emended form (*toyipi* / το είπει) is an excellent example of a medieval infinitive—i.e., the neuter definite article and the third person singular subjunctive of the verb—which survived in Epirus dialect.

36. I have emended from ویلاوي (vilevi).

37. I have emended the copyist's بِیُوۡنَه (piyune).

38. This is an Arabic term for "intellectual" or "scholar."

39. Literally, "their obscurity"—i.e., fields of knowledge obscure to them.

40. I.e., γνώρισαν.

41. The term *bīd'āt* refers to new innovations in religious doctrine, most often used in the negative sense of heresy or heretical doctrines.

42. The term *rek'āt* refers to the ritual movements during daily prayer.

43. I.e., 1667 CE.

44. I.e., the ritual movements during prayer.

45. See for example Zilfi, *Politics of Piety*, 129–181; Terzioğlu, "Sufi and Dissident"; and Sariyannis, "The Kadizadeli Movement."

46. Terzioğlu, "Where 'Ilm-i ḥāl," 110.

47. One prominent example is the 1711 "Great Sedition" in Egypt, when a Turkish preacher turned hundreds of Turkish-speaking soldiers stationed in Cairo against the perceived heterodox practices of the local Arabs. See Peters, "Battered Dervishes"—in particular, pages 105–107, which discuss the differing interests of the centralized, higher-echelon Turkish-speaking jurists, appointed from Istanbul by the Sultan, and the lower-level scholars drawn from the province's own population.

NOTES TO CHAPTER 1

48. This point further confirms Şānī's familiarity with the Christian scriptures and the prestige that they conferred to Greek.

49. A reference to the prominent Hanafi Jurist Ebussuud Efendi (1490–1574), also known as "al-Imadi."

50. Arabic term meaning "cause" or "suit."

51. This argument is made more explicit in other passages, such as fol. 165b lines 5–7.

52. Quoted in Zadeh, *Vernacular Qur'an*, 5.

53. Zadeh, *Vernacular Qur'an*, 53–59.

54. Uysal, *İzahlı Mülteka*, 1.93.

55. I am emending from the copyist's أَخَانَي (ehani).

56. I read this passage as significantly altered by copyist error. It reads مَتِي مُوْدُوْنْ (mati muðun / μάτι μου δουν), which seems to me nonsensical ("my eye, [may] they see"). I interpret it instead as "ma timo[r]un" (μα τιμορούν, "but they punish") or possibly "ma[s] timo[r]un" (μας τιμορούν, "they punish us").

57. In the Greek, there is no attribution to whose judgment this is, but it seems logical that it belongs not to Şānī but his opponents. Alternatively, because the verb κρίνω meant both "to speak" and "to judge," the line could possibly also read as follows: "whoever judged Greek [negatively] has forfeited their soul." In this case, Şānī would be speaking the line and condemning those who have condemned Greek.

58. I am emending from the copyist's كُوْلُدُرْ (koldur).

59. *Manzum Fıkıh* (Jurisprudence in Poetic Verse) is one of the titles traditionally given to Devletoğlu Yusuf's work.

60. For a recent discussion on the debates surrounding Quranic translation, see Basalamah and Sadek, "Debates Around the Translation of the Qur'an."

61. Burak, *Second Formation*.

62. Quoted in Yıldız, "Hanafi Law Manual," 292.

63. That this vision of imperial authority continued to inform many Turkish-language catechisms in later centuries is confirmed by Terzioğlu, "Where ʿIlm-i ḥāl," 110.

64. Kappler, "Fra Religione e Lingua," 104.

65. This is likely αχρεία (the initial "a" having been elided into the terminal "a" of the previous word), meaning "vulgar" or "common."

66. An Arabic apotropaic meaning "God forbid."

67. I am emending from the copyist's بِسْتَفْيَقُوسْ (pisteftikos).

68. I emend the copyist's "ḥoris oston" (χωρίς ως τον) to "ḥoris tonus" (χωρίς τόνους).

69. Here, the manuscript reads "titustoni to ḥarfitu nalakṣun vriskun topo" (i.e., "[για]τί τους τόνοι το χάρφι του να αλλάξουν βρίσκουν τόπο), which does not quite make grammatical sense. The suggested changes above normalize the line to "[για]τί τους τόνους του χαρφιού να αλλάξουν βρίσκουν τόπο"—i.e., "they can easily change the diacritics of the letter."

70. Here I am indebted to Brown, *Remember the Hand*, 23.

71. The second surviving manuscript witness that I noted earlier (yazma bağışlar 3954) is likewise from Fener—i.e., not Ioannina—and dates to fifty years earlier than Hasanis's hand.

72. For the assimilationist pressures facing Greek-speaking Muslim refugees in Republican Turkey, where their language and culture were often discriminated against, see Yalçın, *Emanet Çeyiz*, 265–267.

73. Latour, *Inquiry*, 420.

74. In 2017, an eleven-year-old Afghan refugee was chosen to carry the Greek flag for his class parade in Athens; the decision was later revoked by school administrators, but even the initial announcement was enough to spark a far-right attack on the boy's house and threats to his family.

Chapter two, in which Cavafy is scattered and gathered up and scattered again

1. See for example Papanikolaou and Papargyriou (eds.), *Journal of Modern Greek Media and Culture* vol. 1, no. 2.

2. In 2013, Cavafy's poems were translated directly from the Greek into Turkish (*K.P. Kavafis: Bütün Şiirleri*) and framed explicitly by the publisher Istos as part of a "global YEAR OF CAVAFY." That same year, the Egyptian writer Tarek Imam also released his novel *al-Ḥayāh al-thāniyah li-Qusṭanṭīn Kafāfīs*. In New York, PEN America organized a *Tribute to C.P. Cavafy* on November 18, 2013.

3. Saint-Amour, "Weak Theory, Weak Modernism," 447–452.

4. Halim, *Alexandrian Cosmopolitanism*, 60.

5. Halim, "C. P. Cavafy as an Egyptiote," 132–3; 140–1.

6. Halim, *Alexandrian Cosmopolitanism*, 55.

7. Halim's reading of Cavafy does have one important predecessor: Stratis Tsirkas, *Καβάφης; Πολιτικός*.

8. Kayalis, *Cavafy's Hellenistic Antiquities*, especially pages 209–267.

9. For the ambivalence, see Kazamias, "Another Colonial History," 110–112; for the interlocutors and readers, see Kayalis, *Cavafy's Hellenistic Antiquities*, 230–236.

10. The word "most" here is important, because the vast multiplicity of Cavafy's own textual assemblages nonetheless continues to escape standardization today. More than half a century after Savidis attempted to nail Cavafy's *Poems* in place, editions continue to appear in unexpected and unlikely forms, ranging from mere reproductions of Savidis to unlicensed or outright bowdlerized editions.

11. Savidis, *Καβαφικὲς ἐκδόσεις*, 149–150; 194; 197. To reach these conclusions, Savidis often resorted to the following rhetorical structure: "Why Cavafy [did A, B, or C] remains an object of conjecture: perhaps because [X, Y, or Z]; but the most likely explanation, it seems to me, is that [...]" ("Τὸ γιατὶ ὁ Καβάφης [ἔκανε τὸ ἕνα ἢ τὸ ἄλλο] [...] παραμένει ἀντικείμενο εἰκασίας: μπορεῖ ἐπειδὴ [ἐκεῖνο ἢ ἐτοῦτο][...]. ἀλλὰ τὸ πιθανότερο, μοῦ φαίνεται, εἶναι πώς..."—for this specific example, see page 129).

12. Emmerich, *Literary Translation*, 133–4; Papanikolaou, *Σαν κι εμένα*, 9–10; 63–65.

13. Hirst, "Philsophical"; "Cavafy's Cavafy."

14. I have learned this term from Meredith McGill, who insists that by "disaggregating the corpus" we "avoid presuming that an author unifies or is unified by his published work. The regional and ephemeral nature of most of the periodicals in which [early American authors] published [...] meant that complete or even coherent bodies of their work were unavailable to readers," See McGill, *American Literature*, 17.

15. Sykoutris, *Μελέται καὶ ἄρθρα*, 245.

16. For a much deeper dive into Cavafy's life, see Jeffreys and Jusdanis's forthcoming critical biography, previews of which can be found in Jeffreys, "Cavafy's Levant."

17. Jeffreys, *Eastern Questions*, 91–92.

18. Quoted in Jeffreys, *Eastern Questions*, 76.

19. One early reader remarked in 1924 that "within his work, as multiform as it is brief, all of eternal Greece pulses with life across every period, from its height to its decadence. And Cavafy has remained a perfect Greek in his work" ("μέσα στὸ ὅσο σύντομο τόσο καὶ πολύμορφο ἔργο του ἀναπάλλεται ὅλη ἡ αἰώνια Ἑλλάδα ὅλων τῶν ἐποχῶν, τῆς ἀκμῆς καὶ τῆς παρακμῆς. Κ' ἔμεινε τέλειος Ρωμιὸς στὸ ἔργο του ὁ Καβάφης," *Νέα τέχνη*, no. 7–10, p. 110). Konstantinos Dimaras, whom we met in the introduction, similarly suggested that Cavafy "conceived [...] of Greece within a historical unity [...]. His national stirrings inspired some of his best verses [...] [in which] he expressed his faith in the Race" ("Συνέλαβε κι αὐτὸς [...] τὴν Ἑλλάδα σὲ μιὰ ἱστορικὴ ἑνότητα [...] Οἱ ἐθνικὲς συγκινήσεις του ἐνέπνευσαν μερικοὺς ἀπὸ τοὺς

καλύτερους στίχους του [...] [στοὺς ὁποίους] τὴν πίστη στὸ Γένος τὴν ἐξέφρασε"). See Dimaras, Σύμμικτα, Γ, 123.

20. Jeffreys, *Eastern Questions*, 99.

21. E.g., Fahmy, "For Cavafy." Hala Halim's work provides for a welcome complication to Fahmy.

22. McKinsey, *Hellenism and the Postcolonial*.

23. Ideologically, Cavafy avoided public pronounciations on most contemporary politics. Some scholars have resorted to Cavafy's supposed "self-commentaries," yet such exercises are dangerous. See Seferis, Μέρες Ε', 157, and Saregiannis, Σχόλια, 120 for the limits of this method. Linguistically, Cavafy was active during the height of the so-called Language Question: What form should written Modern Greek take? Would it be the archaicized and artificial *Katharevousa* or the supposedly oral (yet also artificial) *Dimotiki*? Cavafy's mature poetry hewed closer to the second but maintained countless idiosyncrasies that alienated most Demoticists. See Seferis, Μέρες Ε', 162; Saregiannis, Σχόλια, 41–42; and Savidis, Καβαφικὲς ἐκδόσεις, 162–163.

24. Lambropoulos, *Literature as National*, 183.

25. I draw my Greek text from the digital facsimile of the manuscript, housed in the Onassis Foundation's Cavafy Archive (https://cavafy.onassis.org/object/r8r7-gfx3-t9ye/).

26. Stroebel, "Some Assembly."

27. Savidis, Καβαφικὲς ἐκδόσεις, 65.

28. See for example Alithersis, Πρόβλημα, 20; Malanos, Ποιητής, 44; and Savidis, Καβαφικὲς ἐκδόσεις, 164–165. Among these, Savidis offers the most nuanced explanation, based on Cavafy's drive for aesthetic independence from the market forces of commercial publishing. Jusdanis, *Poetics of Cavafy*, offers this same interpretation through a close reading of the poems themselves.

29. Tsirkas, Καβάφης and Πολιτικός.

30. The idea that authorship is shaped by a larger social field belongs to McGann, *Critique*.

31. Cavafy, Πρῶτο ταξίδι, 29–30.

32. Karaoglou, Τὸ περιοδικό Μούσα, 20.

33. See for example advertisements on the inside cover of Μοῦσα 4, no. 1 (August 1923) or Νέα τέχνη, nos. 7–10 (1924), p. 127.

34. Savidis, Καβαφικὲς ἐκδόσεις, 173.

35. Βωμός vol. 1, no. 19 (August 1919), page 248.

36. Liata, "Εἰδήσεις."

37. Heliou, "Βιβλία με συνδρομητές," part 1, 103–104.

38. Heliou, "Βιβλία με συνδρομητές," parts 1 and 2.

39. Βωμός vol. 1, no. 19 (August 1919), page 248.

40. Dimaras, Σύμμικτα, Α,' 226.

41. In fact, the works of leading Helladic authors, from Xenopoulos to Kazantzakis, were frequently republished by local firms in Egypt—i.e., rather than importing prints from mainland Greece, Egyptian Greeks chose to print their own (and vice versa).

42. Παναθήναια, nos. 141–142, page 231.

43. I choose *Alexandrian Art* merely as an indicative example. Similar Panhellenic gestures and inter-periodical discussions can be found in the editorials of most other major Greek-language journals, from *Muse* to *Macedonian Letters* to *Rythmos*.

44. See Loughran, *Republic in Print*, 17–18, for a similar phenomenon in early American print.

45. An editorial of Βωμός (*Altar*), one of the leading literary journals of Athens at the end of the First World War, states the following: "The time is still far away when we'll be able to recover from the terrible costs of publishing (the price of paper has risen and makes no signs of dropping, and the cost of printing has doubled since we started the publication [i.e. in less than a year])" ("ἀργεῖ ἀκόμη ὁ καιρὸς ποὺ θὰ μπορέσουμε ν'ἀνακουφιστοῦμε ἀπ' τὰ φοβερὰ ἔξοδα,

(τὸ χαρτὶ στάθηκε σὲ μιὰ τιμὴ καὶ δὲν ἐννοεῖ νὰ κατέβει, τὰ δὲ τυπωτικὰ ἔγειναν τὰ διπλὰ ἀπ' ὅτι ὅταν ἀρχίσαμε τὴν ἔκδοση)," no. 19, August 1, 1919, page 247).

46. Karaoglou, *Το περιοδικό Μούσα*, 17–37.

47. For economy of space I note here only in its bare essentials the well-documented narrative of the rise and fall of Alexandria's leading Greek-language journals, beginning with *Νέα ζωῆ* (*New Life*) in 1904. In 1910, an important core of the journal's editorial team resigned in disagreement with the decision to reject Varnalis's socialist poem "Thysia." The following year, this group (at the heart of which lay Stephanos Pargas), founded the journal *Letters*. After its final closure in 1921, Alexandria remained without a major journal for two years, until the appearance of *Argo* in 1923 and *Alexandrian Art* in 1926.

48. Edwards, *Practice of Diaspora*, 115–118.

49. Moullas, "Καβάφης"; Karaoglou, *Αθηναϊκή κριτική*.

50. Lagoudakis moved to Alexandria in 1918 to direct the leper clinic there. He was also a prolific writer, publishing novels, essays, and studies on topics as arcane as "The Production of Human Life from a Dead Body." In 1934, he intentionally infected himself with leprosy as an experiment and died ten years later. For an extended description of the "Lagoudakis affair," see Moschos (ed.), *Καβάφη: Επιστολές*, 82–91.

51. Melas, "Ἡ ἀνώτερη ποίηση."

52. The neologism "Xevafy" (*Ξεβάφης*) plays on the verb *xevafo* (*ξεβάφω*), meaning to remove paint, thus transforming Cavafy's name into "paint remover." The journal in question is Vaianos's *New Art*.

53. Ultimately derived from "Arabia," this geographic slur vaguely denotes Islamic Africa.

54. Like *Arapia*, this is a deeply offensive term that can mean anything from "African Muslim" to the n-word.

55. The journal had a short but "loud" life, from 1933 to 1934. Karaoglou et al., *Περιοδικά*, 392–401, characterize the publication as stridently anti-communist: "*Idea* accepts no class distinctions in Greek society; to the contrary, it projects the unifying significance of 'nation'" (397). In one issue, Melas embraced the Italian fascist Giovanni Gentile as a model intellectual.

56. The geographic racialization of Cavafy lasted for at least another decade. Writing two years after the poet's death, Petros Vlastos conjured up the image of a Cavafy "blasted by the scorching winds of North Africa, who lived among the dirt-floor hovels of the Muslim peasants of Egypt," and whose style of poetry "deafens you like the vomitous dithyrambs of an African gorilla" ("Ὁ Καβάφης ὁ λιβακωμένος ... [εἶναι] ἀπὸ τὰ φελλάχια χαμώγια" ... οἱ στίχοι του "σὲ ξεκουφίζουνε σὰν ἐμετικὸς διθύραμβος ἀφρικανοῦ γορίλα"). See Vlastos, *Ἑλληνική*, 163.

57. Papanikolaou, *Σαν κι εμένα*.

58. I draw my Greek text from the 1918 broadsheet printed by Kasimatis & Ioanas.

59. As a son of Julius Caesar, Caesarion represented an obvious political threat to Octavian, whose claim to Roman power lay within his legitimacy as the former's legal heir.

60. Kayalis, *Cavafy's Hellenistic Antiquities*, 113–122.

61. Kayalis, *Cavafy's Hellenistic Antiquities*, 107; 219.

62. Blanshard, "Mahaffy and Wilde."

63. Kayalis, *Cavafy's Hellenistic Antiquities*, 108–109.

64. Kayalis, *Cavafy's Hellenistic Antiquities*, 112–113.

65. Agras, "Σύντομη ἀπάντηση," 280.

66. See Yılmaz and Doğaner, *Cumhuriyet Döneminde Sansür*, 65–80.

67. 2012 marked the opening of *Istos*, a bilingual Greek and Turkish publishing firm specializing in Greek literature.

68. I am drawing my narrative here primarily from Dalachanis, *Greek Exodus*, and Gorman, "Repatriation." For a wider-frame history of the Greek community, see Alexander Kitroeff, *Greeks and the Making*.

69. Koutsoumis, *Πώς και γιατί*.
70. Leontis, *Topographies*, 89.
71. Found in Saregiannis, *Σχόλια στὸν Καβάφη*, 9.
72. For a summary of the reception of Polylas' edition, see Linos Politis, *Γύρω στὸ Σολωμό*, 284–291.
73. Sykoutris, *Γράμματα*, 103.
74. Sykoutris, *Φιλολογία καὶ Ζωή*, 44.
75. Güthenke, "Editing the Nation," 138.
76. Sykoutris, *Φιλολογία καὶ Ζωή*, 44.
77. Sykoutris, *Μελέται καὶ ἄρθρα*, 516.
78. Manolis Savidis, "From Birth to Boston."
79. McGann, *Critique*, 81.
80. McKenzie, *Bibliography*, 39.
81. Sykoutris, "Φιλολογικὰ θέματα," 349.
82. Malanos, "Λίγα ἐξ ἀφορμῆς," 187.
83. Thanks to this particular history, Cavafy's archive functions as a central metonym for Greek philology and is an important locus of debate. See for example Kargiotis, "Φιλολογία ως φετιχισμός," and Papanikolaou, *Σαν κι εμένα*.
84. In a chapbook released immediately after the edition, Savidis wrote that "until [Cavafy's archive] is published, we cannot embark on the publication of his Complete Surviving Works [Ἅπαντα τῶν εὑρισκωμένων]," and suggested that until such a time he aimed at least to publish Cavafy's "Complete Published Works," in two volumes (prose and poetry). But this programmatic agenda never materialized, leaving what amount to multiple variations in Savidis's usage of "Complete Works" in his early publications. See Savidis, *Γιὰ δύο νέες ἐκδόσεις*, 12–14.
85. Savidis published *Hidden Poems* in 1968, then in 1983 he published Cavafy's early poems (rejected by the poet in his maturity). As for Cavafy's prose writings, Giorgos Papoutsakis and Mihalis Peridis had produced two collections in 1963, which were later expanded by Mihalis Pieris's edition of Cavafy's prose in 2003. Renata Lavagnini's *Ατελή ποιήματα*, a critical edition of the unfinished poems, offered important new views into Cavafy's oeuvre, as well as fruitful provocations for translation, on which see Emmerich, *Literary Translation*, 131–159.
86. In pinpointing this tension, I am indebted to Karen Emmerich's helpful reading of and pushback on earlier drafts of this chapter.
87. Manolis Savidis, "From Birth to Boston," 133.
88. Hirst, "Cavafy's Cavafy."
89. McGann, *Critique*, 101.
90. For a sense of how European scholars repeated this geographic whitewashing of Greek philology, see Halim, *Alexandrian Cosmopolitanism*, 69–70.
91. Leontis, *Topographies*.
92. Emmerich, *Literary Translation*, 157–158.
93. See, for example, the special issues of *Journal of the Hellenic Diaspora* (edited by Alexiou in 1983) and *Αμφί* (edited by Angelakis in 1984).
94. White Paper available online at https://scholarlyeditions.mla.hcommons.org/2015/09/02/cse-white-paper/.

Chapter three, in which witnesses to war tell their truths

1. Certainly, alongside the new genre of testimonial, more traditional historical fiction also continued to circulate in the region—particularly in Turkey. See Kara, *Osmanlı*, 11–56.
2. Latour, *Reassembling*, 115.
3. In fact, the CUP was already building the groundwork for ethno-Turkish hegemony well before the Balkan Wars. See Göçek, "Decline," 49–50. In the wake of the Balkan Wars, these

veiled tendencies toward Turkish exceptionalism became open and foundational platforms of the party. See Findley, *Turkey*, 201–205; 226–231.

4. Akçam, *Shameful Act*.

5. Kostopoulos, *Πόλεμος*, 103.

6. McCarthy, *Death*, 279–283.

7. Nureddin Pasha had already brutally suppressed the Koçgiri uprising and had designed and overseen the death marches of the Pontic Greeks from the Black Sea coast. See Akçam, *Shameful Act*, 323. For on-the-ground reports of suspicions against Nureddin Pasha for the conflagration of Smyrna, see Atay, *Çankaya*, 324.

8. In Kolluoğlu Kırlı, "Forgetting," 31, the estimate of 100,000 deaths serves as the other bookend. In general, many interpretations of demographic losses—including George Horton, *Blight*; Heath Lowry, "Turkish History"; and Justin McCarthy, *Death*, 255–332—have been subject to allegations of bias. For a balanced discussion of available data and the danger of the "numbers game," see Kostopoulos, *Πόλεμος*, 144–149.

9. Mazower, *City of Ghosts*, 361–370; Kyramargiou, *Δραπετσώνα*, 394–395; Balta and Alpan (eds.), *Muhacirname*, 45–47; Yılmaz, *Diplomacy*, 96–97, 154–155, 170–173; Aktar, "Homogenising the Nation," 86.

10. Papailias, *Genres*, 94, italics in the original.

11. Salvanou, *Συγκρότηση*; Gedgaudaitė, *Memories*.

12. For a single exception, see Sabahattin Ali's short story "Çirkince," in *Sırça Köşk*, 93–106.

13. Calotychos, *Balkan Prospect*, 151.

14. Calotychos, *Balkan Prospect*, 131.

15. Doukas likely calls the refugees "captives" because his primary point of contact was a male-dominated space (a tavern), where several of the men may have experienced Turkish internment camps during or after the war.

16. Tziovas, "Η 'Ιστορία.'"

17. Politis, "Review."

18. The explicit metaphor of "pulse" (a term that, as I noted above in the first section of this chapter, İsmail Habib also used in Turkish to describe Halide Edib's testimonial fiction) comes from Fotos Giofyllis: "Life is pulsing within this book" / "Πάλλεται ἡ ζωὴ μέσα σ' αὐτὸ τὸ βιβλίο" (Giofyllis, "Review"). Similar metaphors abound in others' reviews.

19. Kontoglou, "Review."

20. Raftopoulos, "Review," 71.

21. Raftopoulos, "Review," 72.

22. For discussions of Halide Edib's feminism and its political limits, see Durakbaşa, *Halide Edib*; Kandiyoti, "Slave Girls"; and Adak, "Otobiyografik." The political limitations of Halide Edib's feminism become more apparent when one sets her fiction alongside that of leftist contemporaries, such as Derviş, *Bu Roman*.

23. For Halide Edib's declarations against the deportations of Armenians, see Halide Edib, *Memoirs*, 386–388. For her participation in the institutional infrastructure of the Armenian genocide, see Adak, *Halide Edib*, and Deringil, "Your Religion." For Halide Edib's understandings of race and her experience of Ottoman slavery as a child, see Troutt Powell, *Tell This*, 115–148.

24. Halide Edib, *Ateşden Gömlek*, 274.

25. *İkdam*, June 5, 1922.

26. Seyhan, *Tales*, 53; 55.

27. Ünaydın, *Diyorlar ki*, 173.

28. Akçura, *Cumhuriyet Döneminde*, 59.

29. Önder, *Milli mücadelenin yanında*, 8–9.

30. Önder, *Milli mücadelenin yanında*, 24.

31. Akçura, *Cumhuriyet Döneminde*, 62–64.

32. "Towards Baghdad," *Ριζοσπάστης*, January 1, 1921. Cited in Benlisoy, *Kahramanlar*, 40.
33. Carabott, "Greek 'Communists,'" 113.
34. Papalexandrou, "Αἱ ἐφημερίδες," 225.
35. *Κοινωνιολογικόν και πολιτικόν λεξικόν*, 355.
36. Kastritis, *Μπολσεβικισμός και Τροτσκισμός*, 68–71.
37. Carabott, "Greek 'Communists,'" 110.
38. Salonica was home to a vibrant antiwar, internationalist Left, as witnessed, for example, during the May Day demonstrations of 1921, which took a massive, antiwar turn. See Stinas, *Αναμνήσεις*, 53.
39. Tuncay, *Eski Sol*, 191; quoted in Benlisoy, *Kahramanlar*, 25.
40. Carabott cites several communist periodicals clandestinely printed and circulated in Smyrna or elsewhere in Anatolia, such as *Κόκκινος Φαντάρος* (The Red Soldier) or *Ἐρυθρὸς Φρουρός* (Red Army). For a recent assessment of frontline periodicals, see Alpan, "Küçük Asya Seferi'nde."
41. Kastritis, *Μπολσεβικισμός και Τροτσκισμός*, 68.
42. Carabott, "Greek 'Communists,'" 112; Benlisoy, *Kahramanlar*, 27.
43. Halide Edib, *Ateşden Gömlek*, 197.
44. Halide Edib, *Ateşden Gömlek*, 10–11.
45. Göknar, "Turkish-Islamic Feminism," 44.
46. Enginün, *Halide Edib*, 204.
47. Ertürk, *Grammatology*, 95.
48. Çolak, "Language Policy," 80.
49. Çolak, "Language Policy," 81–85.
50. Erdem, *Tarih-Lenk*, 25–60.
51. These attempts at reconciliation were repeatedly undercut by official and unofficial measures on both sides that continued to target minorities. See Özkırımlı and Sofos, *Tormented*.
52. *Ateşten Gömlek* (2011), 13.
53. One might use this same logic to approach the textual history of Halide Edib's personal memoir of the war, first published in English as *The Turkish Ordeal* in 1928, then adapted into Turkish several decades later by Halide Edib and Vedat Günyol (the former gave the latter no attribution for his extensive work). An earlier, lengthier draft of this chapter included a section on this text. For published work on the memoir, see Adak, "National Myths"; Göknar, "Turkish-Islamic Feminism"; and Erdem, *Tarih-Lenk*, 183–200.
54. Kastrinaki, "Πώς το εθνικό," 165–168.
55. Quoted in Kechagia-Lypourli, "Εξωλογοτεχνικές περιπέτειες," 124.
56. I.e., the other captive who was (in the novel) lynched. In reality, this man too had escaped.
57. All of these details are drawn from *Encyclopedia of the Hellenic World* (http://asiaminor.ehw.gr/Forms/fLemmaBody.aspx?lemmaid=4843).
58. Balta, *Beyond*, 55–56.

Chapter four, in which displaced books make a place

1. According to the calculations of Balta, *Gerçi Rum isek de*, 134, Misailidis alone published 92 titles, most notably the impressively long-lived newspaper *Anatoli*. For a discussion of the serialized fiction in *Anatoli*, see Şimşek, "Karamanlidika."
2. Balta, *Beyond*, 81.
3. Turkish for "Sirs"; it is used here, in a Greek-language paper, with obvious intent to demean Turkish-speaking Orthodox Christians.

4. Quoted and translated in Balta and Alpan (eds.), *Muhacirname*, 163.

5. The poetry belongs to Kosmas Çekmezoğlu and Papa-Neophytos, both reprinted and translated in Balta (ed.), *Karamanlidika Legacies*.

6. The person in question is Yorgos Kallinikidis, a retired steel mill worker and third-generation refugee who graciously hosted me in August 2016. For the bibliographic lemma of this version of the Alexander Romance (translated by Agapios Papazoglou), see Balta, *Karamanlidika. Additions (1584–1900)*, no. 122. For a recent study of the work, see Sfoini, "Traduction karamanli."

7. For influential treatments, see Zuwiyya (ed.), *Companion*, and Stoneman, Erickson, and Netton (eds.), *Alexander Romance*.

8. The wording draws from the expression *defterini dürmek*, which means "to roll up his/her notebook" but in practice means to kill someone. Here, the poem implies that military conscription in distant lands has effectively ended the speaker's life.

9. Sultan Abdülaziz ruled between 1861 and 1876, allowing us to roughly date the poem's dramatic time.

10. Mufti, *Forget English!*; Allan, *In the Shadow*.

11. Quoted and translated by Kushner, *Rise*, 53.

12. For a summary of both positions, see Balta, *Beyond*, 50–51.

13. Balta, *Beyond*, 69–70.

14. Balta, *Beyond*, 51.

15. Foti Benlisoy and Stefo Benlisoy, "Reading," 106.

16. Şimşek, "Anatoli," 116.

17. See Renieri, "Xenophone Nevşehirlis."

18. Balta, *Beyond*, 65.

19. Quoted and translated in Balta, *Beyond*, 63.

20. It was also the village in which his wife, who had died young, remained buried. With the Population Exchange in 1924, Agathangelos was torn not only from his homeland but from his beloved—not unlike the Muslim conscript of the poem fronting the Alexander Romance, who had been torn from his Gülşan.

21. A reference to the mural of Jesus, surrounded by angels, painted on the ceiling of the church.

22. Stroebel, "Longhand Lines."

23. For example, "My Sultan, give us permission [/] if you do we'll give you news of victory" (*Aman padişahım izin ver bize* [/] *Zafer haberini verelim size*).

24. From the parish history of Saint Nicholas Orthodox Church, Ann Arbor ("Our Saint Nicholas Parish").

25. From an oral interview with Joanna Sitterlet, Agathangelos's great-granddaughter, July 30, 2017.

26. From an oral interview with Father John Afendoulis, May 5, 2017. Father Afendoulis is from Pontiac Michigan, whose Orthodox community was Turcophone Orthodox.

27. From "Minutes of Special Meeting" (November 7, 1933), in *Fiftieth Anniversary Commemorative Album, 1935–1985*. Printed by Saint Nicholas Greek Orthodox Church.

28. An earlier, multivolume translation of *Monte Cristo* into Karamanli Turkish had been published in 1882. See Balta, *Karamanlidika, Additions (1584–1900)*, lemma 66. It seems unlikely, however, that Agathangelos is adapting his own version from this work, since his title explicitly refers to Greek as its source language.

29. I'm very grateful to Myra Sun for her help in tracking down the series from which these leaves were drawn, as well as her translations of the Chinese. She notes references to editions ranging from 1936 to 1939.

30. Bordin, "Levi Lewis Barbour," 39.

31. Bordin, "Levi Lewis Barbour," 39.

32. Rufus, "Twenty-Five Years," 26.

33. See *Proceedings of the Board of Regents (1936–1939)*, page 846.

34. Karra, "From *Polypathis*."

35. Chapter five features a longer discussion of Katharevousa and Demotic Greek language reforms.

36. Karra, "From *Polypathis*," 207.

37. On the *meddah*, see Köprülü, *Edebiyat Araştırmaları*, 361–412. He notes that only a few *mecmua* containing the prose stories of *meddah* remain from the sixteenth and seventeenth centuries (383; 399–400). For a discussion of the influence of this tradition on late nineteenth-century Ottoman prose fiction, see Moran, *Türk Romanına*, 23–25.

38. While the original Greek is in the past tense, I have shifted to the present here expressly to deploy archaic verb forms in English. This admittedly does some violence to the narrative's time frame but should give a sense of the Greek register.

39. Agathangelos's Turkish-language Theodora is 343 pages, while Kyriakos's Greek text was at least 800 pages long (his novel fluctuated between editions; the first edition was 1,214 pages, while the American edition I consulted is 822).

40. For details of Kyriakos's publications, I draw from Dourvaris, *Αριστείδης Ν. Κυριάκος*. Here, pages 28–29. By far, Kyriakos's most famous novel was *Kassiani* (1905), which had in fact been translated into Karamanli (without attribution to Kyriakos) and published by the newspaper *Asia*.

41. This is confirmed both by the wide geographic distribution of his icons today and through the oral testimonies of his great-granddaughter and Father Afendoulis.

42. Balta, *Beyond*, 58.

43. Balta, *Beyond*, 120.

44. For these examples, see Şimşek, "Anatoli," 113, and Koz, "Bir Âşık," 124–125.

45. In the final leaf of *Monte Cristo*.

46. For a critical discussion of the Center's vision and activities, see Penelope Papailias, *Genres*, 93–138.

47. Dalleggio's notes were themselves deposited in the Gennadius Library and only discovered and published by Balta decades later in *Beyond*, 93–103.

48. Salaville and Dalleggio, *Karamanlidika*, vols. 1–3 (1958–1974).

49. Given the particular historical trajectory of Greece, it is all the more important to conduct a similar survey of Karamanli literature in North America, where different conditions may have led to a very different survival (and production) rate for texts.

50. Loughran, "Books," 48.

51. Loughran, "Books," 50.

Chapter five, in which the script is rewritten

1. Jabotinsky, who was the intellectual founder of Revisionist Zionism, wrestled with the implications of the Greco-Turkish Population Exchange for more than a decade and used it as a model for his late-stage vision of the expulsion of Arabs in Palestine. See Rubin, "Vladimir Jabotinsky," 2019. More broadly, the Greco-Turkish Exchange was a point of fascination for Zionists throughout the 1920s, particularly the Greek State's resettlement projects in Macedonia, which became a model for settler-colonialist visions in Israel. See Moses, *Problems*, 341–348. British plans for a partitioned Palestine likewise drew inspiration and justification from the Greco-Turkish Population Exchange, as Matthew Frank notes. See Frank, *Making Minorities*, 235–236. Frank's larger monograph is crucial for tracing the afterlives of the Greco-Turkish Population Exchange, drawing throughlines from Greece and Turkey to later European and North American diplomatic thought in the interwar period, ranging from fascists like Giovanni Preziosi to liberal democrats like Edvard Beneš and Franklin Roosevelt, each of whom (among many

others) turned to the Greco-Turkish Population Exchange as a model solution for so-called minority problems.

2. Frank, *Making Minorities*, 378–381.

3. Ertürk, *Grammatology*, 5.

4. Kemal, *Writing Cyprus*, 5–23.

5. The book's final chapter concludes, for example, with the superbly ironic sentence: the native speaker has "lost the paradise of his language—but when did he ever possess it?"

6. The work was first published in 2003, just before the opening of certain crossings along the buffer zone. These crossings now offer limited contact, yet Cyprus has yet to reach any lasting solution and the larger de facto partitions remain in place. *The Deported Hours* therefore retains its urgency today, having worked through two editions, the more recent of which I use here.

7. Kinoshita, "Mediterranean," 315.

8. For a literary reenactment of this last case, see Margosyan, *Gâvur Mahallesi*.

9. For a sense of the large number of Sunni Turkish intellectuals reading Armeno-Turkish, for example, see Cankara, "Rethinking."

10. For representative work on Ladino, see Borovaya, *Modern Ladino*. For Romaniyot Greek, see Matsas, *Γιαννιώτικα*. For Ottoman-script Greek, see chapter 1 of this book. For Frangochiotika, see Dalleggio, "Bibliographie"; and Foskolos, "*Φραγκοχιώτικα*." For Karamanli Turkish, see chapter 4 of this book. For Armeno-Turkish, see Berberian, "La literature"; Stepanyan, *Ermeni Harfli*; and Cankara, "Rethinking," and "Armeno-Turkish." For attempts at synthesizing these multiple scriptworlds into a common frame, see Strauss, "Who Read What"; Balta and Ölmez (eds.), *Cultural Encounters*; Uslu and Altuğ, *Tanzimat*; and Mignon, *Uncoupling*. It might be said that all this scholarship shares a common aim: to recuperate the region's forgotten literatures—but almost exclusively *as they existed in the Ottoman period*. After 1923, the strict national paradigm of the field remains largely intact. Balta and Alpan (eds.), *Muhacirname*, stand as an important exception.

11. Quoted in Korinthiou, "Φραγκοχιώτικα," 586–587.

12. Katharevousa began as a "middle-way" solution, countering even more radical archaists who favored the reintroduction of pure Ancient Greek. See Mackridge, *Language*, 127–142.

13. For a more fine-toothed analysis, readers should consult Lewis, *Turkish*; Mackridge, *Language*; and Ertürk, *Grammatology*.

14. Quoted and translated in Mackridge, *Language*, 103.

15. Lewis, *Turkish*, 46.

16. Lewis, *Turkish*, 53.

17. Mackridge, *Language*, 30.

18. Mackridge, *Language*, 297; 329–330.

19. Lewis, *Turkish*, 95; 101.

20. Cankara, "Armeno-Turkish," 185.

21. Mackridge, *Language*, 26; 164.

22. Lewis, *Turkish*, 28; Ertürk, *Grammatology*, 39–41; 86.

23. Mackridge, *Language*, 269; 302.

24. Aytürk, "Script," 119–120; Mignon, "Literati," 17; Çolak, "Language Policy," 74.

25. See for example Kostopoulos, *Απαγορευμένη*.

26. Apostolakou and Carabott, "Ομιλείτε."

27. Quoted in Aktar, *Varlık Vergisi*, 123.

28. For a discussion of both Yalman's article and his larger place in the period, see Baer, *Dönme*, 222–223; 234–236. The Dönme were descendants of the Jewish followers of Sabatay Sevi who, in the eighteenth century, converted along with Sevi himself to Sunni Islam.

29. Aslan, "Citizen," 251–253.

30. Aslan, "Citizen," 253–254; 261–264.
31. The most prevalent examples are postalveolar affricates (tʃ) and fricatives (ʃ), which users of Cypriot Greek represent variously by diacritics (e.g., σ̌έρι for χέρι). The prestige given to Standard Modern Greek in print often produces instances of diglossic disorientation embedded within the script itself, as Hadjioannou, Tsiplakou, and Kappler, "Language Policy," 528, note by example.
32. The velar nasal (ŋ), for example, has become invisible in Turkish, whereas it was represented not only in the Ottoman script (ڭ) but in Karamanli-Turkish as well (γ).
33. Ertürk, *Grammatology*, 15. Mackridge, *Language*, makes similar observations about proponents of Greek vernacular, who either "downplayed" its dialectical pluriformity (232), edited that pluriformity out of their texts (217), or "relegated [it] to an appendix" (285).
34. For a good survey of the population movements and language contacts in medieval Cyprus that produced Cypriot Greek *koiné*, see Terkourafi, "Understanding." For a brief survey of Greek and Turkish in the Ottoman period, see Kappler, "Toward a Common."
35. Karoulla-Vrikki, "Language," 23.
36. Hadjioannou et al., "Language Policy," 522.
37. Hadjioannou et al., "Language Policy," 523.
38. Quoted in Hadjioannou et al., "Language Policy," 523.
39. The measures may ultimately have had a limited impact on the majority of the island's population. See Karoulla-Vrikki, "Language," 23. Nonetheless, it did succeed in elevating English to the status of a privileged language among many of the local elite. See Hadjioannou et al., "Language Policy," 524.
40. Constantinou, "Aporias."
41. Both the Orthodox and Muslim Cypriot communities valued the elevated registers of their languages, as Rebecca Bryant notes, because they unlocked the "long intellectual histories of which each community was proud. To become a fully literate Muslim Ottoman meant that one learned not only Turkish but also Arabic and Persian—the languages of the Koran and of poetry. And to become a fully literate Greek Orthodox meant that one learned the languages of Socrates, of the Bible, and of Byzantium." See Bryant, "Signatures," 83–84.
42. Karoulla-Vrikki, "Language," 25.
43. Hadjioannou et al., "Language Policy," 532. Even following the period of "Cypriotization" after 1974, when many Greek Cypriots began to distance themselves from mainland Greece, Cypriot dialect still did not find its way into classrooms except in "parenthetical" or "occasional" use (531).
44. Kappler, "Toward a Common," 292.
45. Kızılyürek and Gautier-Kızılyürek, "Politics," 40–41.
46. Karoulla-Vrikki, "Language," 22; Kızılyürek and Gautier-Kızılyürek, "Politics," 46.
47. Hadjioannou et al., "Language Policy," 544.
48. Kızılyürek and Gautier-Kızılyürek, "Politics," 46.
49. Gökçeoğlu, *Tezler*, 169.
50. Kızılyürek and Gautier-Kızılyürek, "Politics," 46.
51. Some Cypriot-Greek–speaking Muslim minstrels are detailed in Nicoletta Demetriou's documentary *The Cypriot Fiddler*, 2022. Online. https://thecypriotfiddler.com/.
52. For a recent critical study of the violence and tactics of the Turkish-Cypriot TMT, see Kızılyürek, *Şiddet Mevsimi*, chapter two of which details the attacks, threats, and assassinations carried out against Turkish Cypriot leftists. For a discussion of the Greek EOKA's policing of so-called ethnic traitors and more generally the necropolitics of memorialization, see Demetriou, *Refugeehood*, 25–45. Drousiotis, "Γιατί," offers a concentrated analysis of EOKA's political assassination campaigns.
53. Given the aims of this chapter, I want to maintain a relatively tight focus on language, yet readers interested in a deeper study of conflict in Cyprus, both before and after 1958, should

read Kızılyürek, *Hınç ve Şiddet*. For the geopolitical narrative, see Crawshaw, *Cyprus Revolt*; Dodd, *History*; and Drousiotis, *First Partition* and *Cyprus*. For oral histories of the violence, see Uludağ, *Oysters*.

54. Yashin, "3 Kuşak," 57–63.
55. Hadjioannou et al., "Language Policy," 538.
56. Balta, *Karamanlidika. Nouvelles additions*, 148.
57. Hadjioannou et al., "Language Policy," 508.
58. Le Goff, *Birth*, 205.
59. Quran 7:46–9.
60. Hamza, "Temporary Hellfire," 398–399; 400–402.
61. Kappler, "Contact-Induced," notes several examples, such as *benim arkadaşım şu beraberdik onu gördüm* (I saw my friend that I was with earlier) or *o gelin ki aldıŋ hiş yaramaz* (that wife whom you married is no good).
62. Yashin, *Sınırdışı*, 26.
63. Yashin, *Sınırdışı*, 68.
64. Krstić, *Contested Conversions*, 35–36.
65. Yashin, *Sınırdışı*, 92.
66. A Greek phrase partially assimilated into Turkish, meaning "Here's the head, here's the marble stone"—i.e., *what a blockhead!*
67. Yashin, *Sınırdışı*, 65.
68. Yashin, "3 Kuşak," 44.
69. In 1962, he was threatened by the Turkish nationalists of TMT for not being radical enough. Two years later, Greek nationalists looted his house in Peristerona and destroyed his manuscripts and library, part of a wider series of attacks on Turkish-Cypriot neighborhoods. It marked a turning point in his art. See Yashin, "3 Kuşak," 46–47.
70. Demetriou, *Refugeehood*, 205.
71. Yashin, *Sınırdışı*, 115.
72. Mufti, *Forget English!*, 250.
73. Yashin, *Sınırdışı*, 140.
74. Yashin, *Sınırdışı*, 159.
75. Yashin, *Sınırdışı*, 142.
76. Yashin, *Sınırdışı*, 141.
77. Buran (ed.), *Sâ'atnâme*, 18; 21.
78. Reinburg, *French Books*, 3.
79. Reinburg, *French Books*, 53–83.
80. Yashin, *Sınırdışı*, 179.
81. For a survey of the interpenetration of Latin and Greek churches during Latin rule and the indignation of Latin hardliners, see Hill, *History*, 1099–1104 and, more recently, Kyriacou, *Orthodox*, 19–20.
82. Buran (ed.), *Sâ'atnâme*, folios 3b-7a.
83. Latour, *Inquiry*, 393–394.
84. These are Latour's words, see *Inquiry*, 393–394.
85. Yashin, *Sınırdışı*, 192.
86. I'm grateful to Veli Yashin for this reading.
87. This same phenomenon is found in other regional languages, such as Greek (γραφτό) and Arabic (المكتوب).
88. This is true even in our basic editorial capacity. The commercial book's typesetters, unfamiliar with Greek, have introduced countless typographical errors into the Greek script (see for example figure 19). These errors have in turn evaded the attention of the editors and Yashin

himself in all three editions of the novel. The book thus drafts its readers into vigilant line editing as a preliminary training exercise for their larger transformations.

Afterword

1. See for example Papatheodorou, *Ρομαντικά*; Vasunia, *Classics*; Ahmed, *Archeology*; Kurtz, "Philological."
2. Yıldırım, *Diplomacy*, 9–15; Frank, *Making Minorities*, 88–93.
3. For this last case of the question mark, see Stroebel, "Some Assembly," 298–306.
4. Anderson, *Imagined Communities*.
5. Fitzpatrick, *Generous Thinking*, 13.
6. Latour, *Inquiry*, 262–263.
7. "פיוט נאה בעד פורים" ("A lovely poem for Purim"). I draw these Greek-language verses from page 25 of a manuscript collection of traditional Romaniyot poetry, carefully written out by the polymath Avraam David in 1928, from the same city as Ṣānī: Ioannina. David became a mentor to the socialist poet Yosef Eliya, whose work now holds an important place in Greek poetry. To my knowledge, no research has yet been carried out on David's manuscript codex, now housed in Israel (Ms. Heb. 4°7734, National Library of Israel).

BIBLIOGRAPHY

Adak, Hülya. "National Myths and Self-Na(rra)tions: Mustafa Kemal's *Nutuk* and Halide Edib's *Memoirs* and *The Turkish Ordeal*." *South Atlantic Quarterly* 102, nos. 2/3 (Spring/Summer 2003): 509–527.

———. "Otobiyografik Benliğin Çok-Karakterliliği: Halide Edib'in İlk Romanlarında Toplumsal Cinsiyet" (The Multi-Characterness of the Autobiographic I: Social Gender in Halide Edib's First Novels). In *Kadınlar Dile Düşünce: Edebiyat ve Toplumsal Cinsiyet*, edited by Sibel Irzık and Jale Parla. Istanbul: İletişim, 2004.

———. *Halide Edib ve Siyasal Şiddet* (Halide Edib and Political Violence). İstanbul: Bilgi Üniversitesi Yayınları, 2016.

Agathangelos. [Commonplace Book]. No date.

———. Φρανσανην Μασσαλιασηντα Μονδελχριστο Νακλιετι (The Story of Monte Cristo in Marseille, France). Ann Arbor, MI: 1939.

———. Μυθοστόρημα της Θεοδώρας, Βυζαντινικής αὐτοκράτειρας (The Novel of Theodora, Byzantine Empress). Ann Arbor, MI: 1939.

Agras, Tellos. "Σύντομη ἀπάντηση" (A Brief Response). *Ρυθμός* no. 9 (June 1933): 280.

Ahmed, Siraj. *Archaeology of Babel: The Colonial Foundation of the Humanities*. Stanford, CA: Stanford University Press, 2018.

Akçam, Taner. *A Shameful Act: The Armenian Genocide and the Question of Turkish Responsibility*. New York: Henry Holt and Company, 2006.

Akçura, Gökhan. *Cumhuriyet Döneminde Türkiye Matbaacılık Tarihi* (A History of Turkish Publishing in the Republican Era). İstanbul: Tarih Vakfı, 2012.

Aktar, Ayhan. *Varlık Vergisi ve Türkleştirme Politikaları* (The Wealth Tax and Turcification Policies). Istanbul: İletişim, 2000.

———. "Homogenising the Nation, Turkifying the Economy: The Turkish Experience of Population Exchange Reconsidered." In *Crossing the Aegean: An Appraisal of the 1923 Compulsory Population Exchange between Greece and Turkey*, edited by Renée Hirschon. New York: Berghahn Books, 2003, 79–95.

———. "Türk-Yunan Nüfus Mübadelesi'nin İlk Yılı: Eylül 1922-Eylül 1923" (The First Year of the Greco-Turkish Population Exchange). In *Yeniden Kurulan Yaşamlar*, edited by Müfide Pekin. Istanbul: Bilgi Üniversitesi Yayınları, 2005.

Alexiou, Margaret (ed.). *Journal of the Hellenic Diaspora* 10, nos. 1–2 (1983): 7–166.

Alithersis, Glafkos. *Τὸ πρόβλημα τοῦ Καβάφη* (The Problem of Cavafy). Alexandria: S. N. Grivas, 1934.

Allan, Michael. *In the Shadow of World Literature: Sites of Reading in Colonial Egypt*. Princeton, NJ: Princeton University Press, 2016.

Alpan, Aytek Soner. "Küçük Asya Seferi'nde Cephede Yayımlanan Yunanca Asker Gazeteleri" (The Newspapers Published by Greek Soldiers at the Frontline of the Asia Minor Campaign). *Toplumsal Tarih* no. 345 (July 2022): 50–56.

Anagnostou, Yiorgos. *Contours of White Ethnicity: Popular Ethnography and the Making of Usable Pasts in Greek America*. Athens: Ohio University Press, 2009.
Anderson, Benedict. *Imagined Communities: Reflections on the Origin and Spread of Nationalism*. London: Verso, 1991 [1983].
Andersson, Ruben. *Illegality, Inc.: Clandestine Migration and the Business of Bordering*. Berkeley: University of California Press, 2014.
Angelakis, Andreas (ed.). *Αμφί: Για την απελευθέρωση της ομοφυλόφιλης επιθυμίας* (Amfi: For the Liberation of Homosexual Desire), vol. 2, issues 16–17, 1984.
Anker, Elizabeth, and Rita Felski (eds.). *Critique and Postcritique*. Durham, NC: Duke University Press, 2017.
Apostolakou, Lito, and Philip Carabott. "Ομιλείτε ελληνικά: Σλαβομακεδόνες και κράτος στην Ελλάδα του Μεσοπολέμου" (Speak Greek: Slavo-Macedonians and the State in Interbellum Greece). *Ο ελληνικός κόσμος ανάμεσα στην Ανατολή και τη Δύση 1453–1981*, τ. Β, edited by Asterios Argyriou et al. Athens: Ellinika Grammata, 1999, 121–132.
Apostolidou, Venetia. *Η λογοτεχνία στο πανεπιστήμιο: Η συγκρότηση της επιστήμης της Νεοελληνικής Φιλολογίας (1942–1982)* (Literature at the University: The Formation of Modern Greek Philology as a Science, 1942–1982). Athens: Polis, 2022.
Apter, Emily. *The Translation Zone: A New Comparative Literature*. Princeton, NJ: Princeton University Press, 2006.
———. *Against World Literature*. New York: Verso, 2013.
Aslan, Senem. "'Citizen, Speak Turkish!': A Nation in the Making." *Nationalism and Ethnic Politics* 13, no. 2 (2007): 245–272.
Atay, Falih Rıfkı. *Çankaya*. Istanbul: Bateş Atatürk Dizisi, 1998 [1961].
Avdela, Efi, et al. *Φυλετικές θεωρίες στην Ελλάδα: Προσλήψεις και χρήσεις στις επιστήμες, την πολιτική, τη λογοτεχνία και την ιστορία της τέχνης κατά τον 19ο και 20ο αιώνα* (Racial Theories in Greece: Receptions and Uses in the Sciences, Politics, Literature and History of Art in the 19th and 20th Century). Herakleio: University of Crete Press, 2017.
Aytürk, İlker. "Script Charisma in Hebrew and Turkish: A Comparative Framework for Explaining Success and Failure of Romanization." *Journal of World History* 21, no. 1 (2010): 97–130.
Baer, Marc. *The Dönme: Jewish Converts, Muslim Revolutionaries, and Secular Turks*. Stanford, CA: Stanford University Press, 2010.
Ballinger, Pamela. *The World Refugees Made: Decolonization and the Foundation of Postwar Italy*. Ithaca, NY: Cornell University Press, 2020.
Balta, Evangelia. *Karamanlidika. Additions (1584–1900). Bibliographie Analytique*. Athens: Centre d'Etudes d'Asie Mineure, 1987.
———. *Karamanlidika. XXe siècle. Bibliographie Analytique*. Athens: Centre d'Etudes d'Asie Mineure, 1987.
———. *Karamanlidika. Nouvelles additions et complements*. Athens: Centre d'Etudes d'Asie Mineure, 1997.
———. *Beyond the Language Frontier: Studies on the Karamanlis and the Karamanlidika Printing*. Istanbul: Isis, 2010.
———. *Gerçi Rum isek de, Rumca Bilmez Türkçe Söyleriz* (Although We Are Greek Orthodox, We Don't Know Greek but Speak Turkish). İstanbul: Türkiye İş Bankası, 2012.
Balta, Evangelia (ed.), with Mehmet Ölmez. *Cultural Encounters in the Turkish-speaking Communities of the Late Ottoman Empire*. İstanbul: Isis, 2014.
Balta, Evangelia (ed.). *Karamanlidika Legacies*. Istanbul: Isis Press, 2018.
Balta, Evangelia, and Aytek Soner Alpan (eds.). *Μουχατζήρναμέ—Muhacirnâme: Poetry's Voice for the Karamanlidhes Refugees*. İstanbul: Istos, 2016.
Balta, Evangelia, and Matthias Kappler (eds.). *Cries and Whispers in Karamanlidika Books*. Wiesbaden: Harrassowitz Verlag, 2010.

Basalamah, Salah, and Gaafar Sadek. "Debates Around the Translation of the Qur'an Between Jurisprudence and Translation Studies." In *The Routledge Handbook of Arabic Translation*, edited by Sameh Hanna, Hanem El-Farahaty, and Abdel-Wahab Khalifa. New York: Routledge, 2019, 9–26.

Baskakis, Yannis. "Αυτή είναι η εντολή Μιχαλολιάκου, κυρία εισαγγελέα" (This Is Mihaloliakos's Command, Madam Prosecutor). *Efsyn*, April 1, 2020. Online. https://www.efsyn.gr/ellada/dikaiosyni/i-diki-tis-hrysis-aygis/225526_ayti-einai-i-entoli-mihaloliakoy-kyria-eisaggelea.

Bastias, Kostis. "Φιλολογικὸς ἐπιδρομεύς" (Literary Invader). *Δημοκρατία*, August 19, 1924.

Benlisoy, Foti. *Kahramanlar, Kurbanlar, Direnişçiler: Trakya ve Anadolu'daki Yunan Ordusunda Propaganda, Grev ve İsyan (1919–1922)* (Heroes, Victims, Mutineers: Propaganda, Strike, and Mutiny in the Greek Army in Thrace and Anatolia, 1919–1922). İstanbul: İstos, 2014.

Benlisoy, Foti, and Stefo Benlisoy. "Reading the Identity of 'Karamanli' Through the Pages of *Anatoli*." In *Cries and Whispers*, edited by Evangelia Balta and Matthias Kappler. Wiesbaden: Harrassowitz Verlag, 2010, 93–108.

Berberian, Haig. "La literature arméno-turque." *Philologiae Turcicae Fundamenta* 2 (1964): 809–810.

Beverley, John. *Testimonio: On the Politics of Truth*. Minneapolis: University of Minnesota Press, 2004.

Blanshard, Alastair. "Mahaffy and Wilde: A Study in Provocation." In *Oscar Wilde and Classical Antiquity*, edited by Kathleen Riley, Alastair J. L. Blanshard, and Iarla Manny. Oxford: Oxford University Press, 2018, 19–36.

Boletsi, Maria. 2013. *Barbarism and Its Discontents*. Stanford, CA: Stanford University Press.

———. *Specters of Cavafy*. Ann Arbor: University of Michigan Press, 2024.

Bordin, Ruth. "Levi Lewis Barbour—Benefactor of University of Michigan Women." *Michigan Quarterly Review* vol. 2, no. 1 (1963): 36–40.

Borovaya, Olga. *Modern Ladino Culture: Press, Belles Lettres, and Theater in the Late Ottoman Empire*. Bloomington: Indiana University Press, 2012.

Brouillette, Sarah. *Postcolonial Writers in the Global Literary Marketplace*. London: Palgrave Macmillan, 2007.

Brown, Catherine. *Remember the Hand: Manuscription in Early Medieval Iberia*. New York: Fordham University Press, 2023.

Bryant, John. *The Fluid Text: A Theory of Revision and Editing for Book and Screen*. Ann Arbor: University of Michigan Press, 2002.

Bryant, Rebecca. "Signatures and "Simple Ones": Constituting a Public in Cyprus, circa 1900." In *Britain in Cyprus: Colonialism and Post-Colonialism*, edited by Hubert Faustmann and Nicos Peristianis. Mannheim: Bibliopolis, 2006, 79–97.

Bryant, Rebecca (ed.). *Post-Ottoman Coexistence: Sharing Space in the Shadow of Conflict*. New York: Berghahn, 2016.

Burak, Guy. *The Second Formation of Islamic Law: The Hanafi School in the Early Modern Ottoman Empire*. New York: Cambridge University Press, 2015.

Buran, Ahmet (ed.). *Sâ'atnâme* (Book of Hours), by Hibetullah bin İbrahim. Ankara: Akçağ Yayınları, 2008.

Cabot, Heath. *On the Doorstep of Europe: Asylum and Citizenship in Greece*. Philadelphia: University of Pennsylvania Press, 2014.

Calis, Richard. "Reconstructing the Ottoman Greek World: Early Modern Ethnography in the Household of Martin Crusius." *Renaissance Quarterly* 72 (2019): 148–193.

Calotychos, Vangelis. *Modern Greece: A Cultural Poetics*. New York: Berg, 2003.

———. *The Balkan Prospect: Identity, Culture and Politics in Greece After 1989*. New York: Palgrave Macmillan, 2013.

Cankara, Murat. "Rethinking Ottoman Cross-Cultural Encounters: Turks and the Armenian Alphabet." *Middle Eastern Studies* 51 (2015): 1–16.

———. "Armeno-Turkish Writing and the Question of Hybridity." In *An Armenian Mediterranean*, edited by Kathryn Babayan and Michael Pifer. New York: Palgrave Macmillan, 2018, 173–191.

Carabott, Philip. "The Greek 'Communists' and the Asia Minor Campaign." *Δελτίο Κέντρου Μικρασιατικών Σπουδών* 9 (1992): 99–118.

Carpenter, Edward (ed.). *Ioläus: An Anthology of Friendship*. London: Swan Sonnenschein, 1906.

Cavafy, Constantine. *Ποιήματα* (Poems). Two volumes. Edited by George Savidis. Athens: Ikaros, 1963.

———. *Το πρώτο ταξίδι στην Ελλάδα: Φύλλα ημερολογίου* (The First Journey to Athens: Journal Pages). Athens: Ροές, 2002.

Chapoutot, Johann. *Greeks, Romans, Germans: How the Nazis Usurped Europe's Classical Past*. Translated by Richard R. Nybakken. Berkeley: University of California Press, 2016.

Charrière, Etienne. "Translation, Transcription, and the Making of World Literature: On Late Ottoman and Modern Turkish Scriptworlds." In *Turkish Literature as World Literature*, edited by Burcu Alkan and Çimen Günay-Erkol. London: Bloomsbury Academic, 2021, 36–54.

Clark, Bruce. *Twice a Stranger: How Mass Expulsions Forged Modern Greece and Turkey*. London: Granta Books, 2006.

Cloutier, Jean-Christophe. *Shadow Archives: The Lifecycles of African-American Literature*. New York: Columbia University Press, 2019.

Coddington, Kate, Deirdre Conlon, and Lauren L. Martin. "Destitution Economies: Circuits of Value in Asylum, Refugee, and Migration Control." *Annals of the American Association of Geographers* 110/5 (2020): 1425–1444.

Cohen, Matthew. *The Networked Wilderness*. Minneapolis: University of Minnesota Press, 2010.

Constantinou, Costas. "Aporias of Identity: Bicommunalism, Hybridity and the 'Cyprus Problem.'" *Cooperation and Conflict* 42/3 (2007): 247–270.

Crawshaw, Nancy. *The Cyprus Revolt*. London: George Allen and Unwin Publications, 1978.

Çolak, Yılmaz. "Language Policy and Official Ideology in Early Republican Turkey." *Middle Eastern Studies* 40, no. 6 (2004): 67–91.

Dalachanis, Angelos. *The Greek Exodus from Egypt. Diaspora Politics and Emigration, 1937–1962*. New York: Berghahn, 2017.

Dalakoglou, Dimitrios, and Georgios Agelopoulos (eds.). *Critical Times in Greece: Anthropological Engagements with the Crisis*. London: Routledge, 2018.

Dalleggio, Eugene. "Bibliographie analytique d'ouvrages religieux en Grec imprimes avec des caracteres latins." *Mikrasiatika Chronika* 9 (1961): 385–498.

Damaskos, Dimitris, and Dimitris Plantzos (eds.). *A Singular Antiquity: Archaeology and Hellenic Identity in Twentieth-century Greece*. Athens: Benaki Museum, 2008.

Damrosch, David. *What Is World Literature?* Princeton, NJ: Princeton University Press, 2003.

———. "Scriptworlds: Writing Systems and the Formation of World Literature." *Modern Language Quarterly* 68, no. 2 (2007): 195–219.

Davis, Caroline. *Creating Postcolonial Literature: African Writers and British Publishers*. London: Palgrave Macmillan, 2013.

Dedes, Yorgos. "Was There a Greek Aljamiado Literature?" In *The Balance of Truth: Essays in Honor of Professor Geoffrey Lewis*, edited by Çigdem Balım-Harding and Colin Imber. Istanbul: Gorgias Press, 2000, 83–98.

———. "Blame It on the Turko-Romnioi (Turkish Rums): A Muslim Cretan Song on the Abolition of the Janissaries." In *Between Religion and Language*, edited by Evangelia Balta and Mehmet Ölmez. Istanbul: Eren, 2011, 321–376.

———. "The Eighteenth-Century Greek Aljamiado Mevlid Translation of the Tourko-Yanniotes." *Journal of Turkish Studies* 39 (2013): 323–395.

DeLanda, Manuel. *A New Philosophy of Society: Assemblage Theory and Social Complexity*. New York: Continuum, 2005.
———. *Assemblage Theory*. Edinburgh: Edinburgh University Press, 2016.
Deleuze, Gilles, and Felix Guattari. *A Thousand Plateaus*. Translated by Brian Massumi. Minneapolis: University of Minnesota Press, 1987 [1980].
Demetriou, Olga. *Refugeehood and the Post Conflict Subject: Reconsidering Minor Losses*. Albany: State University of New York Press, 2018.
Deringil, Selim. "'Your Religion Is Worn and Outdated': Orphans, Orphanages and Halide Edib during the Armenian Genocide." *Études Arméniennes Contemporaines* 12 (2019): 35–65.
Derviş, Suat. *Bu Roman Olan Şeylerin Romanıdır* (This Is the Novel of Things that Happen). Istanbul: İthaki yayınları, 2018 [1937].
Dickinson, Kristin. *DisOrientations: German-Turkish Cultural Contact in Translation, 1811–1946*. University Park: Pennsylvania State University Press, 2021.
Dimaras, Konstantinos. *Ἱστορία τῆς νεοελληνικῆς λογοτεχνίας* (History of Modern Greek Literature). Athens: Ikaros, 1949.
———. *Σύμμικτα, Γ΄: Περὶ Καβάφη* (Miscellania III: On Cavafy). Edited by George Savidis. Athens: Εκδόσεις Γνώση, 1992.
———. *Σύμμικτα, Α΄: Ἀπὸ τὴν παιδεία στὴν λογοτεχνία* (Miscellania I: From Education to Literature). Edited by Alexis Politis. Athens: Σπουδαστήριο νέου ελληνισμού, 2000.
Dimiroulis, Dimitris. *Ο ποιητής ως έθνος: Αισθητική και ιδεολογία στον Γ. Σεφέρη* (The Poet as Nation: Aesthetics and Ideology in Seferis). Athens: Plethron, 1997.
Dodd, Clement. *The History and Politics of the Cyprus Conflict*. New York: Palgrave Macmillan, 2010.
Doukas, Stratis. *Ἡ ἱστορία ἑνὸς αἰχμαλώτου* (A Captive's Story). Athens: Ἐκδοτικός οἶκος Χ. Γιαννάρη, 1929.
———. *Ἡ ἱστορία ἑνὸς αἰχμαλώτου* (A Captive's Story). Athens: Βιβλιοπωλεῖον τῆς Ἑστίας, 1958.
———. "Πῶς γράφτηκε ὁ αἰχμάλωτος" (How the Captive Was Written). *Τομές*, 6 (November 1976): n.p.
Dourvaris, Apostolos. *Ο Ἀριστείδης Ν. Κυριάκος και το λαϊκό ανάγνωσμα* (Aristeidis N. Kyriakos and Popular Reading). Athens: Στιγμή, 1992.
Drousiotis, Makarios. "Γιατί ἠταν πολιτικές οι Δολοφονίες των ΑΚΕΛικών: Ὁλοι οι Ελληνοκύπριοι που Εκτέλεσε η ΕΟΚΑ" (Why Were the Murders of AKEL Members Political? All the Greek Cypriots Executed by EOKA). *Politis*, April 10, 2005.
———. *The First Partition: Cyprus 1963–1964*. Nicosia: Alfadi, 2005.
———. *Cyprus 1974: The Greek Coup and the Turkish Invasion*. Nicosia: Alfadi, 2009.
Durakbaşa, Ayşe. *Halide Edib: Türk Modernleşmesi ve Feminizm* (Halide Edib: Turkish Modernization and Feminism). Istanbul: İletişim Yayınları, 2000.
Edwards, Brent Hayes. *The Practice of Diaspora: Literature, Translation, and the Rise of Black Internationalism*. Cambridge, MA: Harvard University Press, 2003.
Ekdawi, Sara, and Anthony Hirst. "Left Out, Crossed Out and Pasted Over: The Editorial Implications of Cavafy's Own Evaluation of His Uncollected and Unpublished Poems." *Modern Greek Studies* (Australia and New Zealand), 5–7 (1999): 79–132.
Elam, J. Daniel. *World Literature for the Wretched of the Earth*. New York: Fordham University Press, 2021.
Emmerich, Karen. *Literary Translation and the Making of Originals*. New York: Bloomsbury, 2017.
Encyclopedia of the Hellenic World. http://asiaminor.ehw.gr/Forms/fLemmaBody.aspx?lemmaid =4843.
Enginün, İnci. *Halide Edib Adıvar'ın Eserlerinde Doğu ve Batı Meselesi* (The East West Issue in Halide Edib Adıvar's Works). Istanbul: Edebiyat Fakültesi Matbaası, 1978.
Erdem, Yusuf Hakan. *Tarih-Lenk: Kusursuz Yazarlar, Kâğıttan Metinler* (Lame History: Spotless Writers, Texts of Paper). İstanbul: Doğan Kitap, 2008.

Ertürk, Nergis. *Grammatology and Literary Modernity in Turkey*. New York: Oxford University Press, 2011.
Evliya Çelebi. *Seyāhatnāme (Book of Travels)*, edited by Seyit Ali Kahraman, Yücel Dağlı, and Robert Dankoff. vol. 8. Istanbul: Yeni Kredi Yayınları, 2003.
Fahmy, Khalid. "For Cavafy, With Love and Squalor: Some Critical Notes on the History and Historiography of Modern Alexandria." In *Alexandria, Real and Imagined*, edited by Anthony Hirst and Michael Silk. Burlington: Ashgate, 2004, 263–280.
Fallmerayer, Jakob. *Geschichte der Halbinsel Morea während des Mittelalters* (History of the Morean Peninsula in the Middle Ages). Stuttgart: J. G. Gotta, 1830.
———. *Περί της καταγωγής των σημερινών ελλήνων* (On the Descent of Today's Greeks). Translated into Greek by Konstantinos Romanos. Athens: Nefeli, 1984 [1835].
Fielder, Brigitte, and Jonathan Senchyne (eds.). *Against a Sharp White Background: Infrastructures of African American Print*. Madison: University of Wisconsin Press, 2019.
Fiftieth Anniversary Commemorative Album, 1935–1985. Ann Arbor, MI: Saint Nicholas Greek Orthodox Church, 1985.
Filelfo, Francesco. *Collected Letters: Epistolarum Libri XLVIII*, volume 2. Edited by Jeroen De Keyser. Alessandria: Edizioni dell' Orso, 2015.
Findley, Carter Vaughn. *Turkey, Islam, Nationalism, and Modernity: A History, 1789–2007*. New Haven, CT: Yale University Press, 2010.
Fisk, Gloria. *Orhan Pamuk and the Good of World Literature*. New York: Columbia University Press, 2018.
Fitzpatrick, Kathleen. *Generous Thinking: A Radical Approach to Saving the University*. Baltimore, MD: Johns Hopkins University Press, 2019.
Foskolos, Markos. *Τα "Φραγκοχιώτικα" βιβλία* (Frangochiotika books). Αποστολικό Βικαριάτο, 2012.
Frank, Matthew. *Making Minorities History: Population Transfer in Twentieth-Century Europe*. Oxford: Oxford University Press, 2017.
Fraser, Robert. *Book History Through Postcolonial Eyes*. New York: Routledge, 2008.
Galanti, Avram. *Vatandaş: Türkçe Konuş! Yahud Türkçenin Ta'mīmi Mese'lesi* (Citizen: Speak Turkish! Or the Issue of Universalizing Turkish). Istanbul: Hüsn-i tabīat Matbaası, 1928.
Garvey, Ellen Gruber. *Writing with Scissors: American Scrapbooks from the Civil War to the Harlem Renaissance*. Oxford: Oxford University Press, 2013.
Gedgaudaitė, Kristina. *Memories of Asia Minor in Contemporary Greek Culture: An Itinerary*. Cham, Switzerland: Palgrave Macmillan, 2021.
Ghosh, Anindita. *Power in Print: Popular Publishing and the Politics of Language and Culture in a Colonial Society, 1778–1905*. Oxford: Oxford University Press, 2006.
Giofyllis, Fotos. [Review of *A Captive's Story*]. *Πρωτοπορία*, June/July 1929.
Gorman, Anthony. "Repatriation, Migration or Readjustment: Egyptian Greek Dilemmas of the 1950s." In *Greek Diaspora and Migration Since 1700*, edited by Dimitris Tziovas. Surrey, UK: Ashgate, 2009, 61–72.
Gourgouris, Stathis. *Dream Nation: Enlightenment, Colonization, and the Institution of Modern Greece*. Stanford, CA: Stanford University Press, 1996.
Goyal, Yogita. *Runaway Genres: The Global Afterlives of Slavery*. New York: New York University Press, 2019.
Göçek, Fatma Müge. "The Decline of the Ottoman Empire and the Emergence of Greek, Armeninan, Turkish and Arab Nationalisms." In *Social Constructions of Nationalism in the Middle East*. Albany: State University of New York Press, 2002, 15–83.
Gökçeoğlu, Mustafa. *Tezler ve Sözler*, vol. 3. Yakın Doğu Üniversitesi Matbaası, 1994.
Göknar, Erdağ. "Turkish-Islamic Feminism Confronts National Patriarchy: Halide Edib's Divided Self." *Journal of Middle East Women's Studies* 9, no. 2 (Spring 2013): 32–57.

Grammatikos, Alexander. *British Romantic Literature and the Emerging Modern Greek Nation.* Cham, Switzerland: Palgrave Macmillan, 2018.

Greene, Molly. *Edinburgh History of the Greeks, 1453 to 1768: The Ottoman Empire.* Edinburgh: Edinburgh University Press, 2015.

Grewal, Zareena. "The Obligation Is the Point: 'Refugee 2 Refugee' Care and Solidarity in Greece." *Anthropology of the Middle East* 16, no. 1 (2021): 70–91.

Güthenke, Constanze. *Placing Modern Greece: The Dynamics of Romantic Hellenism, 1770–1840.* Oxford: Oxford University Press, 2008.

———. "Editing the Nation: Classical Scholarship in Greece, c.1930." In *Classics and National Cultures*, edited by Susan Stephens and Phiroze Vasunia. Oxford: Oxford University Press, 2010, 121–140.

———. *Feeling and Classical Philology: Knowing Antiquity in German Scholarship, 1770–1920.* Cambridge: Cambridge University Press, 2020.

Gvili, Gal. *Imagining India in Modern China: Literary Decolonization and the Imperial Unconscious, 1895–1962.* New York: Columbia University Press, 2022.

Hadjioannou, Xenia, Stavroula Tsiplakou, and Matthias Kappler. "Language Policy and Language Planning in Cyprus." *Current Issues in Language Planning* 12 no. 4 (2011): 503–569.

Halide Edib. *Ateşden Gömlek: Sakarya Ordusuna* (Shirt of Flame: For the Army of Sakarya). Bab-ı 'Âli, Cağaloğlu Yokuşu: Teşebbüs Matba'ası, 1923.

———. *Ateşten Gömlek: Sakarya Ordusuna* (Shirt of Flame: For the Army of Sakarya). İstanbul: Muallim Ahmet Halit Kitap Evi, 1937.

———. *Ateşten Gömlek: Sakarya Ordusuna* (Shirt of Flame: For the Army of Sakarya). Edited by Baha Dürder. İstanbul: Nurettin Uycan Matbaası, 1968.

———. *Memoirs of Halide Edip.* Piscataway, NJ: Gorgias Press, 2004 (First edition 1926).

———. *Ateşten Gömlek* (Shirt of Flame). Istanbul: Can Yayınları, 2007.

———. *The Turkish Ordeal: Being the Further Memoirs of Halide Edib.* New York: The Century Company, 1928.

———. *Türk'ün Ateşle İmtihanı* (The Turk's Trial by Fire). Istanbul: Can Yayınları, 2007 (First edition 1960).

Halim, Hala. "Lotus, the Afro-Asian Nexus, and Global South Comparatism." *Comparative Studies of South Asia, Africa and the Middle East* 32/3 (2012): 563–583.

———. *Alexandrian Cosmopolitanism: An Archive.* New York: Fordham University Press, 2013.

———. "C. P. Cavafy as an Egyptiote." *Boundary 2*, 48:2 (2021): 123–160.

Hamilakis, Yannis. *The Nation and Its Ruins: Antiquity, Archeology, and National Imagination in Greece.* Oxford: Oxford University Press, 2007.

Hamza, Feras. "Temporary Hellfire Punishment and the Making of Sunni Orthodoxy." *Roads to Paradise: Eschatology and Concepts of the Hereafter in Islam*, vol. 1. Edited by Sebastian Gunther and Todd Lawson. Leiden: Brill, 2017, 371–406.

Hanink, Johanna. *The Classical Debt: Greek Antiquity in an Era of Austerity.* Cambridge, MA: Harvard University Press, 2017.

Harpham, Geoffrey Galt. "Roots, Races, and the Return to Philology." *Representations* 106/1 (2009): 34–62.

Hartman, Saidiya. *Lose Your Mother: A Journey Along the Atlantic Slave Route.* New York: Farrar, Straus and Giroux, 2007.

———. "Venus in Two Acts." *Small Axe* 26 (2008): 1–14.

Hatzifotis, I. M. *Ἡ ἀλεξανδρινὴ λογοτεχνία* (Alexandrian Literature). Athens: s.n., 1971 [1967].

Heinsius, Daniel. *Poemata graeca et e graecis latine reddita* (Greek poems, also with Latin translations). Ex Officina Francisci Hegeri, 1616.

Heliou, Philippos. "Βιβλία μὲ συνδρομητές, 1: Τὰ χρόνια τοῦ Διαφωτισμοῦ (1749–1821)" (Books with Subscribers, 1: The Years of the Enlightenment, 1749–1821). *Ὁ ἐρανιστής*, vol. 12 (1975): 101–179.

———. "Βιβλία μὲ συνδρομητές, 2: Ἀπὸ τὰ χρόνια τῆς ἐπανάστασης ἕως τὸ 1832" (Books with Subscribers, 2: From the Years of the Revolution to 1832). *Ὁ ἐρανιστής*, vol. 22 (1999): 172–240.

Herzfeld, Michael. *Ours Once More: Folklore, Ideology, and the Making of Modern Greece*. Austin: University of Texas Press, 1982.

———. *Anthropology Through the Looking Glass: Critical Ethnography in the Margins of Europe*. Cambridge: Cambridge University Press, 1987.

———. "The Absent Presence: Discourses of Crypto-Colonialism." *South Atlantic Quarterly* 101, 4 (2002): 899–926.

Hill, George. *History of Cyprus*, vol. 3. Cambridge University Press, 1948.

Hirschon, Renée. *Heirs of the Greek Catastrophe: The Social Life of Asia Minor Refugees in Piraeus*. Oxford: Clarendon Press, 1989.

Hirschon, Renée (ed.). *Crossing the Aegean: An Appraisal of the 1923 Compulsory Population Exchange between Greece and Turkey*. New York: Berghahn Books, 2003.

Hirst, Anthony. "Philosophical, Historical and Sensual: An Examination of Cavafy's Thematic Collections." *Byzantine and Modern Greek Studies* no. 19 (1995): 33–93.

———. "Cavafy's Cavafy versus Savidis's Cavafy: The Need to De-edit the 'Acknowledged' Poems." Online. Greekworks.com. March 1, 2002.

———. "Correcting the Courtroom Cat; Editorial Assaults on Cavafy's Poetry." In *Standard Languages and Language Standards—Greek, Past and Present*, edited by Alexandra Georgakopoulou and Michael Silk. Farnham, UK: Ashgate, 2009, 149–166.

Horton, George. *The Blight of Asia: An Account of the Systematic Extermination of Christian Populations by Mohammedans and of the Culpability of Certain Great Powers; With the True Story of the Burning of Smyrna*. Indianapolis, IN: Bobbs-Merrill, 1926.

Hume, David. *Essays Moral, Political and Literary*. London: Henry Frowde, 1904 [1758].

Iğsız, Aslı. *Humanism in Ruins: Entangled Legacies of the Greek-Turkish Population Exchange*. Stanford, CA: Stanford University Press, 2018.

Imam, Tarek. *Al-Ḥayāh al-thāniyah li-Qusṭanṭīn Kafāfīs* (The Second Life of Constantine Cavafy). Cairo: Elaine Publishing, 2012.

İsmail Habib. *Edebî Yeniliğimiz* (Our Literary Innovation), vol. 2. Istanbul: Devlet Matbaası, 1932.

Janse, Mark. "Η καππαδοκική διάλεκτος" (Cappadocian Dialect). In *Νεοελληνικές Διάλεκτοι*, edited by Christos Tzitzilis. Thessaloniki: Institouto Neoellinikon Spoudon, 2022.

Jeffreys, Peter. *Eastern Questions: Hellenism and Orientalism in the Writings of E. M. Forster and C. P. Cavafy*. Greensboro, NC: ELT Press, 2005.

———. "Cavafy's Levant: Commerce, Culture, and Mimicry in the Early Life of the Poet." *Boundary 2*, 48:2 (2021): 7–39.

Jeffreys, Peter (ed.). *The Forster-Cavafy Letters: Friends at a Slight Angle*. Cairo; New York: American University in Cairo Press, 2009.

Johns, Adrian. *The Nature of the Book*. Chicago: University of Chicago Press, 1998.

Joshi, Priya. *In Another Country: Colonialism, Culture and the English Novel in India*. New York: Columbia University Press, 2002.

Jusdanis, Gregory. *The Poetics of Cavafy: Textuality, Eroticism, History*. Princeton, NJ: Princeton University Press, 1987.

———. *Belated Modernity and Aesthetic Culture: Inventing National Literature*. Minneapolis: University of Minnesota Press, 1991.

Kamouzis, Dimitris. *Greeks in Turkey: Elite Nationalism and Minority Politics in Late Ottoman and Early Republican Istanbul*. New York: Routledge, 2021.

Kandiyoti, Deniz. "Slave Girls, Temptresses, and Comrades: Images of Women in the Turkish Novel." *Feminist Issues* 8, no. 1 (1988): 35–50.

Kappler, Matthias. "Fra Religione e Lingua/Grafia Nei Balcani: I Musulmani Grecofoni (XVIII–XIX Sec.) e un Dizionario Rimato Ottomano-Greco de Creta" (Between Religion and Language/Script in the Balkans: Greek-speaking Muslims in the 18–19th c. and a Rhymed Greek-Turkish Dictionary from Crete). *Oriente Moderno*, Nuova serie, Anno 15 (76), no. 3 (1996): 79–112.

———. "Contact-Induced Effects in the Syntax of Cypriot Turkish." *Turkic Languages* v. 12, 2008, 203–220.

———. "Toward a Common Turkish and Greek Literary History in Ottoman Cyprus." In *Ottoman Cyprus: A Collection of Studies on History and Culture*, edited by Michalis Michael et al. Wiesbaden: Harrassowitz Verlag, 2009, 285–296.

Kara, Halim. *Osmanlı'nın Edebi Temsili: Tarihsel Romanda Fatih* (The Conquest of Istanbul in the Historical Novel). Istanbul: Hat Yayınları, 2012.

———. "National Literary Historiography in Turkey: Mehmet Fuat Köprülü and His Legacy." In *Routledge Handbook on Turkish Literature*, edited by Didem Havlioğlu and Zeynep Uysal. London: Routledge, 2023, 223–234.

Karagiannis, Christos. *Το ημερολόγιον 1918–1922* (The Diary: 1918–1922). Athens: Αποστόπουλος, 1976.

Karaoglou, Ch. L. *Η Αθηναϊκή κριτική και ο Καβάφης* (Athenian Criticism and Cavafy). Thessaloniki: University Studio Press, 1985.

———. *Το περιοδικό Μούσα (1920–1923)* (The Journal Mousa, 1920–1923). Athens: Εκδόσεις Νεφέλη, 1991.

Karaoglou, Ch. L., et al. *Περιοδικά λόγου και τέχνης (1901–1940), Τόμος δεύτερος (1926–1933)* (Journals of Literature and Art, 1901–1940; vol. 2, 1926–1933). Thessaloniki: University Studio Press, 2002.

Kargiotis, Dimitris. "Η φιλολογία ως φετιχισμός: ο 'Καβάφης' ως παράδειγμα" (Philology as Fetish: The Example of Cavafy). *Νέα εστία* no. 1860 (December 2013): 741–771.

Karoulla-Vrikki, Dimitra. "Language and Ethnicity in Cyprus Under the British." *International Journal of the Sociology of Language* 168 (2004): 19–36.

Karra, Anthi. "From *Polypathis* to *Temaşa-i Dünya*, from the Safe Port of Translation to the Open Sea of Creation." In *Cries and Whispers in Karamanlidika Books*, edited by Evangelia Balta and Matthias Kappler. Wiesbaden: Harrassowitz Werlag, 2010, 201–218.

Kastrinaki, Angela. "Πώς το εθνικό συμφέρον αλλάζει την λογοτεχνία: Το 1922 και οι λογοτεχνικές αναθεωρήσεις" (How National Interests Change Literature: 1922 and Literary Revisions). In *Ο ελληνικός κόσμος ανάμεσα στην ανατολή και τη δύση, 1453–1981*, edited by Asterios Argyriou, Konstantinos Dimadis, and Anastasia D. Lazaridou. Athens: Ellenika Grammata, 1999, 165–174.

Kastritis, Kostas. *Μπολσεβικισμός και Τροτσκισμός στην Ελλάδα* (Bolshevism and Trotskyism in Greece), vols. 1–2. Athens: Εκδόσεις εργατικής πρωτοπορείας, n.d.

Kayalis, Takis. *Cavafy's Hellenistic Antiquities: History, Archaeology, Empire*. Cham, Switzerland: Palgrave, 2024.

Kazamias, Alexander. "Another Colonial History: How Cosmopolitan Was Cavafy's Contemporary Alexandria?" *Boundary 2*, 48:2 (2021): 89–121.

Kechagia-Lypourli, Aglaia. "Εξωλογοτεχνικές περιπέτειες της Ιστορίας ενός αιχμαλώτου του Στράτη Δούκα: αποκαλύψεις τώρα" (Exo-literary Adventures of Stratis Doukas' A Captive's Story: Apocalypseis Now). In *Ο λόγος της παρουσίας*, edited by Maire Mike, Miltos Pechlivanos, and Lizy Tsirimokou. Athens: Σοκόλη, 2005, 123–133.

Kehagioglou, Yorgos. "Τύχες της βυζαντινής ακριτικής ποίησης στη νεοελληνική λογοτεχνία." *Hellenika* 37 (1986): 83–109.

Kemal, Bahriye. *Writing Cyprus: Postcolonial and Partitioned Literatures of Place and Space*. New York: Routledge, 2019.
Kızılyürek, Niyazi. *Şiddet Mevsiminin Saklı Tarihi* (The Hidden History of a Season of Violence). Nicosia: Heterotopia, 2015.

———. *Bir Hinç ve Şiddet Tarihi: Kıbrıs'ta Statü Kavgası ve Etnik Çatışma* (A History of Resentment and Violence: Status Dispute and Ethnic Conflict in Cyprus). İstanbul Bilgi Üniversitesi Yayınları, 2016.

Kızılyürek, Niyazi, and Sylvaine Gautier-Kızılyürek. "The Politics of Identity in the Turkish Cypriot Community and the Language Question." *International Journal of the Sociology of Language* 168 (2004): 37–54.

Kilito, Abdelfattah. *Thou Shalt Not Speak My Language*. Translated by Waïl S. Hassan. Syracuse, NY: Syracuse University Press, 2008.

Kinoshita, Sharon. "Mediterranean Literature." In *A Companion to Mediterranean History*, edited by Peregrine Horden and Sharon Kinoshita. Oxford: Blackwell, 2014, 314–329.

Kirtsoglou, Elizabeth, and Giorgos Tsimouris. "Migration, Crisis, Liberalism: The Cultural and Racial Politics of Islamophobia and 'Radical Alterity' in Modern Greece." *Ethnic and Racial Studies* 41/10 (2018): 1874–1892.

Kitroeff, Alexander. *The Greeks and the Making of Modern Egypt*. Cairo: American University in Cairo Press, 2019.

Knight, Jeffrey Todd. *Bound to Read*. Philadelphia: University of Pennsylvania Press, 2013.

Kolluoğlu Kırlı, Biray. "Forgetting the Smyrna Fire." *History Workshop Journal*, no. 60 (2005): 25–44.

Κοινωνιολογικὸν καὶ πολιτικὸν λεξικόν: Ἐγκυκλοπαιδικὸν λεξικὸν ἐκλαϊκεύσεως τῶν πολιτικῶν, οἰκονομικῶν καὶ κοινωνικῶν ἐπιστημῶν (Social and Political Lexicon: Encyclopedic Dictionary for the Popularization of Political, Economic and Social Sciences). Athens: Anexartitos, 1933.

Kolocotroni, Vassiliki, and Efterpi Mitsi (eds.). *Women Writing Greece: Essays on Hellenism, Orientalism and Travel*. Amsterdam: Rodopi, 2008.

Kontoglou, Fotis. [Review of *A Captive's Story*]. *Ἑλληνικὰ γράμματα*, April 4, 1929.

Konuk, Kader. *East West Mimesis: Auerbach in Turkey*. Stanford, CA: Stanford University Press, 2010.

Korinthiou, Ioannis. "Τὰ Φραγκοχιώτικα: Οἱ παράγοντες ποὺ συνέβαλαν στὴ γέννηση καὶ ἐπιβίωση τοῦ γραφικοῦ αὐτοῦ φαινομένου" (Frangochiotika: The Factors Contributing to the Birth and Survival of This Script Phenomenon). *Πάρνασσος* Κ' ἀρ. 4 (Οκτ.-Δεκ. 1978): 577–592.

Kostopoulos, Tassos. *Η απαγορευμένη γλώσσα: Κρατική καταστολή των σλαβικών διαλέκτων στην ελληνική Μακεδονία* (The Forbidden Tongue: State Suppression of the Slavic Dialects in Greek Macedonia). Athens: Mavri Lista, 2002.

———. *Πόλεμος και εθνοκάθαρση: Η ξεχασμένη πλευρά μιας δεκαετούς εθνικής εξόρμησης, 1912–1922* (War and Ethnic Cleansing: The Forgotten Side of a Decade-Long National Campaign, 1912–1922). Athens: Bibliorama, 2007.

Kotzageorgis, Phokion. *Το Ισλάμ στα Βαλκάνια: Ένα ελληνόφωνο μουσουλμανικό χειρόγραφο από την Ήπειρο του 18ου αιώνα* (Islam in the Balkans: A Greek-language Islamic Manuscript from Eighteenth-Century Epirus). Athens: Association of Megaloscholites, 1997.

———. "Reworking the Ascension in Ottoman Lands: An Eighteenth-Century Miʿrājnāma in Greek from Epirus." In *The Prophet's Ascension: Cross-cultural Encounters with the Islamic Miʿrāj Tales*, edited by Christiane Gruber and Frederick Stephen Colby. Bloomington: Indiana University Press, 2010, 297–312.

Koutsoumis, Dinos. *Πώς και γιατί διαλύθηκε η Παροικία της Αιγύπτου* (How and Why the Greek Colony in Egypt Was Dissolved). Athens: s.n., 1992.

Koz, M. Sabri. "Bir Âşık: Tâlib—Bir Karamanlıca Divan: Divan-ı Tâlib" (A Troubadour: Talib—A Karamanli Divan: Divan-ı Talib). In *Cultural Encounters in the Turkish-Speaking Communities of the Late Ottoman Empire*, edited by Evangelia Balta. İstanbul: Isis, 2014.
Köprülü, Fuad. *Edebiyat Araştırmaları* (Researches upon Literature). Ankara: Türk Tarih Kurumu, 1966.
Krstić, Tijana. *Contested Conversions to Islam: Narratives of Religious Change in the Early Modern Ottoman Empire*. Stanford, CA: Stanford University Press, 2011.
Kupffer, Elisar von. *Lieblingminne und Freundesliebe in der Weltliteratur*. Berlin-Neurahnsdorf: Adolf Brand's Verlag, 1900.
Kurtz, Paul Michael. "The Philological Apparatus: Science, Text, and Nation in the Nineteenth Century." *Critical Inquiry* 47 (2021): 747–776.
Kushner, David. *The Rise of Turkish Nationalism, 1876–1908*. London: Frank Cass, 1977.
Küçük, Harun. "Natural Philosophy and Politics in the Eighteenth Century: Esad of Ioannina and Greek Aristotelianism at the Ottoman Court." *Journal of Ottoman Studies*, 41 (2013): 125–158.
Kyramargiou, Eleni. *Δραπετσώνα 1922–1967: Ένας κόσμος στην άκρη του κόσμου* (Drapetsona 1922–1967: A World at the Edge of the World). Athens: Ethniko Idryma Erevnon, 2019.
Kyriacou, Chrysovalantis. *Orthodox Cyprus Under the Latins, 1191–1571*. Lanham: Lexington Books, 2018.
Kyriakos, Aristeidis. *Θεοδώρα: Ἡ αὐτοκράτειρα τοῦ Βυζαντίου* (Theodora: The Empress of Byzantium). New York: Atlantis, 1920.
Lambropoulos, Vassilis. *Literature as National Institution: Studies in the Politics of Modern Greek Criticism*. Princeton, NJ: Princeton University Press, 1988.
———. *The Rise of Eurocentrism*. Princeton, NJ: Princeton University Press, 1993.
Lammer, Andreas. *The Elements of Avicenna's Physics: Greek Sources and Arabic Innovations*. Berlin: De Gruyter, 2018.
Lange, Johann Michael. *Differentia Linguae Graecorum ueteris et nouae siue Barbaro-Graecae* (The Difference between the Language of Ancient Greek and Modern, or Barbaric Greek). Published by Jodocus Guilielmus Kohles, 1688.
Latour, Bruno. *Reassembling the Social: An Introduction to Actor-Network-Theory*. Oxford: Oxford University Press, 2005.
———. *An Inquiry into Modes of Existence*. Translated by Catherine Porter. Cambridge, MA: Harvard University Press, 2013.
Lausanne Conference on Near Eastern Affairs: Records of Proceedings and Draft Terms of Peace. London: H.M.S.O., 1923.
Lavagnini, Renata (ed.). *Τα ατελή ποιήματα* (The Unfinished Poems). Athens: Ikaros, 1994.
LeGette, Casie. *Remaking Romanticism: The Radical Politics of the Excerpt*. New York: Palgrave Macmillan, 2017.
Le Goff, Jacques. *The Birth of Purgatory*. Translated by Arthur Goldhammer. Chicago: University of Chicago Press, 1984 [1981].
Lemos, Natasha. "Early Literature of the Asia Minor Disaster and of the Turkish War of Independence: Where Greek and Turk Have Yet to Meet." In *When Greeks and Turks Meet: Interdisciplinary Perspectives on the Relationship since 1923*, edited by Vally Lytra, 185–208. Farnham, UK: Ashgate, 2014.
Leontis, Artemis. *Topographies of Hellenism*. Ithaca, NY: Cornell University Press, 1995.
———. *Eva Palmer Sikelianos: A Life in Ruins*. Princeton, NJ: Princeton University Press, 2019.
Levy, Lital. *Poetic Trespass: Writing Between Hebrew and Arabic in Israel/Palestine*. Princeton, NJ: Princeton University Press, 2014.

Lewis, Geoffrey. *The Turkish Language Reforms: A Catastrophic Success*. New York: Oxford University Press, 1999.
Liata, Evtychia. "Εἰδήσεις γιὰ τὴν κίνηση τοῦ ἑλληνικοῦ βιβλίου στὶς ἀρχὲς τοῦ 18ου αἰώνα" (Information on the Movement of the Greek Book in the Beginning of the 18th Century). *Ὁ ἐρανιστής*, vol. 14 (1977): 1–35.
Loughran, Trish. *The Republic in Print*. New York: Columbia University Press, 2007.
———. "Books in the Nation." In *The Cambridge Companion to the History of the Book*, edited by Leslie Howsam. Cambridge: Cambridge University Press, 2015, 36–52.
Lowry, Heath. "Turkish History: On Whose Sources Will It Be Based? A Case Study on the Burning of Izmir." *Osmanlı Araştırmaları*, no. 9 (1988): 1–29.
Lupher, David, and Elizabeth Vandiver. "Yankee She-Men and Octoroon Electra: Basil Lanneau Gildersleeve on Slavery, Race, and Abolition." *Ancient Slavery and Abolition: From Hobbes to Hollywood*, edited by Richard Alston, Edith Hall, and Justine McConnell. Oxford: Oxford University Press, 2011, 319–352.
Machairas, Leontios. *Ἐξήγησις τῆς γλυκείας χώρας Κύπρου, ἡ ποία λέγεται Κρόνακα τούτέστιν Χρονικόν* (Explication of the sweet land Cyprus, which is called cronica, id est, chronicle), edited by Konstantinos Sathas. Μεσαιωνικὴ βιβλιοθήκη (Medieval Library), vol. 2, 1873.
Mackridge, Peter. *Language and National Identity in Greece, 1766–1976*. New York: Oxford University Press, 2009.
Mahaffy, John. *The Empire of the Ptolemies*. London: MacMillan, 1895.
Malamud, Margaret. *African Americans and the Classics: Antiquity, Abolition and Activism*. London: Bloomsbury, 2016.
Malanos, Timos. *Περὶ Καβάφη: Συμπληρωματικὰ σχόλια* (On Cavafy: Supplementary Commentary). Athens: Σεργιάδης, 1935.
———. *Ο ποιητὴς Κ.Π. Καβάφη* (The Poet C.P. Cavafy). Athens: Δίφρος, 1957 [first edition 1933].
———. "Λίγα ἐξ ἀφορμῆς μίας νέας, 'λαϊκῆς', ἐκδόσεως τῶν καβαφικῶν ποιημάτων" (A Few Words by Way of a New, 'Popular' Edition of the Cavafic Poems). *Νέα ἑστία* no. 878 (February 1, 1964): 187.
Mallette, Karla. "Boustrophedon: Towards a Literary Theory of the Mediterranean." In *A Sea of Languages*, edited by Suzanne Conklin Akbari and Karla Mallette. Toronto: University of Toronto Press, 2013, 254–266.
Mangalagiri, Adhira. *States of Disconnect: The China-India Literary Relation in the Twentieth Century*. New York: Columbia University Press, 2023.
Mani, B. Venkat. *Recoding World Literature: Libraries, Print Culture, and Germany's Pact with Books*. New York: Fordham University Press, 2017.
Margosyan, Mıgırdiç. *Gâvur Mahallesi* (Infidel Neighborhood). Istanbul: Aras, 1994.
Matsa, Iosif. *Γιαννιώτικα Εβραϊκά Τραγούδια* (Jewish Songs of Ioannina). Ioannina: Ipeirotiki Estia, 1953.
Mattar, Karim. *Specters of World Literature: Orientalism, Modernity, and the Novel in the Middle East*. Edinburgh: Edinburgh University Press, 2020.
Mazower, Mark. *Inside Hitler's Greece*. New Haven, CT: Yale University Press, 1993.
———. *Salonica, City of Ghosts: Christians, Muslims and Jews, 1430–1950*. London: Harper Perennial, 2004.
McCarthy, Justin. *Death and Exile: The Ethnic Cleansing of Ottoman Muslims 1821–1922*. Princeton, NJ: Darwin Press, 1995.
McGann, Jerome. *A Critique of Modern Textual Criticism*. Chicago: University of Chicago Press, 1983.
———. *The Textual Condition*. Princeton, NJ: Princeton University Press, 1991.

McGill, Meredith. *American Literature and the Culture of Reprinting, 1834–1853*. Philadelphia: University of Pennsylvania Press, 2003.

———. "Copyright and Intellectual Property: The State of the Discipline." *Book History* 16 (2013): 387–427.

McHenry, Elizabeth. *Forgotten Readers: Recovering the Lost History of African American Literary Societies*. Durham, NC: Duke University Press, 2002.

———. *To Make Negro Literature: Writing, Literary Practice, and African American Authorship*. Durham, NC: Duke University Press, 2021.

McKenzie, D. F. *Bibliography and the Sociology of Texts*. Cambridge: Cambridge University Press, 1999.

McKinsey, Martin. *Hellenism and the Postcolonial Imagination*. Cranbury, NJ: Rosemount Publishing, 2010.

Melas, Spyros. "Η ανώτερη ποίηση" (Higher Poetry). *Ελεύθερον βῆμα*, January 23, 1925.

Mezzadra, Sandro, and Brett Neilson. *Border As Method. Or, the Multiplication of Labor*. Durham, NC: Duke University Press, 2013.

Michailidis, Eugenios. *Βιβλιογραφία τῶν Ἑλλήνων Αἰγυπτιωτῶν (1853–1966)* (Bibliography of the Greek Egyptians, 1853–1966). Second edition. Alexandria: Ἔκδοσις Κέντρου Ἑλληνικῶν Σπουδῶν, 1966 [1965].

Miéville, China. *The City and the City*. New York: Ballantine Books, 2009.

Mignon, Laurent. *Ana Metne Taşınan Dipnotlar: Türk Edebiyatı ve Kültürlerarasılık üzerine Yazılar* (Footnotes Moved into the Main Text: Writings on Turkish Literature and Multiculturalsim). İstanbul: İletişim, 2009.

———. "The Literati and the Letters: A Few Words on the Turkish Alphabet Reform." *Journal of the Royal Asiatic Society* 3, 20/1 (2010): 11–24.

———. *Uncoupling Language and Religion: An Exploration into the Margins of Turkish Literature*. Brighton, MA: Academic Studies Press, 2022.

Milkman, Ruth. *Immigrant Labor and the New Precariat*. Cambridge: Polity Press, 2020.

Millas, Herkül. *Türk Romanı ve Öteki* (The Turkish Novel and the Other). İstanbul: Sabancı Üniversitesi, 2005.

Moran, Berna. *Türk Romanına Eleştirel bir Bakış* (A Critical Gaze at the Turkish Novel), vol. 1. İstanbul: İletişim, 1983.

Moschos, Evangelos (ed.). *Κ.Π. Καβάφη: Επιστολές στὸν Μάριο Βαϊάνο* (C. P. Cavafy's Letters to Marios Vaianos). Athens: Ἑστία, 1979.

Moses, A. Dirk. *The Problems of Genocide: Permanent Security and the Language of Transgression*. Cambridge: Cambridge University Press, 2021.

Moullas, Panagiotis. "Ὁ Καβάφης καὶ ἡ Ἄρνηση" (Cavafy and Rejection). *Ἐπιθεώρηση Τέχνης* no. 108 (December 1963): 652–669.

Moustoxydis, Andreas. "Βιογραφικά" (Biographical Writings). *Ἑλληνομνήμων*, no. 2 (February 1843): 94–96.

Mufti, Aamir. *Enlightenment in the Colony: The Jewish Question and the Crisis of Postcolonial Culture*. Princeton, NJ: Princeton University Press, 2007.

———. *Forget English! Orientalisms and World Literatures*. Cambridge, MA: Harvard University Press, 2016.

Mufti, Aamir, and Stathis Gourgouris. "Immigration and Neocolonialism in Greece's European Crisis [Part 1]." *Greek Left Review*, July 2014.

———. "Immigration and Neocolonialism in Greece's European Crisis [Part 2]." *Journal of Modern Greek Studies*, Occasional Papers #1, 2014.

Naci, Fethi. *Yüz Yılın 100 Türk Romanı* (100 Turkish Novels of the Century). İstanbul: İş Bankası Kültür Yayınları, 2000.

Nikolaidis, Nikos. "Καβ-αφίξεις" (Cavaf-arrivals). *Ἡ βραδινή*, July 4, 1932.

Oruç, Fırat. "Rewriting the Legacy of the Turkish Exile of Comparative Literature: Philology and Nationalism in Istanbul, 1933–1946." *Journal of World Literature* 3, no. 3 (2018): 334–353.

"Our Saint Nicholas Parish," St. Nicholas of Ann Arbor, 2017. Online. http://www.stnickaa.org/about-us/history/our-saint-nicholas-parish. 2017.

Önder, Mehmet. *Milli mücadelenin yanında ve safında Öğüd gazetesi: bilgiler-belgeler* (The Newspaper Öğüd, On the Side and in the Ranks of the National Struggle: Information and Documents). Ankara: Güven Matbaası, 1986.

Özkırımlı, Umut, and Spyros A. Sofos. *Tormented by History: Nationalism in Greece and Turkey*. New York: Columbia University Press, 2008.

Özsoy, İskender. *İki Vatan Yorgunları: Mübadele Acısını Yaşayanlar Anlatıyor* (The Exhausted People From Two Homelands: Those Who Lived Through the Pain of the Population Exchange Tell Their Stories). İstanbul: Bağlam Yayınları, 2003.

Pachirat, Timothy. *Every Twelve Seconds: Industrialized Slaughter and the Politics of Sight*. New Haven, CT: Yale University Press, 2011.

Padilla Peralta, Dan-el. "Anti-Race." *A Cultural History of Race*, volume 1. Edited by Denise McKoskey. London: Bloomsbury, 2021.

Palamas, Kostis. "Στὸ γύρισμα τῆς ρίμας" (In the Turn of the Rhyme). *Ἐλεύθερος λόγος*, December 29, 1924.

Panagiotopoulos, I. M. *Ἀνήσυχα χρόνια* (Uneasy Years). Athens: Aetos, 1943.

Panourgia, Neni. *Dangerous Citizens: The Greek Left and the Terror of the State*. New York: Fordham University Press, 2009.

Papada, Evie. "Evolving Moral Economies of Vulnerability in the Aegean Borderscape." *Journal of Modern Greek Studies* 40 (2022): 319–343.

Papailias, Penelope. *Genres of Recollection: Archival Poetics and Modern Greece*. New York: Palgrave, 2005.

Papalexandrou, K. Th. «Αἱ ἐφημερίδες τοῦ μετώπου» (The Newspapers of the Front). *Ἑλληνικὰ γράμματα* no. 41 (February 15, 1929): 224–230.

Papanikolaou, Dimitris. *"Σαν κι εμένα καμωμένοι": Ο ομοφυλόφιλος Καβάφης και η ποιητική της σεξουαλικότητας* (Those Made Like Me: The Homosexual Cavafy and the Poetics of Sexuality). Athens: Ekdoseis Pataki, 2014.

Papanikolaou, Dimitris, and Eleni Papargyriou (eds.). *Journal of Modern Greek Media and Culture* (special issue) 1/2 (2015).

Paparrigopoulos, Konstantinos. *Ἱστορία τοῦ Ἑλληνικοῦ Ἔθνους* (History of the Hellenic Nation), five volumes. Athens: Typographeio Niketa Passare, 1860–1874.

Papatheodorou, Yannis. *Ρομαντικά πεπρωμένα: Ο Αριστοτέλης Βαλαωρίτης ως "εθνικός ποιητής"* (Romantic Fate: Aristotelis Valaoritis as "National Poet"). Athens: Vivliorama, 2009.

Papazoglou, Agapios (translator). *Alexandros Makedoniali Meşhur Padişahın eyyam-i padişahlığında ettiği seferlerin ve cenklerin, ve min evvelinden el ahirine dek, yani doğduğu günden ta vefatine kadar nasıl ve ne tarzile gelip geçtiğinin nakliyeti* (The Story of Alexander of Macedon the famous sultan, and the campaigns and battles that he made in the days of his sultanate, and how and in what way he came and went from origo to terminus, which is to say from the day of his birth until his death). Istanbul: Iohannes-Derthyantz Basmahanesi, 1871.

Park, Sowon. "Introduction: Transnational Scriptworlds." *Journal of World Literature* 1 (2016): 129–141.

Perera, Suvendrini. "A Pacific Zone? (In)security, Sovereignty, and Stories of the Pacific Borderscape." In *Borderscapes: Hidden Geographies and Politics at Territory's Edge*. Edited by Prem Kumar Rajaram and Carl Grundy-Warr. Minneapolis: University of Minnesota Press, 201–227, 2007.

———. *Australia and the Insular Imagination: Beaches, Borders, Boats, and Bodies.* New York: Palgrave Macmillan, 2009.

Peters, Rudolph. "The Battered Dervishes of Bab Zuwayla: A Religious Riot in Eighteenth-Century Cairo." In *Eighteenth-Century Renewal and Reform in Islam*, edited by N. Levtzion and J. O. Voll. Syracuse, NY: Syracuse University Press, 1987, 93–115.

Philliou, Christine. *Biography of an Empire: Governing Ottomans in an Age of Revolution.* Berkely: University of California Press, 2011.

Pifer, Michael. *Kindred Voices: A Literary History of Medieval Anatolia.* New Haven, CT: Yale University Press, 2021.

Piper, Andrew. *Dreaming in Books: The Making of the Bibliographic Imagination in the Romantic Age.* Chicago: University of Chicago Press, 2009.

Politis, Athanasios. *Ὁ Ἑλληνισμός καὶ ἡ νεωτέρα Αἴγυπτος, Β' τόμος: Συμβολὴ τοῦ ἑλληνισμοῦ εἰς τὴν ἀνάπτυξιν τῆς νεωτέρας Αἰγύπτου* (Hellenism and Modern Egypt, vol. 2: The Greek Contribution to the Development of Modern Egypt). Alexandria-Athens: Γράμματα, 1930.

Politis, Fotos. [Review of *A Captive's Story*]. *Ἐλεύθερον βῆμα*, May 10, 1929.

Politis, Linos. "Φιλολογικὰ θέματα: Γύρω ἀπὸ τὸ ζήτημα τῶν κριτικῶν ἐκδόσεων τῆς λογοτεχνίας μας: ἐπιστολὴ 1" (Philological Themes: On the Issue of the Critical Editions of Our Literature: Letter 1). *Νέα γράμματα* 2 (1936): 343–346.

———. *Ἱστορία τῆς νεοελληνικῆς λογοτεχνίας* (History of Modern Greek Literature). Athens: Morfotiko Idryma Ethnikis Trapezis, 1978.

———. *Γύρω στὸ Σολωμό: Μελέτες καὶ ἄρθρα* (On Solomos: Studies and Articles). Athens: Morfotiko Idryma Ethnikis Trapezis, 1995 [1958].

Pollock, Sheldon. "Introduction." In *World Philologies*, edited by Sheldon Pollock, Benjamin A. Elman, and Ku-ming Kevin Chang. Cambridge, MA: Harvard University Press, 2015.

Prins, Yopie. *Ladies' Greek: Victorian Translations of Tragedy.* Princeton, NJ: Princeton University Press, 2017.

Proceedings of the Board of Regents (1936–1939). Ann Arbor, MI, 1939.

Psomiades, Harry. "Fridtjof Nansen and the Greek Refugee Problem (September–November 1922)." *Δελτίο Κέντρου Μικρασιατικῶν Σπουδῶν* 16 (2009): 287–346.

Pyrsinellas, Vasilis. "Οἱ ὁμολογίες τῶν Τουρκογιαννιωτῶν" (The Omoloyies of the Muslims of Ioannina). *Ἠπειρωτικὰ χρονικά* 12 (1937): 160–169.

Qur'an. Translated by Yusuf Ali. Jeddah: Islamic Education Centre, 1946.

Raftopoulos, Dimitris. [Review of *A Captive's Story*, 3rd edition]. *Ἐπιθεώρηση τέχνης*, no. 49 (January 1959): 70–74.

Reinburg, Virginia. *French Books of Hours: Making an Archive of Prayer, c. 1400–1600.* New York: Cambridge University Press, 2012.

Renieri, Irini. "'Xenophone Nevşehirlis ... Greek-Souled Neapolitans': The Persistent Yet Hesitant Dissemination of the Greek Language in 1870s Nevşehir." In *Cries and Whispers in Karamanlidika Books*, edited by Evangelia Balta and Matthias Kappler. Wiesbaden: Harrassowitz Werlag, 2010, 31–44.

Rodas, Michalis. [Book review of *Τὸ νούμερο 31328*]. *Ἐλεύθερον βῆμα*, January 7, 1932.

Round, Phillip. *Removable Type: Histories of the Book in Indian Country, 1663–1880.* Chapel Hill: University of North Carolina Press, 2010.

Rozakou, Katerina. "Solidarians in the Land of Xenios Zeus: Migrant Deportability and the Radicalisation of Solidarity." In *Critical Times in Greece: Anthropological Engagements with the Crisis*, edited by Dimitris Dalakoglou and Georgios Agelopoulos. London: Routledge, 2017, 188–201.

Rubin, Gil. "Vladimir Jabotinsky and Population Transfers between Eastern Europe and Palestine." *Historical Journal* 62/2 (2019): 495–517.

Rufus, W. Carl. "Twenty-Five Years of the Barbour Scholarships." *Quarterly Review* (Autumn 1942): 14–26.
Sabahattin Ali. *Sırça Köşk* (Glass House). Istanbul: Yapı Kredi Yayınları, 2014 [1947].
Said, Edward. *The World, the Text, and the Critic*. Cambridge, MA: Harvard University Press, 1983.
Said, Suzanne. "The Mirage of Greek Continuity: On the Uses and Abuses of Analogy in Some Travel Narratives from the Seventeenth to the Eighteenth Century." In *Rethinking the Mediterranean*, edited by W. V. Harris. Oxford: Oxford University Press, 2005, 268–293.
Saint-Amour, Paul. "Weak Theory, Weak Modernism." *Modernism/Modernity* 25.3 (2018): 437–459.
Salamangas, Dimitris. "Μιὰ Τουρκογιαννιώτικη ὁμολογία" (An Omoloyia of the Muslims of Ioannina). *Ἠπειρώτικη ζωή* 60 (1946): 14–15.
Salaville, Severien, and Eugene Dalleggio. *Karamanlidika. Bibliographie analytique d'ouvrages en langue turque imprimes en caracteres grecs I (1584–1850)*. Athens: Collection de l'Institut Français d'Athenes & Centre d'Etudes d'Asie Mineure, 1958.
———. *Karamanlidika. Bibliographie analytique d'ouvrages en langue turque imprimes en caracteres grecs II (1851–1865)*. Athens: Institut Français d' Athenes, 1966.
———. *Karamanlidika. Bibliographie analytique d'ouvrages en langue turque imprimes en caracteres grecs III (1866–1900)*. Athens: Philologikos Syllogos Parnassos, Epistimonikai Diatrivai ar. 4., 1974.
Salvanou, Emilia. *Η συγκρότηση της προσφυγικής μνήμης: Το παρελθόν ως ιστορία και πρακτική* (The Construction of Refugee Memory: The Past as History and Practice). Athens: Nefeli, 2018.
Saraçoğlu, Ahmet Cemaleddin. *Gazeteler, Gazeteciler ve Olaylar Etrafında Mütareke Yıllarında İstanbul* (Istanbul in the Armistice Years: Newspapers, Reporters, and Events). Cağaloğlu, İstanbul: Kitabevi, 2009.
Saregiannis, I. A. *Σχόλια στὸν Καβάφη* (Commentaries on Cavafy). Edited by Zisimos Lorentzatos. Athens: Ἴκαρος, 1964.
Sariyannis, Marinos. "The Kadizadeli Movement as a Social Phenomenon: The Rise of a 'Mercantile Ethic'?" In *Political Initiatives from the Bottom Up in the Ottoman Empire*, edited by Antonis Anastasopoulos. Rethymno: Crete University Press, 2012, 263–289.
Sathas, Konstantinos. *Νεοελληνικὴ Φιλολογία* (Modern Greek Philology). Athens: Typographia teknon Andreou Koromila, 1868.
———. *Τουρκοκρατουμένη Ἑλλάς* (Greece during Turkish Rule). Athens: Typographia teknon Andreou Koromila, 1869.
———. *Ἱστορικαὶ Διατριβαί* (Historiographic Disquisitions). Athens: Typographia teknon Andreou Koromila, 1870.
Saumaise, Claude. *De Hellenistica Commentarius* (Commentary on Hellenistic Greek). Ex Officina Elseviriorum, 1643.
Savidis, George. *Γιὰ δύο νέες ἐκδόσεις τοῦ Καβάφη* (On Two New Editions of Cavafy). Athens: s.n. (printed by Leonidas Zenakos), 1963.
———. "Τὸ ἀρχεῖο Κ. Π. Καβάφη, Μία πρώτη ἐνημερωτικὴ ἔκθεση." (The C.P. Cavafy Archive: An Initial Informative Exhibit), 1963. Online. http://www.snhell.gr/kavafisarchive/archive/history/content.html.
———. *Οἱ καβαφικὲς ἐκδόσεις (1891–1932): Περιγραφὴ καὶ σχόλιο* (The Editions of Cavafy, 1891–1932: Description and Commentary). Athens: Ἴκαρος, 1966.
Savidis, Manolis. "From Birth to Boston (And Back): George P. Savidis 1929–1995." *Harvard Review* 12 (Spring 1997): 129–134.
Seferis, George. *Μέρες Ε' 1945–1951* (Days, vol. 5, 1945–1951). Athens: Ἴκαρος, 1996 [1975].

Seyhan, Azade. *Tales of Crossed Destinies: The Modern Turkish Novel in a Comparative Context.* New York: MLA, 2008.
Sfoini, Alexandra. "La traduction karamanli du Récit d'Alexandre de Macédoine (1843–1871)." In *Karamanlidika Legacies*, edited by Evangelia Balta. Istanbul: Isis, 2018.
Sharpe, Kenan. "Hellenism without Greeks: The Use (and Abuse) of Classical Antiquity in Turkish Nationalist Literature." *Journal of the Ottoman and Turkish Studies Association* 5/1 (2018): 169–190.
Shih, Shu-Mei. "Race and Relation: The Global Sixties in the South of the South." *Comparative Literature* 68/2 (2016): 141–154.
Sjöberg, Erik. *The Making of the Greek Genocide: Contested Memories of the Ottoman Greek Catastrophe.* New York: Berghahn, 2016.
Skopetea, Elli. *Το 'Πρότυπο βασίλειο' και η Μεγάλη Ιδέα: Όψεις του εθνικού προβλήματος στην Ελλάδα (1830–1880)* (The Model Kingdom and the Grand Idea: Facets of the National Problem in Greece). Athens: Polytypo, 1988.
Slaughter, Joseph. "World Literature as Property." *Alif* 34 (2014): 1–35.
Smith, Helena. "'Nobody knows how many murders': Witnesses Speak Out on Golden Dawn." *The Guardian*, October 7, 2020. Online. https://www.theguardian.com/world/2020/oct/07/its-the-silence-that-hurts-most-joy-and-regret-for-witness-in-golden-dawn-trial.
Spivak, Gayatri. *Death of a Discipline*. New York: Columbia University Press, 2003.
Spyridonos, Georgios. *Πόλεμος καὶ ἐλευθερίαι: Ἡ μικρασιατικὴ ἐκστρατεία ὅπως τὴν εἶδα* (War and Freedoms: The Asia Minor Campaign As I Saw It). Athens: privately published, 1957.
Stepanyan, Hasmik. *Ermeni Harfli Türkçe Kitaplar ve Süreli Yayınlar Bibliyografyası, 1727–1968* (Bibliography of Armeno-Turkish Books and Periodicals, 1727–1968). Istanbul: Turkuaz Yayınları, 2005.
Stinas, A. *Αναμνήσεις: Εξήντα χρόνια κάτω απ' τη Σημαία της σοσιαλιστικής επανάστασης* (Memories: Sixty Years Under the Flag of Socialist Revolution). Athens: Vergos, 1977.
Stoneman, Richard, Kyle Erickson, and Ian Netton (eds.). *The Alexander Romance in Persia and the East*. Groningen: Barkhuis and Groningen University Library, 2012.
Strauss, Johann. "Who Read What in the Ottoman Empire?" *Middle Eastern Literatures* 6/1 (2003): 39–76.
Stroebel, William. "Some Assembly Required: Suspending and Extending the Book with Cavafy's Collections." *Book History*, vol. 21 (2018): 278–316.
———. "Longhand Lines of Flight: Cataloging Displacement in a Karamanli Refugee's Commonplace Book." *PMLA* 136, no. 2 (2021): 190–212.
Stroebel, William, and Kristina Gedgaudaitė. "Borders, Belonging, and Refugee Memory since the Greco-Turkish War and Population Exchange." *Journal of Modern Greek Studies* 40 (2022): vii–xxxvii.
Sykoutris, Ioannis. *Φιλολογία καὶ Ζωή* (Philology and Life). Athens: Hetairia P.D. Sakellarios, 1931.
———. "Φιλολογικὰ θέματα: Γύρω ἀπὸ τὸ ζήτημα τῶν κριτικῶν ἐκδόσεων τῆς λογοτεχνίας μας: ἐπιστολὴ 2" (Philological Themes: On the Issue of the Critical Editions of Our Literature: Letter 2). *Νέα γράμματα* vol. 2 (1936): 347–359.
———. *Μελέται καὶ ἄρθρα* (Studies and Articles). Athens: Εκδόσεις του Αιγαίου, 1956.
———. *Γράμματα του Ιωάννη Συκουτρή από την Κύπρο* (Letters of Ioannis Sykoutris from Cyprus). Edited by Fanis Kakridis. Athens: Morfotiko Idryma Ethnikis Trapezis, 2008.
Şānī. *Tuḥfe-i Şānī be zebān-ı yūnānī* (The Gift of Şānī in the Greek Tongue). Codex graecus 593. Bayerische Staatsbibliothek.

Şimşek, Şehnaz Şişmanoğlu. "The Anatoli Newspaper and the Heyday of the Karamanli Press." In *Cries and Whispers in Karamanlidika Books*, edited by Evangelia Balta and Matthias Kappler. Wiesbaden: Harrassowitz Verlag, 2010, 109–124.

———. "Karamanlidika Literary Production at the End of the 19th Century as Reflected in the Pages of *Anatoli*." In *Cultural Encounters in the Turkish-Speaking Communities of the Late Ottoman Empire*, edited by Evangelia Balta. İstanbul: Isis, 2014, 429–447.

Tangopoulos, Dimitris. "Καβαφισμός" (Cavafism). In *Έθνος*, April 8, 1924.

Terkourafi, Marina. "Understanding the Present through the Past: Processes of Koineisation in Cyprus." *Diachronica* 22, no. 2 (2005): 309–372.

Terzioğlu, Derin. "Sufi and Dissident in the Ottoman Empire: Niyazi-i Misri (1618–1694)." Harvard University, PhD dissertation, 1999.

———. "Where ʿIlm-i ḥāl Meets Catechism: Islamic Manuals of Religious Instruction in the Ottoman Empire in the Age of Confessionalization." *Past and Present* 220 (2013): 79–114.

Theodoridis, Dimitris. "Ein unbekanntes griechisch-aljamiadisches Werk aus dem 18. Jh" (An Unknown Greek-Aljamiadio Work from the 18th Century). *1er Congès International des Études Balkaniques et Sud-Est Européennes, Sofia, 26/VIII-1er/IX 1966* (1966): 88–91.

———. "Über die griechische-aljamiadische Handschrift Cod. Graec. 593 der bayerischen Staatsbibliothek in München" (On the Greek-Aljamiado Manuscript Cod. Graec. 593 of the Bavarian State Library in Munich). In *Anlassich des II. Internationalen Balkanologenkongresses in Athen 7.v–13.v*. Munich: Beitrage zur Südosteuropa-Forschung, 1970, 179–182.

———. "Birgivī's Katechismus in griechisch-aljamiadischer Übersetzung" (Birgivī's Catechism in Greek-Aljamiadio Translation). *Südost Forschungen* 33 (1974): 307–310.

Ther, Philipp. *The Outsiders: Refugees in Europe Since 1492*. Translated by Jeremiah Riemer. Princeton, NJ: Princeton University Press, 2019.

Torunoğlu, Berke. "The Neo-Hellenes in the Ottoman Empire, 1830–1869." *Journal of Modern Greek Studies* 39.1 (May 2021): 49–70.

Triandafyllidou, Anna, and Maurizio Ambrosini. "Irregular Immigration Control in Italy and Greece: Strong Fencing and Weak Gate-keeping Serving the Labour Market." *European Journal of Migration and Law* 13 (2011): 251–273.

Troutt Powell, Eve. *Tell This in My Memory: Stories of Enslavement From Egypt, Sudan, and the Ottoman Empire*. Stanford, CA: Stanford University Press, 2012.

Tsirkas, Stratis. *Ὁ Καβάφης καὶ ἡ ἐποχή του* (Cavafy and His Age). Athens: Kedros, 1958.

———. *Ὁ πολιτικὸς Καβάφης* (Political Cavafy). Athens: Kedros, 1971.

Tsirpnalis, Zacharias. "Μαρτυρίες γιὰ τὸ ἐμπόριο τοῦ ἑλληνικοῦ βιβλίου, 1780, 1783" (Accounts of the Greek Book Trade, 1780, 1783). *Δωδώνη* 10 (1981): 139–165.

Tsitselikis, Konstantinos (ed.). *Η ελληνοτουρκική ανταλλαγή πληθυσμών: Πτυχές μιας εθνικής σύγκρουσης* (The Greco-Turkish Population Exchange: Facets of a National Confrontation). Athens: Ekdoseis Kritiki, 2006.

———. *Old and New Islam in Greece: From Historical Minorities to Immigrant Newcomers*. Leiden: Martinus Nijhoff Publishers, 2012.

Tunçay, Mete. *Eski Sol Üstüne Yeni Bilgiler* (New Information on the Old Left). İstanbul: Belge Yayınları, 1982.

Turner, James. *Philology: The Forgotten Origins of the Modern Humanities*. Princeton, NJ: Princeton University Press, 2015.

Tziovas, Dimitris. "Η 'Ιστορία' του Στρατή Δούκα" (The 'Story' of Stratis Doukas). *Το βήμα*, August 14, 1999. Online. https://www.tovima.gr/2008/11/24/opinions/i-istoria-toy-strati-doyka/.

———. *Ο μύθος της γενιάς του τριάντα: Μυθιστορήματα, ελληνικότητα, και πολιτισμική ιδεολογία* (The Myth of the Generation of the 30s: Novels, Greekness, and Cultural Ideology). Athens: Polis, 2011.

Uludağ, Sevgül. *Oysters with the Missing Pearls: Untold Stories About Missing Persons, Mass Graves and Memories from the Past of Cyprus*. Nicosia: IKME Sociopolitical Studies Institute, 2005.
Uslu, Mehmet Fatih, and Fatih Altuğ. *Tanzimat ve Edebiyat: Osmanlı İstanbul'unda Modern Edebi Kültür* (Tanzimat and Literature: Modern Literary Culture in Ottoman Istanbul). İstanbul: İş Bankası Kültür Yayınları, 2014.
Uysal, Mustafa (translator and editor). *İzahlı Mülteka El Ebhur Tercümesi* (Annotated Translation of the Mülteka El Ebhur). Istanbul: Çelik Yayınevi, 2015.
Ünaydın, Ruşen Eşref. *Diyorlar ki... !* (They say that... !). Istanbul: Kanaat Matbaası, 1918.
Vafopoulos, Giorgos. [Review of *A Captive's Story*]. *Μακεδονία*, October 26, 1929.
Vaianos, Marios. "Κ.Π. Καβάφης: ὁ ποιητὴς ποὺ δὲν ἐπῆρε τὸ ἀριστεῖον (;)" (C. P. Cavafy: The Poet Who Didn't Get the National Medal (?)). *Ἐλεύθερος τύπος*, May 19, 1924.
Vaianos, Marios (ed.). *Νέα τέχνη* (New Art), issue 7–10 (1924).
Van Steen, Gonda. *Theatre of the Condemned: Classical Tragedy on Greek Prison Islands*. Oxford: Oxford University Press, 2011.
———. *Adoption, Memory, and Cold War Greece: Kid Pro Quo?* Ann Arbor: University of Michigan Press, 2019.
Vasunia, Phiroze. *The Classics and Colonial India*. Oxford: Oxford University Press, 2013.
Villavicencio, Karla Cornejo. *The Undocumented Americans*. New York: One World, 2020.
Vlastos, Petros. *Ἡ ἑλληνικὴ καὶ μερικὲς ἄλλες παράλληλες διγλωσσίες* (Greek and Some Other Parallel Diglossias). Athens: Nea Estia, 1935.
Wallace, Jennifer. *Shelley and Greece: Rethinking Philhellenism*. New York: St. Martin's Press, 1997.
Wilson, Bret. *Translating the Qur'an in an Age of Nationalism: Print Culture and Modern Islam in Turkey*. Oxford: Oxford University Press, 2014.
Xenopoulos, Grigorios. "Ἕνας ποιητής" (A Poet). *Παναθήναια*, November 1903, 97–102.
Yalçın, Kemal. *Emanet Çeyiz: Mübadele İnsanları* (The Entrusted Dowry: People of the Exchange). Istanbul: Belge Yayınları, 1998.
Yannoulopoulos, Yorgos. *Διαβάζοντας τον Μακρυγιάννη: Η κατασκευή ενός μύθου από τον Βλαχογιάννη, τον Θεοτοκά, τον Σεφέρη, και τον Λορεντζάτο* (Reading Makriyannis: The Construction of a Myth by Vlachoyannis, Theotokas, Seferis, and Lorentzatos). Athens: Polis, 2003.
Yashin, Mehmet. "3 Kuşak, 3 Kimlik, 3 Vatan Arasında Bir Türk Azınlık Şiiri: Kıbrıslıtürk Şiiri" (Cypriot-Turkish Poetry: A Minor Poetry Among Three Generations, Three Identities, Three Homelands). *Kıbrıslıtürk Şiiri Antolojisi*. Istanbul: YKY, 1994, 19–67.
———. *Poeturka: Deneme* (Poeturca: Essay). Istanbul: Adam Yayınları, 1995.
———. *Sınırdışı Saatler* (The Deported Hours). Istanbul: Yapı Kredi Yayınları, 2015 [2003].
Yashin, Mehmet (ed.). *Step-Mothertongue*. London: Middlesex University Press, 2000.
Yıldırım, Onur. *Diplomacy and Displacement: Reconsidering the Turco-Greek Exchange of Populations, 1922–1934*. New York: Routledge, 2006.
Yıldız, Sara Nur. "A Hanafi Law Manual in the Vernacular: Devletoğlu Yūsuf Balıkesrī's Turkish Verse Adaptation of the Hidāya-Wiqāya Textual Tradition for the Ottoman Sultan Murad II (824/1424)." *Bulletin of SOAS* 80 no. 2 (2017): 283–304.
Yılmaz, Mustafa, and Yasemin Doğaner. *Cumhuriyet Döneminde Sansür (1923–1973)* (Censorship in the Republican Period, 1923–1973). Ankara: Siyasal Kitabevi, 2007.
Yoon, Duncan. *China in Twentieth- and Twenty-First-Century African Literature*. Cambridge: Cambridge University Press, 2023.
Zadeh, Travis. *The Vernacular Qur'an: Translation and the Rise of Persian Exegesis*. Oxford: Oxford University Press, 2012.
Zanou, Konstantina. *Transnational Patriotism in the Mediterranean, 1800–1850: Stammering the Nation*. Oxford: Oxford University Press, 2018.

Zeitlian Watenpaugh, Heghnar. *The Missing Pages: The Modern Life of a Medieval Manuscript from Genocide to Justice*. Stanford, CA: Stanford University Press, 2019.

Zilfi, Madeline. *The Politics of Piety: The Ottoman Ulema in the Postclassical Age (1600–1800)*. Minneapolis, MN: Bibliotheca Islamica, 1988.

Zuwiyya, Z. David (ed.). *A Companion to Alexander Literature in the Middle Ages*. Leiden: Brill, 2011.

INDEX

Abacı, Panayot, 99
Abdul Hamid, 120
Abu al-Layth al-Samarqandi, 43
Abu Hanifa, 53–54, 56–57
Abu Mijlaz of Basra, 214
Academy of Athens, 18, 103, 106
Actor Network Theory, 250n70
Against World Literature (Apter), 249n67
Agathangelos, 30, 33, 168–93, 260n20
Agras, Tellos, 97–98
Ahmed, Siraj, 246n10
Aiolian Land (Venezis), 169
Alexander Romance, 165–72, 260n20
Alexandrian Art (Singopoulou), 84–85
al-Halabi, Ibrahim, 43, 52–54
Ali Bey, 153, 154–61
Alipashiad (Shehreti), 16
Alithersis, Glafkos, 114
Allatios, Leo, 15–16
al-Marghinani, 43
al-Shaybani, Muhammad, 53
alternative media, 194–95, 221, 228–29, 237–38. See also *Book of Hours* (Hibetullah); composite codices; handmade manuscripts; manuscript codices; *mecmua* (Agathangelos); *Monte Cristo in Marseille* (Agathangelos); oral performance; textual handlers; *Theodora* (Agathangelos)
Anatoli, 171–72, 190–91, 259n1
Anthology of Friendship (Carpenter), 95
anticolonialism, 80
Apostolidou, Venetia, 246n13

Apter, Emily, 198, 249n67
Arab nationalization, 99–100
a'raf, 214–15, 219–21, 227. See also purgatory
Archaeology of Babel (Ahmed), 246n10
"Archive of Desire," 68
Armeno-Turkish, 200
Assemblage Theory, 250n70
Atatürk, Mustafa Kemal, 143–44, 203
autobiography, 116–17

"The Ballad of Andaval," 173–76
Ballinger, Pamela, 245n6
Balta, Evangelia, 163, 171–72, 191, 259n1
Barbour, Levi, 184–85
Bastias, Kostis, 87
Baybars, Taner, 223
Bayerische Staatsbibliothek, 40
Beneš, Edvard, 261n1
Beverley, John, 118
the Bible. See New Testament
bibliographic codes, 78
bibliomigrancy, 29–31
bicommunalism, 208, 224, 228
bilingualism, 209
Boletsi, Maria, 114
book history, 27–31, 194, 250n69, 250nn71–74. See also philology
"The Book of Deportation" (Yashin), 211, 213–29, 233
Book of Hours (Hibetullah), 213, 230–36
"The Book of Hours" (Yashin), 213, 229–38

288 INDEX

Book of Travels (Evliya Çelebi), 41
Border as Method (Mezzadra and Neilson), 21–22
border-guard (*akritas*), 20–21
borderscapes, 5–7, 19–25, 66–67, 118–19, 159–60, 198, 200, 207, 229, 238. *See also* philology
border studies, 5
Brouillette, Sarah, 26
Bryant, Rebecca, 263n41
Burak, Guy, 57
Buran, Ahmet, 232

Cabot, Heath, 23
"Caesarion" (Cavafy), 93–96
Calotychos, Vangelis, 122–23, 161
Cankara, Murat, 203
A Captive's Story (Doukas), 32, 118, 122–28, 147–54, 161–62
Carabott, Philip, 137, 259n40
Carpenter, Edward, 95
catechisms, 42–43, 50–51, 53, 200
Catholic Levantines, 201–2
"Cavaf-arrivals" (Nikolaidis), 96–97
Cavafy, C. P., 5, 26, 31–32, 68–98, 107–15, 254n2, 254n10, 254n19, 255n23, 257nn84–85. *See also* Greek publishing; Hellenism; publishing strategies
Cavafy Editions (Savidis), 72, 81
Cave, Nick, 68
censorship, 99, 133–39, 143–44
Central Intelligence Agency (CIA), 196
Cham Albanians of Epirus, 18
Christianity. *See* Armeno-Turkish; catechisms; Catholic Levantines; Frangochiotika; Greek Orthodox Christians; prayer; Slavophone Orthodox Christians
"Citizen, Speak Turkish!," 205–6, 209
civilizational clash, 19
Clark, Bruce, xv
Classical Debt (Hanink), 247n24
The Clown's Daughter (Halide Edib), 144–45

Cohen, Matthew, 250n69
colonialism, 12–13, 22, 71, 95–96, 197, 207–8, 221, 246n10, 250n69
Committee for Union and Progress (CUP), 120
communism, 137–38
"Complete Works" (Cavafy), 72, 108–13
composite codices, 164–65, 194
"Considering the Scholarly Edition in the Digital Age," 115
"Contact Induced Effects in the Syntax of Cypriot Turkish" (Kappler), 264n61
copyright, 29, 38, 249n65
"Copyright and Intellectual Property" (McGill), 249n65
Cornaro, Vincenzo, 202
The Count of Monte Cristo (Dumas), 180–82
the Crete syndrome, 208
Crusius, Martin, 207, 247n20
Cypriot Turkish grammar, 215
Cyprus, 196–98, 200, 206–11, 215–16, 263n53. *See also The Deported Hours* (Yashin)

Dalleggio, Eugene, 193–94
Damrosch, David, 31, 37
"The Dance of Zalongo," 177
Dante, 213–14
Davis, Caroline, 26
decentralized literature, 7, 24, 37, 65–66, 83, 195, 203–4, 236–37, 241. *See also* textual handlers
Dedes, Yorgos, 248n44, 250n2, 251n7
De Hellenistica Commentarius (Saumaise), 9
Demetriou, Olga, 224
deowned literature, 249n67
The Deported Hours (Yashin), 33–34, 198–200, 213–38, 262nn5–6, 264n88. *See also* "The Book of Deportation" (Yashin)
Devletoğlu Yusuf, 43, 55–58
Diakonos, Konstantinos, 208
diasporic print, xv, 73–74, 77–78, 81–84, 86, 91–94, 114, 248n47. *See also* Greek publishing

dictation, 60–63
differential inclusion, 22
Dimaras, K. Th., 18–21, 248n48, 254n19
Dionysios of Larissa, 40
Diplomacy and Displacement (Yıldırım), xv
Divine Comedy (Dante), 213–14
Doukas, Stratis, 6, 32, 122–28, 147–54, 161–62, 258n15
Dream Nation (Gourgouris), 247n24
Dumas, Alexandre, 180–82
Dürder, Baha, 143

Ebussuud Efendi, 52–53
"Editing the Nation" (Güthenke), 248n45
"The Eighteenth-Century Greek Aljamiado Mevlid" (Dedes), 251n7
Ekdawi, Sara, 73
Eleftheron Vima, 163–64
El Shazly, Nadah, 68
emigration, 100–101
Emmerich, Karen, 73, 114
The Empire of the Ptolemies (Mahaffy), 95
Enginün, İnci, 142
Enlightenment in the Colony (Mufti), 250n68
EOKA, 210
Epic of Digenis Akritas, 20–21, 248n47
Ertürk, Nergis, 33, 197, 206
ethnic cleansing, xv, 1–2, 31, 104, 120, 196, 210. *See also* racism; violence
ethnicity, 41
Etienne-Charrière, 37–38
eugenics, 4
Evliya Çelebi, 41
exile, 7
Eyüboğlu, Sabahattin, 246n12

Fallmerayer, Jakob, 10–14, 104, 247n24
Farewell Anatolia (Sotiriou), 6
fascism, 37
Filelfo, Francesco, 7–9
First Balkan War, 119–20
First Language Congress of Turkey, 143–44
first principles (of the border regime), 4
Fitzpatrick, Kathleen, 249n56

forced displacement, xv, 7, 25–27, 245n2. *See also* Population Exchange of 1923; racism
Forget English! (Mufti), 250n69
Forster, E. M., 75
Frangochiotika, 202
Frank, Matthew, 261n1

Galanti, Avram, 41
Gautier-Kızılyürek, Sylvaine, 208
Gavrilidis, Yannis, 172
Gedgaudaitė, Kristina, 2
Generous Thinking (Fitzpatrick), 249n56
Giannaris, Chrysostomos, 122
The Gift of Şānī in the Greek Tongue, 31, 35–67, 92, 219–20, 253n69, 253nn56–57
Gökçeoğlu, Mustafa, 209–10
Göknar, Erdağ, 142
Golfis, Rigas, 92
Gourgouris, Stathis, 247n24
Grand Idea (*Megali Idea*), 71, 101, 113
Great Sedition (Egypt), 252n47
Greco-Turkish War of 1919, 1–2, 26, 100–101, 117, 119–20, 136–39, 168
Greece during Turkish Rule (Sathas), 17
Greek academy, 73
Greek Letters (Bastias), 87
Greek Library series, 18
Greek Orthodox Christians: Catholic opposition to, 15; diaspora of, 70–71, 80, 98, 179–80; and forced displacement, 1–2, 17, 163; history of Ioannina's, 40; and literature, 7, 18, 46–48; and Muslim participation, 251n11; and the New Testament, 10. *See also* Karamanli Christians
Greek publishing, 80–93, 100, 136. See also *Eleftheron Vima*; *New Life*; publishing strategies; *Pyrsos*; *Red Guard*; *Rizospastis*; *Voice of the Refugee*
Greeks in Turkey (Kamouzis), xv
Grewal, Zareena, xvi
Günyol, Vedat, 259n53
Gürkan, Ahmet Muzaffer, 210
Güthenke, Constanze, 248n45

Halide Edib, 32, 117, 128–35, 140–47, 259n53
Halim, Hala, 71, 114
Hamid Bey, 246n6
Hanafi legal school, 53–55, 57
handmade manuscripts, 164–65, 169–70
Hanink, Johanna, 247n24
Hartman, Saidiya, 95
Hasanis (or Hasan Bey), 61–63, 65
Heinsius, Daniel, 8–9
Hellenic (as a term), 74–75
Hellenism: and Asia, 75, 77, 88–92; and assimilation, 7, 19–21; Cavafy's, 74–76, 79, 112–13; as a crossroads, 19–21; and dynamism, 13–14, 20; European, 12–13, 16–17; and historiography, 18–19, 27–28; institutional, 21–25, 31–32, 35, 101–4, 112–13, 127, 160, 171–72, 204; and Modern Greek philology, 5; queer, 69; and weak connections, 70
Hibetullah bin Ibrahim, 213, 229–36
Hidden Poems (Cavafy), 108, 257n85
"Higher Poetry" (Melas), 88–89
Hikmet, Ayhan, 210
Hilali, Ahmet, 136
Hirst, Anthony, 73, 110
historical novels, 117–18
History of Modern Greek Literature (Dimaras), 18–21, 248n48
History of the Hellenic Nation (Paparrigopoulos), 13–14
History of the Morean Peninsula in the Middle Ages (Fallmerayer), 10
Hortatzis, Georgios, 202
"How the Captive Was Written" (Doukas), 148–51, 153
Hristovasilis, Hristos, 83–84
Humanism in Ruins (Iğsız), 4
Hume, David, 11
Huntington, Samuel, 19
"Hymn to Liberty" (Solomos), 102

icon of John the Baptist (Agathangelos), 183
Idea, 89, 256n55
Iğsız, Aslı, 2, 4

Ikaros (Cavafy), 98
İkdam, 133–34
İleri, Selim, 132
Iliad (Homer), 27
Imam, Tarek, 254n2
interlingualism, 152–53
Islam. See *a'raf*; catechisms; Cham Albanians of Epirus; Kadızadelis; Kurds; Muslims (of Greece); Muslims (of Western Thrace); prayer; Quran; Tawhid
İsmail Habib, 117, 119, 130
Iyer, Vijay, 68

Jabotinsky, Ze'ev, 196, 261n1
Jeffreys, Peter, 75

Kadızadelis, 50–51
Kallinikidis, Giorgos, 191, 193, 260n6
Kalpaklı, Mehmet, 145–46
Kamouzis, Dimitris, xv
Kant, Immanuel, 11
Kappler, Matthias, 172, 215, 264n61
Karamanli Christians, 17, 33–34, 163–64, 168–77, 182, 187, 190–95, 219. *See also* Greek Orthodox Christians
Karamanli Turkish, 198, 211, 219, 226–29, 260n28
Karaoglou, Ch. L., 86
Karra, Anthi, 187
Kastrinaki, Angela, 147
Katharevousa, 202–4, 208, 262n12
Kavazoğlu, Derviş Ali, 210
Kayalis, Takis, 71, 95, 114
Kazakoglou, Nikolas, 26, 32, 123, 125–26, 151–62, 168
Kemal, Bahriye, 197
Kemalist state, 2, 120–21, 128, 139, 145–47, 203–4, 221
Kilito, Abdelfattah, 197–98
Kinoshita, Sharon, 200
Kızılyürek, Niyazi, 208
K.K. (Papaioannou), 68
Kontoglou, Fotis, 126, 169
Konuk, Kader, 7

Köprülü, Fuad, 246n12
Korais, Adamantios, 202–3
Kotzageorgis, Phokion, 250n2
Koutsoumis, Dinos, 100
Kurdish language, 200
Kurds, 197
Kyriakos, Aristeidis, 182, 187–90, 261n40

Lagoudakis, Sokratis, 86–87, 256n50
Lange, Johann Michael, 9
language reforms, 201–11, 221, 263nn31–33. See also "Citizen, Speak Turkish!"; Turkish Language Reforms
Lapathiotis, Napoleon, 79, 90
Latour, Bruno, 118
Lavagnini, Renata, 257n85
Law School Students' Association of Istanbul University, 205–6
layers of invention, 197
League of Nations, 1–3
Leontis, Artemis, 113, 247n36
Letters (Pargas), 85, 91
Lewis, Bernard, 53
Lewis, Robin Coste, 68
Library of Modern Greek Literary Authors, 103
Lieblingminne und Freundesliebe in der Weltliteratur (von Kupffer), 95
linguistic codes, 78
linguistic modernity, 200
Linnaeus, Carl, 11
literary studies, xvi, xviii, xix, 6, 24, 27, 195
local dialects, 210–11
Loughran, Trish, 194
Ludwig, Otto Friedrich, 11–12
Luqman, Shahzad, 37

Macedonian Letters, 85–86, 92–93
Machairas, Leontios, 207–8
Mahaffy, John, 95
Malanos, Timos, 79–80, 114
Mani, B. Venkat, 29, 250n73
manuscript codices, 198, 200
"Maria's Prayer" (Solomos), 102
marxism, 80, 137–38, 210

McGann, Jerome, 78, 105
McGill, Meredith, 249n65, 254n14
McKenzie, D. F., 105, 250n69
McKinsey, Martin, 75
mecmua (Agathangelos), 173–79, 182, 261n37
medieval infinitive, 252n35
Melas, Spyros, 88–89, 256n55
Menderes, Adnan, 196
Metaxas, Ioannis, 204–5
Mezzadra, Sandro, 21–22
Michaelides, Vasilis, 208
Michailidis, Eugenios, 100
Miéville, China, xviii
Misailidis, Evangelinos, 163, 259n1
miscegenation, 11, 14–15, 20–21. See also racism
Modern Greek Philology (Sathas), 15–16
modernist studies, 69–70
Monte Cristo in Marseille (Agathangelos), 180–85, 187, 191–92, 260n28
Moore, Julianne, 68
Moullas, Panagiotis, 86
Moustoxidis, Andreas, 247n39
Mufti, Aamir, 27, 198, 250nn68–69
Multaqa al-Abhur (al-Halabi), 52–54
Muslims (of Greece): and assimilation, 51; discrimination against, 54, 60, 66; and forced displacement, 2; and Hellenism, 16, 65; history of the, 40–41; and language, 41–42, 51–60, 63–64, 200; and literature, 6–7, 16–19, 31, 35–53. See also Population Exchange of 1923
Muslims (of Western Thrace), 18, 98–99
My Homeland (Kondoglou), 169
Myrtiotissa, 90

Naci, Fethi, 131–32
Nansen, Fridtjof, 1–3, 245n2, 246n6
Nasihat, 135
Nasser, Gamal Abdel, 99–100
National Turkish Students' Union (MTTB), 206
Neilson, Brett, 21–22
The Networked Wilderness (Cohen), 250n69

New Art (Vaianos), 87
New Life, 91, 256n47
New Testament, 10
nightingale, 64–65, 166
Nikolaidis, Nikos, 96–97
Nikolis, Yiorgis, 137
Nureddin Pasha, 120, 258n7
Nūrī, 58

"Ode to the Nun" (Solomos), 102
Öğüd, 135–36
Onassis Foundation, 68, 108, 113–14
Önder, Fazıl, 210
Önder, Mehmet, 135
oral performance, 170, 190
Ouranis, Kostas, 91

Palamas, Kostis, 92, 247n36
Palmer, Richmond, 207
Pamuk, Orhan, 68
Panagiotopolous, I. M., 116–17, 119
Pancyprian Federation of Labour (PEO), 210
Papaioannou, Dimitris, 68
Papanikolaou, Dimitris, 89, 114
Paparrigopoulos, Konstantinos, 13–15, 19, 21
Papoutsakis, Giorgos, 257n85
Pargas, Stephanos, 85
partitioning, 7, 196–98, 210–11, 214–15, 218–25
pastedown binding, 30, 31
People's Houses (*Halk evleri*), 204
Peridis, Mihalis, 257n85
Petsopoulos, Yannis, 136–37
philhellenism, 12–13
philology: borderscapes, discussion of, 4–5, 22, 34, 40, 66; European, 246n13; Greek, 7–10, 14, 17–21, 31–32, 35, 38, 65, 102–14; and literature, 6–7, 15, 18, 27–30, 35; and philological borders, xv–xvi, 5–7, 22, 24, 27, 31, 65–66, 198; and the undocumented, xvii, 23–24. *See also* book history
phonocentrism, 206
Pifer, Michael, 23

Poeturka (Yashin), 221
politikos stichos, 43–46, 92
Politis, Fotos, 125–26
Politis, Linos, 18–19, 103–7
Polylas, Iakovos, 102
Population Exchange of 1923: background on the, 1–2, 17, 89, 98–99, 196, 261n1; and border regimes, 4–5, 22, 32, 38; and Cyprus, 196–97; effects of the, 30–31, 100–101; and institutionalized Hellenism, 65, 102–4, 113; and language policies, 197–98; and literature, xvi, 5–6, 18, 33, 121–22, 165, 173, 191–94, 251n7; and philology, 4–5; and race, 2–4, 246n6; refugees of the, xv, 120–21, 163–65, 168, 179, 182, 191–94, 211. *See also* racism
The Postman (Koutsoumis), 100
prayer, 53–54, 200, 211, 230–32, 235–36
Preziosi, Giovanni, 261n1
A Prisoner of War's Story (Doukas), 6
procedural precedents (of the border regime), 4
Progressive Party of Working People (AKEL), 210
psychological portraiture, 72
Psyharis, Yannis, 247n36
publishing strategies, 69–70, 78–80, 82, 84, 114–15, 135–40. *See also* composite codices; diasporic print; Greek publishing; handmade manuscripts
purgatory, 213–14. *See also a'raf*
Pyrsinellas, Vasilis, 16
Pyrsos, 99

queer studies, 68–69, 75, 89, 95–96
Quran, 46–47, 53, 55–56, 166–68, 252n21, 252n32. *See also a'raf*

racial families, 11
racism: and literature, 16–19, 33, 86–93, 112, 248n46, 256n56; and migration, 8–10, 12, 14–15; scientific, 10–11. *See also* borderguard; ethnic cleansing; miscegenation; Population Exchange of 1923; violence

Raftopoulos, Dimitris, 126–28, 147
realism, 117
"Reciprocal Exchange of Racial Minorities," 3
Recoding World Literature (Mani), 250n73
Red Guard, 138
refuge, xvi–xviii
"Return from Greece" (Cavafy), 76–78
ritual prayer. *See* prayer
Rizospastis, 136–37
Romiosyne, 247n36
Roosevelt, Franklin, 196, 261n1
Rozakou, Katerina, xvi, 23
Rufus, W. Carl, 185

Saint-Amour, Paul, 70
Sami, Şemseddin, 171
Saraçoğlu, Ahmet Cemaleddin, 136
Saregiannis, I. A., 69
Sathas, Konstantinos, 15–17, 21, 247n39
Saumaise, Claude, 9
Savidis, George, 32, 72–74, 81, 98, 103–4, 107–14, 242, 254n10, 255n28, 257n84
scripts, 236–37
scriptworlds, 31, 33, 37–40, 67, 198, 200–201, 221, 238
secularism, 50–52, 57
Seferis, George, 101–2
Sevastopol Battle, 176–77
Seyhan, Azade, 132
Shaykh al-Islam, 53
Shehreti, Haxhi, 16
Shirt of Flame (Halide Edib), 32, 118, 128–35, 140–47, 161
Singopoulos, Alekos, 107–9
Singopoulou, Rika, 84, 98
Slavophone Orthodox Christians, 18, 197
Socialist Labor Party of Greece (SEKE), 137
"A Soldier's Song from the Russian War," 176–77
solidarity movement (of Greece), xvi
Solomos, Dionysios, 18, 102, 106–7
Song of the Dragomans (Diakonos), 208
Sotiriou, Dido, 6

Spivak, Gayatri, 198
The Survey Journal (*Tarama Dergisi*), 143–44
survivor objects, xvi
Sykoutris, Ioannis, 18, 73, 103–7, 114, 248n45
symbolism, 37, 64–65, 166

Tanpınar, Ahmed Hamdi, 246n12
Tawhid, 46
testimonial novels, 117–19, 121–35, 140–43, 147–54, 162
textual handlers, 24, 26, 29, 32–33, 65–66, 105, 165, 221, 229, 233, 237. *See also* decentralized literature
Theodora (Agathangelos), 180–82, 185–90, 261n39
Theodora (Kyriakos), 182, 187–90, 261n39
Theotokas, Giorgos, 89
threat of indeterminacy, 197
TMT, 210, 264n69
Tomadakis, Nikolaos, 18
Topographies of Hellenism (Leontis), 247n36
translation, 53–54, 56–57, 68, 81, 136, 187–91, 207, 224, 227–28
transmission. *See* copyright; dictation; textual handlers
Treaty of Lausanne, 2
Triantafyllidis, Manolis, 204
Tseng, Katherine Yu, 185
Tsirkas, Stratis, 79–80, 108
Tsitselikis, Konstantinos, 17
Tunçay, Mete, 137–38
Turcograecia (Crusius), 247n20
"Turkish-Cypriot Poetry" (Yashin), 223
Turkish Language Association (TDK), 204
Turkish Language Reforms, 143–44, 204–6
The Turkish Ordeal (Halide Edib), 259n53
Turkish publishing, 135–36. See also *Anatoli*
Twice a Stranger (Clark), xv
Tziovas, Dimitris, 124, 152

Ünaydın, Ruşen Eşref, 132–33
Uneasy Years (Panagiotopoulos), 116–17
unseeing, xviii

Vafopoulos, Yiorgos, 125
Vaianos, Marios, 74, 87, 90
Valaoritis, Aristotle, 102
Valavanis, Ioakeim, 172
value extraction, 22, 26
Venezis, Elias, 169
Venizelos, Eleftherios, 204
violence, 119–20, 139–40, 176–77, 210, 223–24, 226, 252n74. *See also* ethnic cleansing; racism
Vlastos, Petros, 256n56
Voice of the Refugee, 163–64
von Kupffer, Elisar, 95

Wainwright, Rufus, 68
"Was There a Greek Aljamiado Literature?" (Dedes), 248n44, 251n7
Watenpaugh, Heghnar Zeitlian, xvi
weak theory, 70–71, 114
Wilde, Oscar, 95

Wilson, Bret, 53
women, 41–42, 128, 147, 182, 184–85
world literature (discussion of), 6, 25–27, 169–70, 226–27, 249n67
World Philologies (Pollock), 246n10
The World Refugees Made (Ballinger), 245n6

Xenopoulos, Grigorios, 82, 90, 255n41

Yalman, Ahmet Emin, 205
Yanyalı Esad Efendi, 251n12
Yaşaroğlu, Ahmet Halit, 144
Yashin, Mehmet, 33–34, 198, 211–38, 264n88
Yashin, Özker, 223–24
Yıldırım, Onur, xv
Yusuf, Abu, 53

Zadeh, Travis, 53
Zanou, Konstantina, 22

TRANSLATION/TRANSNATION

Series Editor Emily Apter

Writing Outside the Nation by Azade Seyhan

Ambassadors of Culture: The Transamerican Origins of Latino Writing by Kirsten Silva Gruesz

The Literary Channel: The Inter-National Invention of the Novel edited by Margaret Cohen and Carolyn Dever

Experimental Nations: Or, the Invention of the Maghreb by Réda Bensmaïa

What Is World Literature? by David Damrosch

We, the People of Europe?: Reflections on Transnational Citizenship by Étienne Balibar

The Portable Bunyan: A Transnational History of "The Pilgrim's Progress" by Isabel Hofmeyr

Nation, Language, and the Ethics of Translation edited by Sandra Bermann and Michael Wood

Utopian Generations: The Political Horizon of Twentieth-Century Literature by Nicholas Brown

Guru English: South Asian Religion in a Cosmopolitan Language by Srinivas Aravamudan

Poetry of the Revolution: Marx, Manifestos, and the Avant-Gardes by Martin Puchner

The Translation Zone: A New Comparative Literature by Emily Apter

In Spite of Partition: Jews, Arabs, and the Limits of Separatist Imagination by Gil Z. Hochberg

The Princeton Sourcebook in Comparative Literature: From the European Enlightenment to the Global Present edited by David Damrosch, Natalie Melas, and Mbongiseni Buthelezi

The Spread of Novels: Translation and Prose Fiction in the Eighteenth Century by Mary Helen McMurran

The Novel and the Sea by Margaret Cohen

The Event of Postcolonial Shame by Timothy Bewes

Hamlet's Arab Journey: Shakespeare's Prince and Nasser's Ghost by Margaret Litvin

Archives of Authority: Empire, Culture, and the Cold War by Andrew N. Rubin

Security: Politics, Humanity, and the Philology of Care by John T. Hamilton

Dictionary of Untranslatables: A Philosophical Lexicon edited by Barbara Cassin

Learning Zulu: A Secret History of Language in South Africa by Mark Sanders

In the Shadow of World Literature: Sites of Reading in Colonial Egypt by Michael Allan

Leaks, Hacks, and Scandals: Arab Culture in the Digital Age by Tarek El-Ariss

City of Beginnings: Poetic Modernism in Beirut by Robyn Creswell

Vernacular English: Reading the Anglophone in Postcolonial India by Akshya Saxena

The Making of Barbarians: Chinese Literature and Multilingual Asia by Haun Saussy

Sacred Language, Vernacular Difference: Global Arabic and Counter-Imperial Literatures by Annette Damayanti Lienau

Literature's Refuge: Rewriting the Mediterranean Borderscape by William Stroebel

GPSR Authorized Representative: Easy Access System Europe - Mustamäe tee
50, 10621 Tallinn, Estonia, gpsr.requests@easproject.com

www.ingramcontent.com/pod-product-compliance
Lightning Source LLC
LaVergne TN
LVHW090456180925
821343LV00002B/51